WORKADAY

'The Primitive Methodists'
Painted in the early 1890s at St. Ives Primitive Methodist Chapel by W. H. Y. Titcomb
(1858-1930). Evidence regarding the painting suggests that a local preacher is in the
pulpit. The occasion seems to be a prayer-meeting following a summer evening service.
(Dudley Art Gallery).

WORKADAY PREACHERS
The story of Methodist Local Preaching

Edited by

Geoffrey Milburn

and

Margaret Batty

Methodist Publishing House

1995

Workaday Preachers

ISBN 1 85852 058 4 (paperback)
ISBN 1 85852 063 0 (casebound)

Printed in England by Clays Ltd, St Ives plc

Dedicated to all local preachers
of the past, the present and the future

'Thy only glory let them seek:
O let their hearts with love o'erflow!
Let them believe, and therefore speak,
And spend Thy mercy's praise below.'

Charles Wesley

(A verse from a hymn beginning 'Jesus, Thy wandering sheep behold',
first published in 1742 with the heading 'A prayer for labourers'.
Included in *The Methodist Hymn Book* 1933, no.791)

A WORD TO THE CONGREGATION

Judge not the preacher; for he is thy Judge;
If thou mislike him, thou conceiv'st him not.
God calleth preaching folly. Do not grudge
To pick out treasures from an earthen pot.
The worst speak something good: if all want sense
God takes a text, and preacheth patience.

Jest not at preachers' language or expression,
How know'st thou, but thy sins made him miscarry?
Then turn thy faults and his into confession:
God sent him, whatsoe'er he be: O tarry
And love him for his Master: his condition,
Though it be ill, makes him no ill physician.

From *The Church Porch* by George Herbert (1593-1633),
part of a series of poems entitled 'The Temple'.

FOREWORD AND THANKS

Workaday Preachers has its origins in a decision of the Local Preachers' Office of the Methodist Church to commission a serious readable history of local preaching as part of the general celebration of local preaching planned for 1996. The two hundredth anniversary of the general introduction of local preachers' quarterly meetings (the result of a regulation of the 1796 Methodist Conference) has provided a useful peg on which to hang these celebrations. But Methodist local preaching began some fifty years before that date, and our book, which had to begin at the beginning, covers a timespan of 250 years, from Methodism's origins to the present day.

While the conduct of worship by lay men and women is one of the most familiar features of Methodism, the history behind it is by no means simple. Indeed local preachers have played such a large and vital role in Methodism (as well as having been the subject of an ongoing debate as to what that role should be) that it is hard to give a just estimate of their work without almost writing a history of Methodism itself! So the background of general Methodist development (with its complexity and diversity) has had to be reckoned with in this book, but this in turn raises the problem of how to preserve within a broad historical survey the true flavour of the individuality and character of local preachers themselves. We have tried to ensure that a good deal of this individuality does shine through, while also being very aware of the constraints which have often obliged us to sacrifice biographical detail for the sake of the general story.

The difficulties mentioned above (and there are others) may explain why no previous large-scale historical treatment of Methodist local preaching has been published, (though Dr George Lawton's *Reader-Preacher* (1989) went some way towards it). Consequently the contributors to this book, having no substantial earlier histories of preaching to consult, have had to undertake a considerable amount of original work, delving into the archives and printed records of Methodism, as well as drawing upon their own experience.

A glance at the table of contents will reveal the book's plan. Chapters one to six set out the story of local preaching, and in the subsequent chapters (and in the introduction) various related themes are explored. Each chapter, though set within a planned structure, was written largely as an independent essay so that the book does not claim to be entirely comprehensive or to say the last word on Methodist local preaching. Nevertheless what is offered here is the first overall and fully-documented account of its subject to have appeared in print, and fills a notable gap in Methodist historical writing. At the same time it is our hope and belief that any reader who wishes simply to browse in the book will be able to dip in at almost any point and discover much interest and pleasure. Aids to such browsing are the illustrations, and the series of quotations scattered throughout the chapters, illuminating the text but boxed round so as to be distinctive and easily read on their own if desired. These 'vignettes' (culled from a wide range of sources, including reminiscences of present-day preachers) offer vivid glimpses of people and incidents, and serve as examples of the countless personal experiences which lie at the heart of the story of local preaching, as well as some of the humour.

Those readers who wish to know more than is in the book, or would like to do some research and are looking for guidance, are referred to the book's appendices. We ought to stress that this book is a history of local preaching rather than of local preachers, and that there is certainly room for other publications devoted more to the grass-roots history of local preaching, and the life-stories of individual preachers, than has been possible here. It is good to think that this book might stimulate the writing of some of them.

In editing this book over the past two or three years we have become indebted to more people than can be named. Our warm thanks go to them all, but some must be acknowledged: Revd John Lampard and Revd Peter Barber, the two Local Preachers' Secretaries who have held office during the book's progress; the staff of the Local Preachers' office, particularly Wendy Turner and Ken Kingston; Brian Thornton and Sue Gascoigne of the Methodist Publishing House; Peter Nockles and Gareth Lloyd of the John Rylands University Library of Manchester; Joyce Banks, librarian for the Wesley Historical Society; Frances Mather who compiled the book's index; Brunswick Methodist Church, and the Literary and Philosophical Society, both of Newcastle, for the kind provision of rooms in which to hold our editorial meetings; all our contributors whose chapters were written under various pressures, and who, while patiently enduring our editorial requests and revisions, made many helpful suggestions regarding the book; John Vickers and Revd Keith Parr who served on the book's editorial committee; and last, but certainly not least, Mary Milburn and Harry Batty for their support, encouragement and practical help while the book was in progress.

Geoffrey Milburn and Margaret Batty
September 1995

ACKNOWLEDGEMENTS

The editors and publisher express thanks for the material quoted or used as illustrations in this volume, most of which is acknowledged in the book's notes, captions and references.

Other acknowledgements are as follows:

> HarperCollins for permission to quote an extract from D. H. Lawrence, *Apocalypse and Other Writings on Revelation* ed. Maria Kalnis 1980, and an extract from Howard Spring *Fame is the Spur*, Fontana Books, 1953.

> Ruth G. Clemo for permission to print Jack Clemo's poem 'The Harrassed Preacher' from the collection *Broad Autumn* 1975; and the Revd Ray Trudgian for help and advice with this poem.

> Douglas Hyde and Heinemann for permission to quote an extract from *I Believed,* The Reprint Society, 1952.

> J. M. Dent for permission to print R. S. Thomas' poem 'The Chapel' from his *Collected Poems 1945-1990.*

> Cover Photograph – Tom Hall, and Northeast Press Ltd., *Shields Gazette*.

We also wish to acknowledge the help of those who sent items into the Local Preachers' Office in response to an appeal for preachers' reminiscences. Some of this material has found a place in this book. We hope that other outlets might be found for the remainder.

CONTENTS

Appendices

ILLUSTRATIONS

Dr James Hamilton (a local preacher) on the left and Joseph Cole (a travelling preacher) on the right escorting the aged John Wesley along Princes Street, Edinburgh, on his last visit to the city in May 1790. A symbol perhaps of the importance to Wesley (and to Methodism) of the support both of ministers and lay people.

INTRODUCTION

LOCAL PREACHERS AND THE CHURCH'S MISSION

A personal view

Donald English

Much of what follows in this book is the result of scholarly study, with references shown. My aim is to give a much more impressionistic view of our local preachers. Anyone else writing this chapter would no doubt produce something different. Please accept that what I write is what I observe, and has no other value except that it may start readers reflecting about their own experience (active or passive) of local preaching.

How are we to assess the value of local preachers? My own testimony is that I was raised in a very small mining village, in the United Free Methodist mould, and don't remember seeing a clerical collar until I reached about the age of five! The majority of our services were led by local preachers; ministerial work was provided by lay pastors.

My earliest job, at the age of three, was to pump the organ. I can still sense the stickiness of the varnish on that long wooden handle with which I pumped in order to get the little lead mouse, as I was told it was, high enough for the organ to be played by my Uncle George or Mr Huntsman. From that vantage point I watched those men, who I later came to realise were local preachers. Most of them were wearing the one suit they possessed. I would see them in the village from time to time during the week, going about their normal work, as miners or shopkeepers or railmen or steelworkers. But on Sunday there was a grave dignity, or *gravitas,* about them which I will never forget. They somehow seemed to be polished for the occasion. I suppose in that setting the local preacher came about as near to being a Moses-like figure as was possible. One had the feeling they had been on the Mount with God, and what they brought us was his Word, transmitted through their own minds and hearts.

That is how it seemed to that little boy who watched with a certain amount of awe. What do I now see as the benefit to Methodism of its local preachers? I begin with the blunt fact that they have enabled Methodist strategy to be sustained over many decades. I refer to the strategy of forming Methodist societies in particular geographical areas, followed by building chapels for them to worship in. Non-Methodists are amazed at the number of our chapels around the country! Well might they be, since we sustain ourselves even after the local school, the local post office, and sometimes even the local pub, close down. It has to do with a conviction, no doubt closely related to the band and class meetings, that it was in their local setting that people would best be in fellowship and grow together. Without local preachers who could occupy the pulpits in seven out of ten of our places each Sunday? It could not happen.

JOURNEYING HAZARDS

'My father was a Primitive Methodist local preacher in a circuit comprising many miles of central Northumberland. For more than forty years, ending many years ago, he carried his simple message, faithfully and well, to chapels in the quiet country, and to their small congregations – attentive under the soft light of oil lamps . . . I remember the first appointment undertaken by car – a lofty vehicle painted bright red and having a vertical steering-column and shining brasswork. My mother's anxiety at the risks in so dangerous a method of transport was lessened by the fact that my father's travelling companion (another preacher) was by trade the driver of the local steam roller! The skills associated with that occupation, she felt, would enable him to cope with any misbehaviour on the part of the car.

Summer and winter alike the work went on. Once, in a bitter cold and phenomenal snow-storm, my father left a country chapel to walk to a farmhouse a mile or two away. He lost his bearings completely in the darkness and the spinning snowflakes. He wandered in one field, in the circle which traps all pedestrians in similar circumstances. His friend the farmer set out, storm lantern in hand and found my father, exhausted in a deep drift – and very, very near sleep, from which he would probably never have wakened.'

J. D. Watson 'A Son Remembers',
in *The Bridge* the magazine of the churches
of Bury St. Edmunds, Easter 1972.

Local preachers have shown that not only ordained ministers have a vocation to preach. The definitions in our Deed of Union show how equivocal we are about the role of ordained ministers amongst us. Methodism does not easily take to the idea that somehow those who are ordained become different people. For us ordained people are representative people, in the sense that they have been called, trained, tested and then authorised to play a principal and leading part in the life of the Methodist Church. But local preachers also have a call. They too are trained and tested and authorised. Through them Methodists can see that vocation is wider than ordination.

The very fact that local preachers are lay people is also a reminder that their vocation spreads beyond the call to preach. The strength of the lay woman or man who preaches is precisely that they spend their days in the places where most members of the congregation also spend them. They have been in what is called secular employment, or secular unemployment, or secular ex-employment! They have not been protected within or without the life of the church by a title, a particular piece of distinctive clothing, or a traditional status. They have had to win their way as Christians, day by day, on the simple basis of the quality of their lives, their work and their character. Their vocation to preach and lead worship depends to a very great extent on the way in which they live out their lives throughout the week. The local preacher in the pulpit reflects a different life experience from that of the ordained minister.

Local preachers are reminders of what can be achieved when a call is responded to. I remember how as a young boy and a teenager I marvelled at the people who became local preachers. Their spoken styles were in some cases not at all polished. I remember the sermon about Daniel looking out from his window at a moment of high tension. But the preacher leading the worship that evening kept referring to it as the 'winda'. If he said it once he must have said it fifty times! I and my fellow grammar school pupils, mercifully sitting way back in the gallery, were absolutely convulsed. We could tell when the next occurrence of the word would come. Yet that man had about him an aura that was unmistakable. He was an eccentric who, as I discovered later, also had a remarkable gift for healing. How awful if he had been knocked into Oxbridge shape in content and presentation. But he remained himself to the end, and many were grateful for his ministry.

Local preachers bring a *gravitas* to a task which is not their job. They are not in danger, as a minister may be, of leading worship and preaching as bread and butter activities. It all has to be special for them,

3

because it is special. It isn't what they normally do. I do not mean by that that it is better than what ministers do, but I do mean that it is different. Vive la différence!

THE MYSTICAL INSIGHT OF A PREACHER

'Victor Murray has a passage in one of his books referring to the common experience of Christians 'that there comes a point in the soul's progress to God when the seeker becomes aware of himself as the sought'. Augustine, Lady Julian of Norwich, Pascal and Francis Thompson are all quoted by him on this theme. He then goes on: 'As a further illustration of the similarity of authentic Christian experience, I may quote this remark which I heard in the prayer of an unknown Primitive Methodist local preacher in a Yorkshire moorland chapel: "If Thou hadst dealt with us after our sins, or rewarded us according to our iniquities, we should not have been in Thy house tonight in an attitude of pleading with Thee." What is often called "prevenient grace" is really prevenient love.'

Personal Experience and the Historic Faith 1941 edition, London, p.171. Victor Murray (1890-1967) was brought up as a Primitive Methodist, became a local preacher in his teens, and later served as Professor of Education at Hull and President of Cheshunt College, Cambridge.

One wonders on reflection whether we have been too eager to remove the difference. John Wesley's comment that he tolerated lay preaching (not a terribly enthusiastic attitude!) as an absolute necessity, because without it thousands of souls would perish, was a reflection of his need for more preachers than he had ordained clergy available. We may need to ask, however, whether the reason why many are *not* led to faith today, is not because of a shortage of preachers, but because we are all under pressure to conform to a narrower pattern. The fact that Wesley used the model of the earliest apostles as a justification of lay preaching is interesting. He acknowledged that they were not philosophical or lettered men, but defended them strongly in terms of 'substantial, practical, experimental Divinity'. Is that distinction still valid? If so, are our local preachers still examples of it? And if so, should so much of the training of local preachers be carried out by ordained ministers?

Local preachers have also been a reflection of both the condition and the background of our congregations. This is not surprising since they are drawn from those very congregations. But the details which follow in this book concerning the social classes and occupations from which local preachers were and are drawn is extremely significant in this matter. So is the tracing of the development in the nineteenth century whereby congregations, increasingly influenced by people of substance, grew tired of what they believed to be the old-fashioned Gospel sermon aimed at unconverted sinners, and longed for and got more concentration on that which would teach them and build them up in faith. No-one would wish to condemn them for that. But it could just be that in the moving from the one to the other we lost that way of addressing the unconverted sinner, and went for a style of preaching which was more conducive to an increasingly middle class, better-educated congregation, in a way which changed both manner and content. That change, however acceptable to the congregations, increasingly excluded from the ranks of local preachers those who did not fit that pattern, and by so doing may have cut off our capacity for reaching those of different background who would increasingly not feel at home in our churches. (The very change of name from chapel to church is not without its significance in this context).

Since local preachers can be seen as a reflection of the nature and desires of the congregation, and since they are also the source from which ordained ministers are drawn, their attitude, mood, manner and sermon content are a crucial indicator of where the Methodist Church is today. In many ways what we train our local preachers to do, and what we expect of them, provides a sharp reflection of who we are and what we need to be as Christians. Local preachers could therefore be the key to changing the nature and narrow base of our congregations, if they themselves were to become again more widely representative.

The local preachers have without a doubt been a strongly unifying element in the life of the Methodist Church. John Stacey, who has far more qualifications than I have for such an opinion, pays testimony to this element in this book. Despite the provision of lectionary readings an undoubted disadvantage in having a different preacher in the pulpit week after week is the disjunction in terms of what is taught and commended. The congregation has to learn each week to adapt itself to a different person's way of being a preacher and conducting worship. And those who come to lead worship may not know the congregation as well as a person who preaches there every week.

There are great advantages, however. The very variety of person and manner can itself be refreshing, and prevent any one preacher from becoming too dominant either in worship or in teaching. In a curious way the congregation can be more calm about what is going on, since at each service they are aware of the wider variety of which it forms a part. And the sense of belonging to a team of preachers, reinforced by the fellowship of the preachers' meeting, undoubtedly contributes to the unity of the Church not least because it encourages the preachers to play a full part in determining the very life and nature of the Church. The local preachers with whom I first had to do were very different from one another. But they certainly helped to hold us together, and for that I shall be for ever grateful.

We come to what is perhaps the most tantalising question of all. Could the local preachers be the spearhead of a revival of Christianity in this country? I believe they could, and for this very basic reason. Local preachers are probably best placed of all those who hold office in the Methodist Church to sustain and develop the links between what happens in the church and in the world, between which the gap seems to be growing every decade.

A PREACHER'S SATURDAY NIGHT IN ANCOATS, MANCHESTER c.1905

'No one was ever asked into the Stansfield's house on a Saturday night. When Gordon and John returned, high tea was ready in the kitchen, and John well knew the unvarying routine that would follow. This was Gordon's sermon-writing night. As a local preacher, he was not called on every Sunday, but every Saturday he worked on a sermon.

He and Ellen washed up in the scullery; then Ellen put the red cloth on to the kitchen table and brought out from a dresser drawer the blotting-pad, the ink-pot and pen, the half-sheets of note-paper which were the size Gordon liked for writing on. She placed a Bible, Cruden's Concordance and the Methodist Hymn-book alongside the blotting-pad. She pulled out the wooden chair, ready for him to sit down. This was the total extent of Ellen's secretarial work in any week, and not for anything would she have abrogated one gesture of it. Then she sat down with a basket of mending at her side, and put a silence-commanding finger on her lips as she looked at John, sitting with his new book in the Old Warrior's chair on the other side of the purring fire.

The boy snuggled into the chair, aware of the keen cold without and of the warm silence within, a silence broken only by the steady scratching of Gordon's pen, the tinkle of ash into the grate, the tiny rasping of a woollen sock over his mother's rough-skinned hands.'

From: Howard Spring *Fame is the Spur* (first published 1940)

[Howard Spring describes his own beginnings as a local preacher in the part of his autobiography entitled *And Another Thing* (1946). He was for some years on the Wesleyan plan in Cardiff but later ceased to preach, and drifted away from organised religion during World War I. He comments however "In my more depressed moments I still think of myself as a stickit preacher" (*And Another Thing* p.163).]

At the outset of the Methodist movement there lay a fundamental assumption which has now been largely abandoned in our culture. It was that Christian faith and theology were still seen to be operating at the centre of life's big questions, and that those questions could not be properly addressed without faith and theology, and therefore without the experts on those subjects, namely the clergy.

One has only to state the position like that to underline how different things are today. Rather than being seen at the centre of our national life, with authority and perspectives that go to the heart of the issue, the church today is viewed as another of the institutions which is in terminal decline. The current battles over religious broadcasting provide telling evidence of this situation. The major issues which dominate our television screens are not perceived to be either overtly or covertly theological. When church leaders get themselves involved in such debates, they are usually told they would do better to stick to their own area, which is said to be spirituality, worship, and life within the church. Although we know this is not true, since Christian theology relates to, and should be at the centre of, all consideration of every issue of life, many observers of the current situation in our society might well conclude the criticism to be accurate. It is not self-evident that questions concerning European monetary union, new developments in genetic medicine, and the alleged special relationship between Britain and the United States have anything at all to do with theology. Nor, for that matter, is the link evident between theology and wage negotiations, television programme schedules, quangos, and the relationship of trade unions to the Labour Party. They are central topics in the news, but few (including many Christians) recognise their connection with christian faith and theology.

Yet if our biblical theology of Creation and Redemption means anything, then the link is plainly there. The question is who can best be aware of that link and who could best communicate it? The answer to that seems to me to be not the ordained minister, but rather the lay preacher, who has spent or is spending her or his working day closely related to many of these issues, or directly affected by them. Even in the matter of employment or unemployment the Methodist minister is in an entirely different situation from almost everyone else who belongs to the Methodist Church. Speaking as a minister, I have to say that our experience of security or insecurity at work is in an entirely different category. So, in general terms, is our exercise and/or experience of discipline. Within the Church family we also work within a remarkably mild and caring framework.

What are the implications which flow from recognising that the local preacher is more likely to establish a link between theology and daily life than the ordained minister? It means getting rid of the idea that the local preacher is somehow a second-rate occupant of the pulpit, because the ordained minister is the model. It means enabling the local preacher to come to the biblical text with a greater sense of the insight she or he has from daily work, rather than from the influence of ordained ministers upon them. It means encouraging them to grapple in their preaching and in their leading of worship with the issues which they face at work, or which others of their number face at work, rather than copying the prayers and the insights which the ordained minister brings. This may mean giving them a larger part in the running of the Local Preachers' Office than is the case at present.

A CUMBRIAN PREACHER DIES IN HARNESS

'William Malkinson, a Wesleyan local preacher aged 54, died on 21 February 1886 while walking over Irton Fell to conduct two services at Eskdale chapel. It was a damp and foggy morning. William, heavily clothed, was walking up the steep incline with his companion, but collapsed and appeared to die instantly, presumably from heart failure. On 22 February 1986 a commemorative service was held on the exact spot on which he died. The Revd Norman Pickering, then Chairman of the Cumbria District of the Methodist Church, conducted the service, during which a message from the then President of the Methodist Conference, Revd Christopher Hughes Smith, was read out to the eighty folk assembled for the commemoration. Part of the message was:

"In remembering William Malkinson we give thanks for the tradition of Methodist local preachers through the generations and throughout the world".'

Wesley Historical Society, North East Branch,
Bulletin 46, September 1986, p.2.

Most of all, it requires of us the courage to see that mission involves finding the focal point of God's activity outside the church, and in the world he has made, within which he operates, and in which he invites us to join him in mission. If part of the task is discerning where and how God is involved in the affairs of the world, then it is at least arguable that lay preachers are more likely than ordained ministers to perceive and recognise his steps, because of their daily involvement. But they will need to be enabled to do their theological reflection and their faith perception within the working world, outside the Church where eventually they communicate what they have perceived. Too often, one fears, the pressure to be church-based from start to finish is too great for local preachers to resist. And part of that pressure comes from the congregation, which too often has not wished to be troubled by what is going on in the world around them. They have viewed the time at church as an escape from all that. Each time this happens, our engagement in mission become harder.

THE IMPORTANCE OF LANGUAGE

'In presenting the Christian message today, we need to avoid religious-sounding words, which amount sometimes to jargon . . .

A useful discussion was held centring on the "fear" of the Lord. Whilst it was felt there were dangers in minimising the impact of the meaning of the word "fear" thus leading to complacency, nevertheless the discussion brought out the great need for an up to date translation of Biblical words and terminology.'

(From the Minutes of the Nicholson Square Circuit, Edinburgh, LP Meeting, December 1965 and June 1966)

If any of this is to take place, however, the theological training of local preachers will need to include more of what has traditionally been called 'apologetics' – that is how to make sense of the world in the light of Christian faith, and how to make sense of our faith in the light of the world around us. It will be about how to be co-creators with God in the world he has put into our hands, and how to be channels of redemption within that world. It will not detract from the value of Christian worship: indeed it will make it even more vital and necessary. Nor will it in any way detract from the task of calling individuals to personal commitment in Jesus Christ through repentance and faith. This lies at the heart of all our effort and our perception. But it will mean a much greater concentration on the others who do not join us in worship; about how God is present in their lives; and about how they might recognise that presence, and about how those who do attend worship might enable them to recognise that presence, by making sense of the world today.

When the eighteenth and nineteenth century missionaries talked about engaging in their task, they were sometimes told that it was impossible. They would not be able to find their way to the people amongst whom they wished to be missionaries. If they got there they would not know how to survive. If they did survive they would not know how to communicate. And they would miss all the rich fellowship of the church here at home. A precisely similar task faces the missionary church in Britain today, but not about places overseas. The task is how to meet all those challenges in our own culture. If we will not take this missionary task seriously then we cannot expect to survive, let alone grow. If we do take that task seriously, it will be the witness of lay people which will make it possible. At the centre of that witness will be the lay preacher, and we Methodists may yet learn an extra reason to thank God that at the centre of our life is a faithful band called local preachers. Long may they flourish!

1

ORIGINS: THE AGE OF WESLEY

Margaret Batty

Irregular Preachers

'Stop him at your peril:' said Mrs Canning of Evesham to John Wesley. 'He preaches the truth, and the Lord owns him as truly as he does you or your brother!' That was straight enough – but Wesley said he liked plain speaking. 'He' was Thomas Westell, a carpenter who was a member of the first society formed by Wesley at Bristol in 1739, and who had made a preaching excursion shortly after.[1]

When visiting Bristol in 1742 Wesley heard that Thomas Maxfield, a layman, had begun to preach in London. He set off at once to investigate. Though disturbed, he was probably not surprised. The previous year he had told his brother Charles 'I am not clear that Brother Maxfield should not expound at Greyhound Lane; nor can I as yet do without him.'[2] Maxfield had been left at the Foundery, a former armaments store in London, to pray with the members of the Methodist society who met there. Wesley's mother had heard him preach, and when told of John's disquiet said 'Take care, John, what you do respecting that young man, for he is as surely called of God to preach as you are.'[3]

In many lay people the evangelical revival produced an irresistible urge to preach. It came not only to educated people but to the most unlikely and apparently ill-fitted, like soldiers or tradesmen or sometimes women. It had happened periodically over the Christian centuries but that was no help to the Wesleys just then. They were in an awkward position; regarded as 'irregular' by fellow-clergymen of the Church of England because they preached out of doors, they now had to deal with 'irregularity' in their own movement when unordained persons began to preach.

Opposition grew, largely expressed in pamphlets. One such, milder than many, said 'For laymen to officiate in reading prayers to any assembly, except their own families, is an encroachment upon the office of those who are ordain'd to holy functions; and I fear takes off from the reverence and respect due to them. And for unletter'd Laics to take upon them to expound or interpret the Scriptures, is neither justifiable nor laudable.'[4]

SILAS TOLD'S FIRST IMPRESSION OF WESLEY, JUNE 1740

'Exactly at five a whisper was conveyed through the congregation, "Here he comes! here he comes!" I was filled with curiosity to see his person, which, when I beheld, I much despised. The enemy of souls suggested that he was a farmer's son, who, not able to support himself, was making a penny in this manner. He passed through the congregation into the pulpit, and having his robes on, I expected he would have begun with the Church service; but to my astonishment, he began with singing a hymn, with which I was almost enraptured; but his extemporary prayer was quite unpleasant, and I thought it savoured too much of the Dissenter.'

The service described above was at the Foundery, Moorfields, in London. Wesley's sermon on that occasion overcame Silas Told's doubts and misunderstandings. He became an ardent Methodist and one of the first local preachers, spending much time in serving the inmates of Newgate Prison. The incident is quoted in John Telford, *Wesley's Chapel and House* n.d. pp.13-14.

Objections understood and overcome

Wesley admitted that he and his brother had been prejudiced against allowing laymen to preach. But because clergymen would not help, each local society had had 'to find some one among themselves who was upright of heart and of sound judgment in the things of God; and to desire him to meet the rest as often as he could, in order to confirm them, as he was able, in the ways of God, either by reading to them, or by prayer, or by exhortation'.[5]

The Aberdeen society is one example: in 1759 '[The Methodists] met every morning at 5 o'clock. During their meeting they sang a hymn, read a portion of Scripture, with Mr Wesley's commentary, after which they read and sang a second time and then concluded with prayer.' A few months later Wesley sent two preachers on a short visit, and after that 'three of their principal men acted as public speakers. The first began with singing a hymn and praying extempore; the second read a portion of Scripture, with a commentary upon it; and the third sung another hymn, and concluded with a prayer.'[6] This was the pattern of development in many places from the 1740s onwards.

True, allowing laymen to preach cut at the deep roots of John and Charles Wesley's high Anglican view of the office of a clergyman, and at their inbred love of regularity and order. But John, more readily than Charles, could exclude his personal bias. For him, there were two tests, those of Scripture and effectiveness. He said that he allowed no other rule, whether of faith or practice, than the Holy Scriptures [7] and that God would work through men of his own choosing[8] – women also, he discovered later. Swallowing his doubts, he wrote 'It is plain to me that the whole work of God termed Methodism is an extraordinary dispensation of His providence.'[9]

Wesley was no revolutionary. 'I submit' he wrote, 'to every ordinance of man wherever I do not consider there is an absolute necessity for acting contrary to it. Consistently with this I do tolerate lay preaching, because I conceive there is an absolute necessity for it; inasmuch as, were it not, thousands of souls would perish everlastingly.'[10]

Clergy objected that the lay preachers were uneducated. Wesley conceded that they did not understand the ancient languages or any branch of philosophy. But then, did their accusers, or did they rather pretend to a learning which they did not possess? In any case, he said, the apostles themselves, apart from St. Paul, were common, unphilosophical, unlettered men.

Wesley was not ashamed of his preachers. 'I trust there is not one of them who is not able to go through such an examination in substantial, practical, experimental Divinity, as few of our candidates for holy orders, even in the University . . . are able to do.'[11] They could stand up for themselves too: when a clergyman in the North told one of them that he was not qualified to preach he retorted 'Qualified! Why, without your gown ye *dare* na, without your book ye *could* na and without your pay ye *would* na. And I do without all three.'[12]

The great objection was that they were not ordained. Wesley replied that it was not absolutely necessary if they were effective, and drove the point home with a story: 'A peasant being brought before the College of Physicians in Paris, a learned doctor accosted him, "What, friend, do you pretend to prescribe to people that have agues? Dost thou know what an ague is?" He replied "Yes, sir. An ague is what I can cure and you cannot."'13   As Wesley reminded the Earl of Dartmouth, the Reformation itself came about as the result of 'irregular preaching'.14

Charles Wesley's constant fear was that the use of lay preachers would precipitate the separation of the Methodists from the Church of England. In 1756 he told the vicar of Truro, Samuel Walker, that the mere possibility had made him tremble for years past.15 John had already faced it and had written in plain terms to Walker 'If we cannot stop a separation without stopping lay preachers, the case is clear – we cannot stop it at all.'16

He was uncomfortably aware of the risks, but these preachers were successful; there was fruit of their labours and he would not let his own feelings override what seemed to him indisputable proof that God was directing. Unchurched people were being convinced of the truth of the Gospel and built up in Christian fellowship.17

By 1740 this work was becoming organised. The country was divided into 'rounds' [later called circuits]. Men who had shown themselves able preachers in their own locality were called, employed and

---

RICHARD BURDSALL : LOCAL PREACHER
IN THE OLD LEEDS CIRCUIT FOR NEARLY 60 YEARS

'Mr Burdsall's peculiar – they may be called eccentric – talents, were admirably adapted for the season of persecution with which Methodism was assailed when those talents were called into exercise. And subsequently, when time had worn out prejudice, and the public profession of Wesleyanism was no longer considered a reproach, the plain colloquial style of preaching which Mr Burdsall adopted, and that humour, sometimes bordering on coarseness, with which his discourses were intermixed, have often been the means of making an impression on his auditors, which in all human probability more rounded periods and polished oratory might not have been able to effect. The expectation of enjoying a laugh at the drollery of the preacher has unquestionably very often greatly added to the number of his congregation, and as frequently has the fact been verified, that they who came to scoff remained to pray.'

Memoir of Richard Burdsall (1735-1824) –
an autobiography with additional material
by his grandson, Revd Dr John Lyth,
4th edition, London 1884, pp.314-5

---

paid by Wesley as full-time professional travelling preachers ['itinerants'] to take spiritual charge of a round. They worked through it systematically over a period of four to six weeks, and every two years or less Wesley moved them on. He harnessed these itinerant preachers to himself in the belief that God had raised him up to create a force capable of presenting the gospel to all the people.[18] The itinerants were 'in connexion' with him, as were all the societies. It was a safeguard from legal attack. But they were in connexion with each other too; and this principle of 'connexion' became vital to Methodist discipline and government.[19]

How did local preachers fit into Wesley's system?

The quick answer is 'hardly at all, on the face of things'. For example the standard guide for the government of Methodist societies, the *Large Minutes,* six editions of which were published before Wesley's death (an indication of their importance to him), prescribed for the itinerant preachers not only their sermon subjects, but their dress, eating habits, sleep, study and conversation. The precise office and duty of stewards, class leaders, sick visitors; the home life, education of children, leisure and business activities of the ordinary members – all were exactly laid down. But there was nothing about local preachers, despite their obvious importance to Methodism. The reason may be found in what follows.

Exhorters

It is clear is that preachers began as 'exhorters'.

In the *Arminian Magazine* first published in 1778 'exhorters' were frequently mentioned. The formative days of Methodism were over and the term needed no explanation. The exhorter was part of the working system. Maybe the earliest Methodist use of the term in print is a reference in Charles Wesley's *Journal* for 1746. He was on a preaching tour of Cornwall when he met some exhorters who had held the societies together with prayer and encouragement after a number of travelling preachers had been caught by press-gangs. There were four such at Gwennap. Charles met them and reported that 'so far' they had given no cause for him to doubt that God had called them to the work, though he added 'I advised and charged them not to stretch themselves beyond their line by speaking out of the society or fancying themselves public teachers. If they keep within their bounds, as they promise, they may be useful in the Church, and I would to God that all the Lord's people were prophets like these.'[20]

Charles could not shake off the fear that unless carefully circumscribed, lay preaching would be a force destructive to the Church. At Zennor he told a young exhorter to practise the gospel before he preached it. At St. Just he probably thought his fears had been justified because a 'covetous, proud exhorter' had divided the society. Still, another exhorter had taken his place, and he was a solid, humble Christian who had 'kept the trembling sheep together'.21

The following year John went to Cornwall and carefully examined the exhorters. He asked whether they had gifts, grace and fruit, his usual questions. As a result he decided that of the eighteen men, four were unsuitable for the work; one had 'made shipwreck of the grace of God'; ten would be helpful when there was no preacher provided they would do nothing without the advice of those who had more experience of the work than themselves and the remaining three 'had gifts and grace, and had been much blessed in the work'.22

After this first encounter with the Cornish exhorters Wesley went to Wales, where he arrived at Merthyr on a Sunday when 'the exhorter was in the midst of his sermon. I preached when he had done.'23 An unforgettable experience for the exhorter. One wonders, in view of later instruction to exhorters, whether 'sermon' was a slip of the pen.

A few years later, in 1753, Charles once again felt he had to put the brake on. 'I spake with our brother Allen, an exhorter, whom one would fain have persuaded to forsake his business [i.e. give up his job and become an itinerant]. I persuaded him to continue in it.'24 Was the 'one' John?

DR JOHNSON COMMENDS PLAIN PREACHING

'I talked of preaching, and of the great success which those called Methodists have. JOHNSON: "Sir, it is owing to their expressing themselves in a plain and familiar manner, which is the only way to do good to the common people".'

J. Boswell, *Life of Samuel Johnson LL.D* (1794)
Oxford Edn. 1904, 2 vols. i p.306.

Exhorting followed a common pattern. A person spoke first in his own class-meeting, then to the society, usually when the travelling preacher failed to arrive. It was customary on these occasions to read one of Wesley's sermons. At Dudley when William Southall (b.1737) had worked through all of them, he took to reading a chapter of the Bible, making such observations as occurred to him and thus became an exhorter.25

This consisted of reproving sin, pleading with sinners to flee from the wrath to come, describing his own experience in those matters and testifying to his present joy. This framework appears to have been fairly rigid, held together by these topics, but leaving scope for individual emphases.

Members then as now were not uncritical. Edward Hampson (b. 1739) was an exhorter in Macclesfield. He was illiterate and had no obvious gift, and after his first attempt one of the members said 'I looked round with anxiety to see whether any strangers were present when Edward was praying, and when I saw none but our own friends I was glad, for I never heard such a blundering prayer in all my life.' Fortunately another member could see beyond the stammering and answered 'If he hold on his way, the Lord has work for him to do.'[26]

John Scaife lived in Easingwold. Having accompanied Richard Burdsall, a celebrated local preacher from York, whenever he came to the circuit, Scaife became an exhorter. They would begin to sing as they entered a village, and continue until they had collected a crowd, then one of them would speak.[27] When Jonathan Savile of Almondbury was an exhorter he and a band of friends who used to tramp round the circuit holding meetings were known as 'the recruiting sergeants'.[28]

How an exhorter became a local preacher

The rubicon between exhorting and preaching was 'taking a text'. Wesley's letter to Sarah Crosby in 1769 makes it explicit: 'Keep as far from preaching as you can; therefore never take a text; never speak in a continued discourse without some break, about four or five minutes.' Services led by exhorters were to be called 'prayer meetings'.[29] Robert Lomas of Manchester recalled 'In the year 1784 I began regularly to attend prayer-meetings in the town and country and sometimes to pray. . . at length when I had attended the prayer-meetings above a year, I broke through all my shackles and spoke a few words . . . I continued to attend the prayer-meetings and to exhort for a year when I began to think of preaching . . .. About Christmas 1786 I first ventured to take a text at Barton near Manchester, Rev. iii 20.'[30]

When John Allen was invited to preach 'Hitherto he had not formally taken a text, though he had frequently spoken from several passages of scripture to as good purpose as if he had mentioned the chapters and verses in which they are recorded.'[31]

At the 1770 Conference it was asked 'How shall each Assistant [later Superintendent] know the exhorters in his circuit?' The answer was 'Let each give his successor a list of them.' This shows that by now they had a recognised place in the system.[32]

The obituaries and biographies in the *Magazine* relating to this period show that 'taking a text' amounted to a public declaration that the exhorter had shown his qualities to be such as befitted a local preacher.

'Locals' were often travellers

Considering the immense part played by local preachers in pioneering and sustaining the early societies, the paucity of information or comment from Wesley is remarkable. This is partly remedied by the autobiographies of the travelling preachers which he published in the *Arminian Magazine*. And since they were local preachers before becoming itinerants, these *Lives* are a source of contemporary evidence about local preachers too. A striking feature is that most of them had travelled widely to preach before becoming itinerants, and had acted for existing itinerants unable to preach.

One of the first was Christopher Hopper, who began as a young class-leader in the society at Low Spen in County Durham, where they 'prayed, sung psalms and hymns, read the Bible and exhorted one another to fear and love God'. From 1744 he worked as a schoolmaster for a year or two, but he 'spent every Sabbath, and all [his] vacant hours in preaching, reading, praying, visiting the sick, and conversing with all that Providence put in my way'. In 1749 schoolmastering gave way to travelling about Allendale and Weardale preaching successfully but unpaid and seeing no future 'but beggary and great afflictions'.[33]

A local preacher who 'supplied' for years without ever becoming an official itinerant was James Sugden of Keighley, a poor weaver for whom the circuit had to buy a coat. In 1780 he was paid 9s. for supplying 9 days.[34]

Hopper said that in 1749 'God raised up many preachers; men, eminent both for gifts and graces. Some of them continued to be local, and some [like himself that year] became itinerant, preachers.'[35] Hopper wrote his 'Life' for the *Arminian Magazine* begun in 1778; would he have used the term 'local preacher' in 1749? An 'informed guess' is that it was coming into use at that time, as will be shown.

Contemporary evidence for the development of local preaching

This is not plentiful in the early years, though after it had been practised for fifty years or so it was recognised in obituaries, memoirs and a little later in local histories for the remarkable strength it had given to Methodism.

(i) The Minutes of Conference

The Minutes of Conference during Wesley's lifetime provide some information about local preachers.

In 1744 the office of an assistant (the itinerant in charge of a circuit, later called a superintendent) was defined.[36] Part of it was 'To see that the Stewards and the Leaders, Schoolmasters and Housekeepers faithfully discharge their several offices'. That is to say, the assistants had authority over all office-bearers. Other preachers based at home or travelling, are not included. The reason may be that at that early period Wesley knew them all and they were under *his* authority not the assistants'. A minute of 1746 [37] reinforces the impression that local preachers were not then differentiated from travelling preachers as far as their discipline was concerned: it was stated that the 'properest persons' to be present at the Conference were: 'as many of the preachers as conveniently could, the most earnest and sensiblest of the band leaders where the Conference was, and any pious and judicious stranger who might be in the place'. At the same time, regulations were formulated for the examination and admission of would-be preachers, under the general question 'How shall we try those who believe they are moved by the Holy Ghost and called of God to preach?'

The requirements were grace, that is a personal love of God reflected in the preacher's behaviour; gifts of sound understanding, right judgment, a just conception of salvation by faith and an ability to speak so that hearers could understand, and lastly, fruit of his labours manifested in persons who had come to understand God's forgiveness and love through his preaching.[38]

There was no indication that these terms referred solely to the travelling preachers. Indeed Wesley said that as long as these three marks occurred in any man, he was called to preach.[39]

An interesting feature of the 1747 *Minutes* was the list of preachers. As well as the twenty-three travelling preachers there were thirty-eight who 'assist us in one place'[40], i.e. in their own localities. So it is perhaps unlikely that 'local preacher' was an official designation just then. Another five years' experience led the brothers in 1751 to make their judgment more explicit. Men had to be prevented from rushing into preaching so none would be allowed to preach until the assistant had examined him and had received permission from the Wesleys to 'admit him a local preacher'.[41] So we can be sure that the name 'local preacher' existed by 1751 at the latest.

By a rule of 1753 any itinerant who married a woman unable to support herself had to go back to his former work and 'so commence a local preacher'. The *Minutes* of 1755 included three lists of preachers: thirty-four itinerants, fifteen 'chief local preachers', among them Thomas Maxfield and Thomas Westell, two of the earliest preachers, and Alexander Mather who eventually became President of the Conference, and twelve 'half-itinerants'. An indication of the contemporary high status of the local preachers came in the *Minutes* of 1758 when it was agreed that if the Assistant were 'straightened for time' when investigating the lives and experience of the band members, any of the local preachers might supply his place.[42] Since this examination was held to be of great importance in maintaining the quality of a society's life, it is evidence of Wesley's regard and trust in those early years.

'In several parts of England,' the Conference was told in 1763, 'there are local preachers who have both gifts and graces equal to those of most itinerants. Why then do they not travel?' Perhaps they could not afford it; a general fund was begun that year, mainly to pay off debts on preaching houses but also the debts of local preachers who were suitable to become itinerants, another indication that Wesley still thought of local and travelling preachers as one species, who differed only in the extent and location of their work.[43]

That local preachers' expenses were already part of the regular budget at Leeds is shown by the account book the circuit dating from 1768. On the second page is a list of regular 'disbursements'. The first twelve concern the expenses of the travelling preachers, then the thirteenth is 'Horsehire and turnpike for the local preachers'. At the bottom of the page is written 'and whatever other expence (sic) relates to the Circuit, or belonging to the whole of it'.[44] This is valuable evidence too that by 1768 in Leeds local preachers were a recognised body there, regarded as a responsibility of the circuit as a whole. This must have been a fairly recent development because Thomas Taylor wrote that in 1760-61 he 'supplied' for several absent preachers in the Leeds circuit and added 'what I did was gratis, not even having a penny for the turnpike.'[45]

The Leeds account book cannot to be taken as evidence necessarily applying to any other circuit. For example, in the

Staffordshire circuit book, also begun in 1768, there were no disbursements other than for the travelling preachers, the quarterly meeting dinner, tickets and (in 1785) preaching plans.

In 1767 the Conference discussed the problem of smuggling. Part of the answer surprisingly perhaps was 'Silence every local preacher that defends it.' The following year Wesley told those present to use his tracts, recommend only those he recommended and sell no others. In this way they would 'effectually prevent the improper publications . . .either of itinerant or local preachers'. The last Conference minute in Wesley's lifetime which referred to local preachers came in 1769, when he said 'I am a centre of union to all our travelling, as well as local preachers.'[46]

These were the regulations made in Wesley's day which had bearing on local preachers: in the last twenty years of his life nothing was said about them in the *Minutes*. Clearly they do not indicate any formulated expression of the office of local preacher as opposed to that of the travelling preacher. One is forced to conclude that in his mind, at least till about 1770, there was one body of men, the preachers; the locals were, for one reason or another, just his non-travelling men.

(ii) Wesley's Journal and Diary

A fairly close search of the *Journal* has revealed no person specifically named as a 'local' preacher. On three occasions, all toward the end of his life, he mentioned them as a group. In London, 31 December 1778 Wesley wrote 'We concluded the old year, and began the new, with prayer and thanksgiving. Four or five of the local preachers assisted me.'[47] He added that he was agreeably surprised by their manner of praying, which was natural but scriptural. When he was in the Isle of Man in 1781, he wrote 'I met our little body of preachers. They were two-and-twenty in all. I never saw in England so many stout, well-looking preachers together. If their spirit be answerable to their look, I know not what can stand before them.' There were only two itinerants on the island, so these were all local preachers. 'The local preachers are men of faith and love, knit together in one mind and one judgement. They speak either Manx or English, and follow a regular plan, which the assistant gives them monthly.'[48] Lastly, and again in London, he wrote in 1789 'Being the quarterly day for meeting the local preachers, between twenty and thirty of them met at West Street and opened their hearts to each other.'[49] This reads as though there was a regular local preachers' meeting in London: if so, this is the first mention of it. Probably it had been customary for some time for the local preachers to meet the assistant on the quarterly meeting days to receive their plan of appointments for the next quarter, though at West Street it seems to have been a time of fellowship too.

In the *Journal* and the *Diary* many persons are named, but not as local preachers, who from other sources are known to have been eminent and influential in this field.[50] Here is a small selection of them. William Holmes, one of the earliest, farmed at Sykehouse, not far from Epworth. Wesley called him 'an Israelite indeed'. His house was one of the earliest meeting places for Methodists outside London, and he suffered for his preaching from the mob at Grimsby.[51]

His school-master brother-in-law William Green became a class leader and local preacher in 1741. He introduced Methodism into Rotherham and used his school for preaching until 1761 when he led the society to build the 'Octagon'. He kept horses for local preachers to ride to their appointments, and his house was home for the itinerants. When he died Wesley said he 'had been as a father to them [the members at Rotherham] from the beginning'.[52] Thomas Capiter was a retired sailor who lived at Grimsby. He organised the building of a preaching-house and Wesley preached in it in 1757. In a letter to him, Wesley said that he advised the preachers not to preach for more than an hour at a time, and not to speak louder than necessary. When he died in 1772, Wesley said 'He was, between twenty and thirty years, a pillar and an ornament of the society' but we have to learn that he was a local preacher from local history and other sources. [53]

Thomas Garforth, a miller, had houses in Skipton and Leeds. He pioneered the building of a preaching house at Woodhouse. His name was on the Leeds plan of 1777, and he preached all over the West Riding – he once said he would not give a fig for a man who would not wade up to the chin in snow to fulfil an appointment to preach. Wesley mentioned him once, merely remarking that he had intended to preach in the market place but the rain prevented him so he stood near Mr Garforth's house.[54]

Matthew Mayer was the young son of a prosperous Cheshire farmer when he met Wesley at Stockport in 1763 and was invited to accompany him to Birmingham. On the way Wesley told him he must preach at the 5 o'clock service the next day. Mayer said that he had never preached except in small houses, but Wesley replied that the Lord would help him. This did not prevent Mayer from spending a sleepless night, relieved only by knowing that Wesley would not be there to listen. It was the start of his long career as a local preacher who undertook preaching tours far from home, to Lancashire, Derbyshire and Yorkshire. Wesley mentioned him in the *Diary* four times, but only to say that he had meals at his home.[55]

PERSECUTION IN CUMBRIA IN 1768

'Now it was that persecution began to lift his iron hand . . . The most serious attack was at Scaleby Hill, a small village six miles from Carlisle. Robert Bell (an exciseman of Carlisle and a local preacher), Robert Wilkinson (a schoolmaster and local preacher from Barnard Castle – shortly to become an itinerant) and a Mr Wilson, a local preacher from Cockermouth, had agreed to go there and Wilson was to preach. At the hour appointed a mob was fully prepared to meet them. Numbers were dressed in the most fantastical manner, and those who were known or suspected to be Methodist were ushered into the village with the beating of drums, and the playing of various musical instruments. A quantity of eggs had been provided, which were soon disposed of; and when these were exhausted, stones supplied their place. The scene now became serious. The moment the preacher had read his text, and was on the point of commencing his discourse, a stone struck him on the side of the head with such violence that the blood flowed profusely . . . The attacked sought shelter in a house but neither here were they secure. The doors of the house were burst open, and the windows broken to pieces . . . Two of the company went out for the purpose of endeavouring to appease their fury. But . . . they were thrown into the pond of a dunghill, and trampled upon . . . In those days there was no law for the Methodists. Instead of affording some redress, the worthy Magistrate, or some of his family, set the dogs upon them, and drove them from the house when application was made to him by some friends.'

Thomas Bridgman 'Methodism in Carlisle' in the *Wesleyan Methodist Magazine* 1826, pp.60-61. The account given here is typical of very many similar incidents in early Methodism.

Abraham Brames worked in the dockyard at Chatham. He began to preach in 1771 and at the end of his life calculated that he had walked 4,622 miles to preach the gospel, though he never counted the miles he had ridden. He was also chapel steward, and Wesley had a high regard for his judgment in this office: 'Tell the travelling preachers whatever you think or fear concerning them, if you love either them or your affectionate brother, J. Wesley.' He was not mentioned in the *Journal*.[56]

Philip Guier was the schoolmaster and local preacher in the settlement of German refugees at Ballingarrane [Ballingarry] near Limerick. He was present at the first Irish Conference, in 1752. One of his pupils, Philip Embury, also a local preacher, emigrated to New York in 1760 where he became a founding father of American Methodism. [57]

Dr James Hamilton FRCP (Edinburgh) was a town councillor of Dunbar who attended Wesley during an illness in Edinburgh in 1772. He later moved to Leeds and in 1795 was appointed Physician to the London Dispensary. He and Wesley did not always see eye to eye, either on medical or religious matters, but he was the only local preacher ever to preach the sermon during the Conference. This was at Leeds in 1789, pleading with Methodists not to separate from the Church. It was later printed, a sign of Wesley's approval. He said 'The case of separation from the Church was largely considered, and we were all unanimous against it' but did not refer to Hamilton.[58]

W. Ridley Sculp.

James Hamilton MD 1740-1827, Fellow of the Royal College of Physicians, Edinburgh, and a leading figure in Scottish affairs. Both as local preacher and physician he gave notable service to Methodism in London as well as in Scotland.
(Portrait from the *Arminian Magazine*, 1794.)

Of the hundreds of local preachers in Methodism in the eighteenth century he mentioned only three by name, though with the title 'preacher' not 'local preacher'. One was William Parker, the first class-leader in Bedford, and later its mayor. Under his governance, Wesley said, there was no open wickedness. Parker was 'an artless preacher . . . not destitute of pathos . . . of much use among honest, simple-hearted people'.[59]

Another was Lieut. Thomas Webb, who lost an eye when fighting for General Wolfe in 1758. He preached regularly in the Methodist chapel in New York in the 1760s and later settled in Bristol. Wesley wrote in 1773 'The captain is all life and fire; therefore, although he is not deep or regular, yet many who would not hear a better preacher flock to hear him.' In 1780 he said that he had 'found the fruit' of Webb's preaching, and three years later the flame that Webb had kindled had not gone out.[60]

The third 'preacher' was Robert Carr Brackenbury, a Lincolnshire landowner, scholarly, fastidious and precise. Wesley, who met him in 1776, came to regard him with the affection of a father. He preached (not acceptably to some) in Edinburgh, substituted for Wesley in Buxton, accompanied him to Holland and began Methodist work in the Channel Isles from his estate in Jersey. In 1782 Wesley wrote to him 'It is exceedingly clear to me, first, that a dispensation of the gospel is committed to you; and secondly, that you are peculiarly called to publish it in connexion with us . . . you are welcome to preach in any of our preaching-houses . . . whenever it is convenient for you.'[61]

Brackenbury was not typical of Wesley's preachers, if only in this, that he could do as he liked as far as Wesley was concerned.

In the *Journal* he told of the risks of preaching. After a terrifying attack on preachers in Cornwall in 1744 he wrote 'For what pay could we procure men to do this service? – to be always ready to go to prison and to death?'[62]

At Roughlee near Colne in 1748, he was accompanied by William Grimshaw the Methodist curate of Haworth, and Thomas Colbeck a grocer and local preacher from Keighley. He was cut off from them by the mob, which, incited by the Colne curate and deputy constable, 'tossed them to and fro with the utmost violence . . . and loaded them with dirt and mire of every kind'. The next day he sent a letter to the constable, ending with an effective threat 'This is flat rebellion against God and the King, as you may possibly find to your cost.'[63] Wesley always defended the preachers with his knowledge of the law and his rapier pen. At Hatfield in 1772 he was reminded of an earlier occasion there, when 'a justice levied a fine on a local preacher, on pretence of the Conventicle Act. So did a justice in Kent three or four years ago; but it cost him some hundred pounds for his pains.'[64]

> ## LOCAL PREACHERS AS PIONEERS
>
> 'The first sermon by a local preacher in Preston was delivered from the steps of the court of the Quarter Sessions under the following circumstances; John Wood was a weaver and a zealous layman. He had come from Padiham to Preston Sessions, to obtain a licence to preach. Having obtained it, and as he was leaving, a noisy rabble outside disturbed the business of the courts within, when one of the magistrates said to him contemptuously "There, go and reform that crowd." John Wood immediately in obedience to the high authority, availed himself of the opportunity and preached the first Methodist sermon those rude Prestonians had ever heard. It took place about 1778.'
>
> W. Pilkington *Makers of Methodism in Preston*
> London and Manchester 1890, p.18.

Local Preachers' Sermons

The local preacher's sermon was less subjective than the exhorter's. He had to deal with specific doctrines brought out by his 'texts'. John Phillips of Ossett who began to preach in 1772 wrote 'The doctrines I preach are, the fall of man, repentance towards God, faith in our Lord Jesus Christ, and the holiness without which no man shall see the Lord.' The friend who wrote his obituary said that he generally dealt with one doctrine at a time and explained it, then applied it to the needs of his hearers with considerable skill. He was 'a son of thunder', and 'vehement' in the pulpit and while some might have preferred a preacher of milder temperament, few persons slept while he preached. His sermons were short, energetic and full.[65]

What John Phillips' friend called a 'vehement' manner was less charitably described by non-Methodists. It seems however to have been a characteristic of much Methodist preaching because most of the critics seized on it as typical. 'The Preacher . . . endeavours all he can to increase the rising consternation which is sometimes spread over a great Part of the Assembly in a few minutes from its first Appearance. And, to compleat the work, the Preacher has his recourse to still more frightfull Representations; that he sees Hell's flames flashing in their Faces, and that they are Now! Now! Now! dropping into Hell! into the bottom of Hell!'[66]

Unlike the Anglican clergymen, who, in William Cowper's words

'. . . mount the rostrum with a skip,
And then skip down again; pronounce a text,
Cry, hem, and reading what they never wrote,
Just fifteen minutes, huddle up their work,
And with a well-bred whisper close the scene,'[67]

the rough, ill-bred and ill-educated lay preachers made electrifying contact with their congregations. Goldsmith corroborated this, if back-handedly: 'When I think of the Methodist preachers among us, how seldom they are endued with common sense, and yet how often and justly they affect their hearers, I cannot avoid saying within myself, had these been bred gentlemen, and been endued with even the meanest share of understanding, what might they not effect!'[68] Goldsmith, who was Irish, conceivably had heard John Carr, a Dublin local preacher. In 1766, Dr Davis, the surgeon of a regiment of dragoons and a noted wit, was persuaded to go and hear him. He admitted he went 'merely to take him off', but 'while I was leaning on my cane, looking at him through my fingers, during his first prayer, an arrow went to my heart which sent me home bruised and wounded.' He became a preacher too.[69]

Reports in the public press depicted local preachers as practically illiterate but clever enough to patch together an emotional harangue of scriptural phrases; carpenters, bricklayers, tallow-chandlers or butchers peddling piety. It was made to appear as though any person could get up and preach to his fellows if he felt moved to do so.[70]

Adam Clarke, Methodist itinerant and profound scholar, wrote in his *Commentary* (referring to I Cor. 13) about a local preacher who certainly was illiterate: 'I have quoted several passages from the heathens of the most cultivated minds in Greece and Rome to illustrate passages of the sacred writers. I shall now quote from an illiterate collier of Paulton in Somerset . . .. Josiah Gregory, whose mind might be compared to a diamond of the first water . . .. Among various energetic sayings of this great unlettered man I remember to have heard the following: "People of little religion are always noisy; he who has not the love of God and Man filling his heart is like an empty waggon coming violently down a hill: it makes a great noise because there is nothing in it."' Gregory became a local preacher in 1756. Once, while preaching at Bath in the presence of 'some fine ladies and gentlemen' he tried to speak more correctly than was natural to him and, as he put it, he 'began crimping the dishclout; but I made such miserable work on't, and was so hobbled up, that I said to myself: The Lord forgive me this time, and I'll never crimp the dishclout again.' Some of the Bath congregation having complained about his poor grammar, on his next appointment there he gave out the text 'He that believeth shall be saved, and he that believeth not shall be damned' then closed the Bible, looked at the congregation and said 'There's grammar for yo' Bath chaps.'[71]

Robert Phillipson's account of his beginnings as a local preacher in Weardale in the 1770s may be taken as a usual experience. He said that soon after his conversion in 1771 he felt called to act 'in a more public way'. He then spoke in prayer meetings and with others exhorted in the society. One Sunday evening at a meeting in his master's house he 'ventured to speak' alone. In 1777 the travelling preacher pressed Phillipson to preach in the chapel at Barnard Castle while he listened. 'I attempted to speak from Titus iii 5, 6. Giving way to the fear of man brought a snare, and I was much embarrassed and for some time after much ashamed to look my friends in the face again. Not having a proper command of my voice, setting it too high at the beginning . . . it was two or three days before I was well again. Soon after this I was put on the local preachers' plan.'[72]

Lecky, in his history of the eighteenth century, said that the secret of Methodism's success was that it satisfied the deepest and most persistent needs of human nature by preaching doctrines long neglected by the Church of England: the depravity and lost condition of men, the atonement of Christ, the necessity of rebirth, and the sustaining grace of the Holy Spirit. He said that these doctrines were driven home because the preachers spoke extempore and completely disregarded the conventional dignity and pose of the preacher. Nevertheless Lecky thought that these preachers preyed on the nerves of their hearers, scaring them to the verge of insanity, and concluded that 'a more appalling system of religious terrorism has seldom existed'.[73]

There is no doubt that many Methodist preachers did often deal with death, judgment and hell. But after the warning they presented the 'hope of glory'. And it was noticed that 'Methodists die well.'

Conclusions

Judging by the *Minutes of Conference*, Wesley's *Journal, Letters*, and the *Lives of the Early Methodist Preachers*, it is probably true to say that in the first quarter century of Methodism little was said specifically about local preachers because in Wesley's eyes they were simply preachers who were not travelling. He was closely connected with them.

He had known many of them from the beginning. Many were the pioneers of Methodist work, 'fathers' of their societies and influential in their community.

He told George Whitefield in 1767 that some of them were equal both in grace and gifts to most of the itinerants.[74] Nevertheless by about this time he was beginning to feel some anxiety, even mistrust, towards them. He had claimed to be a centre of union to both travelling and local preachers but in the rapid expansion of the movement he increasingly sensed that he was losing close control of the local preachers. Now he began to fear the effects of their preaching and to regret their lack of training and oversight. He doubtless had seen reports in newspapers and magazines attacking them. In the *Letters* we can see how his attitude developed. He wrote in 1761 'If local preachers who differ from us will keep their opinion to themselves, they may preach in our societies; otherwise they must not.' In 1776 he was sharper: 'Several of them talk

---

WESLEY'S CHAPEL, LONDON – BUILT BY A LOCAL PREACHER

'As far as information on the subject is accessible we believe that the contracts (for the building of Wesley's Chapel) were all taken up by Mr Samuel Tooth, a builder of influence who resided in the neighbourhood, who was one of the leaders and local preachers in London, and who, a few years previously had travelled one year as a preacher. The personal knowledge which Mr Wesley had of Mr Tooth, and the confidence which he is known to have reposed in him, only confirm the belief that Mr Tooth was responsible for the entire erection of the chapel, the morning chapel and of the one house, in which Mr Wesley afterwards resided.'

G. J. Stevenson *City Road Chapel, London, and its associations* 1872, p.66

---

nonsense and some of them speak against perfection. This must not be suffered.' So the assistant in the Dales was told to 'Fix a regular plan for the local preachers and see that they keep it.' 'Perfection' or 'perfect love' was a doctrine he insisted on, though many baulked at the idea that a person could be so filled with the love of God that he would not knowingly commit a sin. In 1781 he told the assistant at Bradford to stop local preachers who were in debt and to 'clip the wings' of the local preachers who did not do exactly as they were told. He repeated the wingclipping order to another assistant the same year.[75] At Margate in 1785 he noted that some years before, there had been a small society 'but a local preacher took them to himself'. This was Thomas Coleman, a schoolmaster who used his schoolroom for Methodist preaching. Wesley said he had no confidence in his behaviour and severed all connection with him.[76] In 1789 and 1790 he took up the matter of 'perfect love' again, and said that if any local preacher or leader spoke against it he must be removed from office.[77]

The travelling preachers had to obey Wesley. He could discipline them into habits of study and self-control, and remove them from the itinerancy if they did not meet his standards. But there was no machinery to train or supervise the ordinary local preacher and by 1790, in the rapid expansion of Methodism, Wesley had lost grip on him.

It was largely because of attacks on the quality of local preachers that the rule was made in the Conference of 1787: 'Let no person that is not in connexion with us preach in any of our chapels or preaching houses without a note from Mr Wesley or from the Assistant [superintendent] of the circuit from which he comes; which must be renewed yearly.'[78] 'A person in connexion' with Wesley was an itinerant preacher. So a local preacher was authenticated by the possession of a note to preach from the assistant or himself. A similar rule for exhorters was made in 1790: 'Let none exhort in any of our societies without a note of recommendation from the assistant. Let every exhorter see that this is renewed yearly. Let every assistant rigorously insist on this'.[79]

In the *Deed of Declaration* of 1784, Wesley's Will for Methodism, he did not give local preachers a place.[80]

Yet all over the connexion ordinary local preachers continued faithful. They pioneered new work, prepared the way for his itinerants, and built chapels. Three examples will serve.

In Wesley's last years William Wilkinson of Masham, comfortably off, 'spent the profits of two estates in doing good' and 'rented rooms for divine service and thus introduced the gospel into many villages' though, like many of us, 'his talents were not of a superior kind'.[81]

In 1780 Wesley 'preached at Joppa, a settlement of colliers three miles from Edinburgh. Some months ago, as some of them were cursing and swearing, one of our local preachers, going by, reproved them. One of them followed after him and begged he would give them a sermon. He did so several times. Afterwards the travelling preachers went' and a society was formed.[82]

Many local preachers gave sacrificially to make sure there was a chapel. William Buxton of Gunnerside was a lead miner. In 1788, a time

of great poverty, he found a vein of ore, dug it out by himself and gave all
the £50 he was paid for it to building the chapel.[83]

These men were untrained, unsupervised and largely unsung, but
'God works by whom he will work' and Wesley knew it.

Closer control 1791-1796

'What shall we do now? The time we have long looked for with
fear and trembling is come at last.'[84] Wesley had just died, and after the
first burst of sorrow John Pawson, like many itinerants and members,
realised that the dissatisfactions and problems of the last decades,
contained fairly well while Wesley lived, would now break surface. Chief
among them were whether itinerants should be allowed to administer the
sacraments, and Methodists allowed to hold services at the same time as
the Anglicans, either of which would cause the final separation of the two
bodies.

The Conference, now taking Wesley's place, recognised that
without immediate and firm direction the connexion would disintegrate in
factions. They were uncomfortably aware of the possible reaction of the
government to any liberalising reforms within Methodism; in the
atmosphere of the day 'democracy' evoked for many the same fear and
revulsion that 'communism' did in this century.

The discipline of the growing army of local preachers, who
conducted the majority of Methodist services, was a serious if lesser
concern. A rule of 1793 should be seen in this light: 'All Local Preachers
shall meet in class. No exception shall be made, in respect to any who
have been Travelling Preachers in former years,' and 'no [travelling]
preacher who has been suspended or expelled shall on any account be
employed as a Local Preacher, without the authority of the Conference.'[85]
The establishment of this rule indicates that some preachers, both itinerant
and local, thought themselves above Methodist discipline.

After much struggle and prayer, it was agreed by the Conference
of 1795, and set out in the so-called 'Plan of Pacification', to allow the
administration of the sacraments, and services in church hours, if a
majority of the trustees, and a majority of the stewards and class-leaders,
decided in favour of it. We notice immediately that local preachers, as a
body, were not to be involved in the decision, presumably on the grounds
that theirs was a circuit and not a society function. However, many of
them held office as stewards, class-leaders or trustees anyway. There was
to be no argument, for 'if any Local Preacher, Steward or Leader shall

disturb the peace of the Society, by speaking for or against the old or new plan, so called, the Superintendant [sic] of the Circuit, or the majority of the trustees, Stewards and Leaders of the Society so disturbed shall have the authority to summon a meeting of the Travelling Preachers of the Circuit, and the Trustees, Stewards and Leaders of that Society. Evidence shall be examined on both sides; and if the charge be proved, the Superintendant Preacher shall expel from the society the person so offending'.[86] Local preachers could not sit as judges of an offending local preacher except in their other capacities.

KIND WORDS IN DIFFICULT TIMES

'Our (local) preachers are men of God; we sincerely love them and I believe they love us. The Lord I trust is with us, and we hope that he will not suffer us to labour in vain, but that he will carry on his own work in the midst of us. Let us go forward, my dear brother, in the name of the Lord.' (18 December 1789)

'My mind, I hope, is fully bent to live and labour for the glory of God and if I can live and labour in peace with our people and preachers, my fixed design is to live and die among them, and if this cannot be, then peaceably to withdraw and so retire into some obscure corner as I trust that I shall never be the unhappy instrument of making any division in the church of God.' (4 May 1791)

From J. C. Bowmer and J. A. Vickers (eds) *The Letters of John Pawson, Methodist Itinerant* MPH 1994, vol i, 85, 101.

Alexander Kilham, an itinerant with a devastating pen and ideas ahead of his time, put a searchlight on Methodist practices. Until then local preachers were appointed by the superintendent and subject to his judgment alone. In a series of pamphlets Kilham pressed for the examination of the would-be local preacher by his own society's leaders' meeting and then by the circuit quarterly meeting. He also wanted a preachers' meeting for study and mutual criticism. His proposals did not evoke universal agreement even among preachers, so he published a letter from local preachers of the Leeds circuit, who felt it their duty 'to rectify the judgments of their misinformed brethren' who thought that reform meant the same as revolt.[87]

What most alarmed the connexional leaders was his outright advocacy of separation from the Church, and of lay representation in District meeting and Conference. The understandable anxiety at the top was that in the heady atmosphere of 'reform' the careful framework of responsibility erected by Wesley would be destroyed, a fear reflected in the title of a negative response to Kilham's proposals: *Christian Order, or Liberty without Anarchy, Government without Tyranny, and Every Man in his proper place.*[88] How were local preachers to be kept in their 'proper place'? This caused the Conference to ask in 1796 'what can be done to bring certain local preachers more fully to observe our discipline?' The answer indicates that some were free-lancing: the rule about meeting in class was repeated; preaching in another circuit was not permitted without at least three documents – former plans showing that the local preacher did preach regularly, a note from his superintendent and an invitation from the other circuit's superintendent. Further, he was forbidden to hold a lovefeast without being appointed to do so by the superintendent.[89]

After fifty years of such ad hoc adjustments, something radical was needed: the collective regulation of local preachers. Until this time

---

LOCAL PREACHERS: WARTS AND ALL

'Many . . . are men of mean birth, without education, accustomed to earn their livelihood by manual labour . . . their manners may be unpolished, their language coarse, the sound of their voices unharmonising, and their expressions vulgar, yet with all their defects, they may preach with power and be instrumental in bringing many souls to repentance.'

Arminian Magazine 1796 pp.368-9

---

they had usually met the superintendent at the time of the quarterly meeting to receive their plan of appointments, and perhaps their travelling expenses. Regular meetings may already have been established in many places, but the model for the Conference was probably that of the Sunderland circuit, which had set up a local preachers' quarterly meeting in 1794, with stringent rules for their examination and subsequent conduct.[90]

So in 1796 the Conference established the Local Preachers' Meeting. It gave security to the circuits, because now there was a frequent check on the standards of preaching, and security to the preacher, because his peers as well as the superintendent were now together judges of his fitness to preach. 'Let the Superintendent regularly meet the Local Preachers once a quarter, and let none be admitted but those who are proposed and approved at that meeting; and if in any circuit this is not practicable, let them be proposed and approved at the quarterly meeting.'[91] Two hundred years later this decision of Conference has become the occasion of our celebration of the contribution made by local preachers to the life and work of Methodism from its very beginning.

MRS. TAFT.

Mary Taft (née Barritt) (1772-1851) a notable Wesleyan preacher of the late eighteenth and early nineteenth centuries mainly in northern England. After her marriage in 1802 to Zechariah Taft, a Wesleyan itinerant, she continued preaching, virtually acting as assistant to her husband in the circuits to which he was appointed.

2

YEARS OF TENSION AND CONFLICT 1796-1850

John Munsey Turner

The First Schisms and the Sidmouth Bill

By 1796, then, we have the constitutional setting for later developments. In 1797 the rules laid down in 1796 were re-affirmed but with the covering statement that no disrespect was implied to the local preachers – 'our worthy brethren whom considered as a body we greatly respect' which sounds slightly patronising.

The effort to resolve the disputes of the early 1790s had preserved connexionalism despite the wishes of some wealthy trustees, but the outcome was tantamount to virtual independence from the Church of England. Moreover the political tensions of the day began to find echoes within Wesleyanism, forcing further changes. Kilham, using the political clichés of the time rather in the way liberation theologians in the 1970s used Marxist methodology, espoused a more democratic constitution [with lay representation in Conference] to reduce the powers of the itinerant preacher. His stream of pamphlets, culminating in *The Progress of Liberty among the People called Methodists* (1795) envisaged control from below and unwisely suggested dishonest thinking among the preachers who opposed him.

The ministerial leadership moved against such Methodist 'jacobinism', unfairly calling Kilham both Painite and Leveller. As a result Kilham, aided by William Thom (1751-1811), superintendent at Halifax, founded the Methodist New Connexion in 1797, draining off about five per cent of Wesleyan membership, ironically at a time of great expansion. Around Ashton-under-Lyne and in parts of Cheshire, Lancashire and the West Riding – Mount Sion, Halifax, is a good example – it proved possible for the New Connexion to take whole congregations, buildings and all. In Sheffield, always prone to gusts of radicalism, fifteen out of thirty-two local preachers joined the new grouping. Even so the New Connexion did not grow rapidly. By 1808 there were only 174 local preachers in the MNC, compared with probably 2,000 in the Wesleyan Connexion.

Kilham had advocated more training for local preachers with study groups in the towns for all preachers.[1] It is doubtful if his dreams were ever realized, though in later years United Methodism gave some priority to the training of local preachers. Kilham's basic demand for lay representation in the Wesleyan Conference was not to be met until 1878.

The second great wave of revival in England came in part as an off-shoot of the frontier tradition of church life in the USA, beginning in the 1790s. One consequence in the north west and the north midlands, especially the Potteries, was an outbreak of revival which appeared threatening to Wesleyan itinerants who could not always reconcile order and ardour. Some groups like the Magic Methodists of Delamere Forest with James Crawfoot as leader, and the Quaker Methodists around Warrington led by Peter Phillips, came closer to the apocalyptic groups and millenarians who evoked memories of the Ranterism of the 17th century. The Independent Methodists (1805), with no paid ministry, stemmed from the Quaker Methodists and the Band Room Methodists of

---

A PRIMITIVE METHODIST HERALD COMES TO MANCHESTER (1819)

'There is a long-standing tradition to the effect that Primitive Methodism was first carried to Manchester by "a local preacher from Macclesfield; that he had a wooden leg; that he walked from Macclesfield on the Sunday morning to Manchester; that he preached at the New Cross after dinner; and that he walked home after preaching in the evening, thus performing a journey of thirty six miles on foot!" Now tradition is often very tenacious in its hold on essential fact . . . and the mental picture of the unknown missionary with his artificial limb, stumping his way to Manchester and back, has stamped itself on the imagination. Who else could the hero of our tradition be than "Eleazar Hawthorn of the wooden leg" – the convert of Lorenzo Dow and an active participant in the first Mow Cop Camp Meeting?'

H. B. Kendall *The History of the Primitive Church c.1905* vol.ii p.15.

Manchester. It should be noted here, too, that the revivalist Wesleyan itinerant William Bramwell influenced James Sigston, a Leeds schoolmaster and local preacher, who seceded, setting up the 'Kirkgate

Screamers'. Sigston moved back into Wesleyanism later and was to be a prime mover in the affair of the Brunswick organ in 1827.[2]

Primitive Methodism should be seen as a separate revivalist movement, rather than simply a revolt against an insensitive and cautious Wesleyanism which was in due course to hound out the PM founders.[3] Hugh Bourne (1772-1852) and William Clowes (1780-1851) were expelled from Wesleyanism not merely for 'not meeting in class' (as required under the 1796 Regulations) nor for 'upholding other than normal style of worship' but for taking out preaching licences without the sanction of the itinerants and the quarterly meeting. Bourne clearly wished to legitimise camp meetings, which were a central feature of Primitive Methodism with much praying and preaching, and as far as possible keep the movement free from the restraints of Wesleyan superintendents. Early Primitive Methodism however copied much of the older system, including the use of local preachers, but with little distinction between local and travelling preachers other than the payment and administrative responsibilities which belonged to the latter. The local preacher could preside at the Lord's Supper though this in practice may not have been frequent. Among some Primitives a Quaker view of worship prevailed, and some PM Methodist congregations never celebrated the Lord's Supper.[4] Indeed the lovefeast was for a time as significant, and sometimes more popular, than holy communion, and frequently conducted by local preachers.

This is the background to the great crisis of 1810-11 when Lord Sidmouth's Bill almost put an end to local preaching.[5] This was Methodism's first experience of involvement in national politics against a background of war, the Luddite movement in the north and the midlands, and widespread revival. Itinerant preaching was in no way a Methodist monopoly as Dr Lovegrove[6] has recently shown in great detail. 'Indeed it would', wrote R. W. Dale, 'have been as difficult in 1820 to find a Congregational church without a body of lay preachers as it would be to find a Congregational church without a Sunday School.' There was a fear of jacobinism in governmental and ecclesiastical circles, but if thousands were being attracted to the new infidel societies, hundreds of thousands were being drawn to hear nonconformist preachers and to join chapel and cottage meetings. There were 251 licences for permanent meeting houses in the 1780s , but 832 in the 1790s. From 1795 to 1801 in the country as a whole the figure for all places of worship (permanent and temporary) was 3,578 and from 1802 to 1808, 3,680. In the West Riding licences for temporary places of worship rose from 73 in the 1780s to 401 in the

1790s, the numbers clearly being much greater in the period of the Napoleonic wars. There was an almost paranoid fear in government circles of insurrection and a parallel literary campaign against Methodism (the term was often used loosely and inaccurately) by Sidney Smith (who called it 'lunacy'), Leigh Hunt, Robert Southey, T. E. Owen and, later, William Cobbett. Hazlitt's bitter and belittling description of a Wesleyan congregation is typical: 'Never was there such a set of scarecrows: melancholy tailors, consumptive hairdressers, squinting cobblers, women with child or with ague make up the forlorn hope of the cavalcade.'[7]

The exemption of licensed preachers from the militia caused the Wesleyan Conference in 1803 to ban the practice of local preachers claiming exemption by taking out licences. In 1803 the very important Committee of Privileges was set up by the WMs, paralleling the older Dissenting Deputies. An example of what might happen occurred in October 1810. William Kent, a local preacher, held a service in an uninhabited and unlicensed house in Berkshire, and was fined £20 under

---

LOCAL PREACHERS IN THE PENINSULAR WAR 1811

'It has come to my knowledge that Methodism is spreading very fast in the army. There are two or three Methodist meetings in this town, of which one is in the Guards. The men meet in the evening and sing psalms, and I believe a sergeant (Stephens) now and then gives them a sermon. Mr Briscall has his eye on these transactions, and would give me notice were they growing into anything which ought to be put a stop to . . . These meetings likewise prevail in other parts of the army. In the 9th regiment, there is one, at which two officers attend, Lieut--- and Dr---, and the Commanding Officer has not yet been able to prevail upon them to discontinue this practice. Here, and in similar circumstances, we want the assistance of a respectable clergyman [to] moderate the zeal and enthusiasm of these gentlemen.'

The Dispatches of Field Marshal the Duke of Wellington, during his various campaigns. An enlarged edition in 8 vols., compiled from official and authentic documents by Col Gurwood, CB. KCTS. Vol 4. London 1844 pp.584-585.

---

the Toleration Act. Quarter Sessions at Reading upheld the fine, though King's Bench later quashed it.[8] Lord Sidmouth, former Prime Minister and now Home Secretary, stated on 1 June 1809 that he believed licences were being taken out to dodge service in the militia. The prohibition of camp meetings by the Wesleyans and the subsequent establishment of Primitive Methodism, must be seen in this context. Sidmouth had received information from Justices of the Peace like Mr Sparrow of Stafford who stated that fifteen men, nine of them journeymen potters, had presented themselves to take the oaths as Methodist preachers. Ten had declared they had no particular congregation, i.e. were not resident pastors. On 18 June 1810 Sidmouth gave notice that he would bring in a Bill to prevent anyone taking out licences as preacher or teacher unless he was twenty-two, was appointed to a congregation and could give testimonials for his fitness for office.

The Bill was presented in May, 1811, and Sidmouth noted that the list of people taking the oaths included 'blacksmiths, cobblers, tailors, chimney sweepers and what not' – carpenters were not mentioned! He and his friends clearly had anxieties about the established church being eclipsed by a 'sectarian people', which was not a foolish fear by any means, and indeed was to be increasingly justified, as the results of the 1851 Religious Census were to bear out a generation later.

The debate within Methodism became furious. Adam Clarke and Thomas Coke (who greatly disliked the American evangelist Lorenzo Dow who had promoted the Camp Meeting movement in England)[9] were interviewed by Sidmouth. Their fears were apparently allayed, but the interests of the Connexion and the preachers were better served by the Connexional solicitor, Thomas Allan, whose place in Methodist history has been underestimated. He was supported by Thomas Thompson MP (1754-1828)[10] who was significantly part of that group cohering around William Wilberforce, the Hull evangelical 'cousinhood'. Wilberforce called him 'a true Christian as well as a man of great acuteness and tried integrity'. It is significant that both Allan and Thompson were local preachers, and knew where the shoe might pinch. A scholarly man, who left a large library to the Connexion, Allan would only officiate as a local preacher in workhouses and small chapels, 'delighting mostly to address Gospel truth to the poor, the aged, the infirm, the friendless and the afflicted'.[11]

The Wesleyans approached Prime Minister Spencer Percival, and his successor, Lord Liverpool. Allan produced from Wesleyanism 520 petitions with 30,000 signatures[12] while 700 petitions came from dissenting sources for whom Sir William Smith, the Unitarian, was a tireless advocate. The Whigs pursued a policy of mild toleration and the bill was lost without a division under government pressure. A Tory attempt to destroy religious toleration had failed, not least because Tory ministers were unwilling to court opposition. England was becoming a plural society in religious matters.

Dissenters wished to go further. The Protestant Society for the Protection of Religious Liberty presaged a more militant mood. The battle shifted to the localities where justices of the peace (of whom a quarter were clergymen) interpreted the Toleration Act harshly. Typical of what could happen was an occasion at Swansea where two Methodist ministers had their appeal against the militia ballot refused as they were not ministers of distinct single congregations but had wider circuit responsibilities. Likewise in Leeds in 1812 several preachers were refused licences. Not all cases went against the preachers. In one riot against a Methodist congregation at Pershore those responsible were reminded by the judge that 'the parties assembled were not a private meeting to hear an enthusiast but to hear a licensed preacher in the licensed meeting house'. In Berkshire a penalty on a local preacher of £3 for unlawful preaching was quashed.[13]

Timothy Hackworth (1786-1850), a leading north-eastern locomotive engineer and designer, and loyal Wesleyan local preacher. He did much to promote Methodism in the Bishop Auckland area of County Durham.
W. D. Lawson *Wesleyan Local Preachers* 1874. p.169.

However the overall opposition could have been fatal to local preaching, especially among the raw lads and lasses of the Ranters. Local uncertainty led the Committee of Privileges to strike while the iron was hot. A bill was produced which owed much to Thomas Allan and the dissenting leader, Sir William Smith, as well as Thompson and Joseph Butterworth MP, a founder member of the Committee of Privileges and MP for Coventry 1812-1818. It embodied the views of Dissent against the Five Mile and Conventicle Acts which had been a thorn in Wesley's flesh. On 25th July 1812 the Bill (52 George III C.155), a new Toleration Act, received the Royal assent.[14] 'The Five Mile and Conventicle Acts were repealed, magistrates were compelled to administer the oaths to those who asked to take them, and the law protected itself against abuse by stating that exemption from military and civic duties could only be claimed by ministers without any other calling but that of schoolmaster.'[15] This Act is still the basis of Free Church toleration. Conference in 1812 duly rendered thanks to the Committee of Privileges while exhorting its members to 'fear the Lord and the King and meddle not with those that are given to change' – radicals and Luddites one presumes. The Wesleyan leaders certainly believed that their movement was a bulwark against working class radicalism.

Allan privately stated, 'In times of scarcity and distress we may safely say that among colliers, miners and mechanics, Methodism has been the grand instrument of preserving subordination, and if government were but acquainted with the happy effect of Methodism both in England and Ireland they would do their utmost to protect them rather than discourage them. . . . We are not a political people, we simply wish to worship God and promote Christianity in the land by all means and have been the steady friends of government.'[16] Elie Halévy was to build his famous thesis about the stabilising influence of Methodism on sentiments like this.

The passing of the Bill was of particular importance to local preaching in the smaller Methodist groups, for in that very year Primitive Methodism launched itself as an independent movement, followed up by the Bible Christians in 1815 in the south west. Local preaching in all its forms had secured legal authorisation – a vital matter for all lay preachers including those extraordinary female preachers of Primitive Methodism and the Bible Christians, though the days of distress and persecution were by no means over, as innumerable stories in Primitive Methodist folklore testify.[17]

Later Schisms and Controversies

Later schisms were of a different order due not so much to revivalism as to the inner tensions within Methodism, stemming from a growing desire for increased local autonomy. In the first instance this involved Sunday Schools. The Bolton Wesleyan Refugees[18] are an interesting example. Some called for more democracy in the circuits and societies. There was also resentment at the division of large circuits which was taking place at that time in Liverpool, Sunderland, Leeds and other large centres where membership had grown rapidly since Wesley's death.[19]

Methodism's social composition was changing also. While still predominantly artisan,[20] there was a growing number of more affluent congregations where pew holders tended to put pressure on trustees who themselves were often rising in the social scale. Some of these prominent laymen formed the groups which gave support to Jabez Bunting (a representative figure for many itinerants) as well as to laymen like James Wood (1777-1849, first President of Manchester Chamber of Commerce) and W. Gilyard Scarth (1780-1853) of Leeds, both of whom were local preachers.

The Leeds Organ case (1827) was a notable example of class conflict within Methodism as the lists of the Brunswick Chapel trustees and of the circuit leaders indicate.[21] The circuit leaders, as a whole, were lower in the social scale than the trustees. Brunswick chapel, opened on 9th September 1825 with Jabez Bunting as preacher, was a prime example of the large chapels being built for affluent worshippers in urban areas, with a taste for Morning Prayer as well as for organs, for which Conference permission was needed. Brunswick in fact never used Morning Prayer, but later had its own service book. With the further details of this fascinating case we cannot be concerned; Dr Batty has given a clear account (see note 1). But we need to make clear the rôle of local preachers on both sides of the controversy which began with a request by the Brunswick trustees for an organ countered by opposition from the circuit leaders and the local preachers whose part in the affair was a prime cause of Conference's intervention. The opposition was led by James Sigston (of 'Kirkgate Screamers' fame) and Matthew Johnson, a cloth glosser and local preacher who became prominent among the breakaway groups who later formed the Wesleyan Association. Sixty out of sixty-two local preachers opposed the organ, no doubt associating it with 'high church' tendencies and ministerial pulpit monopoly. On the other side was the redoubtable William Gilyard Scarth, a master dyer, trustees' secretary and member of the lay groups which supported Jabez Bunting in his financial re-floating of Wesleyanism. The local preachers, led by Johnson, undoubtedly broke the constitution by holding meetings

---

TENSIONS IN SUNDERLAND IN THE MID-1830S

'At a special local preachers' meeting in January 1836 charges were made against John Thompson for: 1. Holding a lovefeast at Phoenix Lodge or elsewhere in Sunderland without the appointment or approbation of the Superintendent. 2. For preaching and holding the said lovefeast in factious opposition to the regular ordinances of the connexion, and during the times of preaching, and a lovefeast being held in Sans Street chapel. Mr Thompson having admitted that he had preached and held a lovefeast at Phoenix Lodge, after some conversation on the subject it was agreed that if Mr Heape would plan him more frequently he would pledge himself not to preach anywhere in future from factious motives nor attempt any factious measures when he was planned to any of the places.'

From the Sunderland Circuit LP Minutes. Phoenix Lodge was the Masonic temple in the east end of the town, much used by various religious secessions as a temporary base.

---

without the permission of the superintendent, but could claim that the Conference had contravened the spirit of the 1797 regulations by upholding the trustees. These had voted only eight to six (with one neutral) for the organ, while the leaders voted sixty to one against. This was at first a wholly lay revolt, provoked by harsh expulsions, no itinerant preacher joining the resulting secession of the Protestant Methodists (1828). It was ironically stated that the Brunswick organ cost Leeds Wesleyanism £1,000 and 1,000 members. Bunting (reported as asserting that 'Methodism was as much opposed to democracy as it is to sin') was quite prepared to 'ditch' the rebels for the sake of order.[22]

The trustees, circuit leaders and local preachers who clashed here are an interesting case of quite different approaches to church life. The 'Organ Case' was a revolt not so much about organs (even the Protestant Methodists soon acquired them) or even liturgy, for the rebels accepted that too, in their London chapel, but a revolt against the pastoral office as practised in Wesleyanism and against the growing dominance of a clerical élite, backed by a group of leading West Riding and Lancashire business men who provided both political 'clout' and money. The opposition stood for local autonomy with little or no interference from either District or Conference.

In the next schism (the Wesleyan Association) it was reformers in congregations of such chapels as Baillie Street, Rochdale, who were not only radical in their desire for autonomy but had the financial means to support it, leaving the poor to the Wesleyans.[23] The Association held its first Assembly in 1836 in Manchester, a result of agitation against the introduction of a Wesleyan Theological college and also of the manner in which the matter was rushed through Conference against the spirit of the 1797 regulations. In 1837 the Association made clear the role of the local preacher: 'We believe that those who are called by Christ to preach the Gospel, and who render their services gratuitously, are not thereby less qualified to exercise any of the offices of the Christian ministry than those who are maintained by the contributions of the church; they therefore are eligible to be appointed by the Quarterly Meeting of the Societies to discharge any of the offices of the Christian ministry.' This meant that local preachers could conduct both Sacraments. They continued to do so in the various branches of what was to become United Methodism up to 1932, using normally a non-liturgical form, though Service Books were later introduced.[24]

The final and largest schism followed the prolonged 'Fly Sheets' controversy of the late 1840s, in which the main targets of the critics were the secularisation of Wesleyanism, as well as its centralisation and the concentration of its leaders in London. There was angry abuse on both sides, with rival magazines and newspapers, and mass expulsions of 'rebels', including many local preachers. In 1857 the United Methodist Free Churches embraced most of the rebels of 1828, 1835 and other minor schisms like the Arminian Methodists. The much smaller Wesleyan Reform Union (1859)[25] remained and still remains outside the main Methodist grouping [with its headquarters in Sheffield] though its local preachers are associated with the LPMAA.

We must note that local preachers played a considerable role in all these painful controversies which split chapels and circuits and even families, halting the progress of Wesleyanism for a decade with a total of almost 100,000 members lost to that Connexion, many of whom never linked with any other Christian group. It was men like Sigston and Johnson of Leeds who epitomised the local, decentralised revivalist tradition which was so often in conflict with the 'high Wesleyanism' led by Jabez Bunting, the more affluent Wesleyan cousinhoods, and those who still hankered after closer relationships with the Church of England. Some of these laymen were local preachers, so the laity lay athwart the social tensions and conflicts of the time. We need to remember that the

Methodist Churches were religious societies primarily, not political parties.

> 'Mr Bunting took the lead in the measures necessary to accomplish the recognition of the itinerant preachers' ministerial character. It had been usual in Quarterly Meetings of local preachers, when the examination of character took place, to read all the names on the plan beginning with the Superintendent. Mr Bunting objected to have his name thus read, on the ground that it was not the place for any examination into his character, that being done at District Meetings and the Conference. By this means he drew a distinction between the itinerant and the local preachers, which to some extent recognised the proper pastoral *status* of the former. This, and other apparently trivial, but significant circumstances prepared the people to regard those who were so truly their "pastors and preachers" as Christian "ministers".'
>
> George Smith *History of Wesleyan Methodism* 1864 vol.iii p.35.

High Wesleyanism stressed the connexional, the national and indeed the international stance of the church. It was the minister (the itinerant preacher) who was the linchpin of the system, the spokesman for the Conference, with the circuit superintendent an 'episcopal' figure with power any Anglican diocesan would envy! The itinerant preachers acted as a shuttle, weaving the Connexion together, the three year itinerancy producing a monochrome style of Wesleyan minister never in circuit long enough to be truly part of the community. This style of Methodism was increasingly conscious of its standing within society. High Wesleyanism tended to be conservative both liturgically and politically, though the old stereotype of a dominant toryism and underlying liberalism is too rigid, as local studies like those of Dr David Gowland have shown. There was an air of clericalism about all this, the marks of a Connexion struggling to become a church[26] but having to attain too quickly the maturity of a national institution. It was easy for the local preachers to believe themselves to be considered inferior by the itinerants, and for them to regard the itinerants as 'jumped up laymen'[27] from the same background as themselves, but giving themselves unseemly airs after being received into full connexion. Low Wesleyanism was more local, more lay, more democratic in style, more prone to support revivalism and high-powered trans-Atlantic revivalists and evangelists from Lorenzo Dow to James Caughey.[28] It was orientated towards chapel culture, to lay prerogatives and leadership. It was more consciously dissenting. Localism threw up the Sigstons and Johnsons and that glorious 'Dad's army' of local preaching characters like the irrepressible handicapped Jonathan Saville of Halifax[29] who believed 'You can catch more flies with honey than with vinegar' and later William Thornton, also of Halifax, a Primitive Methodist who, after leading prayers at the great Chartist meeting at Peep Green on Whit Monday, 1839, was clapped on the shoulder by the Chartist leader, Feargus O'Connor, shouting 'Well done, Thornton, when we get the People's Charter I will see that you are made archbishop of York.'[30] Thornton could not wait and emigrated to the USA! Men like him made high Wesleyans shudder – and Hugh Bourne too! – but it was not accurate to claim that the local preachers were necessarily politically radical. Religious radicalism was often politically quietist. Methodism was heterogeneous enough to produce all styles of political thinking. These two strands have always lived together uneasily in Methodism and still do, though there has been no national schism since 1849. Sociologists refer to the division as one between 'locals' and 'cosmopolitans' – (Gesellschaft and Gemeinschaft are the words used by F. Tönnies) – the 'locals' being tied to chapel, home and work loyalties, while the 'cosmopolitans' are more mobile – socially, spatially and cognitively.[31] The itinerants, often unconsciously, represented a wider loyalty and a wider church, and the alliance with the intelligentsia and the bourgeoisie of Methodism – often through marriage – is perfectly intelligible.

Patterns of Worship

What was Methodist worship like in the early nineteenth century? The evidence is patchy and caution is wise. Authoritative-sounding statements are not always genuinely authoritative and legislation is better evidence for what it proposed to prohibit than for what it sought to promote.[32] Wesley had always urged attendance at the parish church. This was often observed well into the nineteenth century especially when the rector or vicar was an Evangelical. Avoidance of 'church hours' tended to push Methodist worship into the evening. Preaching services, lovefeasts and other 'prudential' means of grace, as Wesley called them, grew in popularity and were increasingly open to a wider public than society members alone. Local preachers would conduct the majority of such services in the smaller chapels.

Their style was varied. In the large town chapels there was some continuance of the Morning Prayer tradition – often thought 'high' by some of the 'low' Wesleyans though certainly no innovation, being part of the original pattern.[33] Most large towns like Bolton had at least one 'Morning Prayer' chapel, up to quite recent times. In these chapels the evening service – much more popular after the introduction of incandescent gas mantles[34] – would be of an extempore nature. And a less formal pattern was the norm in smaller urban and all rural chapels.

> 'In the Pocklington circuit at the time there were few chapels; so that our meetings for preaching and public worship were mostly held in the kitchens of farm houses and the cottages of labouring men. The preacher usually stood behind a chair, the back of which supported a moveable desk upon which stood his bible and hymn book, the people standing or sitting upon chairs, tables, stools or chests of drawers as the case might be. In these humble sanctuaries the people worshipped God in spirit and in truth as their entire behaviour indicated. The sermons to which they listened contained no elaborate phraseology, no disquisitions on dark and doubtful questions and no hard technical terms; their substance being the essential truths of Christ's Gospel and their garb pure Saxon English which even the children understood, delivered with a broad Yorkshire accent. The sentiments embodied in the hymns that were sung and in the prayers that were offered, the people felt in their hearts. There was nothing artificial in their services . . . at lovefeasts many a tale of true personal conversion was told and listened to with tears of grateful joy.'[35]

This was typical of a village community in 1800.

Norman Wallwork has traced the factors that lay behind the preaching service, though one would add the fact that early Methodism owed much to the ethos of field preaching which gave chapel worship the feel of being an open air service with a roof on, and a strong sense of the experiential. Worship could be, and still is, judged by its immediate effect on the worshippers. Norman Goldhawk is also right to observe that 'although Methodists felt no direct responsibility to conform to any older non-Anglican tradition of worship such as that which lay behind the nonconformity of the time, they could hardly escape the influence of the pattern of worship found in the dissenting chapels.' We need, also, especially in assessing Primitive Methodism, to remember the influence of the frontier tradition and worship patterns like camp meetings and prayer meetings.[36]

Methodist worship was usually simple and short compared with dissenting worship – an hour in the morning, longer in the evening. Curiously Scripture readings were not always included though they became normal by 1820. The basic units were extempore prayer, extempore (though not unprepared) preaching and the singing of hymns, at first 'lined-out' by the preacher. This created an 'oral tradition' of hymnody which was of great importance to the Methodist people who imbibed Evangelical Arminianism through remembered songs in a way almost unique in Christendom. The service would later – when 'lining-out' ceased – be filled out with more hymns and later still (in the large chapels) introits, anthems, canticles, with organs and choirs.

Two contemporary accounts can be compared. Joseph Nightingale's *A Portraiture of Methodism* (1807) is somewhat satirical – 'Here is no pomp, no parade, no vain shows of unmeaning ceremonies, nor irksomeness of tedious liturgies; all is simple and intelligible, agreeable to the easy decorum and decent order of a Christian temple.' But the simple order he outlines is confirmed by Jonathan Crowther's *Portraiture of Methodism* of 1815. Hymn, prayer, hymn, sermon, hymn, prayers, benediction. An early Methodist New Connexion order of 1823 shows a similar pattern – hymn, prayer, scripture, hymn, sermon, notices, intercession for the sick, thanksgiving, solemn prayer. It is, unconsciously, the classic Genevan shape! Primitive Methodists (1829) and Bible Christians (1838) produced similar orders. The Bible Christian order was:– hymn led by precentor, congregation standing, prayer and Lord's Prayer (all kneeling), scripture reading (at least in the morning), verses of a hymn, sermon, infant baptism when required, hymn, prayer.[37] What is notable is the rôle of the sermon which was not yet the great climax as it tended to become in later Victorian styles, though we must not assume these practices universal.

Preaching services could easily be transformed into revival meetings. Bunting was put off for life by the eccentricities of local preaching in Macclesfield in 1803. Earlier Joseph Entwistle in Halifax in the 1790s spoke of 'an outpouring of the spirit'. 'Our warm friends from Woodhouse were there, they had gone beyond all bounds of decency, such screaming and bawling I never heard. Divided into small companies in different parts of the chapel, some singing, some praying, others praising, clapping of hands etc. All was confusion and uproar ... they continued till five o'clock in the morning. What shall we say of these things? God is working very powerfully in the minds of many but I think Satan or at least the animal nature has a great hand in all this.' That was in the chapel where Thompson, Pawson and Thom had ministered and where Bunting was to be superintendent also.[38]   There has always been great variety of style in Methodism and no doubt local preachers were to be found not only of different styles themselves but, chameleon-like, adapting to different chapels, a skill which every Methodist preacher has to learn and which is different from a parish or pastorate style. This still remains the case today.

Patterns of Training

What training did local preachers receive? There is here a quite extraordinary continuity of practice with a strangeness of language like 'on Note' and 'on Trial' and 'on full Plan' which have continued for two centuries. The local preacher would begin with a period 'on Note' with an experienced preacher, the novice trying out his praying and exhortations in a remote chapel, as the writer did in Staffordshire and in the Fens in 1950.   Then followed the period 'on trial' at the end of which the preacher would conduct a whole act of worship, preach a trial sermon before his or her peers and an itinerant, and endure an oral examination before the preachers, to test his or her required knowledge of 'our doctrines' and Wesley's Sermons. These remain and, strikingly, were reproduced in all the smaller non-Wesleyan bodies as was the original stress on gifts and grace and fruit – a genuine call to preach and an ability to convince hearers. This was basically an apprentice system which would be familiar at the time to the artisan groups from which many preachers came. William Clowes met with preachers on Saturday evenings almost on the lines of the old Puritan 'prophesyings'. In Sunderland there was a Reading Society as there was in distant Mousehole when J. H. Rigg was a young minister there. London preachers in 1806 were promised a series of bible lectures by ministers of the calibre of Adam Clarke and Joseph Benson. Traces can be found in Leeds, Salisbury, Calderdale, Brierley Hill, the Isle of Man and Sheffield of useful schemes of what today we would call lay training, but the lack of any Connexional policy is a strange commentary on the consequences of Wesley's espousal of lay preaching. Properly organised Connexional training of local preachers comes well after the period of this chapter though we ought not to underestimate the rôle of Connexional magazines.

'Our literature' was not as diverse as in the days of Wesley, though the Bible Commentaries of Thomas Coke and Joseph Benson, Adam Clarke and Joseph Sutcliffe circulated widely as did the *Theological Institutes* of Richard Watson. And under the editorship of Thomas Jackson the *Lives of the Early Methodist Preachers* (1837-8)

A CALL FOR LOCAL PREACHER TRAINING (MID-19TH CENTURY)

'The pulpit ought not to be left to the casualties of the ever-changing circumstances of the Church, which is too much the case amongst us. The consequence is, under pressure of urgent necessity . . . hands are laid suddenly upon men . . . congregations fall away, and Christianity is dishonoured. These deplorable results can be prevented only by a systematic provision. There ought, in every circuit, to be a systematic course for the training of local preachers . . . Some simple and effective plan might be adopted and efficiently worked out, by the ministers of each circuit; or better still, the local preachers might originate and maintain it themselves.'

John H. Carr (of Leeds) *The Local Ministry : Its Character, Vocation and Position Considered* London, 1851, pp.186-7.

---

provided a link with Wesley's Helpers who first began to make the Methodists a reading people, with their saddle bags filled with Wesley's books. Methodism at this time was theologically self-supporting though perhaps dangerously inbred. The general range of literature as a tool of evangelism and cultural edification was severely limited. Jackson himself went so far as to say that the Methodists 'had no time for light literature and chiefly read the Methodist Hymn Book and the Bible'.[39] This may have been more true of the countryside than the towns; there is evidence by the 1840s of urban preachers reading reviews, newspapers and even novels.

The Influence of Local Preachers

The demands of preaching played a part in the movements of working class and bourgeois self-education and self-improvement in the early nineteenth century and later. Sunday Schools could be visited by waves of radicalism, and were much more dominated by working-class people than was previously thought[40] and often restive (as were many local preachers) at Conference's dictates. The radical element in Manchester awakened the wrath of John Stephens, superintendent at the time of the 'Peterloo' massacre there in 1819.[41] He made no bones about suppressing radicals ('crushing them one by one when they notoriously commit themselves . . . they are down and we intend to keep them down',) and (writing in the vein of E. P. Thompson[42]) 'They have grown tired of radicalism and as that dies religion will revive . . . Methodism stands high among the respectable people . . .'. In Burnley[43] there was the same attitude to radicalism. In December 1818 the local preachers there asked themselves the question, 'What is the opinion of the meeting respecting local preachers abetting the cause of combination and encouraging revolutionary measures?' The answer given is, 'We are unanimous in our opinion that as preachers of righteousness and followers of Christ whose Kingdom is not of this world, we ought to respect every ordinance of man for the Lord's sake whether of the King as supreme governor of this realm or of magistrates acting under authority.' A contrary view might bring swift retribution. William Stephenson, a local preacher of North Shields, protested at Newcastle about 'Peterloo'. Robert Pilter, the superintendent, advised Stephenson to hold his tongue. Edmund Grindrod and Jabez Bunting became involved as did the Committee of Privileges. Stephenson lost his job as a teacher in a colliery school, was expelled from Wesleyanism and as a consequence fourteen Independent Methodist societies were founded in the Newcastle area.[44] The price of protection under the law was silence on politics – or rather on radical politics.

We must not assume that the smaller Methodist connexions were supporters of radicalism. The New Connexion expelled preachers for Chartist activities. Hugh Bourne had no time for 'speeching radicals' such as Joseph Markham of Leicester, expelled from the connexion for damaging religious peace. Methodism may not have provided many prominent leaders to Chartism, but there were some notable local preachers involved. One was Joseph Capper who was converted at the first camp meeting held on Mow Cop in 1807. As a prominent Staffordshire Chartist he was arrested in 1842 and having stood trial for 'sedition, conspiracy and rioting' he was sentenced to two years imprisonment. It was said of Capper that 'his tongue was like the sledge hammer he used in his shop'. His description of life in prison makes grim reading. 'I have been in prison near six months and the prison diet has made my insides so raw that one time I thought I should have died and gone to my Saviour . . . my only consolation in prison was that I had one who came to visit me through bars and bolts and no one could deprive me of communion with my Saviour.'[45]

Local preachers often enough learned skills in the chapel which they took into other areas of life – local politics after the Municipal

Corporation Act of 1835, Chartism, and the early Friendly Societies, the trade unions and later the Labour Party. Many Methodists were from the artisan groups in society – tailors and carpenters, saddlers and harness makers, hand loom weavers and stockingers and other independent craftsmen, the skilled men in the extractive industries, small shopkeepers, school teachers and petty clerks. The same groups provided leadership in early unionism and Friendly Societies. Several of the Tolpuddle Martyrs[46] of 1834 (ignored by Conference) were Wesleyans, George and James Loveless being local preachers. Many of the early mining or agricultural union leaders were Primitive Methodists, men trusted by their mates, and (if we are to include lapsed or expelled Methodists) the list is long.[47] The 'no politics' rule which applied just as much in Primitive Methodism as in Wesleyanism[48] did not deter the Cappers, Wilsons and Thorntons of this world from their activities.

LOCAL PREACHERS AND TRADE UNIONISM

'Perhaps the extensive openings for lay service attracted to the Methodist churches the natural extrovert who would also tend to be a leader in his trade-union, co-operative society or reform association. Something more is required, however, to explain why the Methodist lay preacher took his Bible with him when he went into politics or into industry, why he infused the spirit of Methodism into his secular pursuits. He did so because he sensed, in a rough and ready fashion perhaps, the relevance of his religion to his craft. At its worst this perception degenerated into a crude moral certainty which identified the workers with the Israelites in bondage and the employers with the Pharaohs who oppressed them . . . At his best the Primitive Methodist trade-unionist showed a firm grasp of Christian responsibility for the affairs of this world, exhorting masters and men to join in prayer to God for guidance in their disputes and earnestly restraining his followers from resort to violence in the pursuit of their quarrels.'

F. C. Mather, 'The British Layman in Modern Times, 1780-1962' in *The Layman in Christian History* eds. Stephen Neill and Hans-Ruedi Weber, SCM 1963.

A Few Vignettes of Preachers

Local preachers from Wesley's day have been found at every level of Methodism and on all sides of political conflict. This has been a continual factor in Methodist life. Here are some varied examples. Thomas Thompson (1754-1828) we have already encountered in connection with Sidmouth's bill. He fits into the banking and commercial world of Hull and the Wilberforces, represents those Methodists who kept their links with the Church of England, and was the first local preacher to enter Parliament where he served from 1807 to 1818. The first lay treasurer of the Wesleyan Methodist Missionary Society, he was typical of the way in which the church Methodists developed into the high Wesleyans, being one of the initiators of the Plan of Pacification of 1795. Thompson's wife – Philothea Briggs – was the daughter of William Briggs an early Book Steward and related to the Perronet family whose links with the Wesleys was very close. In Parliament Thompson was a valuable ally for Allan and Butterworth in representing Methodism to government and we find him speaking about a minimum wage for weavers and against the national lottery! We would agree with Robert Southey that it was men like Thompson who enabled Methodism to survive and grow.[49]

Samuel Thomas Drew (1765-1833) of St. Austell was an extraordinary character, perhaps the first Methodist layman to make his mark on literature. Originally a shoemaker, he became a local preacher, deeply influenced by Adam Clarke and had the confidence to reply to Tom Paine's *Age of Reason* and Richard Polwhele's *Anecdotes of Methodism*. There followed an *Essay on Immateriality* and *Immortality of the Human Soul* (1802), an essay on the *Identity and Resurrection of the Human Body* of 1809 and the *Being and Attributes of Deity* in 1811. Aberdeen conferred on him an MA and he was offered the Professorship of Moral Philosophy at London. Drew wrote a history of Cornwall and a poorish life of Dr Coke, who like Clarke, was one of his mentors. He edited the *Imperial Magazine*, acting as secretary to Adam Clarke. In London, he seems to have occupied a semi-ministerial position.[50]

Very different was William (Billy) Dawson (1733-1841). Born at Garforth, near Leeds in 1733 he moved to and remained at Barwick for the rest of his life. Joseph Benson inspired him as did Alexander Mather.

**LOSSES OF PREACHERS IN THE LATE 1840S
DUE TO HARDSHIP IN THE COUNTRYSIDE**

'Brother Craig has left the Society.
Brother Musgrove has removed to Middleham.
Brother Brown is gone to America.
Brother Oates is gone to the Institution.
Brother Stobbart has removed to Bishop Auckland.
Brother Watters is gone to Jesus.'

From the Reeth (N. Yorks) Local Preachers'
Minutes, 21 September 1850.

Beginning to preach in 1803 he worked in mining and later he had a small farm, so he never itinerated in any official sense but became an outstandingly effective 'itinerant local preacher', and advocate of missions, with extraordinary powers in winning converts. Nevertheless he cherished no illusions about contemporary Methodism. Preaching at Brunswick, Leeds, he was greatly vexed to find a notice in the circular announcing the service to be held: 'The trustees wishing to accommodate the respectable friends who may attend on this occasion propose to reserve the entire gallery of the Brunswick chapel for their use. To facilitate this, silver will be taken at the foot of the stairs.' Small wonder Bunting (with Machiavellian *realpolitik*) could dismiss the organ rebels as 'very little missed'.[51]

William Dawson (1773-1841) a Yorkshire farmer who became a local preacher in 1801. His remarkable abilities as a preacher took him further and further afield until in 1837 he became a travelling speaker within Britain for the Wesleyan Missionary Society.
W. D. Lawson *Wesleyan Local Preachers* 1874 p.88

As a character Dawson may be compared with Sammy Hick (1779-1849),[52] the Aberford blacksmith, who after 1826 was able to preach throughout Yorkshire and Lancashire, offering a message of entire sanctification which he himself had claimed in 1794. He professed to have worked physical miracles as well as miracles of soul winning. Like Dawson, he was a missionary advocate and a great believer in the power of prayer. Perhaps only Methodism could make full use of the eccentricities of a man like Hick or the physically handicapped Jonathan Savile (born in 1770) who lived in a cottage attached to the chapel in Halifax. Savile preached at South Parade after Bunting had refused to bury a Luddite though he attended the funeral. He was stoned in the street afterwards for his pains but was never deterred from his earthy style of offering the Gospel. His pithy sayings are remembered. Of wandering thought in prayer he said, 'Nah! Ye cannot stop birds flying over your 'ead but you can stop 'em building nests in yer 'air.'

Thomas Dixon (1794-1867), a Lincolnshire business-man and local preacher. On a typical Sunday soon before his death he was at a prayer meeting at 7 a.m., Sunday School at 9.15 a.m., preached 3 times during the day, and conducted an evening prayer meeting. 'I returned home just as well as when I started.'
Joseph Dixon *The Earnest Methodist : a memoir of the late Thos. Dixon of Grantham*. Wesley Conference office 1871.

The Calder Valley generated characters of this style – 'Fiddler' Thompson who was a juggler; Jonathan Dodgson whose voice could be heard for miles; Benjamin Rushton, who always wore clogs and a tall hat and supported Chartism. Chartism certainly divided the Calderdale preachers. Abraham Hanson of Elland, a preacher for the Halifax Wesleyans, was expelled by the District Meeting along with Benjamin Haigh of Huddersfield. The charge was that they had taken part in the famous West Riding meeting at Peep Green near Liversedge (where as we have seen O'Connor praised Thornton). He is reported to have said, 'We shall break away if need be from a sectarian church, we want Christ and a full belly, Christ and a good house, Christ and universal suffrage. Loud cheers!' Methodism, as John Kent[53] put it, was both producing men and women whose religion spilled over into politics and represented new forces within society, and then rejecting them if their views became compromising and appeared to disturb the peace of the societies. The comment of the veteran itinerant William Myles to Bunting was quite typical: 'I have some fears respecting the local preachers. They know well we cannot do without them. Some of them appear to be jealous and envious of us.' Perhaps the tragedy of Methodism in the period of this chapter is that the possibility of a genuine partnership of the preachers, lay and ministerial, could not be achieved. Methodism was divided[54] and each of the divisions was not able to function without its local preachers of whom the MNC had 776 in 1847, the Bible Christians in 1850 had 1,153, the Primitive Methodists 8,524, the Wesleyan Association 946. The Wesleyans were always by far the largest group. The first year they were counted was 1883 when there were 17,568, but one pamphleteer writing in 1794 when there were 300 itinerants says that there were 2,000 local preachers in England.[55]

GETTING TO AN APPOINTMENT IN THE 19TH CENTURY

'It really was a treat to see him driving out to preach (in his pony and gig). There he sat, with his large umbrella which had lost its original colour and become a faded brown in the service of the Lord; his whip, which often fell, though making but little impression upon poor Taffy's back, held loosely in his hand; his rug wrapped closely round his knees; his greatcoat buttoned up to his chin, a blue-spotted handkerchief tied around his neck; his broad-brimmed hat half burying his head. Rain, hail, snow, blow – it was all the same; away he went, singing and praising God from the beginning to the end of the journey.'

Joseph Dixon, *The Earnest Methodist,*
a Memoir of the late Mr Thomas Dixon
of Grantham, London 1871, p.98.

3

THE LOCAL PREACHER'S ROLE, STATUS AND TRAINING IN DIVIDED METHODISM 1850-1932

Geoffrey Milburn

The lengthy period covered by this chapter was one of vast economic development and social change, and included also the traumas and upheavals of the first World War.[1] Those men and women born about the middle of the nineteenth century and still alive at Methodist Union in 1932 might well have been expected to think in their old age that the familiar landmarks they had known as children had passed away for ever. Yet some aspects of social life are surprisingly resistant to change. This certainly applies to organised religion, especially in the customs and practices of local church life, which can reveal a remarkable depth of conservatism and continuity (often to the despair of those urging change!).

The *Methodist Local Preachers' Who's Who* published in 1934 reveals the names of a number of men and women, some still active as preachers, whose lives spanned all or most of the eighty years of this chapter. Let us name some of them: John Trenmouth of Devonport, born 1849, grocer; Edward Williamson of Woolstanwood, Crewe, born 1850, joiner; Hannah Salway of Hapthorne Lane near Chesterfield, also born in 1850; John Boulton of Goole, born 1851, tax collector; John Harriman of New Seaham, born 1851, coal miner; Edwin Jones of Swindon, born 1852, sub-postmaster; William Rich of Barrow-in-Furness, born 1852, coal miner, one of those still busy in his preaching work; and Elizabeth Williams of Penalt, Monmouth, born 1855, housekeeper. I suspect that if we could have chatted to these men and women in their old age about their memories of their preaching work we would have discovered that in some essentials it had not changed very much, if at all, from when they had first come on the plan, up to sixty years before. This is not of course to deny that society, and Methodism itself, had changed in this period, but simply to recognise that there was (and to some considerable extent still is) a pattern associated with the work of local preaching which can persist unchanged in the midst of change.

Our awareness of this continuity comes not from pondering connexional policies, nor from attempting to grapple with the vast numbers of local preachers, whose annual totals exceeded 40,000 in the later years of the nineteenth century. It comes rather from those precious surviving personal documents, such as letters and diaries, which can suddenly illumine the past, bridge time and space, and bring us almost face to face with the writers of long ago. Let us therefore, at the start of this chapter, go back a century and a half to share if only briefly the experiences of one particular preacher, John Young of Sunderland, as recorded in a diary he kept for a couple of years in the early 1840s, not long after Victoria came to the throne.[2]

One preacher's experience

John Young's father, T. B. Young, was one of the most active leaders on Wearside of the Wesleyan Methodist Association which in Sunderland in the mid-1830s, as elsewhere in the country, emerged as one of the products of the turbulent developments within Methodism in the first half of the nineteenth century, which have been described in the preceding chapter. T. B. Young carried on his own shoulders much of the organisational responsibilities of the WMA in Sunderland, and it was through his anxiety to have a vacant appointment filled that John Young came to preach his first sermon. John records the conversation that took place when he came down to breakfast on that particular Sunday in May 1842:

> ' "You must take Monkwearmouth this night; there is no one else at liberty." I replied "I can't." He said "You must begin, and this is a favourable opportunity. Never mind preparation. Go and exhort sinners to flee from the wrath to come." I considered, and resolved to go, though I felt little confidence in my resolution.'

We may well have some sympathy for John in being so brusquely pitch-forked into preaching, but in fact he managed remarkably well, speaking more or less extempore for 40 minutes on Joel 2:32 ('All who call upon the name of the Lord shall be saved'). About a month later one of the circuit preachers proposed him as a preacher 'on trial', which was agreed to, and a few days later he and six others were formally received as trainee preachers by the Circuit Quarterly Meeting.

A lesson soon learned by John Young was his need for preparation and study. There was no formal training programme for local preachers in the WMA, nor in fact in any of the other Methodist connexions at that time, so that the rigorous course of study upon which he then embarked was largely self-imposed, no doubt with help and advice from more experienced preachers, and the circuit ministers. The range of his reading is striking and indicates the seriousness with which an earnest preacher at that time might seek to equip himself. The books he read included Wesley's *Notes on the New Testament*, Matthew Henry's Bible Commentary, and other annotated editions of the Bible by Burkitt, Benson, and Conquest; theological tomes by George Campbell, Adam Clarke and Richard Watson; and guides to English grammar and the techniques of preaching. John also perused serious magazines (Methodist and general) and the literary reviews of the day, read a good deal of history, and enjoyed novels, though felt it necessary to justify the pleasure they gave by arguing that they improved the style and illustrations of of his sermons. Newspapers also absorbed him when he could find the time, but likewise had to be justified. Such were the strict evangelical constraints of the time.

His work as a preacher was from the beginning arduous. A quarterly plan for the Sunderland WMA Circuit in 1843 shows him taking fourteen appointments, mainly at chapels in the pit villages which surrounded Sunderland.3 However he also preached occasionally at the larger urban chapels, including Salem at South Shields, the most flourishing and prosperous cause in the circuit. His mode of travel varied. Often it was in a hired gig or phaeton, usually in the company of other preachers heading to their own appointments along the same route. At other times he would go on foot, walking along country lanes, field paths, or colliery waggonways. Occasionally he used the new-fangled railways.

Inclement weather, obscure preaching places difficult to locate, ill-designed pulpits, noisy children, over-kindly hosts who fed him large dinners before warm afternoon services, lack of conveniences for preachers in the chapels, and simple weariness as he faced his Sunday labours after an arduous week's work in his chemist's shop – these and other hazards of the preacher's lot were very familiar to John Young. It must be admitted however that they were mole-hills compared with the

A THOUGHTFUL FARMER-PREACHER

Saturday November 4th 1871

'I have been thinking of assisting my treacherous memory by commencing an orderly succession of books. That is to say constantly have a history on hand, a work on ethical science, on the physical sciences, or natural theology, on the great compass of Christian evidence, on logical science, on rhetoric, on poetry, on the arts. This would naturally reduce the great chaos of thought into encyclopaedic order.'

Friday November 8th 1872

(He had been thinking about Darwin's theories) 'Is it in the minds of men of science to bow God out of His Universe? Shall He be deprived of his personality and black and blank law be enthroned as an abstract Deity or Natural Selection or some other imaginary being or nonentity?'

Journals of a Methodist Farmer 1871-1875 (Cornelius Stovin of Binbrook in Lincolnshire, 1830-1921, a local preacher in the United Methodist Free Church.) Ed. Jean Stovin, his grand-daughter, 1982. pp.38, 112.
Jean Stovin in the Introduction (p.17) says that in a later journal (May 6th 1893) Cornelius came to honour the 'sublime discovery of Charles Darwin', putting him on a level with Newton, Harvey and Galileo.

extremely demanding journeys of the larger rural circuits, and the active opposition and persecution which some local preachers of his period endured in the course of their labours.

As time went by, despite periodic bouts of self-doubt as to his adequacy and worthiness, we sense in John's diary a growing pleasure in the companionship in the work, in the stimulus to study, in his own competence and effectiveness in the pulpit, and in the conviction that he was doing the Lord's work. Within ten months of his first service he was called to submit himself for assessment and examination as the necessary step in his progress from being a local preacher 'on trial' to fully accredited status. The process, (as daunting to John Young as to most local preachers, ancient or modern) was in his case carried out in a single evening at the Brougham Street chapel in Sunderland, to which he walked by a circuitous route to allow time to compose himself, his pockets 'stuffed with mint lozenges, liquorice and coffee berries to stimulate and clear the voice'. In the chapel schoolroom he directed the entire service before about 150 attenders, leading the prayers and the singing of the hymns, and preaching a 35 minute sermon on Psalm 90, verse 12. That ordeal over he was summoned into the vestry for an oral examination by the assembled ministers and local preachers, who put questions to him on a variety of topics – proofs of the existence of God, the authenticity of scripture, the conditions of Man's salvation, and the rules and polity of the WMA John acquitted himself competently it seems, but all was not yet over. At the circuit quarterly meeting on the following Monday he was called publicly to declare his conversion experience, his call to the ministry of preaching, and his understanding of the doctrines and disciplines of the WMA A show of hands then indicated a unanimous affirmation of his acceptance as a local preacher, and the superintendent minister addressed both the church and John Young himself in words suited to the occasion. The next day one of the younger ministers, the able and attractive Aquila Keene, walked down to John's shop and over a pipe chatted with him about his examination. He was congratulatory but advised John to guard in his sermons against 'a profusion of images and illustrations which tend to confuse the common hearers'. Too much novel-reading perhaps!

ADVICE ON READING TO A YOUNG LOCAL PREACHER

'Let him eschew tales, fictions and romances. He must regard this class of literature as forbidden fruit . . . or only to be indulged in by snatches . . . Yet it is in reading of this sort that some young men spend all their time. And indeed nothing is easier than to live in a whirl of this enervating literature . . . descending through the swarm of romantic rubbbish and fiddlestick fictions till they come to silly songs and lewd ballads of the class of 'My charming, blue-eyed Sally' and 'We won't go home till morning' . . . Let this course be persevered in for some time and he will become mentally puny, poor, feeble, sickly and drivelling. His soul will be emasculated – robbed of its vitality . . . From such a mental prostration – from rubbishy books – from sentimental love tales – from wishy-washy penny periodicals, let all our religious young men devoutly say "Good Lord, deliver us".'

The Wesleyan Methodist Penny Magazine
published by the Wesleyan Reformers August 1853, p.115

Continuity and change

John Young's story has of course unique and personal elements. For one thing he had more opportunity and inclination for study than many preachers. Yet accounts of the work and experiences of other individual preachers throughout the nineteenth century, and into the early twentieth, bear a striking resemblance to his. The sense of call (no matter how it came); the anxious beginnings; the probationary periods 'on note' and 'on trial'; the disciplines of the circuit plan, and of preparation and examination; the journeyings on foot or by some variety of horse-power, supplemented by an occasional railway journey perhaps, and increasingly by the ubiquitous bicycle, and later, for some more fortunate, the motor car; the growing sense of freedom and confidence in the work; the comradeship of fellow preachers; the weariness at the close of a busy Sabbath, joined with a deep yet humble sense of satisfaction at work done out of faith and love, with no remuneration, on behalf of God's people – such was the staple experience of the countless local preachers who filled three quarters or more of the pulpits of Methodism throughout the long years covered by this chapter. It was work largely unrecorded and unsung yet without it Methodism as it was would have virtually collapsed.

Yet while allowing for this underlying stability, and common shared experience, there was both variety and change in the local preachers' lot. One obvious reason was the division of Methodism into several separate connexions, each with its own ethos and polity. At a deeper level ecclesiastical changes within Methodism generally, and social changes in the wider society within which Methodism operated, impinged sooner or later upon local preachers and faced them with new challenges and opportunities. In particular we may note first an increasing 'churchiness', which came to pervade all the Methodist Connexions in the later Victorian period; and second a heightened expectation among congregations with regard to the educational and cultural quality of worship, preaching and chapel life in general.[4] Let us examine each of these more closely.

Divided Methodism

Despite the union in 1857 of the Wesleyan Methodist Association and the Wesleyan Reformers to form the United Methodist Free Churches, and the coming together in 1907 of the UMFC the Methodist New Connexion and the Bible Christians as the United Methodist Church, the period from 1850 to 1932 was the great era of divided Methodism.

The accompanying table sets out some of the relevant statistics for the various connexions for one sample year, 1907, which falls just about at the turning point in the story of institutional Methodism, when the growth associated with the nineteenth century was giving way to the decline of the twentieth.[5] The table shows the figures for the constituent parts of the UMC just before their merger.

1907	Members	Chapels	Ministers	Local Preachers
Wesleyan	496,430	8,520	2,445	19,672
Primitive	211,673	5,214	1,169	16,259
United Methodist Free Churches	79,948	1,269	438	2,983
New Connexion	37,009	457	204	1,123
Bible Christians	32,202	622	206	1,515
Wesleyan Reform Union	8,689	197	17	530
Independent Methodist	9,614	153	399 (Lay Ministry)	
Totals	875,565	16,432	4,878	42,082

There was in Britain at that date one Methodist local preacher for every 880 people, a statistic which to the optimistic might have even suggested the possibility of evangelising the entire nation. In relation to Methodist membership the overall ratio was 1:21, but with some significant variation between the different connexions with the Primitives at 1:13, and the remainder (apart from the Reform Union) much lower, between 1:21 (BC) and 1:33 (MNC). Leaving aside the IMs and the WRU, the average ratio of ministers to local preachers was 1:8, with a range between 1:6 (MNC) and 1:14 (PM).

Assuming that each chapel had two services on a Sunday, and that each minister took two Sunday appointments, the services available to local preachers average out at something like one a fortnight for each preacher, assuming all preachers were active. However this takes no account of preaching places other than chapels.

What about the potential size of congregations? In the nineteenth century congregations in general were made up largely of adherents, who outnumbered members by up to three times. This ratio was assumed to be still applicable in the first decade of the twentieth century by the editors of the *New History of Methodism* published in 1909, though if so, the pattern was very soon about to change, due to a fall-off of adherents.[6] However if we assume the 3:1 ratio to have been operative in 1907, and divide the total adherents and members by the number of chapels, the overall

An enthusiastic entrepreneur seeking to tap the considerable market which local preachers
constituted. The Primitive Methodists alone had over 16,000 local preachers at this date.
(*PM Conference Handbook*, 1906).

average is 213, though once again with considerable variation between the different connexions, with the PMs (162) lowest and the MNC (323) highest.

WILLIAM SMITH, BREAM.
50 YEARS A LOCAL PREACHER FOR THE BIBLE CHRISTIANS

'His sermons were characterised by common sense, sound theology, and abounded in practical exhortations to his hearers, whom he frequently addressed in a serious and impassioned strain, bringing forth and enforcing the experimental and doctrinal portions of the text in such a manner as to address himself to the understanding, the conscience, and the heart of those who heard him.

William Smith was ill for 18 months before his death. He suffered severely but said often "My sufferings can be put in a nutshell."

"Are you afraid to die?" said his wife shortly before the end. He replied "No. If I am unconscious at the last, whisper *Jesus* in my ear."'

Bible Christian Magazine 1907
pp.118-121

Rude things have been said about the reliability of statistics and those above are offered with some hesitation. They provide some insight into aspects of the local preachers' lot in the early years of the present century, but many imponderables were at work to affect the neat averages offered here.

A clearer lesson to be learned from the table is that although the Wesleyans had 117,000 more members than all the other connexions added together, they had fewer local preachers by a considerable margin – over 3,000 less if the IM lay ministers are included among the local preachers. This must be a reflection of the lower view of the ordained ministry, and the correspondingly greater freedom and role open to local preachers, within the non-Wesleyan connexions, a state of affairs due in large part to the origins of these connexions, which as has been clearly shown in chapter two were the result of impatience with, or outright revolt against, Wesleyan ministerial domination whether in circuit or in Conference.

Local preachers were at the very heart of these new movements and played a key role in establishing and extending them in the crucial early years, often being as active as were the travelling preachers, who were regarded, essentially, as different from the local preachers only in that they worked full time, received remuneration for their labours, and moved from circuit to circuit. In the early years of Primitive Methodism when the itinerants were missioning very large areas, their occasional visits to the various scattered preaching places must have made them appear almost as assistants to the local preachers, rather than in any sense superior to them. The practice of the Primitive Methodists to enlist some local preachers to work full time on short term arrangements (as temporary itinerants or 'hired local preachers') further weakened any distinction between the two ministries.

The greater freedom and scope of the non-Wesleyan local preachers is evidenced in other ways. They baptised children, and conducted funerals (though in some areas Wesleyan local preachers did so too); they might share in the making of the circuit preaching plan; their initial recruitment was not dependent on a note from the Superintendent but on the agreement of the leaders' meeting and quarterly meeting; women were able to serve as local preachers equally with men; as trusted lay leaders they could be called on to chair meetings which in Wesleyanism were exclusively chaired by a minister; they were able to conduct love feasts; and they were allowed to celebrate the sacrament of the Lord's Supper. How widely some of these rights were actually claimed in practice is a subject in need of research. Lay celebration is a good example. But it is significant that in the negotiations preceding the Methodist Union of 1932 the principle that a lay person could preside at a

---

BURIAL PRACTICES IN SWALEDALE (Wesleyan)

'Between 1826 and 1847 Jonathan Daykin buried 288 Gunnerside people, and between 1848 and 1887 William Coates buried 277. George Dougill was the next local preacher to conduct burial services, and between 1888 and 1902 he buried 41 people. Clearly the practice was altering because in 1889 the minister, Revd Joseph Cartwright, began to countersign the local preachers' signatures and 1903 was the last occasion when a local preacher officiated ...

The cortège was met at the top of the village by the oldest local preacher, who then led the proceedings. He intoned a dirge line by line, which was repeated very slowly by all those following until the procession reached the Chapel. Miss Elizabeth Rutter (b.1883) remembers hearing it as a child, and being 'terrified at the doleful sound'. She used to run away and hide until the funeral was over. Her father, George Rutter, was the last to lead the dirge, which dropped from use during the First World War.

Once as William Coates [local preacher, d.1888] lay ill in bed, he heard a funeral procession coming down the other side of the valley singing the dirge out of tune. So he got up and shouted the correct version out of the window.'

M. Batty *Gunnerside Chapel and Gunnerside Folk* 1967

communion service was so staunchly upheld by non-Wesleyan leaders as to ensure its survival in the united church, though limited to particular circumstances, and requiring the authorisation of conference.[7]

Victorian vicissitudes

Like any living and complex organism Methodism has never stood still, and is notoriously difficult to generalise about. Any description of Methodism which over-simplifies is always bound to be to some extent misleading, and we need therefore to look more closely at the state of affairs outlined in the previous section, and in particular to consider ways in which the patterns there described were shifting and changing in the second half of the nineteenth century and the early years of the twentieth.

Let us begin with the Wesleyans. In 1850 they were reeling from the major upheavals of the 1830s and late 1840s which had resulted in disastrous secessions from the 'old body'. One deep cause of the troubles was the sense of divided interests between ministers and laity, and the censorious and vindictive official voice of the connexion with regard to what was seen as disloyalty or unjustified complaint against the system by lay folk. Local preachers were in the forefront of these clashes and many of them parted company with Wesleyanism to join the new connexions. What was to be the Wesleyan policy towards those who remained faithful, among whom must have been many uncertain folk whose continued loyalty to the old connexion could not be taken for granted? Wesleyan local preachers in particular must have looked with some envy at their brethren (and sisters) in Primitive Methodism and Free Methodism, and at the status and freedom they enjoyed there.

Thoughtful Wesleyans were well aware of this situation and the more far-seeing ministers, without desiring to sacrifice their love of ministerial order or their traditional spiritual oversight of the Wesleyan societies, realised that a new humility towards the laity must prevail. The Revd Alfred Barrett, addressing his fellow ministers in 1850, confessed that 'our sins against brotherly confidence and love have been many and serious', and called on them all to 'acknowledge and affectionately recognise our faithful leaders and local preachers as fellow helpers in the work of the Lord'.[8] There is no word here of any constitutional change in the status of local preachers, but Barrett's tone and mood are significant, and as a man with a high view of the pastoral office his words would carry especial weight.

A generation later we find Revd Dr William B. Pope, another leading high Wesleyan, and Methodism's pre-eminent theologian of that time, endeavouring to persuade a gathering of local preachers in Manchester (in March 1879) of the reality of the new mood. In doing so he made one of the most significant and interesting Wesleyan statements of that period with regard to local preachers.[9] Pope was not the man to concede ministerial authority, and was careful to remind his hearers of the need to maintain careful control over the selection and conduct of local preachers. This said, however, he sounded a generous and encouraging note. Local preaching was 'an honourable vocation'. Pastors and local preachers were 'ministers of the word in common and that should be and is a very precious bond between them'. The ministers' probationary period as local preachers, insisted on by the Wesleyan Conference since 1797, was 'a pledge of unity and brotherhood and good fellowship between the two orders'. (The final phrase is significant – one wonders whether Pope was the first Wesleyan leader to designate local preachers as an order.) He went on to urge local preachers to take pride in their 'noble fraternity', to have a high view of their office, not to feel ignored or underrated: 'if you test the pulse of the connexion you will find that it beats kindly towards its old servants, the local preachers'.

Fine words, and doubtless deliberately up-beat, in an attempt to rally the troops. Pope had indeed already shown that he was a man of deeds as well as words since it was under his presidency that the Wesleyan Conference in 1877 had agreed to admit lay representatives into its deliberations, beginning from 1878, when well over forty local preachers (mainly drawn from the professional and business classes) found themselves among the official lay representatives attending that body for the first time (or at least since some of the early conferences summoned by John Wesley).[10]

Yet despite the kindlier expressions from on high, and despite lay representation, Wesleyan local preachers were not at ease in their

---

TIGHT REINS IN NOTTINGHAM

'The Wesleyan superintendent minister in 1861 had an unruly horse that landed the trap in a ditch from which he was rescued by a local preacher who later made the comment: "He holds the reins in each hand and keeps them tight. He does the same in affairs ecclesiastical but it does not answer!"'

R. C. Swift, *Lively People:*
Methodism in Nottingham 1740-1979
(1982) pp.145-6

---

connexion as the nineteenth century drew to its close. What was the trouble? A complex of causes was at work. The democratisation of society was heightening the longing for greater equality in general, and not least between Methodist lay folk and their ministers. Yet, deliberately or not, ministers seemed to be once again elevating their status so as to re-emphasise the old distinctions. College training was pretty well universal for ministers by the later part of the century, high-lighting the much humbler educational attainments of the majority of local preachers, and also helping to foster in ministers themselves a more clerical and professional view of their office. One outward sign of this was the growing preference for clerical vestments, further distinguishing ministry from laity.

Protest was forthcoming. One of the most eloquent and distinguished critics was Samuel Waddy QC, one of a well-known Wesleyan dynasty (with several ministers among his forebears and relatives) who was a local preacher and had been one of the first lay delegates at the Wesleyan Conference of 1878. Waddy launched a remarkable broadside against developments in Wesleyanism in the august forum of the first Methodist Oecumenical Conference held at Wesley's Chapel in September 1881.[11] Gazing round on the cream of the Methodist ministry of Britain and North America he scorned them for 'affecting too much the uniform and livery of other churches', and went on to remind them that despite their titles and their doctorates and even (in the case of some American delegates) their episcopacy, they were still essentially *lay preachers* since their 'setting apart' for the Methodist ministry was not a true ordination in the eyes of the historic episcopal churches. Come off your pedestals, urged Waddy in effect; lessen the distinction between minister and local preacher; let us stand together in the same work. If local preachers are expected to do the rough work in mission halls and the open air (as many did) let the ministers join them. 'Let there be fair play, equal work, equal rank, equal call in the sight of God Almighty.'

It is ironic to find towards the end of the nineteenth century expressions of frustration and anger about Wesleyan lay-ministerial relations similar in tone to those voiced fifty years before or more. Waddy's protest is the more significant because of his impeccable Wesleyan credentials, and his high standing. Other Wesleyan voices of a humbler kind made themselves heard, and we will return to them, but first let us draw the non-Wesleyan connexions into this aspect of our survey.

**OLD-STYLE VERNACULAR PREACHING
BY A SUNDERLAND KEELMAN (MID-19TH CENTURY)**

'The preacher describes how the father in the parable of the Prodigal Son recognised his son as he walked in rags and tatters down the long road home:

'Now when the awd man pulled the blind ti one side on the perticler moanin', according tiv 'is custom, his two eyes beheld a chap toiling away alang the dusty lonnon. Poor feller! Eff ye'd ha' puttin him in one o'Ralphy Lawson's fields, Ralphy's flae craw (scare crow) wad ha' been that much annoyed at the disgrace that he wad ha' run away through Pennywell, and niver stopp'd till he gat tiv Offerton. But spite of all this, my friends, the awd man knew him thereckly. His eyes wasn't as good as they used ti be, but he wasn't lukin' at the lad through his bodily vishon. He was lukin' strite at him through the magnifying eye ov FAITH! Tears o'joy and thenkfulness streamed down his cheeks, and he cried out aloud – "It's my son! it's my son! Aw knaw him, aw knaw him bi the cut ov his jib".'

From *Tales and Ballads of Wearside*
by John Green, 4th edition 1885

From connexion to church

A familiar theme in ecclesiastical history is the tendency for religious enthusiasm to gradually solidify into institutional forms. Charisma gives way to committees; movements become churches. Methodism embodies this perfectly. Each of the connexions, no matter how fluid and unformed at its origins, developed within a few decades into an organised and structured denomination, with an increasingly sophisticated life of its own. The Wesleyans of course went through the process first; the others, sooner or later, mirrored the Wesleyan experience.

In the process something of the early excitement, freedom, and spontaneity was lost, in favour of order, reliability, and respectability. Inevitably the distinctions between lay and clerical became more heavily drawn, even in such previously open and lay-dominated connexions as the Primitive Methodists. Indeed the Primitives demonstrate the inexorable onset of 'churchiness' as clearly as any of the Methodist connexions, after the Wesleyan. From the mid-nineteenth century they showed an increasing concern for improved chapels, college training for their ministers, a general raising of the education and culture of their members, a higher tone in their magazines, an enrichment of hymnody, more dignity and reverence in worship, a strengthening of the social and communal elements of congregational life, and a tighter connexionalism.[12]

95, YORK ROAD.

WEST HARTLEPOOL.

March 24th 1904

My dear Bro,
        It is a great joy to me to authorize
you to take services in the Circuit during
the coming quarter,
        You are represented on the Plan by
Parallels (II) & are appointed at Greatham
on Sunday Morning May 1st
Wishing you every Blessing & Success
                I am
                        Yours faithfully
                                W. Kendrew.

Mr. W. E. Stoddings
        Seaton Carew

A note to preach written for a Hartlepool Wesleyan local preacher, 1904.
The large chapel with its handsome portico (shown on the letterhead) still stands, though
is in secular use. Preachers 'on note' were often represented by a symbol on the plan, and
accompanied another preacher until more experienced.

The PM itinerant preachers were key agents in this process and the middle and later years of the century saw them transformed from itinerants into circuit ministers and thence into pastors as PM circuits (like those of the Wesleyans) were extensively reduced into ever smaller areas. The PM Connexion had 189 'Home' circuits in 1852, 499 in 1882, and 681 in 1903, the increases being explained almost entirely by a process of subdivision. In each reduced circuit there was of course only a handful of chapels, and in many cases only one minister. In fact by 1924 out of the 684 PM circuits 486 were 'single minister stations'. A similar process had developed within the United Methodist Church, which in 1924 had single ministers in 250 of its 330 circuits.[13]

The Wesleyans did not use single ministers to anything like this degree but had nevertheless pursued a policy of circuit subdivision, increasing their total number of circuits from 580 in 1868 to 756 in 1924. In all the Methodist connexions therefore the trend was towards a more concentrated style of ministry, more like the pastorates of the dissenters than the old-style Methodist circuit strategy. Some Methodists complained that they were becoming Congregationalist. Certainly the ministers were now devoting most of their energies to building up the religious, social and educational life of their own congregations, rather than to evangelical outreach.

SATAN CHALLENGED BY TWO OLD WEARDALE PREACHERS

George Watson, a Weardale leadminer, once said: 'I'd been preaching at Stanhope and was coming home on a very stormy night when Satan came to me about Park House and said –

"Thou's just a poor slave for Jesus Christ."

"I know that well enough Satan, but I was in thy service four-and-twenty years and thou promised great things, but thou was very slow about paying anything."

At last he left me and I came on my way.'

John Kellet, another Weardale local preacher, walked large distances in the dale. He once caused a smile in a great public meeting at High House by commencing his speech thus:
'I sometimes think Satan and I are not unlike each other. Satan went to and fro up and down the earth, and so do I – but I undo what Satan has done.'

Methodist Recorder, Winter No.1898
pp.29 and 34

Some of the laity were in favour of these developments, but there were serious tensions also, similar to those in the Wesleyan Connexion several decades earlier. In the Sunderland Primitive Methodist circuit in the mid-1870s great bitterness was aroused by what was seen as an increasing 'clericalism' among the ministers, and by the building of an expensive new chapel, followed by the division of the circuit enforced by a connexional committee against considerable local opposition. All this was to lead to a secession in 1877 of several hundred members, who abandoned their old loyalties in order to establish a circuit of Christian Lay Churches with a completely lay ministry, which in due course forged a natural link with the older Independent Methodists in West Yorkshire and Lancashire.[14] The Lay Church leaders included some of the best of the former PM local preachers on Wearside, who looked back nostalgically to what Primitive Methodism had been, and regretted what it was becoming.

> 'Primitive Methodism, in regard to its polity and the relationship subsisting between its paid ministers and the Lay Agency and Members, is no longer what it once was. . . . If Primitive Methodism is to be maintained in its original simplicity and power the lay preachers must organise themselves throughout the connection and arrest the progress of priestly power . . . Two thirds of the local preachers have declared their intention to sever their connection with Primitive Methodism so that they may pursue their beneficent labours free from the trammels of ecclesiasticism.'[15]

The language is excessive, but the passion very evident. The Lay Church secession in Sunderland is in fact an extreme example of a widespread sense of crisis affecting local preachers throughout Methodism in the closing decades of the nineteenth century. At the heart of the problem there lay the fundamental question of what Methodism was – an evangelising movement or a fully-fledged Church? There was (and still is) a genuine tension between these two concepts. It could be a fruitful tension but it was also the cause of much disquiet, not least with regard to the role and status of the local preacher within a church which was steadily becoming more institutionalised, with a settled pastoral ministry, and with congregations which, having benefitted from the enhanced educational and social opportunities of Victorian England, expected to find their increasingly refined tastes catered for within the life and worship of their churches. If the local preachers were to stay loyal to their own connexions and not to desert the ship, as the Lay Church seceders had done, could they without compromising their integrity, adapt to the changing times? And were they sufficiently equipped to cope with what was now being demanded of them?

'An ecclesiastical dodo?'

On the 16th November 1886 Helen McKenny, the daughter of the minister at Wesley's Chapel, London, wrote an entry in her diary:

> 'Went to service. Heard the queerest sermon from a 'local' on the advantages accruing to us from Sin entering the world. We ought to be very thankful indeed for it, he said, otherwise Adam would have stuck to the Garden of Eden, and never got beyond it, while we have *Heaven* to look forward to. Adam, he said, only communed with God "in the cool of the evening" but we may commune with Him at any moment of the day, and so on.'[16]

Helen, though kindly by nature, was a sensitive and intelligent young woman and was obviously hurt by the incongruities of such a sermon.

Local preachers often complained that they never got a chance to preach in the big chapels, or that if they did people stayed away. This preacher had his opportunity but unfortunately does not appear to have been able to make the most of it. Less sophisticated congregations than that at City Road might have smiled at his quaintness and not been offended. But from worshippers of a more critical and intellectual turn of mind he could not expect such sympathetic consideration. And with the sermon carrying so much weight in Methodist worship (a fact which Helen McKenny in fact regretted) any disappointment with the preacher left congregations feeling that they had been short-changed by the entire service.

The hard truth was emerging that congregations were wanting more than many local preachers seemed willing or able to deliver – that is to say they looked for more teaching, more thoughtful help and encouragement to Christians already 'on the way', and less old-fashioned Gospel sermons aimed at unconverted sinners which had been the local preacher's acknowledged forte. A leading Methodist historian of today (Henry Rack) goes so far as to say that 'in the increasingly education- and culture-conscious late nineteenth century local preachers had come to seem a liability' – a pretty devastating judgement.[17] A hundred years ago Henry Martyn, a local preacher, addressing fellow preachers at a meeting in 1893, made the same point in more graphic terms: 'Is the local preacher speedily doomed to become an ecclesiastical dodo? Is there no sphere for him in the future of these churches?'[18]

The question sounds rhetorical, and indeed was, and yet expressed a very real anxiety. Henry Martyn himself saw a continuing and vital role for local preachers as witnesses in plain language to other working men, but this kind of work was increasingly having to be done on the fringes of, or completely outside, normal Methodist circuit life. The stimulus to this came in part from the revivalism which affected wide areas of Britain around 1859-60, and again from the early 1870s onwards, largely associated with evangelists from the USA. As a result many local preachers began to seek a variety of evangelical outlets, often of an inter-denominational or non-denominational kind – Brotherhoods, Town

---

SABBATARIANISM IN EARNEST

'As William Bell, a PM local preacher, was passing along the streets of Penrith one Sabbath morning on an errand of mercy he observed a number of men in a barber's shop getting shaved. After proceeding a few yards, he returned, entered the shop, and meekly pointed out to them the wickedness of their conduct, warned them to flee from the wrath to come, and left them, praying that God might bless what he had been enabled to say to them for the good of their souls.'

PM Magazine 1885 p.643

Missions, Temperance organisations, Bible classes, 'Sunshine Hours' and so forth. This in effect allowed them to perpetuate a traditional religious life-style but did nothing to resolve the dilemma of the deployment of local preachers within Methodism itself. If anything it diverted local preachers' attention away from what was increasingly seen by connexional leaders as a fundamental requirement to help resolve that dilemma – a system of training and mental discipline which would better equip preachers to speak more convincingly to the needs of modern Methodist congregations. Some local preachers sought training and inspiration for their work at Thomas Champness' Joyful News Mission (founded in Rochdale in 1886) to train men for evangelical work, mainly in rural areas. Thomas Cook and Samuel Chadwick later extended and developed this work at Cliff College. Those who undertook such training might move on to become full-time paid evangelists, but others remained as local preachers with an especial bent towards revival work, and an emphasis on personal holiness. All this however made little impact on the general problem with regard to local preachers' training.

SCRIPTURAL ECONOMY

Jim Calvert (late 19th cent.) was a preacher who believed in economy in words. He was reading from Daniel 3:5ff, the command of Nebuchadnezzar to the people to fall down and worship him when they heard 'the sound of the cornet, flute, harp, sackbut, psaltery, dulcimer and all kinds of music', words which recur three times in six verses. He looked up when he came to the second time and said 'Ah isn't gean to read it all ower, friends; it were t'same band.'

M. Batty, *Gunnerside chapel and Gunnerside folk* 1967

The battle over training

An insight into the state of English education in the 1890s is offered by some items found among the documents of a formerly well-known Leicestershire local preacher, Fred Burton JP, a grocer of Hinckley, who was born in 1875 and died in 1963.[19] Fred offered himself for the Wesleyan ministry at around the age of 20 and his preliminary examination papers have survived in his personal archive. Here are some sample questions:

> 'If a straight line were drawn from Cardiff to Sunderland through what counties and across what rivers would it pass?
>
> Sketch the history of literature *or* religion in Great Britain during the first quarter of the present century (i.e. the nineteenth).
>
> Write a short history of the reign of Stephen *or* William III.
>
> The yield of a gold-mine increases from .0043 to .0048 per cent; how much more gold does a ton of ore yield now than before?'

The standard of this examination obviously indicates what was considered to be a reasonable test of what a young local preacher who aspired to the ministry, could reasonably be expected to know. But it must also throw some light on general educational standards among many young adults who had grown to maturity in the last third of the nineteenth century, and hence on many of the worshippers in Methodist chapels of that period. It requires an effort of imagination today to realise the surprising degree of intellectual liveliness that was to be found among the more progressive congregations in the late Victorian and Edwardian periods. Such congregations were not confined only to prosperous urban areas, nor was the liveliness in question simply a matter of increasing knowledge, but included an openness to ideas and awareness of the conflict of beliefs and philosophies of the day. Women were likely to exhibit it as well as men, and Helen McKenny, who was quoted above, provides a good example.

Local preachers were in a quandary. If they were excluded from what were referred to as the 'better' or 'more respectable' pulpits they (or at least some of them) felt aggrieved. If they were appointed to such pulpits and a portion of the congregation deliberately stayed away they were equally aggrieved. In any case the prevailing trend towards smaller circuits meant a restriction of the number and variety of chapels open to local preachers within their circuits, and they were increasingly likely to face the very congregations who might be most critical of their efforts. Even if the preachers concerned admitted their shortcomings they were not necessarily convinced that more learning on their part was the answer since a traditional view, widely held within Methodism, was that Gospel piety was the vital requirement and that education might stifle it.[20]

Serious battles had been fought within Methodism on this very ground when ministerial colleges were introduced into the various connexions, and there were likewise many who felt acutely suspicious over formal training schemes for local preachers, which were being increasingly called for in the later decades of the nineteenth century. The Wesleyan Conference of 1876, for instance, while being careful to express appreciation of the service rendered by local preachers, also urged the need to improve their efficiency: 'The spread of education renders it necessary that the standard of qualification for this most important work should be raised'.[21]

Some local preachers reacted very strongly to such suggestions. The Wesleyan Member of Parliament for Cheadle (Staffs), William Shepherd Allen, who was himself a local preacher, was roused, as he put it 'to stand up for my order' who had 'made Methodism' yet were now disparaged and undervalued. He went on: 'Allow me in humility to say "Let us alone". We are plain, homely, unlettered men so don't harass us with exams and courses of study – but let us alone.'[22] Allen's image of the local preachers was that of 'plain and simple laymen, who could tell in the market place the grand old story of the Cross', and whose proper sphere was the smaller chapels, mission halls and the open air. For a preacher who was an MP to hold such views as late as 1881 may seem both odd and anachronistic, but doubtless he was expressing the views of a considerable number of the more humble and conservative-minded local preachers of that time, certainly on the matter of training schemes.

Against such views stood the modernising party within Methodism who believed that the march of change and progress was demanding a new urgency with regard to the training of local preachers. Such training from the beginning of local preaching had been acquired 'on the job', on something like a craft apprenticeship system, with skills learned by practising them, under the watchful eye of more experienced operators, and with the trial sermon and oral examination as the final tests of competence and suitability. Preachers on trial were generally urged to study on their own and some (like John Young) conscientiously did so, but the obstacles were great. Here and there self-help initiatives resulted in preachers setting up their own libraries, study groups and training classes. William Clowes describes such a class (he terms it a 'theological institution') which met at his house on Saturday evenings – this was c.1805-6 when he was still a Wesleyan.[23] The Sunderland local preachers were establishing their own library at about the same time.[24] By 1850 the Bible Christian local preachers on the Isle of Wight were meeting twice a year for prayer and discussion, considering such questions as 'Why are not the services of lay preachers attended with greater success?' and 'What can be done to render the lay ministry more efficient?'[25] In that same year the Primitive Methodists in the Sunderland District launched a preachers' theological association, to encourage serious study among ministers, probationers and local preachers.[26] To publish the association's lectures a scholarly journal (*The Christian Ambassador*) was begun, which in due course developed into the *Primitive Methodist Quarterly Review*. Manchester was another go-ahead area and W. B. Pope in his 1879 lecture (mentioned above) spoke of the example set by a 'centre for local preachers' mutual instruction' in that city.[27]

Encouragement and advice in magazines and books was also forthcoming in increasing profusion. A Bible Christian minister, Thomas Garland, published *The Young Local Preacher's Guide* (1860), aimed at 'young men in the pursuit of knowledge under difficulties'. In the *Local Preachers' Magazine* for 1865 W. B. Carter offered comprehensive advice in eleven articles addressed to young preachers who were 'overwhelmed with how much they don't know'. Connexional and district

---

A SERMON CRITIC

'Mr Fernley read much and variously on theological subjects. One of the fruits of this habit was of course a keen readiness of criticism under the pulpit. He was a good judge of a sermon. If indeed it was full of the truth and tenderness of the Gospel his criticism was merged in something far better. But if the preacher failed to give that certain sound, or glaringly trifled with the meaning of Scripture, he would have no severer critic than Mr Fernley. This however refers chiefly to a time preceding his infirmity of partial deafness. After that came upon him it was his habit to resign himself not to hear what might tend only to chafe his mind!'

W. B. Pope *A Memoir of John Fernley Esq. JP of Southport* 1874 pp.48-50

---

local preachers' committees were established by the Wesleyans in 1883 and in the following year a new magazine, initiated by the Wesleyans but aimed widely, was launched called the *Local Preachers' Treasury*, changing its title to the *Preachers' Magazine* in 1890, and adopting a more ambitious format. As well as articles on special themes the journal served as the information outlet of the 'Wesleyan Union for Biblical and Homiletical Study', which was the brain child of the WM Connexional Local Preachers' Committee. A prospectus of study with recommended reading was regularly published, organised as what we would today call 'distance learning'. The curriculum was graduated and wide ranging. These developments had resulted from a marked heightening of the pressure for the improved education and preparation of local preachers. A number of small but influential books, all published in the 1890s, both resulted from and helped to intensify this pressure. Among them were two books by the Wesleyan minister C. O. Eldridge, *Local Preachers and Village Methodism* (1895) (a particularly interesting volume) and the *Lay Preacher's Handbook* (1898); and the *Local Preacher's Manual* (1896) by the Primitive Methodist ministers James Travis and Henry Yooll.

By the 1890s the Primitive Methodists had elaborated a proposed system of local preacher training, with set books, and examinations held locally. The seriousness with which it was applied no doubt depended on local initiative, and requires research in circuit archives to unearth. The LP Minutes for the Hetton-le-Hole (County Durham) PM Circuit show a high degree of efficiency in the training process and a demanding work

Examination certificate awarded to Fred Milburn (1891-1934), of Hutton Rudby,
a local preacher in the PM Stokesley Circuit.

load for the candidates. We can sympathise with the resignation from preaching in 1900 of Brother Nattress 'on grounds of nervous prostration of a severe kind which invariably precedes his work'.[28]

> 'The future of our Church and the cause of evangelical Christianity in this land must largely depend on the spiritual and intellectual fitness of our lay preachers. On the whole we are inclined to think that the work of our LPs is as good as the Church has any right to expect, considering how little she has done to promote their advancement. Has she not, generally speaking, left them to their own resources, to get on as best they can? . . . Have not many regarded the lay ministry as a temporary provision to meet an emergency, rather than as one of the permanent agencies of the Church? Do many, even some lay preachers, turn away from the sanctuary when a layman is in the pulpit?'
>
> J. Travis and H. Yooll *The Local Preachers' Manual* 1896 p.3
> (The authors were both Primitive Methodist ministers)

In 1904 the PMs introduced new legislation for the training and equipment of local preachers. A central committee was established for the general organisation and oversight of LP correspondence classes, and district committees were to be set up to oversee locally the appointing of tutors, the arrangements for examinations, and the encouraging of study circles, conferences, circuit libraries and so forth. The Hetton-le-Hole minutes show oral and written examinations being held periodically at Clowes Villa, the PM manse.

From 1914 to 1932 the *Preachers' Magazine* was printed in two editions, one of them containing a special Primitive Methodist supplement edited by PM scholars and containing detailed information of the PM correspondence courses and examinations. As I write this I can look up and see on my study wall the Certificate of Merit awarded to my father by the PM Local Preachers' Central Training Council in 1914, for having passed the general examination in the New Testament and its writers, Homiletics, PM Church History and English Grammar. The central council's examinations were not, however, compulsory, and candidates could opt to be examined within their own circuits by some kind of local arrangement. The same held true of the other Methodist connexions, none of which before Methodist Union felt able to enforce on volunteer local preachers a compulsory and uniform system of discipline, training and examination, let alone a programme of continued study and development. The consequences for the Wesleyans (for example) were seen in the figures for 1914:[29]

Local Preachers	19,463
On trial	1,477
Number taken on full plan 1913-14	624
Number taking most recent connexional examinations	67
Numbers making use of reading circles, theological classes, etc.	335

The Primitive Methodists showed greater success, with 170 taking the connexional examinations in April 1914. 'Our movement seems as though it is just getting into its stride and it is destined to render conspicuous service to the lay preachers of our church' commented A. L. Humphries (tutor at Hartley College) in August of that year.[30] Sadly the imminent onset of war was to pose Methodism more urgent problems.

The Impact of World War I

A book needs to be written here, but let us consider briefly some of the ways in which the war affected preachers and preaching. Many preachers either volunteered for military service or were compulsorily conscripted as a result of the Military Service Acts of 1916, and the manpower legislation of early 1918, which directed some of the conscripts into high-priority industrial work. By June 1918 the Wesleyans reckoned that 3,231 of their local preachers were in the armed forces and another several thousand more on some kind of vital national service – in all well over one third of the total number of their preachers.[31] One obvious consequence was a serious shortage of local preachers, some of the worst affected Wesleyan Districts being South and North Wales, Newcastle and Carlisle. 119 Wesleyan circuits had more preaching places than preachers by 1918, and in another 238 preachers exceeded places by only one or two.[32] Presumably the Primitive and United Methodists were affected in somewhat similar proportions. Apart from the obvious difficulties caused by the shortages, they did in fact have some positive consequences, helping to stimulate fresh awareness of the importance of recruiting new preachers (including lads still at school); to highlight the long overdue admission (granted in 1918) of women into the ranks of Wesleyan local preachers on equal standing with men; and to rouse a fresh appreciation of local preachers in general, Sir Henry Lunn being moved to describe them in 1918 as representing the greatest work by an unpaid lay agency in the history of Christianity since Paul the tentmaker! [33]

A vast number of local preachers must have found that military service widened their mental and religious horizons beyond all previous imagining, posing challenges to traditional views and practices, and stimulating the need for a faith robust enough to survive the experiences of the front line, the casualty hospital and the prison camp. A few vignettes from letters in the *Recorder* are as follows:

> 'A Methodist padre held a little Local Preachers' Meeting at the front, with five preachers present. They shared tea, serious talk, the Sacrament – and a little humour. One brother, on trial, when asked what progress he'd made with Wesley's *Notes* and *Sermons* confessed his only recent reading was company orders and army regulations.[34]
>
> Where chaplains were not available the men often led worship themselves. One Wesleyan local preacher led worship regularly for up to 500 men in a POW camp, using Common Prayer in the morning and a Methodist order at night. The men pressed him to celebrate Communion but he declined.[35]
>
> A private in a Labour Company, however, wrote that scarcely a Sunday passed without divine worship, and that they had not forgotten to celebrate the Lord's Supper 'in our simple manner'.'[36]

It is interesting to note that just about the time that last letter must have been written, the Revd F. Luke Wiseman was urging the 1918 Wesleyan Conference to entrust 'saintly' local preachers with the administration of holy communion in rural home circuits, where the ministers were hard-pressed.[37]

Religious and ethical convictions led some local preachers to espouse the pacifist cause, and become conscientious objectors. This became a sharp issue in 1916 when military service was declared compulsory for all men between 18 and 41, first for unmarried men and a few months later for the married also. Victor Murray, a Primitive Methodist local preacher and an Oxford graduate then working for the Student Christian Movement, was one of those who stood fast by his pacifist convictions before a series of tribunals in Oxford. The tribunals at times worked clumsily and unsympathetically, and Victor Murray had a gruelling time, at one point facing a possible prison sentence. Professor A. S. Peake wrote supportively: 'I am proud that you should face the consequences rather than do violence to your convictions. I hope the authorities will prevent the extreme thing from happening . . . But if not the prison is not to be dreaded. We shall honour you for choosing it.'[38]

Epilogue

Some sixteen years after the incidents just referred to, Victor Murray stood before the last Primitive Methodist Conference, held in Middlesbrough in June 1932, as its vice-president. Within three months Methodist Union was to be finally consummated. In the years since the ending of World War I the Methodist connexions had all endeavoured to adjust to peace-time conditions and tackle the work that had to be done in a changed world. Most of the problems and challenges facing Methodism before the war were as urgent as ever, in some case more urgent, and the recruitment, training and deployment of local preachers were high on the agenda. The work of the Wesleyan Local Preachers' Commission, and especially its report of 1919 (see inset on the next page) had cast a chilly light on the realities of the situation in that connexion, and the Primitive and United Methodists were in no better state.[39] After 1932 the three major Methodist connexions would in unity face the problems and possibilities which they had for so long faced in separation. By this date Methodism had a full-time local preachers' connexional secretary, a layman Arthur Button, whom the Wesleyans had appointed in 1923 and who from 1932 served the united church (see next chapter).

In his vice-presidential address to that final Primitive Methodist Conference Victor Murray mused over what Primitive Methodism's particular contribution to the united church would be. He defined it as making 'the consideration of ordinary people regulative of the Church's life and thought. I think of this,' he went on, 'not as a class thing, or a social thing, but as a necessity for the clear perception of truth. And the aim of it is to glorify God . . . not in systems or institutions but in people.'[40] The work of local preachers within united Methodism would be as vital for the maintaining of this principle as it had been for almost two centuries before.

THE WESLEYAN METHODIST LOCAL PREACHERS' COMMISSION 1918

The difficult war years 1914-1918, and the shortage of local preachers, high-lighted both the importance of local preachers, and the urgent need for their training and encouragement.

The Commission consisted of 18 members, half ministerial and half lay. Its terms of reference were:

'To enquire into the conditions relating to the selection, training, appointment, numbers and distribution of local preachers throughout the Connexion; to report whether present arrangements are satisfactory; and to make recommendations as to methods which may be adopted to secure the more efficient conduct of worship.'

A wide representation of 268 circuits was investigated; 261 questionnaires were returned. Some of the findings and conclusion were:

- out of a total of 7370 local preachers in the 261 circuits only 4343 were active and only 1885 were considered as fit to preach in all the circuit churches.
- only 44 of the 261 circuits had training classes.
- only 427 of the 7370 local preachers had used the connexional cheap books scheme.
- comments from the circuits included 'LP's don't read, won't read . . . To most of my LPs the reading of a book is a formidable task.'
- recruiting was lamentable. Many able young Methodists refused to consider preaching because of the low regard in which it was held. The growing interest of the young in politics and social questions made them impatient with traditional chapel life. The decline of the class meeting has meant a drying up of one valuable source of recruitment. The shortage of LPs resulted in pulpits being filled by 'supply' preachers, often ill-equipped for their work.

Some of the Commission's recommendations (from the Report of 1919):

There was an urgent need to enhance the status of LPs and the regard in which they were held.

Ministers were urged to attend LP meetings.

Public services of recognition of LPs, with the sacrament, should be much more widely celebrated.

LPs should be used in the 'best' pulpits.

Two grades of LP were recommended – 'local' and 'connexional' the latter being able to transfer anywhere without any further examination.

The mental and spiritual development of LPs was a matter of the utmost importance.

A connexional LP Department, with central offices and a ministerial Secretary, should be established to encourage training and generally stimulate the circuits with regard to the work of local preaching.

The Wesleyan Connexion spent the next decade digesting this report.

THE CONNEXIONAL LOCAL PREACHERS' COMMITTEE.

Secretary: Mr. R. Arthur Button, 1 Central Buildings, Westminster, S.W.1.
Tel. WHItehall 1455.

LOCAL PREACHERS' STUDIES.

WINTER SESSION: OCTOBER—MARCH.

WORK FOR OCTOBER.

GROUP A.

LOCAL PREACHERS ON TRIAL.

Circuit Training Classes and Correspondence Classes. Connexional Written Examination, March 27, 28, and September 25, 26, 1936.

FIRST SECTION.

April—September Classes continued.

1. OLD TESTAMENT INTRODUCTION.
What is the Old Testament? (Smith.) 4s. (Postage 4d.) Pp. 147-161.
Questions:
1. What is meant by the *School* of Deuteronomy?
2. Discuss the question of the date and authorship of Deuteronomy.
3. Describe the chief characteristics of the book.
4. 'The master idea of the book of Deuteronomy is the old one of Covenant.' What is the content of this idea?

2. NEW TESTAMENT INTRODUCTION.
New Testament and Its Writers. (M'Clymont.) 1s. (Postage 2d.) Pp. 77-90.
Questions:
1. Write a brief outline of the contents of the Epistle to the Romans.
2. Show how 'the universality of the Gospel' is set forth by St. Paul in Romans.
3. What do you know of Philippi and of St. Paul's visits to that city?
4. The Epistle to the Philippians breathes 'a spirit of the warmest sympathy and approval.' How would you explain this?

3. THE ENGLISH BIBLE.
It is preferable that the Revised Version be used.
Read Amos and Hosea; Romans and Philippians. Learn Prov. ii. 1-11; Rom. viii. 31-39, and Phil. ii. 5-11.
Questions:
1. Relate the story of one of the Patriarchs. Give the reasons for your choice.
2. Outline the story of David and Jonathan.
3. What impressions of the early Christians did you gain by reading the *Acts of the Apostles*?
4. Name *three* outstanding characteristics of Paul as a Missionary, stating your reasons.

4. CHRISTIAN DOCTRINE.
Christian Foundations. (Hughes.) 4s. (Postage 4d.) Pp. 127-145.
Questions:
1. What is the New Testament teaching about the Holy Spirit?
2. What relation does this New Testament teaching bear to that of the Old Testament?
3. What is the evidence for belief in the Trinity?
4. Give four instances which illustrate the great practical importance of the doctrine of the Trinity.

5. WESLEY AND METHODISM.
Forty-Four Sermons. (Wesley.) 5s. (Postage 5d.) Pp. 173-197.
Questions:
1. Give an outline (300 words) of Sermon xiv.
2. Explain the phrase, 'Progress from grace to sin.'
3. What does Wesley state 'the life of God in the soul of a believer' to be?

434

A page from the *Preachers and Class Leaders' Magazine*
Methodist Publishing House, October 1935, p.434.

4

NEW VENTURES IN HARD TIMES: LOCAL PREACHING FROM METHODIST UNION TO THE LATE 1960s

Tim Macquiban

The Methodist Union of 1932 brought with it high hopes for the revitalization of the Church, heralded in the *Preachers' Magazine* for September of that year:

> 'Could we not set ourselves to promote that union of forces which would so mightily advance the Kingdom of God?'[1]

There were over 37,000 fully accredited preachers and preachers on trial contributing to the life of the new church.[2] One reason for an increase in recruitment in the Wesleyan Methodist Church in the late 1920s was the allocation of resources by the Conference and the appointment of the first full-time Secretary to co-ordinate local preachers' affairs. In addition, the growing emphasis not only on continued studies but also on fellowship and summer schools, resulted in a feeling that the work of God through the contribution of such a mighty body of preachers could be revived.

The Vice-President, Sir Robert Perks, addressing the Uniting Conference of 1932 in London, spoke of one of the finest sermons he had ever heard, preached by a railway goods guard at Banbury and welcomed the influence that local preachers might exert upon national life. Their ministry was 'a fine sphere for the exercise of Christian influence'.[3]

Sadly, such hopes were not realized, with continued decline a constant pre-occupation. The need to stimulate revival was never far away, a persistent and nagging problem for the Connexion. While union at higher levels was effected quickly and smoothly, at the lower levels the problem of redundancy, of surplus chapels and the distribution of resources locally, was a drain on effort and morale. J. M. Turner has characterized the period around 1932 as one of 'an uneasy compromise with very little experimentation . . . a lack of vigour, drive or new ideas'.[4] From 1921 onwards, decreases in the overall number of local preachers were noted with depressing regularity in denominational magazines and agenda. It was observed that this decline was parallel to and a consequence of the decline of the class meeting. Indeed, proportionally, the number of local preachers diminished more rapidly than that of the church members they served.[5]

The great celebrations of the bi-centenary of the conversions of the Wesleys in 1938 reminded the connexion of the importance of outdoor preaching. But it failed to reverse the decline of the hoped-for aggressive evangelism. The example of Wesley was paraded as a model for preachers who were, in his own day, told that they 'must either read or give up preaching'. The courses offered by the Local Preachers' Department and Methodist Study Centre were designed to foster such Wesleyan scholarship. Nevertheless there was a constant tension between the demand for practical piety over against the fears of lettered learning which might deaden the spirit.[6]

PREACHING UNDER GERMAN OCCUPATION

Leslie Roussel, formerly of Guernsey, became a local preacher in 1933 and vividly recalls the German occupation of the islands during World War II. Worship continued during that period and Leslie himself averaged ten or more services a quarter, walking or cycling to his appointments. At one service a uniformed German soldier entered the church. Leslie was somewhat taken aback but decided to carry on as he had planned. He writes:

'I need have had no reason for concern at all, for at the end of the service, as I came out of the church, he was walking towards me. Straightaway he opened up the conversation, and after thanking me for the service, he started to cry. He pulled out from his wallet a photograph of himself, his wife and his family. . . . He appeared to be a good Christian and I am absolutely certain he was not supporting the Nazi cause. He soon made a hurried retreat, as he would have been punished if caught worshipping with us.'

(With acknowledgements to Leslie Roussel and to the editor of *The Local Preachers' Magazine* for permission to print this story, part of an article in the magazine, May 1995, pp.3-4).

The Second World War caused a major disruption of the social and religious fabric of the nation, creating a need to focus on how spiritual oversight of preachers in the Forces could be maintained, through chaplains. How might arrangements for their studies and exams sometimes thousands of miles from home in difficult conditions be made? At home, as in the First World War, there was the problem of unfilled pulpits requiring the use of unqualified persons to preach and pressing into action the readers' services prepared for emergencies. This brought about a legacy of 'helpers' who had not undergone the same level of training or preparation as others. Some pressed into service without proper training were to recognize their inadequacies later. Even after the war in Europe finished, there was still a need to follow up young men conscripted into national service so that potential preachers were not lost through an interruption to their studies.[7]

After the War the 'critical situation' regarding local preachers was reported to the Conference of 1948, particularly as it related to the future existence of rural Methodism. The opening paragraphs describing 'further losses' and 'emergency measures' had a sombre tone focussing on the 'tragic wastage of man-power' and unequal distribution of resources in the Connexion. The serious decrease in the number of local preachers, once relocation had taken place, was noted and the challenge issued: 'what is your circuit going to do about it?' The task confronting the church on the safe return of those who had served in the Forces was 'sobering in its immensity and urgency'.[8]

The Local Preachers' Department tried to stimulate renewed activity in the Connexion by holding an important retreat at Eastbourne on *The Local Preacher and Evangelism* which resulted in a report published in 1950 which went to Conference. The early 1950s witnessed a determined effort to stress the importance of the place of preaching and how preachers might be better equipped, with a major conference at Swanwick on *Offering Christ : the Relevance of Doctrinal Preaching*, led by Dr E. Gordon Rupp. Eight schools for preachers were held during the presidential year of Dr William Sangster, attracting audiences of over 1,000 at each location throughout the Connexion. These were built upon in years following, with more conferences, and participation in the worldwide evangelistic campaign emanating from the World Methodist Conference of 1952. Local preachers were to take initiatives in 'aggressive and effective evangelism'. Yet the hoped-for year of revival in 1953 witnessed not an increase but a further decline in local preachers' numbers, albeit the smallest for seventeen years. Much confidence was placed in the involvement of Methodism with higher education, through its colleges at Westminster and Southlands and the new growth of Methodist Societies at universities and other colleges. In Oxford and Cambridge there were many small groups which nurtured young Christians and encouraged many to offer to preach. But it was noted also that the pressures of higher education caused some to postpone their local preacher studies. However the decline in numbers of new local preachers experienced in the period 1933 to 1944 was reversed in the period after the War.

In the 1950s, with the example of the great pulling power of Sangster and Weatherhead, and the Billy Graham crusades, belief in the power of preaching was revitalized. In the 1960s, this all collapsed. The confidence of the 1950s was dispelled in an era of increasing uncertainty in matters of theology and denominational survival. Reports to Conference talked repeatedly of decline and difficulties. The word 'crisis' headed the summaries of the situation in 1959 and 1966. The question was even asked 'Was there a future for the local preacher?' The incumbency as Local Preachers' Secretary of David Francis, a quiet but visionary character, marked a watershed in the development of new understandings of ministry. Among them, a fresh look at the ministry of lay people, and a new awareness of the local preacher's potential service to the community as well as in the leading of worship, were significant developments within the life of the Church. The role of women too in preaching was enhanced by the contribution of those like Dorothy Farrar, tutor at the Deaconess training institution at Ilkley and a vice-president of Conference. She wrote regularly in the *Preachers' Magazine* and many of the women she and others trained as deaconesses were also preachers. By 1965, one can see that consideration of the role of local preacher as lay witness within the community was far more prominent. The importance of the 'fourth subject' (Worship and Preaching) in studies was stressed.[9]

The 1961 statement entitled the *Work of the Local Preachers' Department* paid homage to those 'who rendered vital service in their own locality':

> Methodism's use of her laity has been a great characteristic of our Church, and one of which we are righly proud. In the 'Coming Great Church' this frank dependence on lay men and women will be of increasing significance, and in a much wider context.

Note that women are mentioned here, in contrast to earlier Conference reports which, in exclusive language, assumed a predominantly male order of local preachers. While that was so in 1934, when only some 3% of preachers were women, by the 1950s recruitment of women far outstripped the men and the proportion of women rose to 14% in 1958 (3,492 out of a total of 23,093). This trend was to continue.

The Local Preachers' Department

In the period covered by this chapter there were four local preachers' secretaries: **Arthur Button** (1923-1937), **Fred Farley** (1937-1946), **Greville Lewis** (1946-1958) and **David Francis** (1958-1967). They headed a small department at Westminster which constantly struggled to match the task of equipping lay preaching within the Church with the slender resources at their disposal. There were very few years when the financial situation was healthy and much reliance had to be placed not only on the generosity of the Methodist people, but also on the Rank Trust and others for gifts to support its work.

HELPING WEAKER CIRCUITS

'In April 1937 your committee appointed a sub-committee to try and devise some means whereby local preachers who resided in the town circuits could help the country circuits, where help was needed.

The sub-committee met on several occasions, and after much consideration came to the conclusion that the best way of accomplishing this object was for each of the strong Birmingham Circuits who had a redundance of local preachers, to 'adopt' or 'father' one of the weaker country circuits, where there was a shortage of local preachers, and arrange to send teams of preachers in motor cars, two or three times per quarter (or as often as practicable). We are pleased to report that such arrangements are in operation between the following Circuits:

Moseley Road and Redditch	Belmont Row and Evesham
Sutton Park and Tamworth	Wesley and Presteigne
Oldbury and Hereford	

It is earnestly hoped that this scheme will prove to be of great benefit:
    a) To the local preachers who desire more work.
    b) To those circuits who require outside help.'

(*Birmingham and Shrewsbury District LP Committee Report* March 1938)

In order that the Connexion could become more widely involved in the wider concerns of local preaching, steps were taken in 1947 to increase district representation on the connexional committee and circuit representation at district level.

Arthur Button, appointed Secretary to the Wesleyan Methodist Connexional Local Preachers' Committee in 1923, was a Lincolnshire man who trained as a teacher at Westminster College and taught for some years. An able organiser, he was required to cope with the stress of the many-sided work demanded of the Secretary, including not only the central administration of schemes for training but also much personal contact with hard-pressed local preachers in circuits up and down the country. His was the unenviable task of bringing together the three strands of training of the uniting conferences of 1932.

His retirement in 1937 occasioned some dissent when the local preachers' connexional committee recommended that his successor should be a minister. 17 District synods opposed the provisional legislation but the 29 Districts who supported the change carried the day. The feeling that this was inappropriate lingered on and memorials in support of a lay connexional secretary were proposed at Conference, but rejected, in 1942 and 1945. The appointment of additional lay personnel, as field workers, in the mid-1940s seems to have defused the debate.

On his own retirement in 1946, Fred Farley, the minister chosen as Button's successor, defended the decision of the connexional committee not to appoint a lay person. He argued that it was not good that a connexional office be advertised. It might be difficult to get a lay person because of the salary. It could be difficult to end the appointment. Such problems have since been overcome in order to introduce diversity into other connexional offices. He went on to describe the necessary qualifications of a secretary. He needed to be able to conduct conventions and preach every weekend, to be responsible for written examinations and correspondence courses, to have a thorough knowledge of the Bible and theology, and to visit colleges and universities. For that reason it was desirable that he should be a minister with a degree in theology, who could liaise with colleagues in ministerial training. Such arguments persuaded the connexion to continue to appoint ministerial secretaries.

Fred Farley came in 1937 with those qualifications and a distinguished ministry in different situations, with a determination to restore the confidence of the local preachers in their role. He wrote in his first article for the *Preachers' Magazine*:

> We believe in the vocation of the preacher [who is] a
> vital part of the ministry of the Church.[10]

The officers of the Methodist Connexional Local Preachers' Committee shortly after
Methodist Union. From left to right: Mr R. Arthur Button (General Secretary),
Revd W. H. Phipps (Hon. Sec.), Mr. R. A. Richards (Hon. Sec.),
Mr G. Knight (Hon. Treasurer), Mr H. Ibberson (Hon. Sec.)
and Mr J. Longstaff JP (Treasurer).
Source: R. N. Wycherley *Pageantry of Methodist Union* 1936, p.387.

To this end, he gave particular attention to the equipping and training of preachers, the provision of correspondence courses for those on trial, the scheme for travelling tutors to assist areas of deprivation and need, the central Lending Library and its resources, and schemes to assist preachers' travel in country circuits. He sustained the work of the department through the difficult war years and saw a halt to the decline in recruitment in the years immediately following. His sudden death in November 1951 was much lamented.

Greville Lewis came with 18 years' experience of working on the connexional committee. He developed the work which had been initiated by Farley, particularly the series of residential conferences for local preachers at Pembury and elsewhere. Under him the series of *The Preachers' Handbook* was launched, putting into the hands of local preachers a valuable resource for reflection and for equipping them in practical skills. Communication with preachers changed in style, with a more informal newsletter bringing information and encouragement, regarding recruitment, fellowship and evangelism. The latter was something that concerned Lewis from the beginning; in his first letter he urged all preachers that they should read the *Message and Mission of Methodism* report and take up with new conviction the divinely appointed mission of Methodism of which they were an integral part. His promotion of the Eastbourne Report relating the work of local preachers to evangelism was a key feature of his time as secretary.

The contribution of **David Francis** who succeeded him in 1958 was to act as a catalyst for new ideas in an unsettling period of theological and institutional uncertainty. This made for a somewhat uncomfortable time for him, and for preachers struggling to come to terms with profound changes in the relationship of the church with society. Inevitably, the numerical decline of the church, its preocupation with ecumenical conversations with the Anglicans and others, and the need to address the place of the church in the world, were factors which shaped the fundamental shift in outlook of this important period. From an emphasis on the preacher, proclaiming the gospel through sermons, we see an emergence of more emphasis on the leading of worship and on the pastoral links between the witnessing community and the wider community in the world around. He stressed in his many writings the need for more attention to the quality of worship and for local preachers to be more local and less peripatetic.

Under Francis, the series of *Handbooks* continued to be issued with a wide circulation along with other pamphlets and books written in his arresting style.   With his deeply devotional mind and grasp of ecumenical opportunities, he broadened the scope of what local preachers were challenged to be.

In 1967, the Conference Report noted the changing attitude, as the writer looked back and looked forward.   It welcomed the closer relationship with LPMAA and the Anglican lay readers through links which had developed.   It rejoiced in the ministry of the printed word which had put so much good material in the hands of preachers.   It challenged them to be 'a wholly dedicated and disciplined and close-knit' order with a special vocation. Looking back, we can see that many of the issues which all four secretaries had had to wrestle with are still with us today – the need for more sustained planned preaching with increased use of the lectionary and awareness of the Christian Year, the need for a lively teaching ministry fed by continuing training of a high calibre, the need to use preachers' personal resources more effectively, and for circuits to share expertise and personnel, with closer co-operation between the ordained ministers and preachers.

It will be helpful to look at aspects of these in a little more detail to discern patterns of development in the forty-five years after Union.

Status and Identity of Local Preachers

One of the major obstacles to Methodist Union had been in the areas of doctrinal definition, and lay presidency of the sacraments. What constituted a minister of the Methodist Church and how did he differ from fellow preachers?   Rattenbury and those of the 'Other Side', high churchmen of the Wesley tradition, pressed for references to the apostolic faith, the historic creeds and the protestant reformation, and a higher view of ordination. But the principle of a representative ministry as part of the priesthood of all believers united the three bodies. The Wesleyans were forced to give way on the principle of lay presidency of the sacraments though in fact, despite some reluctance from UM and PM circuits to give up lay presidency, the practice was exercised rarely and lay dispensations were generally granted only in cases of severe deprivation through shortage of ministers, mainly in rural areas.[11] While in theory the status of lay preachers was equal to that of the itinerant, with the same testing of the call and the necessary approval of local courts before authorization 'to minister in holy things', in practice the ministers jealously guarded their privileges in the ministerial session of Conference and their separate synods.   They continued to control the local preachers through the chairing of their meeting and that of the circuit quarterly meeting, where both ordained and lay preachers were ex officio members.

Much of the quarterly local preachers' meeting was taken up with the regulation of those who came under its jurisdiction, considering 'the character of the local preachers, their fidelity to doctrine, and their fitness for the work of the circuit'. This disciplinary function of the meeting was important as the names on the circuit plan were scrutinized, complaints received and charges heard. The body also made recommendations for the inclusion as well as the exclusion of preachers, having orally examined those who had generally served at least two years on trial, during which time fellow preachers had heard and reported on services they had conducted and sermons preached. The oral examination covered various stipulated areas on doctrine and Methodist ethos including

> the Fatherhood of God; the Deity of our Lord Jesus
> Christ; the Person, Mission and Work of the Holy Spirit;
> the Universality of Sin; the Atonement; Salvation for All
> by Grace through Faith; the Believer's Privilege of
> Assurance and of Perfect Love; the Christian Church; the
> Future Life.

Reference was to be made to Wesley's *Notes on the New Testament* and his *Forty-four Sermons*, copies of which appeared as foundation sources in most libraries of local preachers until fairly recently. The emphasis upon giving an account of one's conversion to God, present Christian experience and call to preach remains as fundamental as ever to the task of self-regulation and self-examination amongst local preachers.[12]

There was no automatic right for local preachers to be on the leaders' meetings of the local church in which they were members, though, in practice, many were such by virtue of the other offices they held within the church, as stewards or class leaders as well as fulfilling their preaching ministry.

While the ordained ministers were at times loath to share administration of the sacraments with local preachers, such dispensations and practices did occur, though usually only with the concurrence of the superintendent and the permission (in the case of the sacrament of holy communion) of Conference. For baptisms, the permission of the minister was all that was required and in general this was regularly given. In some situations, particularly in the United Methodist tradition, a Sunday School superintendent of a small church who was also a local preacher might on occasion conduct baptisms.

Despite the theological balance expressed in the Deed of Union and the reassurances given in the 1946 debate on the issue of lay administration of the sacraments, it is clear that local preachers were often regarded by others or regarded themselves as second-class citizens, filling in the appointments on the plan which the ministers could not or would not fill, particularly in rural areas.[13] 'Harold King', writing in the *Preachers' Magazine* of March 1958, remarked on the jealousy of churches to secure their share of ministerial appointments in a series of fictitious letters highlighting disparities in the system:

Dear Mr Super,
It is our Chapel Anniversary at - - - on Easter Sunday, so we would be glad if you would plan the young minister Revd - - -, failing him Revd - - - and if both are booked, please plan yourself, and oblige . . .. Bro - - - wants to know why he has never been planned at the Circuit Chapel same as Bro - - -. This special treatment for one and 'fowl' for the other is not leading to the best feeling in the Circuit in his opinion . . .

One older local preacher at Wolverhampton is reported to have complained to the superintendent about the limitation of his preaching appointments: 'It's not cricket – I never get planned at so-and-so', he said, to which the Superintendent replied: 'No, it's not cricket, it's making the plan.'[14]

Ministers were, of course, ever anxious to stress the importance of local preachers, as was Benson Perkins, in his preface to the first *Preachers' Handbook*, referring to the 30,000 local preachers as 'the greatest lay ministry in the world conducting 16,000 services per Sunday'.[15] The collegiality of preachers, ordained and lay, became increasingly stressed with a real searching for the meaning of the office in the 1960s. David Francis thought the very title, local preacher, was too limiting. He urged them to see themsemselves 'as shepherd with a pastoral role among individual people as class leader, visitor, pastoral worker', as well as worship leader 'to lead the people worthily as they praise and pray'. This emphasis on the place of preachers within the 'laos', the whole people of God, with different yet complementary roles from those of the itinerant ministers, bridging the gap between the institutional church and the local community, served to remind preachers of their special responsibilities and to assure them that they were not stop-gaps on the plan but an integral part of the leadership of the worshipping and witnessing local churches they served. It was this reassurance which was needed to restore and boost morale in a declining church. The challenge was issued to individuals to join this order, with its discipline, its regularity of worship and its commitment to continuing education. The culmination of Francis' thinking is to be found in the Report to the 1964 Conference on *The Place and Functions of the Local Preacher*, in which their key position in the life and mission of the church in the world was stressed. Nevertheless, in a system of theological education and ministerial training where ordained and lay were in the main treated separately, it was all too easy for a more educated ministry to undervalue the contribution of local preachers who struggled with limited resources and the pressures of employment to maintain their theological reading and reflection.

Recruitment and training

The foundations within the Wesleyan Connexion for the better training and recruitment of local preachers had been laid at the end of the 19th century with the establishment of the Union for Biblical and Homiletical Study in 1893. As shown in chapter four, attempts to make training compulsory, through prescribed studies and written examinations,

---

TRAINING AT THE GRASS ROOTS!

George Wilfred Humble, a Weardale local preacher, ran a Christian Endeavour group at Frosterley which in the late 1920s and 1930s proved to be a seed bed of local preachers, some of whom went on to become ministers. One of those local preachers writes as follows:

'Before services Wilfred Humble would take himself off to the moors for meditation and sermon preparation. More than this, as local preachers' tutor he would have us individually up on the same moors to preach in the open air to the sheep. It was there we learned to project our voices, and think on our feet. I doubt if many of the sheep were converted, but I'm sure that GWH would have been gratified to know that his work with John Davis, Billy Dagg and myself was fully appreciated in later life.'

From a communication from Mr George Davis, of Arbroath.

---

were resisted in the period before Union, though in 1927 the first WM connexional examination in Biblical Knowledge was framed. By 1934, resistance to the pressure for raising standards through directed study had crumbled. The advice for local preachers to avail themselves of the connexional examination on the bible, doctrine, and Methodist studies, in part to prepare them for the all-important oral examination at the local preachers' meeting, was supplemented with two papers, on Biblical Knowledge and Christian Doctrine, which were introduced in 1936. In addition there was a number of correspondence courses, including one on homiletics, which were optional. In 1947, questions about exams were added to the agenda of the local preachers' meeting: 'Has any local preacher on trial sat for the connexional examinations? With what result?' This accentuated the trend towards a greater emphasis on further training.[16]

The three strands of the uniting churches responsible for the equipping of local preachers, the Wesleyan Union, the Local Preachers' Training Movement (PM) and the Scheme of Studies for Local Preachers (UM) were brought together and merged under the title of Local Preachers' Studies. Through the full-time Secretary of the Department, the courses were offered, organized and the monitoring of progress more centrally controlled. From the start, there was continual encouragement for preachers to exercise self-discipline in making the most of opportunities offered to improve their knowledge and skills. Henry Strawson in 1936 recommended a period on trial of at least two years and urged further studies beyond accreditation. The temptation to cease studying once one's name was on the plan was to be resisted. Each circuit should have a training class for local preachers, like the one in a Halifax circuit where three ministers took it in turns to lead the group in studies of the bible, theology and homiletics. There was, he said, a pressing need for more district conventions, and a more systematic method of preparation and study.[17]

What resources then were to be made available if this more sustained study was to be made possible?

Books were obviously a vital tool in the hands of preachers. To make these fully available, the centrally located library at Westminster was to be built up as a lending library. In the early 1930s this was a circulating library, comprising 36 boxes of up to 20 books which were loaned for up to six months to circuits requesting them. In addition, preachers could buy from a catalogue books of up to 30/- in value at half-price. This scheme was further developed into a stock which was more readily available for individual preachers. On deposit of 2/6d to cover postage, books would be circulated around the connexion 'to improve a preachers' equipment for this work'. It started in 1938 with 11 books. Sadly, all the indications are that the stock was never as large as it needed to be to service the requirements of all local preachers, and the use of the stock was restricted, even though it had increased to 600 books by 1955. The library is now located at Wesley College, Bristol, and is a good, if small, example of a working library containing the sort of books which local preachers in earlier years were urged to read.[18]

Of greater impact were the correspondence courses which were developed, linking preachers with tutors who offered advice and guided reading. While many of these were in the areas of biblical studies, theology and homiletics, courses were also offered for preachers considering offering as candidates for the ministry for whom preparatory courses in English grammar, general knowledge, history and literature were important. These courses were offered by the Methodist Studies Centre which catered for the wider needs of lay people in Methodism, for Sunday School teachers, those involved in Women's Work overseas and candidates for the Wesley Deaconess Order. Some confusion ensued which required closer co-operation between the two arms of lay training but the purpose of the Local Preachers' Department was to move towards a more controlled compulsory system of examination while the MSC was voluntaryist in its approach.

While the local preachers were well served by their magazines, it was felt in the 1950s that more weighty publications ought to be available. The excellent, and well-circulated, series of *Preachers' Handbooks* were produced with sustained contributions on different aspects of the preachers' tasks, in bible and theology and in practical skills. These, and the *Epworth Preachers' Commentaries* commenced in 1955, put into the hands of preachers inexpensive but substantial tools for their theological formation. 14,000 copies of Volume One of the *Handbook* were sold. It comprises such articles as 'The Preacher's Life of Prayer', 'The Conduct of Public Prayer' and 'The Use of the Bible in Public Worship'. The series continued into the mid-60s and was well-received as a valuable help for preachers.

Of significance in local preacher development was the series of conferences and schools organized by the Department. Starting before the Second World War at Ashville College near Harrogate, Culford in East Anglia and Shebbear in the West Country (all Methodist residential schools), they provided, over a few days or a week at Easter and in the summer, times of fellowship, leisure and information-sharing sessions which were a stimulus for further study and preparation for preaching. The Ashville school owed its inception and progress to Mr Herbert Ibberson of Barnsley, who regularly gathered about 40 preachers to such conferences. The residential schools for preachers, and the weekend and Saturday schools arranged by districts and circuits, were of major importance in stimulating a sense of fellowship among preachers which

---

HOW TO DISCOURAGE A YOUNG PREACHER!

'Before conducting my first Methodist service, it was decided that I might make a useful start by one night taking the weekly Friday night prayer meeting . . . . . I was at the time reading with considerable enthusiasm a book which set out to relate modern psychology to Christian practice . . . . . so I based my notes on ideas which flowed from what I had been reading . . . . As we were still all getting down on our knees, a white-bearded octogenarian with egg-bald head and creaking joints started off with the first prayer. In a cracked but unmistakably furious voice he began: "We thank thee, O Lord, that we don't need any psychology, nor sociology, nor zoology, nor any other ology to bring us to thy throne of grace but only the saving blood of thy Son, Jesus Christ our Lord. Ah-men".

He spat out the "Ah-men" with such fury that it was clear that what he really meant was, "Now put that in your pipe and smoke it".'

Douglas Hyde, *I Believed, the autobiography of a former British Communist*, Reprint Society 1952, pp.15-16. At the time of the episode described above Douglas Hyde was a youthful Primitive Methodist.

---

circuit meetings had often failed to provide. Of outstanding value was the series of conferences held after the war at Kent College for Girls at Pembury. Starting in 1948, with an Easter School for five days, and a week in August, these continued to be a significant contribution by Greville Lewis and his successors in bringing key speakers and scholars to share with preachers in concentrated sessions which dealt with such matters as group sermon construction and practical speech therapy as well as the more traditional approaches. By 1955, over 500 local preachers had attended twenty-four schools, at which all age groups were represented with a number of overseas students.[19] These were not just times for serious discussion but great fun too. As the Conference Report of 1958 said:

> The lectures have always stretched the minds of the
> students to the limits but scholarship and humour have
> never been divorced.

Not all could afford the time or money to go to such conferences. So districts were encouraged to organise a yearly training day, sometimes in collaboration with neighbouring districts. Leslie Davison, when

Chairman of the Wolverhampton and Shrewsbury District, organized such schools. Days of reflection were often resourced by tutors at the theological colleges such as Didsbury at Bristol, which had a fine reputation for its biblical and theological scholarship in the 1950s and 1960s. In 1958, such district days were held in Nottingham and Derby, Darlington and Newcastle, Durham, East Anglia, Cardiff and Swansea, North Lancashire, York and Hull, Plymouth and Exeter and West Yorkshire. This still represented only about a quarter of the Connexion and secretaries were constantly encouraging districts to take initiatives which they were willing to support by their presence. In 1953, the secretary commended the work of William Graham, MBE, tutor for the Darlington District, who had formed his first training class 40 years earlier. He organized an annual conference at Brockley Hall, Saltburn. Through him, 157 local preachers on trial had received instruction and guidance. In that year he had 80 students in four weekly classes. 'Oh for more William Grahams in Methodism!' was a heartfelt plea for the rest of the Connexion to take training and recruitment seriously.[20]

To remedy this, Fred Farley instituted a system of travelling tutors in the 1940s. Deaconess Bessie Higgins made a fine contribution: she started in 1941 to assist mainly rural circuits to reinforce the preaching strength of rural Methodism. Commencing in Derbyshire, she moved into Cornwall and Lincolnshire and then Somerset to hold classes and meet with local groups. Her work was not as easy as the first report indicates:

> An unusually difficult winter ensued, the black-out,
> heavy snowfalls and widespread epidemics all make
> travel and attendance at study groups difficult.

By 1948 she had two colleagues, Seymour Simpson in Sunderland and Durham, and later Halifax and Hull, and Marjorie Thorn in East Anglia. She was succeeded by Elsie Camplin who travelled in Chester and Warrington and then Hull Districts. By the end of the decade, equal attention was being given to urban areas as to rural, though the need remained greater in the latter.

In 1955 the Newmarket circuit, with 26 churches, wrote of the challenge of filling 550 appointments a quarter with only three ministers, 41 local preachers and 60 auxiliaries. This left a shortfall of 39 appointments a quarter. The remedy proved to be a crisis letter spelling out the need for more preachers, which led to the happy result of twelve new preachers on trial! For many rural circuits, such a scale of recruitment was needed simply to replace the loss of local preachers through death. This pattern was repeated up and down the connexion. Without aggressive recruitment, rural Methodism would face further crises.

With more books, more courses, more conferences, the pressure for a more generally educated and highly-trained 'Order' of local preachers became irresistible. The extension of examinations as part of the process of training no longer raised widespread opposition. In 1955, as well as the oral examination, candidates for full plan were to be required to produce a written sermon. In 1963, the pressure to include more formal training in worship and preaching was met with the inclusion of an extra paper on that subject in the examination process. Standards were being raised and a new generation of local preachers brought forward for whom study and discussion in a wider context than the local circuit had been made possible by the exciting initiatives of a department which served the connexion well.

Worship and Preaching

What then were the main influences on the practice of local preachers and how did they respond to changes? Quite clearly, the books and printed material that they read helped shape the way in which they preached and led worship, as well as the role models which they sought to emulate. The period began as one in which the centrality of preaching was secure and unquestioned. It ended with all in doubt. Methodism was wrestling with decline, and the inability to reverse this trend resulted in a growing questioning of the content and practice of worship, especially as the effects of the 'Ecumenical Movement' became increasingly felt.

W. E. Sangster, through his pulpit ministry at Westminster and through his extensively-read writings, moulded a whole generation of preachers, reminding them of the need for more systematic teaching on the centralities of faith, warning them of the dangers of entertaining topical addresses which drew the crowds but lacked substance and integrity. He described such sermons as a 'string of loosely related pictures illustrating nothing important'. Sadly some congregations seemed to enjoy them, but the long-term effect on the church was harmful. In his memorable phrases in *Power of Preaching*, he urged the preachers to make it plain and practical, based on sound doctrine, prayed over, and with passion. This renewed Wesleyan emphasis marked a revival of interest in the Methodist heritage which helped shape preachers' studies and practice in the mid-century.[21]

His was not a narrow evangelical emphasis, for he urged on preachers a range of approaches which would include biblical interpretation, ethical teaching and doctrinal exposition, philosophic and apologetic in tone and social and evangelistic in application. This, and his earlier books on *The Approach to Preaching* and *The Craft of the Sermon*, indicate a revival of interest in the sermon as a medium of effective communication of the Gospel. Along with W. R. Maltby in his *Precepts for Preachers*, which urged the need for less about sin and more good news, for offer and demand as well as the story of salvation, these two mighty preachers influenced a whole generation. William Temple once said of Maltby that he was the best preacher he had ever heard for students.[22]

TWO PREACHERS' STORIES FROM ARKENGARTHDALE

'In the early 'thirties Matthew Bell, a local preacher of Swaledale, told this story to the minister, the Revd W. H. Small. After a week of broken nights and weary days during lambing time, he was walking over the moor to a preaching appointment at Arkengarthdale, worrying because he hadn't a new sermon ready. On the way he prayed "Thoo knaws, Lord, Ah's nut hed a minute this week." The Lord said "Preach about Burnin Bush, Matt." He replied "The've heerd that yan, Lord, and Thoo knaws Tommy Hind allus writes preachers' texts in his little book, and he'll be settin lewkin down at ma." The Lord answered "Thee preach it, lad, ther's mair in yon text nor Tommy Hind can chow in yan go."

* * *

'When in the 1960s it became customary to address God in public prayer as "You", J. G. Stones (1896-1976) said "I can't do it, friends; it makes the Lord too far away. For old dalesfolk like me, "Thou" is for relations and friends, and how much more for Him, our father and our best friend".'

M. Batty, *A View of Arkengarthdale*, Barnard Castle, 1982, p.52 and p.55.

In parallel, others were urging more of a teaching style, placing preaching in the wider context of word and sacrament amongst the committed, in a rediscovery of the 'Catholicity of Protestantism'. Lay people, as well as ministers, were affected by two organizations very different in ethos, the Fellowship of the Kingdom and the Methodist Sacramental Fellowship. Later a significant report edited by Newton Flew and Rupert Davies appeared in 1949 as *The Catholicity of Protestantism*. Gordon Rupp's Swanwick lecture in 1952 on doctrinal preaching, mentioned above, may also be recalled here.

For some the stress on personal evangelism was all-important. George Gifford defined this in his article on *The Preacher's Methods and Means*, as leading 'men and women into a real and definite acceptance of Jesus Christ as their Saviour and Lord' by a variety of methods which would show the depth and reality of religious experience to the unawakened by persuading the mind and moving the feelings.

For others the work of the Temperance and Social Welfare (later Christian Citizenship) Department, led by Henry Carter and E. C. Urwin in the 1930s, was important, in 'awakening a new sense of responsibility for social order' and the 'growth of a Christian social conscience' with its roots in the social action of the ministry of John Wesley, offering the gospel of free grace and perfect love for all.[23] The inspiration of William Temple and others made social witness a powerful theme for preaching in the 1930s, still maintained in the late 1940s with the birth of the Welfare State and high hopes for the radical political programme introduced by the Labour Government of 1945. With Temple's death and the difficulties of delivering such a programme in post-war Britain, the centrality of such an approach gave way to the more urgent need for a return to an evangelistic emphasis in the 1950s.

The Eastbourne Report focussed on the need for a systematic and planned approach to the whole business of preaching, to combat the disconnected preaching in country chapels where the 26 sermons in the quarter might be quite unrelated and unbalanced. One might conceivably hear nothing but sermons on the parables of the Sower or the Good Samaritan! Teams of four or five preachers, balanced in experience and technique, were urged to provide services for three churches each, meeting together regularly for corporate study and planning, and liaising with the minister in pastoral charge who would follow up their services. While in the mid-1950s 100 circuits are said to have tried this scheme, there is no indication that it was any more than a brave but limited experiment followed by relatively few.[24]

Of more impact were the lessons of the so-called Liturgical Movement, which brought a heightened awareness of the Christian Year and the value of a lectionary in ordering the life of the Church. The work of Morrow, Billington and Bates, first published in 1956, and the scholarship and ecumenical involvement of college tutors such as Raymond George and Gordon Wakefield, started to plant new ideas in the minds of local preachers regarding the place of worship, and of children in worship, in the life of the Church. This was worship which could not fail to be influenced by the style and content of other churches, notably those with more formal liturgies. Thus the earlier work of William Maxwell, Horton Davies and Nathaniel Micklem was reinforced and given new emphasis within the urgings of the Local Preachers' Secretary, David Francis, an enthusiast for ecumenism and liturgical change. The formal curriculum of local preachers' studies was increasingly shaped by such developments. He did not, however, despair of preaching as a vehicle of communication, but set its circumstances and methods within the wider context of worship and teaching. The people of God needed to praise and serve and not merely listen and be entertained.[25]

Conclusion

Local preachers of outstanding significance have made a contribution to the wider religious and social life of the nation, particularly those who sought to make the bridge between preaching and the social and intellectual life of society. Two names are prominent in their standing in the academic environments in which they were placed. In the apologetic role of interpreting Christianity in the world of science and technology, Charles Coulson (1910-1974), professor of Applied Mathematics of Oxford University, made a powerful contribution, while Herbert Butterfield (1900-1979), Regius Professor of Modern History at Cambridge University, was influential in making a coherent understanding of Christian history intelligible to generations of Methodists who came to appreciate more fully their place in the wider history of the church. Two preachers who made important contributions to political developments in this century were Sir Isaac Foot (1880-1960), MP for Bodmin, representing the then declining strength of west country Liberalism strongly rooted within Methodism, a Vice-President of Conference in 1937, and Arthur Henderson (1863-1935), one of the architects of the modern Labour Party, serving as Home and Foreign Secretary, and representing the links between trade unionism, co-operative societies and local preaching so prominent in the north-east. From Birmingham, Charles Simmons served both in local and central government.[26]

There has since the Second World War been a crisis of confidence for local preachers who began to wonder whether there was any place for them in the Methodist Church. By 1967, there were serious suggestions that the rate of decline would mean the extinction of the group by the end of the century.[27] In the ecumenical climate of conversations with the Church of England, some felt that local preachers were a liability whose status and identity had to be radically re-examined. In what sense were they 'local' and did the title 'preacher' contain their functions too precisely in changing patterns of ministry?[28] While such fears have not been realized, the important questions raised in the 'Francis years' have set the agenda for a revival of interest in the role of local preachers in the ministry of the whole people of God.

An old snapshot of Tom Glasson.
Kindly supplied by his granddaughter, Mrs Ruth Exley.

5

ONE PREACHER'S STORY:
THOMAS GLASSON 1870-1940

T. Francis Glasson

This chapter is a reduction of an account of Tom Glasson's life published in 1943. We are grateful to the author (Tom's son) and the original publisher (Epworth Press) for permission to print this abridged version here, using one preacher's story to illuminate and bring into sharper focus the wider story told throughout this book.

One dark winter night in February 1871, a middle-aged man was seen driving a trap towards Colchester. He was returning from Peldon Mill, where he had been superintending the fixing of an engine. His name was John Glasson, and he had on his person a substantial sum of money. Unfortunately, a thief knew of his journey, and when he drew up outside the Abberton 'Lion' and went in for a whisky the thief stealthily unfastened the reins and the seat-straps. When John Glasson re-entered the trap and the horse started off, he had no control over the animal, and after a short distance the seat overbalanced, he was thrown out and his neck broken. The thief took possession of the money, made off and was never caught. The injured man lived for a fortnight, but he had no sensation below the neck. He was forty-eight years of age. Two years later the thief-murderer, who had joined the Army to try and forget his crime, died after confessing his responsibility and admitting that he had had no rest since.

John Glasson's last injunction to his wife concerned their eleven children: 'Keep them together like a bundle of sticks.' On the funeral card appeared the words: 'Leave thy fatherless children; I will preserve them alive: and let thy widows trust in Me.' The youngest of the eleven was a tiny baby not yet five months old; this was Thomas Glasson (born October 4, 1870) the subject of these pages.

In spite of his last wish, it was impossible for John Glasson's widow to bring up all the children herself. It was decided to send the infant Thomas to an aunt and uncle named Gundry who lived at Wheal Alfred, near Hayle, a seaside town in St. Ives Bay in Western Cornwall. He was thus early separated from his mother and his brothers and sisters; in fact, it was many years before they met again.

The aunt died when he was seven, and Mr Gundry and the boy moved to Hayle, by the sea. A few years later they settled at St. Erth Praze, a small village not far from Hayle. In coming to Cornwall, he was really returning to the original home of his family. His grandfather, Josiah Glasson, had also lived at Hayle, where he was foreman for Richard Trevithick (1771-1833), the famous maker of the road locomotive which carried the first load of passengers ever conveyed by steam (Christmas Eve, 1801).

As a result of his early experiences at Hayle and St. Erth Praze, the sea and the countryside left an abiding influence on his life and character. In later years, as a town dweller, he used to say how much he would love to show me the lanes and fields amongst which he revelled as a boy, and he would look back longingly to those days when the earth and common face of Nature spoke to him rememberable things. 'I spent my boyhood,' he would tell, in one of his talks 'in a lovely countryside, and much of my leisure time was spent in the fields, first as an aimless rambler, then as a youthful workman.'

Christian commitment and the call to preach

Tom would not consent to his uncle's design to send him to a secondary school, and a year or two of his adolescence were spent in idling. At the age of fifteen he was apprenticed to a wheelwright in the village, but a few weeks after the beginning of his apprenticeship, his uncle died, and he was now virtually alone in the world. He stayed on at St. Erth Praze, living with a housekeeper, and continued with his apprenticeship. Thrown on his own resources, he began to drink and live carelessly, without any worthy aim. At length, when he was eighteen, the great event of his life occurred (March, 1889), described here in his own words:

> 'Let me try and sketch a picture for you. A little country chapel, a small congregation, an ordinary local preacher, a simple, pointed discourse. One young man in that congregation was leading a dissolute life; his presence there was more out of curiosity than otherwise. But the preacher preached, and the young man believed, and although he may not be a paragon of virtue, he is filling the role of preacher to you to-night'.

That transaction in the village chapel marked the real turning-point of his life; here was the seed from which all his later life grew.

Among the St. Erth Praze Methodists was a genial farmer named John Trewhella, who became his class-leader, his counsellor, and his most intimate friend. John Trewhella was some twenty years older than my father, but their friendship was like that of David and Jonathan. It was of great importance at this critical point that someone was ready to follow up the decision which had been made and to give guidance and friendship. John Trewhella was a typical Cornish Methodist, large-hearted and loyal, a big man in every way, in physique and in personality. He and several brothers lived at a fine old farm named Tregenhorne, a sturdy and roomy farmhouse with a real old-world atmosphere. This place became like home to the young apprentice. Here he was always welcome. He was looked on almost as a member of the family. In fact it was through this association that he met his future wife, Eliza Trewhella, John's cousin.

Encouraged by John's friendship and by other influences in the small Methodist Society, he steadily grew in grace. He began to serve in the Sunday School and also as a class-leader. In the old-fashioned type of class-meeting, where everyone spoke, it was easy to find those who had any special gifts. Readiness in speech was developed, and wider spheres of service were opened to young people of promise. And so it was not long before he was recognised as a potential preacher. At first he fought against the idea. Finally he allowed his name to be placed on the circuit plan. His first sermon indicates the victory of the Spirit's constraint over natural reluctance. The text was: 'For though I preach the gospel I have nothing to glory of; for necessity is laid upon me. Yea, woe is unto me if I preach not the gospel' (I Corinthians 9:16). We may perhaps quote the opening sentences of the sermon :

> 'Perhaps you will excuse me if in my introductory remarks I make some reference to myself in connexion

with these words. The reason I chose them as my first text is because of their relation to my own personal experience. As to the prophets and apostles of old the Word of the Lord came, so it has come to me, not in an audible voice, but by the still small voice of His Spirit, by an inward impression on my soul. The Spirit of the Lord God has come upon me and He hath anointed me to preach the gospel. My entrance into the work is not the result of any natural inclination or tendency, for with truthfulness I might say, in face of the responsibilities of the office, I would far rather live a private Christian life. I have received the call from God.'

In order to equip himself for this new task, he began to study hard in the limited time at his disposal. Many of his books at that period were obtained from the Joyful News Book Depôt, Rochdale, which was then in the hands of Thomas Champness, that great friend of village Methodism. His copies of such works as Wesley's *Sermons, Notes on the New Testament,* Field's *Theology*, and Cruden's *Concordance* bear embossed on the fly-leaf the name of the Rochdale Book Depôt. The work which Champness began at Castleton Hall, Rochdale – the training of evangelists – was, of course, transferred early this century to Cliff College; it is significant that his work for lay preachers threw its light and help as far as a remote village near Land's End.

The sphere of my father's early preaching was the Hayle Circuit, in which the village of St. Erth Praze was included. It is interesting to notice that Wesley, who was often impressed by the loyalty and fervour of the Cornish societies, visited Hayle on several occasions; indeed, he was once nearly drowned there. It was at Hayle Copper-house that my father preached his trial sermon – not the 'preaching-house' mentioned by Wesley, for this had been replaced by another building in 1817. The slag sanctuary was not destined to remain in use till heaven and earth passed away, as Wesley expected, but for some thirty years only.

In a children's address Tom Glasson used to tell that hardly anybody could read or write in his Cornish village. Let us hear his own words:

'Now I didn't have a very thorough education, but I could always read pretty well. And the villagers soon knew it. The result was that if there were any murders, or any fatal accidents or other unusual affairs happening in the district, a paper would be bought and a company of young and old men would assemble in the kitchen of someone's house. I should be sent for, to read the news. Now it is quite natural for me to have felt proud in being the hero on these occasions, and I assure you they esteemed me quite as highly as I deserved.

'Then there was another thing. Many of the families in the village had sons or daughters away from home. Scarcely a week passed without some mother calling me to her door, and whispering in my ear, "I've got a letter from Jim in America, or Mary in London; will you come in dinner-time and read it. And then I want you to answer it some evening for me.' And so I used to know all the secrets of half the village and had the confidence of them all . . . It was a great thing to a boy like me to have such a warm place in all their hearts and a welcome in all their homes.

'After a time, I offered to teach a lot of the young men in the village to read and I obtained a room and furnished it, with the help of one or two others, as a Village Institute. Then we had draughts and dominoes and other games as a relaxation from study. But instead of learning to read, as I wished, they one and all remained satisfied to play games or sit and smoke while I read to them . . . [Nevertheless] it was an experience that did me good, for I read things to please them which I should never have read from choice and so got a taste for variety.'

In another of his talks (fortunately preserved) he said:

'I knew an old miner many years ago who had lived a rather gay life and he was eventually overtaken by what we called the miner's decline. He with several other miners, when on the night shift, used to spend their afternoons in the shop in which I was apprenticed to talk politics and general gossip. Sometimes the question of religion would share the conversation and with boyish pride I used to join in, and when as sometimes happened it was ridiculed and derided through the inconsistencies of some of its professors I used to step in with a pardonable amount of righteous indignation and tell these men, some of whom were old enough to be my grandfather, to give the subject an unprejudiced study apart from its adherents, and I used specially to implore this old man to forsake his drunken habits and irreverent demeanour and enthrone Christ in his heart. But he would always reply in a tone of jocularity, "None of your nonsense, Tommy boy. None of your nonsense." But after ceasing work for a year or two he fell ill. And Tommy was almost immediately sent for to talk and pray with him.'

Tom Glasson was compelled for health reasons to leave Cornwall for the Midlands at the age of twenty-five, as nearness to the sea had induced chest trouble. After a brief period at Biggleswade, where he met his mother for the first time since infancy, he joined his brother at Derby, remaining there for over forty years. He was now doing the work of a joiner and carpenter, and succeeded his brother as foreman. He married soon after coming to Derby, and lived there in the same house for the rest of his life, worshipping chiefly at the Rose Hill church in the Green Hill circuit.

His methods as a preacher

For many years he left home for work at 7 am and did not return until 6 pm But what time remained was spent in reading and study, and it is true to say that preaching the Kingdom of God was the master passion of his life. His sermons were prepared with great care, everything being written out often as many as three or four times. He used to refer to 'a Spanish artist who, when dying, turned away from the crucifix held before his eyes, declaring he could not bear the sight of such miserable workmanship. And so the most beautiful truths may be rendered of none effect by their crude presentation'. There was nothing slipshod about his preparation; he sought to be a workman that needed not to be ashamed, handling aright the word of truth.

His usual method was as follows. First he would be arrested in the course of Bible reading by some theme and would allow it to simmer in his mind. Then he would write down notes and passages relating to the main subject. Then a rough draft of the whole sermon in pencil would follow, and finally the finished article would be written in ink in a large book like a ledger. The final version would be read through again and again until it was firmly fixed in his mind. He did not set out to memorise slavishly the written words, but found this mode of preparation the most helpful. He did not recommend it to others, but it was the way for him.

In addition to this immediate preparation, there was a great amount of more general reading. He was keenly interested in theological and devotional books, giving special attention to the Cross and prayer. He was particularly attracted to R. C. Moberley's *Atonement and Personality*. He was conservative in theological outlook and read the great Victorians (Liddon, Dale, W. B. Pope, Dr Parker, etc.) as eagerly as contemporary writers; but he was by no means obscurantist, and in later years agreed with that attitude to the Scripture which is represented by C. H. Dodd's *Authority of the Bible*.

He kept books of extracts in which were entered passages of value and importance from his reading. A glance at these shows that his intellectual menu included solid enough fare. A whole note-book is filled with extracts from only four works – Romanes's *Thoughts on Religion*, Hibbert's *Materialistic Philosophy*, Hugh Price Hughes's *Ethical Christianity*, and Walsh's *In Relief of Doubt*.

Not that his reading was purely religious. Though the Bible itself always formed his staple diet, he had a profound love for all good literature. He was particularly interested in the great poets and delighted in the works of Shakespeare, Milton, Tennyson, Browning and Keats. When a man has come under the influence of Christ, he inevitably feels attracted to the best and noblest in every department of life. He would no doubt have been studious in any event – though that is not certain – but the religious impulse drove him to seek goodly pearls, and to steep his mind in the highest thoughts of the human spirit.

His own advice on sermon preparation was based on Psalm 39:3. 'While I was musing, the fire burned: then spake I with my tongue.' He interpreted it thus: 'Meditation and Aspiration (while I was musing), Inspiration (the fire burned), Proclamation (then spake I with my tongue).' 'Don't be afraid,' he would say, 'of being styled a mystic. Cultivate acquaintance with the secret place of the Most High . . . The soul speaking to God, that is aspiration. God speaking to the soul, that is inspiration. Can we say, "I AM hath sent me," if we have not heard His whisper of grace? Oh let us treasure these moments possible to all when God whispers in our ears messages as direct and imperious as any received by prophets of old. To this end let us cultivate that sensitiveness of soul, bred of meditative aspiration, which can hear the still small voice as readily as the din of earthquake or the crackling of fire.'

In the pulpit though he had not the presence and voice of an orator, his delivery was effective and arresting. He was a true Cornishman and retained the Celtic vision and fire.

He kept a register in which each sermon was entered and the places where it was preached, together with the appropriate hymns and Bible readings. Some were given as many as forty times, others only once. The early sermons are all of an evangelistic character; notice the texts: 'Behold, I stand at the door and knock.' 'Redeemed by the precious blood of Christ.' 'How shall we escape if we neglect so great salvation?' Throughout his preaching life he made central the call of Christ and the offer of divine grace. One is impressed by the earnestness and the note of urgency. Preachers are sometimes told that the most important part of a sermon is the application. Most of his sermons are exemplary in this respect; the hearers were not left to make their own deductions, the truth was not set before them in a take-it-or-leave-it fashion, but was faithfully applied to their own lives. He preached for a verdict and appealed for immediate decision. What, for instance, could be more direct and plain that this concluding appeal of an earnest message?

> 'I am led to beg you with all the passionate entreaty of which my soul is capable to take your stand on the side of godliness and righteousness. The world is speaking to you, the flesh is speaking to you and the Devil calls upon you to keep with the crowd in the broad way. But a voice conjoined with mine hushes them all into silence at this moment, and says, "Follow Me; come unto Me; I will give you rest. I will invest your life with a nobler purpose and give you a more abundant life, and on My constancy you can rely. The world will turn its back on you in adversity and age. The flesh will torment you for every sinful indulgence. The Devil will laugh at you in you direst calamity. But I will be with you always, sharing your every burden, nerving your arm in every conflict, soothing your every pain, and when your last day's work is done take you to My Father's House". Young man, heed the voice addressing you, yield to the Spirit now prompting you, and resolve here and now to make the Lord your God.'

Broader views and a deepening faith

After coming to the industrialised and urban Midlands he found himself in a new religious atmosphere. The simple unquestioning faith fostered by village Methodism was suddenly brought up against the fact of sheer unbelief. 'Determinism' and its shallow philosophy seriously affected thousands of working men. All this meant a re-thinking of the Christian message. The simple appeal of earlier years had to be reinforced by more solid argument. This second period included a 'polemical' or 'Christian evidence' note, in addition to the evangelistic motive which was never absent. At the same period came a new interest in social questions and what was then known as 'altruism'. This again was partly the result of witnessing poverty and slumdom in town life, and partly the effect of the awakening social conscience of those days.

Gradually this second phase of his preaching style merged into the third and last, a mature and full-orbed message, the fruit of the experience and thought of years. There was a wider range of subjects but to the very end the main burden was the call of Christ, the offer of grace, the reality of conversion. Many times he turned to the problem of pain. Some one has said that there is a broken heart in every congregation, and as the years passed he sought increasingly to heal the broken in heart and to bind up their wounds. He himself had learned in the school of suffering. As already hinted, he was an asthmatic and in later years had, in addition to this distressing complaint, heart weakness, failing sight, and also sorrows that were not physical. His commission had clearly included the injunction, 'Comfort ye My people'.

Like many other local preachers, Thomas Glasson was a class-leader. He received his first class-book at Green Hill in March 1904, without a class. For fourteen weeks he sat alone in the vestry, was joined by one other in June, then three, and by the end of the quarter, six. By 1909 there were thirty-eight class-members and six on trial. From beginning to end his Christian life was linked with the class-meeting. Side by side with his life of private devotion was the life in the Body of Christ nourishing and upholding it.

He was a true Methodist in that he combined an inner experience of the Spirit's power with regular use of the means of grace. Like Wesley, he carefully noted items of personal expenditure, living abstemiously, making sacrifices for others, spending little on himself.

He valued the place which Methodist polity gives to the layman. The many thousands of local preachers form but one regiment in a great army of lay workers on whose loving and gratuitous service Methodism depends. Perhaps more than any other church, she has from the start recognised that the call of God comes from men like Amos the herdman, who was outside the regular prophetic schools, men whose daily contact with the workaday world gives their message an added authority.

I count it a source of pride that my father was a carpenter, like Jesus. Life's secrets were revealed to him not in the study alone but at the bench among the shavings. His hands were rough and scratched with splinters – and perhaps the hands of Jesus were not as white and smooth as artists represent them. He was short, vigorous, wiry and strong, and he could cobble shoes, mend locks, and sweep chimneys as well as make furniture and build. He was a craftsman with words, too, and his sermons were constructed and mortised with a cabinet-maker's care. Sometimes for illustrations and children's talks he would go to his tool-chest.

When his own preaching days were done he was just as keen a hearer as preacher – and the two do not always go together.

His son recalls 'one sacred memory' of him: During a serious illness my father felt that he was dying, and though on this occasion he recovered, he gave me what he thought was his parting message. The words, he said, which had sustained and guided him throughout his varied course were these:

> 'Trust in the Lord with all thine heart; and lean not unto
> thine own understanding. In all thy ways acknowledge
> Him, and He shall direct thy paths.'

6

TODAY AND TOMORROW

John Lampard

The first problem I have to face with a title such as this is to decide when 'today' begins. If it is literally 'today' then nothing can be said about events in the past and I could only write about the possibilities of tomorrow. I will resolve the difficulty by defining 'today' as roughly the last ten years and 'tomorrow' as being up to the early years of the next millennium.

A second problem lies in the fact that I was connexional local preachers' secretary during the period 1985-94, and it is very difficult to write with any objectivity about events in which I participated. The only solution to this problem is to warn a reader of likely bias!

Recruitment

Ever since Methodist Union, and probably since the beginning of the century, the total number of local preachers has declined, as the table shows. (The figures do not include those on trial.)

1933	34,948
1943	29,934
1953	24,387
1963	21,791
1973	17,291
1983	13,996
1993	13,126

This decline roughly matched the rate of closure of Methodist chapels, but no serious research had been carried out on its implications until Professor David Bartholomew was commissioned in 1982 by the Local Preachers' Office to produce a report which was entitled *Methodist Local Preachers: a Statistical Review*. A summary of the report was presented to Conference in 1983 in the following terms.

This Report looks at the national situation and makes projections of the number of fully accredited local preachers to the end of the century. It then provides projections of the numbers of members, ministers and churches and relates them to the preachers likely to be available. Because the national picture hides a good deal of local variation, the report deals with inequalities between and within Districts. A further section examines the recruitment aspect of the problem by analysing the figures for preachers on trial. The final section of the report attempts to relate the conclusions of the analysis to the courses of action which might be taken to improve the situation. Two paragraphs from this final section need to be quoted:

'For the connexion as a whole the present balance between supply and demand is unlikely to change radically by the end of the century but there may well be a modest deterioration in the availability of preachers. Although recruitment has stabilized there are no clear signs of an upturn. With membership likely to go on decreasing, the pool from which preachers are drawn will inevitably shrink. Against this it must be noted that some Districts have been much more successful in recruiting than others. If all Districts could be brought up to the level of the best there would be a marked easing of the situation especially in some of the hardest pressed areas. With an annual intake of about 300 fully accredited preachers it will hardly be possible to maintain the status quo and some circuits will undoubtedly cease to be viable units. It would take 600 a year to maintain the present preaching strength but this is hardly necessary in view of the declining number of appointments to be filled. A figure of 400 or 450 would be compatible with a steady improvement on provision without being unrealistic (it is below the numbers recruited as recently as 1966).

I, therefore, recommend that the Committee [the connexional local preachers' committee] consider ways by which the numbers offering themselves as local preachers might be increased by, perhaps, 30 or 40%. The evidence from the efforts to recruit more ministers shows that increases of this order are entirely feasible. Because of the large variation in conditions across the country it might be better if the main thrust is made at District or circuit level'.[1]

This report galvanised action over recruitment both connexionally and locally, although complaints were made by a few that the word 'recruitment' denied the empowering work of the Holy Spirit. A letter from the Local Preachers' Office was addressed to every member of local

---

FOOLS IN GOD'S SERVICE

A young preacher on note, aged 17, was sitting in the chapel with his fiancée waiting for the evening service to begin. The preacher did not turn up and he was asked to take the pulpit. His fiancée said 'Don't you go Ernie, you'll make a fool of yourself.' But he did, and groped his way through the opening part of the service as best he could. He had never preached before but only taken small parts in other services. However 'when it came to the sermon I just felt the words come into my mind. They were not my words – and yet in a mysterious way they were. I was saying them, albeit hesitatingly and nervously. I cannot remember my text or subject; I only remember a vivid experience of my first real encounter with a God I was only beginning to understand. I felt, and still feel it, to have been a unique experience, which I treasure and look back upon with wonder. Yes, we are fools in God's service, and I am proud to be one of them.'

(From Ernie Slarks of Sittingbourne, in a communication responding to a request by Revd John Lampard in the *LP Magazine* for preachers' experiences.)

---

church councils; local preachers' meetings were encouraged to discuss Bartholomew's report; and new recruitment literature was prepared. A guide to holding a 'Sharing Day', at which local preachers were to speak about their call and training, proved very popular and effective. At least two circuits reported that they had more people on note and on trial than they had local preachers to supervise them.

Two slightly controversial posters were produced for display in every church. One featured a wooden spoon, and spoke about the stirring of the Holy Spirit. The other had an illustration of a burning telephone box, and a young man kneeling down in front of it. This modern equivalent of the burning bush raised the question of the ways people are called by God, although one writer complained that it was an incitement to commit arson! However, several people wrote to say that they had received a call through the posters, one as she was pinning it to the notice board.

The stirring within Methodism resulting from all these efforts produced a significant increase in the number of people offering to become local preachers in the early and mid-1980s. Although no detailed statistical research was carried out, it is clear that much of the growth was due to an increasing number of women offering to become local preachers. The reasons for this are probably numerous and include a greater awareness of feminist issues and the rôle of women in society, growing confidence among women in leadership positions in the church, a decline in the outlet for traditional vocations for women with the decline of Sunday Schools and the fact that an increasing number of women ministers offered widely-observed role models for women in the pulpit. By 1990 the numbers of new men and women local preachers was almost exactly equal, and in 1994 the proportion was 45% men and 55% women.

The following table gives an indication of the changing numbers of those admitted as local preachers. (It should be noted that the 1991/92 figures are 'distorted' by the inclusion of auxiliaries and helpers who were admitted as local preachers, further details below).

1982	301	1989	394
1983	316	1990	418
1984	304	1991	620
1985	354	1992	528
1986	353	1993	398
1987	387	1994	448
1988	427		

The figure for 1994 is a 49% increase over the pre-Bartholomew, 1982 figure. No research was carried out on whether or not the new local preachers were coming from the areas of greatest need, as defined by Bartholomew.

Although the continuing reduction in the number of churches lessened the demands made on some local preachers, a less obvious change may well have had a greater impact. The decision in a growing number of circuits to drop the evening service has meant that for each service dropped there are thirteen fewer appointments on the quarterly plan. Taking the widely accepted quarterly figure of an average of 6.5 appointments by a local preacher, this is the equivalent of a circuit needing two fewer local preachers for each service dropped. It is much quicker to drop one evening service than to train two new local preachers!

The number of new local preachers was artificially inflated in the early 1990s by the introduction into the ranks of local preachers of many of those who had served through the years as auxiliaries or helpers. These were Methodists who regularly took services but often had no formal training and held no status as preachers. Their presence in some circuits was seen as a discouragement to others to accept the discipline of training to become a local preacher, and many of them were outside the fellowship and discipline of the local preachers' meeting. Over the years there had been some pressure to incorporate them into the ranks of local preachers. For example, a memorial from the West Somerset circuit in 1982 asked that people over fifty years who had offered more than ten years service as helpers, five years of which had been in their current circuit, might be accepted as local preachers.[2]

Such pressure had been resisted by the Local Preachers' Office, and Conference, but in 1986 at my first Conference I brought a discussion document approved by the Connexional Local Preachers' Committee. It invited the Church to consider a policy that 'responsibility for acts of worship on the plan should be in the hands of those who are accredited or on trial'[3]. The intention behind the report was partly to grasp a nettle which had existed too long, but also to provide a 'deck-clearing' exercise before a major shift in training took place. Responses to the report were probably coloured, in some instances, by my unwise decision to give it the negative title 'Phasing out auxiliaries', rather than the more positive intention of phasing in at least some of them.

Over the following two years circuits responded, generally favourably, to the idea, although there were anguished letters from auxiliaries both to the Office and in the *Methodist Recorder*. Some writers particularly objected to 'the humiliation' of being placed 'on trial' for up to two years.

Two years later, in 1988, a further report, more wisely entitled 'The Future of Auxiliaries' (although its thrust was that auxiliaries had no future!) was accepted by Conference with little debate. It proposed that circuits could invite auxiliaries who wished to continue as preachers to follow a two-year training scheme, devised and monitored locally, and then become local preachers. The names of about 350 people were registered by circuits and most were duly admitted as local preachers in the period 1989/92. A random examination of circuit plans suggests that only a few circuits continue to use some form of auxiliaries, so the scheme was largely successful. However, in some instances the continuing pattern of 'local arrangements' may disguise the use of people who were not part of the auxiliaries scheme.

The sudden influx of former auxiliaries meant that the early 1990s showed an increase in the total number of local preachers, certainly for the first time since Methodist Union, and possibly for the first time this century. However, this did not represent 'new blood' as far as the total number of people available to serve were concerned. Recruitment may have nearly reached the figures predicted as necessary by Bartholomew, but the search for new preachers was to continue in an ever-shrinking pool.

Training

The pattern of training for most local preachers had altered little over the years since study and examinations were required. Most people on trial studied a series of text-books and then sat written examinations. About one-third of them used a correspondence course, sending their essays to a distance tutor. With some honourable exceptions, the local preachers' meeting did not involve the circuit in supervising the study of the person on trial by appointing an active local preachers' tutor. This produced a syndrome not unfairly called 'the loneliness of the long distance local preacher'! In the early 1970s two innovative steps were taken by the Local Preachers' Department. The first was the introduction of a continuous assessment course which was devised ecumenically with the United Reformed Church and the Baptist Union. Those on trial worked through a series of study units, and then wrote two assignments for each unit which were marked locally, but assessed connexionally. There were no unseen written examinations.

The second, and more significant innovation in 1972, was to end the right of a circuit to admit people as local preachers even though they had failed the connexional examinations. Until that time examinations had to be sat, but ultimately did not have to be passed if a local circuit wished to accept the person as a local preacher. This change, which was potentially very unpopular with circuits which saw their autonomy being decreased, was skilfully steered through Conference by linking it with the introduction of the new non-examination course. As John Stacey said:

> Our strategy for getting this through Conference was to offer the choice of written examinations, continuous assessment course or (carefully protected) connexional oral examinations, and it succeeded.[4]

Linked with this 'tightening-up' was the decision to end the unlimited time that a person could be on trial. Some plans had people on trial for 30 or 40 years who might have taken only one examination but had progressed no further. Only in exceptional circumstances, with the permission of the District Local Preachers' Committee, could a person in future be on trial for more than five years. Like many innovations this took some time to be implemented in some circuits!

COMMENTS ON THE PROPOSED NEW TRAINING COURSE

'Do you approve of the proposal to end all exemptions?

In other walks of life the general trend is to move towards greater flexibility in entrance and eligibility criteria, particularly to reflect qualifications and experience gained in related fields. It is odd, and unwelcome, that the opposite approach is to be adopted so far as concerns local preachers.'

From the minutes of the Edinburgh and Forth
Local Preachers' Meeting, December 1989.

The continuous assessment course never proved very popular, being followed by no more than 7% of those on trial. It was updated in the early 1980s, but by then that course and the text book examination method were in need of review, particularly in the light of changes in the philosophy and methods of learning pioneered by the Open University. After a five-year gestation process, involving wide-spread consultation, publicity and preparation, an entirely new course and method of education and formation, called *Faith & Worship* was launched in 1990. Mrs Thatcher resigned the day after the launch!

The new course involved study units which used an inter-active approach, a 'tool-kit' of books, audio-tapes, and the input of local tutors. The units were written with an integrated approach in mind so that biblical studies, theology and liturgical practices were combined in each unit, instead of the more traditional separation of subjects. It was strictly designed to help those wishing to become local preachers to develop spiritually and intellectually as well as give them the skills needed for good communication. Half of the assignments were of a practical, rather than a theoretical, nature, requiring students to prepare service and sermon material. It was examined by a combination of marks awarded for assignments, completed at the end of each unit, and two examinations at the half-way and end stages of the study. No final grades were given (apart from pass/fail) in an attempt to avoid the possibilities of students falsely linking examination marks to their ability (or lack of it) as local preachers.

Faith & Worship also expanded the educational and training role of the local circuit by requiring a circuit, or group of circuits, to appoint a local tutor to supervise the training and study of those on trial and mark their assignments. Fears that circuits would not be able to do this proved groundless and the system developed smoothly. A sense of circuit involvement with those on trial was extended by requiring circuits to pay the cost of the study units, leaving the person on trial to purchase the 'tool-kit' books.

The decision to write units in an integrated way led to one of the grounds on which *Faith & Worship* has been most criticised. Because the units were integrated anyone who wished to become a local preacher needed to study all of them, regardless of previous training. (Under the traditional systems exemptions from one or more subjects could be sought.) The course was thus criticised as belittling previous training and experience, and as being monolithic, in a time of increasing flexibility between courses in the wider educational field.

Attempts to make it an ecumenical course also failed, mainly because the United Reformed Church was engaged in the early stages of a rethink of its training of all lay people. It wanted to move in the direction of a modular course which could be used to train people for a wide variety of offices in the church. Also it was wedded to a non-examination approach to training and its officers did not think the partial examination approach of *Faith & Worship* suitable for its lay preachers in training. At the time of writing the United Reformed Church has not yet produced an alternative to the continuous assessment course which was shared with Methodism. However, a number of members of the United Reformed Church, who were members of Local Ecumenical Projects, started to study *Faith & Worship* with Methodist colleagues and the United Reformed Church produced a short URC Supplement to *Faith & Worship* for such students.

A second criticism made of *Faith & Worship* was that the material was culturally and philosophically unsuitable for many of the growing number of people on trial from ethnic minorities, whose education and experience was different from that of many within the majority culture. This has led to a higher drop-out rate among them. The Local Preachers' Office is presently exploring how to respond to both these important issues. In spite of these and other legitimate criticisms, *Faith & Worship* has been widely accepted in the church as a method for training a new generation of local preachers.

Continuing Local Preacher Development

What local preachers should do, as far as their studies were concerned, after admission as local preachers was a matter which was first formally addressed in the major reforms in the early 1970s. In 1971 circuits were consulted on the possibility of introducing compulsory refresher courses for all local preachers. Predictably this ran into strong opposition, although the principle was widely accepted. In the face of this resistance Conference was asked to endorse a voluntary scheme of Refresher Courses.[5] Circuits would either arrange eight study evenings or a weekend conference for study.

The concern for continuing study was broadened out in 1992 when I took to Conference, for discussion, a report on Continuing Local Preacher Development (CLPD). It attempted to address two issues. First, many local preachers felt the need for a more systematic, but flexible, programme of development which consisted of more than just academic study. Second, there was the need to stir a minority of local preachers who had become stale and whose laxness was evident in their leadership of worship. The pattern proposed was a development of the three key areas in *Faith & Worship* namely, spiritual, intellectual and practical. There was also a recognition that initial training needed to be supplemented during the life-time of a local preacher.

Isaac Foot (1880-1960), member of a famous West country family –
solicitor, fervent Liberal (MP for 8 years), devoted Methodist,
life-long local preacher, Vice-President of the Methodist Church 1937-8.
His sermons "were framed and composed with admirable clarity, and
lapped round and incensed with that rich Devon speech which he never lost".
Stanley Goodman in DNB 1951-1960 p.369.
(Acknowledgements to Sara N. Foot *My Grandfather, Isaac Foot* 1980 for the portrait.)

Because it was a discussion document it raised the issue whether those who refused to engage in development should be allowed to continue as local preachers. The report was widely accepted by local circuits although the compulsory nature of it (as in 1972) was rejected by a majority. The report also touched on the matter of appraisal, and although informal methods of appraisal are increasingly being used in many circuits, the very word 'appraisal' produced a disproportionate amount of anger.

Because of the wide support for the principles involved, I returned to Conference in 1994 with a re-written report. This emphasised the need for supported self-evaluation as a basis for guiding further development. Although it remains optional for existing local preachers it will be a requirement for those admitted after 1995, when CLPD begins.

Changes in the pattern and leadership of worship

Changes that have taken place in worship, apart from declining congregations, can easily be listed. They include the impact, mainly through the *Methodist Service Book*, of the liturgical movement; a wide use of the lectionary and increased recognition of the liturgical year; and the introduction of *Hymns & Psalms* and a wide variety of modern songs and choruses. Other changes are explored in the following sections. It is more difficult, in the absence of detailed survey material, to elicit the ways in which local preachers have either led or responded to these changes. Inevitably, a consideration of the role of local preachers in relation to the worship they lead will be impressionistic and based on anecdotal evidence, but certain trends can be widely observed. What is clear is that none of the changes that have taken place has made either the preparation or leadership of worship any easier for a preacher.

Commissions on Worship and Music

Let the People Worship, the product of two years work by the Commission on Worship,[6] encouraged local preachers to think again about the worship they lead. It was a creative and readable document, selling over 15,000 copies. As far as local preachers were concerned it made recommendations in four areas. While these reflected practices that were already being established in at least some parts of the Church, it is helpful to examine summaries of them in some detail.

1.   Local preachers might in some situations be planned more regularly at particular churches so that a special relationship might be established. This would also encourage local participation in acts of worship and the development of a more pastoral relationship.

The traditional role of a local preacher as an all-purpose member of a preaching order ('have sermon, will travel') is challenged by this recommendation. It is, perhaps, surprising that there has not been a more widespread desire among local preachers also to develop their role as local pastors, more in line with the Anglican pattern of lay readers. The reasons for this are not easy to draw out. It may be that it has never been included as an item in local preacher training; or because Methodist lay offices are more specialised than Anglican ones; or because local preachers do, in the main, see themselves as preachers rather than pastors (without denying that worship is a pastoral act). From a congregation's point of view there is some indication that in circuits where local preachers are widely used congregations like to have a variety of preachers.

2.   Co-operation between preacher, organist and congregation, particularly through the use of a Consultation on Worship, could help all of them to affect the quality of worship for which they all share responsibility.

Traditionally, though operating within a basic structure to which they conform, local preachers have been able to exercise a fairly individualistic and self-directed approach to the content of worship. Their individuality and character are expressed through their choice of hymns, readings and prayers. In this they have echoed the way in which ministers had habitually conducted worship. The appointed preacher was master or mistress in the pulpit, planning, choosing, and conducting the whole service. Consultations on Worship were introduced in the 1970s in a very patchy way because they were optional and not mandatory. For the first time in a structured way ministers, local preachers, stewards and church musicians were brought together to discuss the worship of the church. Although some Consultations were little more than an opportunity to fix dates for the coming year, others were able to discuss matters which were traditionally the preserve of preachers, lay or ordained. This sense of participation was enhanced by the influences of both the charismatic movement and the liturgical movement as together they encouraged a greater sense of sharing and responsibility within the membership of the congregation.

THE NEED FOR PREACHERS!

'Some years ago I happened to meet my old Sunday School Superintendent. He asked me about my family. I proudly told him that both my children were local preachers, also my wife. Then added "I am the black sheep of the family." I thought he might remind me of my years as Circuit Steward, Society Steward, Trust Secretary, etc. But instead he said dourly; "Well, you know, if there were no black sheep there would be no need for preachers."'

(Will Bromwich of Aldwick, Bognor Regis, in a reply to Revd John Lampard's request for preachers' experiences.)

Not all local preachers found it easy to share the preparation and conduct of worship with others. Everyone who has tried it discovers that it takes longer to prepare if you do not do it all yourself. But the benefits to a congregation, when worship preparation is shared and skilfully presented, are apparent. It is increasingly rare for a local preacher to lead every part of the service, with at least lessons being read by a steward or other member.

3.   There was a need for the training and retraining of preachers in the skills of all-age worship, and the use of visual arts, music and silence in worship.

There can be little doubt that the development of all-age worship (out of parade services and family services) has proved one of the most challenging and difficult changes for all preachers, not just local preachers. The skills required are very different from those necessary for a traditional act of worship. All-age worship requires a different attitude in both the preacher and the congregation, and an approach which is relational rather than the traditionally didactic one. Although education and worship are very different, the educational method which children have experienced over the last thirty years has emphasised learning for yourself rather than sitting quietly and being told. Such an experience does not make attendance at worship an easy experience for children.

Much help has been offered in the content and leadership of all-age worship, particularly by the Division of Education and Youth (DEY)[7], but something of the unease felt by many who attempted to lead all-age worship was reflected in 1993 in the title of an ecumenical conference for preachers in Birmingham, 'Is all-age worship all age worship?'. All-age worship may be an event, educational, and enjoyable, but does it have that quality, which is so difficult to define, that enables all ages to worship God?

Certainly the training material for local preachers in *Faith & Worship* attempted to take the conduct of all-age worship seriously, and was prepared in collaboration with DEY, but more needs to be done by the Church, both in its liturgical thinking and in skills training.

4.   Recognition needed to be given to the fact that some people had a vocation to lead worship but not to preach. Such worship leaders needed to be affirmed and ways discovered to train them.

The role of worship leaders has developed out of the growth in participation by members of the congregation. Churches which cherished continuity in the leadership of worship, rather than valuing a variety of approach, have been in the lead in producing worship leaders. It was the policy of the Local Preachers' Office not to step in too quickly with rules and guidelines for worship leaders, although it was aware of the danger of allowing a new generation of 'helpers' to develop, just after auxiliaries had been phased out.

As the result of a memorial from the London North-East Synod, guidelines were drawn up and approved by Conference in 1993.[8] These did not carry the authority of Standing Orders but were deliberately introduced in this way in order not to formulate hard and fast rules. The main guidelines were that worship leaders should be appointed by the church councils of the church or churches in which they were to operate; that they should always work with a local preacher or minister; and that they should undergo a training scheme in the local circuit. It remains to be seen whether or not the number of worship leaders will grow and the Methodist Church develop a new group of people paralleling the American Methodist 'liturgists', or whether many of them will, in due course, become local preachers. This is something which only the next millennium will answer.

The continuing impact of the liturgical movement has made itself felt in a number of ways. A lectionary is now widely used by local preachers and the popularity of aids to using the lectionary such as *Worship & Preaching* and the series *Companion to the Lectionary* have been evidence of this. However, this development has made it more difficult for local preachers to 'take the same sermon around the circuit'. The breadth and sense of continuity which the combined use of a lectionary and Church Year gives to worship may be applauded as a significant improvement in worship. However, it has put preachers under a greater pressure of time for preparation, and some sermons, if preached several times, can improve with use. The introduction of a four-year lectionary in 1992 (in place of a two-year one) made the task of a preacher who followed the lectionary even more demanding.

The choice of hymns and music has also become a more difficult area for local preachers. Until 1983 the *Methodist Hymn Book* provided an almost universally shared resource wherever a preacher went. The introduction of *Hymns & Psalms* in 1983 meant that many old favourites, of some congregations if not of all preachers, were no longer available in those churches which had the new hymn book. But the early eighties also saw an explosion of new hymns, songs and choruses which can be broadly grouped under the 'charismatic' label, although many of those who use them would not wish to be labelled as 'charismatic'.

The popularity of this type of music and singing was boosted by the increasing numbers of people who attended large religious gatherings such as Spring Harvest, Easter People and the Methodist Association of Youth Clubs (MAYC) Weekends. Churches started buying and using new books such as *Mission Praise, Songs of Fellowship, Power Praise, Songs of God's People*, and *Let's Praise*. Other churches, sometimes flouting copyright law, produced their own collections of material drawn from this new writing. A circuit might use up to eight different hymn books with no two churches having identical collections.

Pressures for and against modern music were faced by a Commission on Music in the Church which reported to Conference in 1994. Its recommendations, as far as they affect local preachers, are twofold. First, the guidelines for Worship leaders should be expanded to include practical training in music and the development of its role in worship. Second, consideration should be given to the inclusion of practical training in music-making in both the initial training of local preachers and in CLPD.

The liturgical movement has also brought conflicting pressures, on the one hand for greater liturgical formality through styles of worship, and on the other hand less formality through the encouragement of greater participation by all the people in worship. Worship may begin with either a solemn biblical call to worship, or an informal greeting to which the congregation respond, or both. There has also been a widening of the preferred style of worship among different churches in the same circuit. Local preachers are more or less welcome, according to their theology and the style of worship they lead. These 'party' tensions have replaced the post-1932 party tensions, which were mainly between Primitives and Wesleyans.

Local preachers have had to face two issues as they ponder these changes. The first is the question as to where the individual local preacher stands in relation to the rapid and substantial changes. On the whole those who have become local preachers in more recent years have been able to accept and adapt to the changes more easily, in fact some have led them. The second, and more difficult question, is how far local preachers can, with integrity, lead worship in a church which wishes to worship in a style and manner seriously different from the inclination of the person planned to lead worship at that service. Whether or not the fractures developing here continue to grow will be evident in the new millennium.

What are local preachers?

Although it may seem strange to pose this question almost at the end of a book dedicated to the history of local preachers, the question remains both permanent and important. While it may not be an issue that often surfaces in the mind of a local preacher, its significance is never very far from the surface. Study and analysis of the issues involved can, most helpfully, centre around an examination of such concepts as 'order', 'office', 'ministry', 'status' and 'leadership'.

A PUZZLE

The *Guardian* crossword No 20,038 contained the following clue:

Pass up to high mountain; one who gets there can provide services.

No prizes for the answer!
Our thanks to Alan Rose for this item.

Order or Office?

The first question to examine is whether or not local preachers can be said to be members of an order or whether they simply hold an office in the church. The word 'office' implies a function or duty, while 'order' suggests a fraternity or sorority (or a mixture of the two). Within the history of the universal Church an order has at least two marks; it is entered into by some form of ordination and it involves a disciplined life, particularly in a pattern of prayer. Local preachers are certainly not ordained and in spite of having a discipline, as set out in Standing Orders, they do not represent the collegial quality of an Order. The 1936 *Order of Service for the Public Recognition of Local Preachers* included both 'Order' and 'office' in its opening:

> We are gathered together in the sight of God, publicly to recognise these our Brothers and Sisters as members of the Order of Local Preachers. We believe they have been called of God to this great office.[9]

It is somewhat strange that the service does not use the word 'order' again and its operative clauses read:

> (we) joyfully recognise you as Local Preachers' and 'in recognition of your place and office as Preachers'.[10]

There is no rubric to explain the meaning of 'Order' or to indicate any sense of admission to one. The right hand of fellowship is extended by the minister conducting the service and not by fellow local preachers.[11]

Whether consciously or unconsciously, the term 'order' has slowly slipped out of Methodist usage. In 1967, in his final report to Conference, the connexional local preachers' secretary, Revd David N. Francis, spoke of a growing sense of interdependence among local preachers.

> We now want to become – what our Recognition Service indicates we should be – a disciplined *Order* (italics in the original), a body in which the effectiveness of each member depends on the quality of our corporate life.[12]

Although he used the phrase 'Order of Local Preachers' several more times in the report there was no attempt to say what it meant. His successor, Revd John Stacey, in his first report in 1968, used the phrase only when writing about the dramatic decline in the number of new local preachers in the mid-1960s:

> At this rate (of decline) the Order of Local Preachers will cease to exist in 34 years time.[13]

Fortunately the rate of decline did not continue, but this is the last time the word 'order' appeared in the Conference *Agenda*.

The word 'order' was deliberately not included when a new Recognition Service was drafted in 1975. John Stacey, who prepared the first draft for the Faith and Order Committee, used the phrases 'recognised and commissioned' to the 'office and work' of a local preacher.[14] There is no evidence from the *Agenda* that there was any debate over the term, and there was no reference to the new service in the Local Preachers' Office report to Conference, because the new service came to Conference as part of the Faith and Order business.

Until 1994 people were actually admitted as local preachers by the decision of the quarterly (later circuit) meeting. The Agenda of the circuit meeting included an item inviting it to approve any recommendations of the local preachers' meeting for admission to the office of local preacher.[15] The Conference in 1993 was asked to change the *Deed of Union* so that the actual moment a person became a local preacher was in an act of worship, rather than during the circuit meeting, which was a closed meeting at which the person concerned might well not have been present.[16] The right and power of the circuit meeting to be the final arbiter of whether or not a person became a local preacher was not affected by the change. The meeting approved the name of the person to become a local preacher, but no longer actually admitted them. The change met with little resistance partly on the basis that most people, including many local preachers, thought that the Recognition and Commissioning Service was the moment that they became local preachers anyway!

TWO 'CRIS DE COEUR'

From a local preachers' meeting in the Darlington District (1987)

'We believe that we are generally meeting the wishes of our congregations but not their needs . . . We meet with generally ageing and diminishing congregations and in the membership we see little enthusiasm for change. We believe that amongst our congregations and sometimes our preachers there is rarely an expectation that 'anything will happen', and rarely does it.'

From a local preachers' meeting secretary in Lancashire (1987)

'I too like others have gone to the parish church or cathedral to escape, to find that essential depth when I need nourishment. There are times when "ordinariness" flies in the face of the heights and depths that many yearn for, and go away unfilled.'

It is also significant that the Deed of Union, in defining who was a local preacher, did not refer to an 'order of local preachers'. It referred to the means by which people become local preachers (the admission by the quarterly (circuit) meeting). There has always been a theological gap caused by a failure to explain what it is to which people were admitted.

The generally accepted phrase 'office' is not appropriate on its own to describe the position a local preacher holds, although it is the one most commonly used. An office in the Methodist Church is one to which people are appointed, generally for a limited period, or annually; which requires no specific method of selection or training; which does not have a corporate sense of identity or spirituality; and which has no disciplinary procedure. There are no lifelong offices in the church, although some people may feel they have been burdened with one!

Local preachers are selected and trained locally, but they are examined as to their knowledge and understanding at a connexional level. They are then admitted to at least something. They then remain local preachers until death, unless they resign, cease to be members of the Methodist Church, or have their status removed after formal disciplinary procedures. If they move circuit they have the right to be received as local preachers in the new circuit without further examination or official appointment or approval.

Neither 'order' or 'office' adequately expresses what a local preacher is.

Ministry

The unique position of local preachers was explored in the report to Conference in 1993, as the basis for the argument that admission, like that of membership of the church, should take place in an act of worship. The report uses the phrase 'order of ministry', which was the first time it had been used in a Conference report relating to local preachers. But if this route is followed to its logical conclusion, there is the possibility that someone will argue that local preachers should, in some way, be recognised in the doctrinal clause of the Deed of Union, thus creating another order of ministry unique to Methodism. The strongest argument against this is that presbyters and members of the Methodist Diaconal Order are subject to stationing by the Conference in a way that local preachers are not. The 'stationing' of local preachers, if that word can be used, is limited to where the superintendent plans local preachers on the circuit plan.

Perhaps the 1993 report to Conference was correct in identifying elements of 'office','order' and 'ministry' in what it meant to be a local preacher, so no fundamental change in understanding is necessary, although greater clarification might have been helpful.

Status

The word 'status' was introduced in a previous paragraph because it is one word which has echoed within the Church, particularly since the reorganisation of the local church and circuits in the 1970s. Before the recommendations of the *Restructuring Report* 1972 were accepted, local preachers were ex-officio members of both the quarterly meeting and the leaders' meeting. This right came to an end with restructuring, when local preachers lost their ex-officio seats on the new church councils and circuit meetings. There was no provision for them to sit on church councils and no more than ten local preachers could sit, as local preachers, on the new circuit meeting.

This decision led to a continuing protest that the 'status' of local preachers had in some way been diminished. A number of memorials was sent to Conference in the years following restructuring, but to no avail. It could be argued that local preachers had a stronger case for the right to sit on the Circuit Meeting, because they were, in a sense, circuit appointments. Many local preachers were likely to know the circuit churches and their memberships better than the majority of other lay people appointed to the meeting by a local church, and know it better than some ministers.

However, the case of those who argued for the right of local preachers to sit on the circuit meeting was weakened by the fact that in reality many circuits could not find sufficient local preachers willing and able to fill the seats, who were not already members of the meeting in another capacity. The argument was thus seen as a narrow 'status' matter and not one relating to the well-being of the circuit. However, the radical 1993 de-structuring of the circuit left the position of local preachers more precarious, if the circuit decided to adopt new structures. While the constitution of the local preachers' meeting remained untouched, only its secretary was guaranteed a place on the new-style circuit meeting, as the right to up to ten seats for local preachers disappeared. In effect the lay composition of the circuit meeting, apart from the treasurer and one church steward from each church, was a matter for decision by the meeting.

During and after the 1970s the Local Preachers' Office did not take up the cudgels on behalf of those local preachers who felt aggrieved.

This suggests that the Connexional Local Preachers' Committee concurred with the judgement of Conference that the 'status', which some local preachers felt had been diminished, was not related to significant aspects of the office or ministry of a local preacher.

Leadership

Comparisons are sometimes made between Anglican readers and local preachers, often by local preachers who wish to see their rights and duties expanded. The Bishops' regulations for reader ministry divide the role of a reader between pastoral and liturgical work in the parish or area where they are licensed and in accordance with what is agreed with the minister to whom they are responsible. The regulations state that, subject to these provisos:

> Readers are permitted to undertake the following pastoral duties:
> a. to visit the sick and pray with them
> b. to teach in Sunday School
> c. to catechise
> d. to assist the minister in undertaking pastoral and educational work as the bishop directs.
> Readers are permitted to undertake the following liturgical duties:
> a. to read Morning and Evening Prayer (omitting the Absolution)
> b. to read the Scriptures
> c. to preach
> d. to receive and present the offerings of the people
> e. to distribute the Holy Sacrament to the people
> f. to publish banns of marriage in certain circumstances
> g. to officiate at funeral services subject to certain conditions.[17]

While these are the prescribed regulations, in true Church of England style, the Bishops' Regulations go on to point out the fact that the duties may vary between different dioceses, at the discretion of the bishop. Compared with the duties of a local preacher as set out in Standing Orders, the potential duties of a reader included here are very much wider. But there is a difference between 'actually doing things' and the 'right to do things'. Many readers are not treated as part of a leadership team, sharing such duties with an incumbent. Many local preachers do far more in the local church and circuit than are included in their duties. Comparisons are therefore not as clear cut as they might seem.

Two matters can, however, be noted. The first is that there has generally been a reluctance among local preachers to exercise a pastoral role outside that of local preacher, such as taking on pastoral responsibility for a church, or leading a class meeting, as a direct extension of their ministry as local preachers. The pastoral work that many have carried out has been in their local church, as class leaders or pastoral visitors. This duty has been carried out as a team member with other class leaders and pastoral visitors because they were members and not because they were local preachers. Local preachers have not, in the main, seen their local preacher duties as extending to pastoral responsibilities on a circuit basis. This reluctance may be partly because the lay roles in the Methodist Church are more highly developed than they are in the Church of England. There is no reason why local preachers should not officiate at funerals or at weddings, and some do so.

Second, the question may be asked whether they have not developed these roles because they have not been encouraged to do so by ministers, or because they themselves have not seen these activities as part of their calling. Part of the answer to this can be seen in the growing participation of lay workers in the Methodist Church since the early 1980s. Ten years later there were nearly 400 lay workers equally divided between full- and part-timers. While no complete survey has been carried out, it was estimated by those involved in their oversight that about two-thirds of them were either local preachers or training to become local preachers.

Local preachers of the new millennium

Anyone who attempts to predict what the situation will be among local preachers in the next millennium inevitably offers a hostage to fortune. But a glance through the reports to Conference over the last sixty years can give a measure of confidence to anyone who attempts to make predictions, because trends develop slowly over time and radical alterations are unlikely. In the years after 2000 AD local preachers will continue each Sunday to conduct services in about two-thirds of the pulpits of Methodism. They will be better trained and, because of the rising educational level in the country as a whole, will be more likely to have higher educational qualifications. All local preachers will recognise that their initial training was not sufficient to carry them through a life-time of preaching, so varied patterns of continuing local preacher development will be evident in every circuit. An increasing proportion of local preachers will be female, and a growing number of preachers will be black.

Local preachers will be more likely to consult and co-operate with members of the local church and will have shared in the preparation of the service with one or more of its members. It is likely that there will be increasing differences between local preachers who welcome the move towards broadly 'charismatic' styles of worship and those who favour a more formal style of worship, influenced by the 'catholic' tendency within the church. The new *Service Book* will be available by the millennium. If it contains the variety of preaching services which are already in experimental use, it will appeal to those who favour a more formal style of worship. While there will not be any 'no-go' areas, local preachers are

---

PREACHING AND RENEWAL

'We have to picture the principles of our religion, and particularly New Testament Love or Christian Charity, existing as a kind of fermentation in society, perpetually moving as a spontaneous and original spiritual force . . . *Those who preach the Gospel, nurse the pieties, spread New Testament Love, and affirm the spiritual nature of man are guarding the very fountain, dealing with the problems of civilisation at its very source, and keeping open the spring from which new things will arise* . . . The continually renascent power of our religion seems to consist in this unlimited opportunity to return to the original spring, the original simplicities of our faith'.

(From *Christianity in European History*, 1951, pp.54-55, by Herbert Butterfield (1900-1979). historian, local preacher, Master of Peterhouse, and Regius Professor of Modern History in the University of Cambridge.)

---

more likely to be planned at churches which prefer the distinctive style of worship which they lead. A developing spirit of collaboration and support between minister and local preachers will mean that plan-making and circuit preaching policy will be a shared exercise.

In the years after 2000 AD a presumed continuation of the decline in Sunday schools and junior churches will mean that all-age worship will be more common, although the number of younger worshippers will be smaller. Because of a continuing reduction in the number of services held (one per Sunday instead of two) the pressure on the majority of preachers for appointments will be reduced. In spite of fewer members, the increase in morale evident in recent years in many local churches will continue and attendance may well be boosted by a 'millennial surge' such as appeared, we are told, around the year 1000 AD. Despite occasional requests to change the title of local preachers to 'lay preachers', or just 'preachers', it is likely that 'local preacher' will remain the preferred title.

Even if none of these predictions proves to be correct, one thing is certain. Local preachers of the third millennium will continue to be 'called of God, to be worthy in character, to lead God's people in worship and to preach the gospel'.[18]

LOCAL PREACHERS AND THE PREACHING PLAN

E. Alan Rose

The preaching plan is taken for granted by Methodists but is unfamiliar to Christians of many other traditions who expect their worship to be led by the same person Sunday by Sunday. Throughout Methodism's existence the unit of ministry has been the *circuit* and not the individual preaching places which comprise it. In most circuits there have always been more preaching places than ministers and in consequence the preaching ministry has been (and is) shared between ministers and lay preachers. This has necessitated the regular production of a rota of preaching appointments, known as the 'plan'.

In the beginning circuits had separate plans for the travelling preachers and local preachers. The travelling preacher moved round the circuit day by day and preached in a succession of different places until he had completed his 'round'; usually this took four or six weeks after which he would begin his travels all over again. Adam Clarke, writing of his first circuit, Bradford-on-Avon, describes how he had 'more than one place for every day in the month and the preachers rarely stopped two days in the same place'.[1] To guide the preachers round the circuit, the superintendent wrote out a six-week itinerary, with the places and times of the services and details of where to go for meals and a bed.

This type of plan was very different from the plan of Sunday appointments provided for the local preachers, which took the form of a grid with the preaching places down the left hand side and the Sunday dates across the top. It was similar in essence to our plans today but it gave the appointments of the local preachers only. The period covered varied at first from circuit to circuit. In the Isle of Man in 1786 John Wesley described how the Manx local preachers 'follow a regular plan which the assistant (superintendent minister) gives them monthly',[2] while in Leeds the plan was for three months.

Such plans were handwritten. Joseph Entwistle, later a President of Conference, remembered how they were produced in Manchester in 1783:

> There were no *printed* plans in those days. The superintendent of the Circuit, or the Assistant, when he had prepared the draught (*sic*), used to employ a person to write out a copy in a fair and legible hand for each of the Local Preachers.[3]

Plans like this had a long history in Leeds. In the 1760s, John Pawson was, as he wrote later, '. . . put into the Plan among the local preachers before I had ever preached at all'.[4] The earliest plan to have survived anywhere is for the Leeds circuit and it covers the quarter from May to July 1777.[5] From the illustration it will be seen that the circuit was divided into two sections, supplied with preachers on alternate Sundays. Most of the preaching places were small towns or villages which were at that time distinct from Leeds itself; some, like Wetherby, were a considerable distance from the circuit town. Only a minority had purpose-built chapels at this date. The remaining places would be cottages or hired buildings. Often two places are coupled, inferring that the first-named had a morning service and the second an afternoon or evening service, although the times of services are not stated – perhaps they were not even fixed precisely. The 'Old Boggart House' chapel in the centre of Leeds apparently had one evening service in the quarter conducted by a local preacher. The remainder of the services at the circuit chapel were the responsibility of the travelling preachers and therefore do not feature at all on this plan.

The local preachers are indicated by their initials, carefully written in the squares. There is no list of preachers but some can be identified. 'WS' was William Shent, the Leeds barber who invited John Nelson to Leeds in 1742 and before whose shop door in Briggate the first Methodist sermon in Leeds was preached. 'RB' was Richard (Dicky) Burdsall, a native of Kirkby Overblow, near Harewood and a local preacher in the Leeds circuit for about twenty years before his removal to York. 'DP' was David Pawson, a native of Thorner and a brother of John Pawson who became a leading itinerant preacher after Wesley's death and President in 1793 and 1801. 'TG' was Thomas Garforth, a pioneer of Leeds Methodism who died in 1784. Dicky Burdsall once heard him

1777	May				June					July			
Sundays	4	11	18	25	1	8	15	22	29	6	13	20	27
Rippon Garforth & Berwick				WS			JG					JN	
Saxton & Etberford		Rip				WF				JW		DP	
Seacroft Chapeltown & Woodhic		JB		JW		Scr	HS		RB			DP	
Becup & Harewood		WF		WP		JSt		Rip		PB		JS	
Thorner & Keswick		JS		JG		PB		JSt		WF		MP	
Wetherby		WS		Rip		JW		JN		DP		JG	
Pannal & Kearby		Scr		JM		RB		WF		JP		JW	
Wortley Bramley & Armley		RB		JN		JS		JW		WP		RN	
Morley		JN		DP		WP		WS		JG		RB	
Brotherton & Ferrybridge		JG		RB		DP		WP		Rip		WS	
Ackworth		DP		JS		JG		RN		JW		Rip	
Knaresbro & Ribston		JW		JB		WS		Scr		JN		WP	
Woodhouse	JS		JG	SW	WJ	JN	JG	RB	JJ	JS	JG		JS
Yeadon	JN		JS		Scr		JW		WS		Rip		DP
Otley	DP		WP		JS		Rip		WF		WS		JS
Rothwell	WS		RB		JN		JS		DP		WP		JG
Weeton & Harewood	WP		DP		Rip		JN		RB		JW		WS
Staincroft & Cudworth	JS		JN		JB		JW		RN		WF		JS
Horbury & Wakefield	JG		JW		DP		JS		WP		RB		JN
Housforth & Branhope	WJ		JSt		MP		WP		PB		Scr		JB
Clifford & Collingham	JW		PB		WF		Scr		JS		JSt		Rip
Killinghall & Pannal	Rip		MP		JSt		DP		JN		JM		WP
Pontefract & Castleford	PB		JS		WP		RN		MP		DP		RB
Thorner & Bardsley	JSt		Rip				RB				JN		
Hunslet & Holbeck	MP		WF		PB		MP		JW		JS		RN
Belisle & Beeston	RB		JW		RN		JB		JSt		JS		WF
Seacroft & Thorner	RB												PB
Bramley & Armley					JG								
Woodside & Leeds									JG				

The earliest surviving preaching plan, Leeds Circuit May-July 1777
(see opposite page for details).
(Details from James Wray *A Compilation of facts illustrative of
Methodism in Leeds 1735-1835*, ms. volumes, Leeds Reference Library.
For the plan itself acknowledgements are due to the
Wesley Historical Society's Library, Westminster College, Oxford and to Colin Dews)

preach and quoted him as saying that 'he would not give a fig for a man who would not wade up to the chin in snow for Jesus Christ'.

Leeds plans continued to be handwritten until 1790, when the places were printed but the preachers' initials were written as before. Plans were printed in full from 1795 onwards and at the same time preachers were given numbers, a development which had already taken place at Rochdale by 1789. The use of numbers to indicate preachers soon became universal and continued in some circuits (usually Primitive Methodist or United Methodist) until the 1960s. A key to the numbers was provided down the right hand side of the plan, which would be a single sheet, and so, from this time on, the plan provides a list of the local preachers in the circuit, usually arranged in order of seniority although there was at this time no official date of recognition. These lists constitute the only reliable evidence of who the preachers were, since no central lists were kept; indeed, until 1883 the Wesleyans did not even know how many local preachers they had!

**REVD RICHARD WATSON AND THE
LONDON LOCAL PREACHERS (c.1830)**

'Mr Watson, during the time of his residence in Mr Wesley's house, regularly had the local preachers to breakfast with him there on Sunday morning, according to a plan which had been continued from Mr Wesley's time. The plan of labour for the day was read over, and vacant places supplied. On these occasions Mr Watson introduced some question of Christian theology, on which he elicited remarks and enquiries, and then summed up by some remarks which tended to promote their piety and increase their knowledge. By these interesting and affectionate interviews their attachment to him became unbounded, and his regard for them was cordial and sincere. Of the local preachers he often spoke with great esteem and love.'

G. J. Stevenson, *City Road Chapel
and its associations* 1872, p.200.

A more fundamental change occurred when more and more circuits began putting the appointments of both travelling and local preachers on one plan from the 1790s. London was perhaps the first to achieve this integration, closely followed by Manchester (an inversion of the way things usually happen, at least as Mancunians would like to think). Leeds dithered between 1799 and 1807 with only intermittent use of travelling preachers. Bolton did not change until 1811 and some rural circuits took longer. Only from about 1815 did almost all plans become

THE GOSPEL TRUMPET

1. Again the new made plan
   Presents itself to view.
   Sit down awhile my friends
   And I'll explain to you.
   The plan will do but little good
   Except by you it's understood.

2. The line across the top
   The circuit's name does show.
   The places where we preach
   Are down the left below.
   The preachers in the centre stand;
   A pious, plain and zealous band.

3. The figures in a line –
   One, eight, fifteen and so –
   Describe the sabbath days
   On which the preachers go
   To preach the soul-reviving word
   Of Jesus Christ, our risen Lord.

5. The letters here and there –
   P, C, S, L and T –
   According to request
   Shall now explainéd be.
   P the prayer meeting time does
   show,
   And L for Lovefeast you must
   know.

6. S stands for sacrament –
   So far I'm understood.
   C for collection, T –
   Tickets will be renewed.
   Nothing I think does now remain
   Which you may wish me to explain.

7. Now tell me where I'm planned!
   My number's So and So,
   How many times to preach
   And where I have to go?
   Have we a Lovefeast? Please to say.
   And am I planned from home that day?

8. Art thou a preacher here?
   Then search thyself and see
   What work it doth contain
   To be performed by thee.
   When thy appointment thou
   hast found.
   With pen and pencil mark
   them round.

23. The Holy Scriptures take –
    And read them on thy knees.
    Of all the books on earth
    None can compare with
    these;
    A lamp to guide thee in the
    way
    Leading to everlasting day.

24. Respecting other works
    Get all the help you can.
    But do not try to ape
    Or mimic any man.
    Aim to be pithy, plain and
    clear.
    And never mind who comes
    to hear.

34. No controversy hold
    But know the truth you
    preach.
    Let those who know not
    God
    Erroneous doctrine teach.
    What is the chaff compared
    to wheat?
    The people want good
    bread to eat.

(Part of a poem of 35 verses which was written on the back of a plan for 1859 and copied into a commonplace book belonging to the Peacey family of Oakridge Lynch, near Stroud. With acknowledgements to Revd A. J. Triffitt who supplied a copy of the poem.)

what they are today – complete records of the appointments of both ministers and local preachers. Initially some circuits denoted ministers by letters and local preachers by numbers but soon numbers were used for both. The ministers headed the list of preachers and so had the numbers '1', '2', or '3', followed by the local preachers, with the youngest recruits at the bottom of the list.

Along the lower edge of the Manchester plan for 1799 are the words: 'The Bearer hereof . . . is an approved Local Preacher here and may be employed as such wherever he comes.' The superintendent filled in the name and added his signature, and the plan, thus endorsed, constituted the local preacher's credentials. This may have been a response to the regulation in the 1796 *Minutes of Conference*: 'Let no Local Preacher be allowed to preach in any other circuit, without producing a recommendation from the Superintendent of the Circuit where he lives . . .'[6] Other circuits too used this device at a time when there was the danger of imposture and considerable debate both inside and outside Methodism about the precise status of local preachers. It also had a more down-to-earth purpose – it excused local preachers, like ordained clergy, from paying tolls while travelling to their appointments on the Sabbath.

The Liverpool circuit also was using the plan to validate its local preachers by 1806 and was more unusual in printing a set of rules 'agreed to at a Meeting of the Local Preachers'. The preachers met weekly 'to inquire into the state of their minds and help each other on to Christian holiness'; every preacher on trial had to preach 'in the vestry at Pitt Street [Liverpool] some Morning' – where he would be heard by his seniors before being put on full plan. So trial sermons have a long history.

NOT A REST-CURE!

'The local preacher could expect a day's work similar to one completed by Thomas Harwood in 1830 when he preached in the open air at 7 a.m., then at New Basford at 10.30 a.m., at Old Basford at 1 p.m., followed by a funeral service in the Chapel grave-yard, and then on to Kimberley for the 6 o'clock service followed by the prayer meeting and the walk home to Nottingham. Local preaching was not a rest cure! At least the local preacher found there was no escape. His letter of resignation to the superintendent brought no reply except the next quarter's plan on which he was given more appointments than ever before!'

Rowland C. Swift, *Lively People: Methodism in Nottingham 1740-1979*, 1982, p.144,

---

This Liverpool local preachers' plan is a further illustration of the total exclusion of local preachers from the Sunday services at the central town chapels, which do not appear on the plan at all. However, the local preachers were graciously allowed to take the weekly service in Liverpool on Tuesday mornings – at 5 a.m.! – a sure sign that these early services, which went back to Wesley's time were not well attended. The ministerial monopoly of the big congregations produced a sense of grievance among some local preachers, which contributed to the turmoil in Liverpool and elsewhere in 1834, when a sizeable number of preachers left Wesleyan Methodism to help establish the Wesleyan Association. There had been an earlier and smaller secession in some areas in 1797, which had led to the formation of the Methodist New Connexion and in the excitement which surrounded these events the Bolton New Connexion local preachers saw an opportunity to even things up. They were determined to ensure that they should preach in the town chapel on alternate Sundays and that the travelling preachers should take their share of the outlying country appointments. That they did not succeed in their campaign was the result of opposition, not so much from the ministers, as from the congregation at Bolton, who insisted on ministers every Sunday.[7] Such evidence as survives suggests that most MNC circuits followed Bolton and continued the Wesleyan pattern, although an early Huddersfield MNC plan shows appointments at the town chapel shared equally between ministers and local preachers.

Thus, on Sundays at least, it was the local preachers who had the most travelling to do and usually the smallest congregations at the end of it. Transport was both difficult and expensive; meeting places were sometimes difficult to find and liable to change at short notice and ill-health was common. In these circumstances it is not surprising that sometimes appointments were missed. The neglect of appointments was a problem in every branch of Methodism throughout the nineteenth century and well into the twentieth. Exhortations about it were frequently printed on the plan. The Ipswich plan in 1825 carried the following:

> How can we be assured that no Preacher will ever disappoint a Congregation? Ask every one, 1st., Do you see the great sin and fatal consequences of it? 2nd., Will you break a limb rather than wilfully break your word herein? 3rd., If you do not, can you blame us for not employing you any more? MR WESLEY.

The Barnard Castle plan of 1807/8 was more terse: 'Rather break a leg than miss your appointment. Mr Wesley.' Sometimes the exhortation took a subtler form. In 1838 the plan of the Wangford Primitive Methodist circuit in East Anglia printed some verses entitled 'The New Plan' which were clearly directed to the local preachers:

> My worthy brethren, dear,
> You see the new made plan,
> And your appointments there,
> So take them if you can.
> But if you should be call'd aside –
> Be sure to get them well supplied.
>
> Satan will oft suggest,
> That you have naught to say;
> And flesh and blood cry out,
> 'Tis dark and a long way:
> Perhaps there may be no-one there,
> So stop, and go to meeting here.
>
> Perhaps, through some neglect,
> For which we now are blamed,
> Someone who waited there,
> Is now both dead and damned –
> Whereas if we had preached the word,
> They might have sought and found the Lord.[8]

When exhortation was ineffective, sanctions were applied. The conduct and character of local preachers were considered as part of the normal routine of the local preachers' meeting. Much the commonest charge was that of missing preaching appointments. Each case was examined individually and sometimes sub-committees met to examine the circumstances. Reasonable excuses were accepted, as in the case of the Retford preacher who missed his appointment on 23 December 1832 'but being delicate in health, and the day being stormy, he was thought excusable'.[9] The 1806 Liverpool plan cited earlier included a rule: 'That if any Brother be accused of neglecting his appointment and the accusation be proved to the satisfaction of the Preachers . . . he shall be suspended from preaching for three months.' The Primitive Methodists, for whom the problem was more serious than for the Wesleyans, operated a different system. Preachers who neglected appointments were reduced one number on the list of preachers for each offence. This explains the otherwise ambiguous entry in the Tadcaster Primitive Methodist circuit records: 'That Bro J. Stones sink for missing Sherburn'. As at Retford, the rules were applied with some compassion:

> That Bro W. Dale's reasons for not taking his appointment at Wistow on 10th September be deemed satisfactory, he being an aged man, and the day very wet, and on such a day the distance too great for his strength.[10]

We are not told what happened to a preacher who was already at the bottom of the list! It is worth noting that Primitive Methodist preachers could also be demoted for long preaching or long praying.

The local preachers were defended in a book published in 1832 in which a whole chapter is devoted to 'Punctuality in attending Appointments'. The author sympathised with the situation when 'after a week of fatiguing labour, a preacher has an appointment on the Sabbath six or eight miles distant [and] the journey he has to perform on foot, on bad roads, and perhaps in bad weather . . .'[11] The author did not mince his words: 'Much of the blame of non-attendance on the part of local preachers is often due to the injudicious formation of the plan which prescribes their Sabbath labours.' He believed that the local preachers had the right to block dates: 'When he can assign solid reasons either for or against visiting certain places or preaching at certain times or hours, he is entitled to be heard . . . the geographical situations of the preachers ought to be carefully considered, together with their talents and bodily strength . . . and their predilections also, as well as those of the people.'[12]

It was many years before such radical ideas became widely accepted. At this time the superintendent made the plan and every preacher was assumed to be available most if not all Sundays. The Sheffield MNC plan for the six-month period November 1797 to May 1798 had ten appointments to be filled every week and thirteen preachers available, numbered at the foot of the plan. On the first Sunday of the plan, numbers 1-10 were out on the Lord's business, planned in order down the list of places so that the column closes with number 10. On the following Sunday, number 2 takes the first appointment and so on in order down the column to number 11. So it continued with perfect regularity for the whole of the six months, so that we have a grid with consecutive numbering both horizontally and vertically. Every preacher took his turn

THE SABBATH-DAY'S PLAN

FOR THE

Travelling and Local Preachers in Barnard-Caſtle Circuit.

"Rather break a Leg than miſs your Appointment."—Mr WESLEY.

"Our Sufficiency is of GOD."—St PAUL.

Preachers:

No.	Preacher.
1	C. Whiteſide.
2	J. Forſter.
3	L. Barlow.
4	S. Holroyd.
5	J. Wilkin.
6	W. Dixon.
7	H. Oliver.
8	R. Clarkſon.
9	G. Powell.
10	T. Blackburn.
11	A. Race.
12	J. Myers.
13	J. Phillipſon.
14	X. Featherſton.
15	X. Davyſon.
16	X. Parker.
17	X. Vickers.
18	X. Vipond.
19	X. Thompſon.
20	J. Forſter.

Places (Year 1807 – 1808; Months: November, December, January, February, March, April):

- Barnard-Caſtle
- Bowes
- Newſham
- Scargill
- Mickleton and Eggleſton
- Cotherſton
- Staindrop
- Evenwood
- Biſhop-Auckland
- Newbiggin and Middleton
- High-houſe
- Weſtgate
- Ditto
- Eaſtgate
- Rookhope
- Stanhope
- Froſterly
- Wolſingham
- Thornley
- Crook

N. B. January 5th Quarter-Day at Barnard-Caſtle, and April 3d at High-Houſe, and a Love Feaſt.

Printed by Edward Walker, Newcastle.

The first printed plan for the Barnard Castle Wesleyan Circuit, newly formed out of a larger circuit to cover the chapels of Teesdale and Weardale. Weardale places and preachers begin half-way down with High House and Anthony Race respectively. (Durham County Record office.)

at all the preaching places. Thus in the half-year, each preacher had twenty appointments with two breaks of three weeks each. Since eight out of the appointments were doubles, each preacher took 36 services in six months, often travelling considerable distances, since the circuit extended as far as Barnsley to the north and [Stoney] Middleton to the south-west.

DEVOTION TO THE PLAN!

Matthew Braithwaite in his *History of Wesleyan Methodism in Bishop Auckland* 1885, page 222, tells of the following incident which occurred as a result of his search for a full set of circuit plans:

'From one family to which application was made, the reply came that they had possessed a full set, but the father, prior to his death some five or six years ago, had requested they should be put in his coffin as a pillow, which request had been complied with.'

In some large circuits the geographical location of the preachers was taken into account, as in the Barnard Castle Wesleyan circuit in 1807-8, which covered both Weardale and Teesdale. Recognising that travel along the dales was easier than travel across the intervening fells, here the local preachers were planned only in the dale in which they lived. On the list of preachers, numbers 4 to 10 are Teesdale preachers and numbers 11 to 20 are Weardale men; thus in this instance the order of the list is not an indication of seniority.[13] At the other end of the country, the St. Ives (Cornwall) circuit in 1791 was thirty miles long and again the local preachers worked within defined areas and were not expected to travel to more distant parts of the the circuit. John Fennell of Penzance was planned no further away than St. Just (10 miles). In 1812 he became the first headmaster of Woodhouse Grove School, West Yorkshire, where his niece, Maria Branwell, met Patrick Brontë.

For Wesleyan Methodism there survives a set of plans for all circuits in the connexion for the year 1825, giving us a unique snapshot of preaching arrangements across the country at that date.[14] Most of these plans were for a period of six months. Evening services were invariably held at 6 pm and most morning services began at 10.30 am One hundred and seventy years and several social revolutions later, times of services have changed little. However, in 1825 there was still a handful of early services, usually 7 am, in the urban centres. Afternoon services were common in rural areas. In High Wycombe and in Waltham Cross, the preachers were required not only to conduct the service but also to meet the classes afterwards. Throughout the Knaresborough circuit in summer preachers were urged to preach out of doors at 1 pm 'if the weather permit and a majority of the Friends in the Place desire it'. Similarly at Newark the preachers were to 'continue Field Preaching at suitable places'. Gravesend insisted that 'in all our chapels, the regular lessons are to be read during morning service'. The preachers in the Dudley circuit were requested 'to be at their place a quarter of an hour before the time, to begin worship the moment the clock strikes and not to continue the service much above an hour' – and at Cleckheaton they were 'not to keep the Congregations too long at one time' – still very sound advice.

A few circuits recognised the problems many preachers had with transport. A note on the Margate plan regarding the village of Westmarsh stated: 'On account of the great distance of this place, it is optional with the Preacher supplying whether he preach in the evening or not . . .' Presumably he told the stewards in advance what to expect! Leicester and Birmingham circuits held collections for local preachers' travelling expenses and Malton requested that (in returning home) 'every Preacher may be provided with a Horse, when necessary'.

In circuits such as Hull or Salford the preachers met weekly or monthly for fellowship and study but the quarterly 'business' meeting was very often held either before or after the Quarterly Meeting, of which all the preachers were *ex-officio* members. In Primitive Methodism this became almost an invariable rule. Meetings were generally in daytime, presumably to avoid the difficulties of travel after dark. Christmas Day was a popular date.

A few places were woefully short of preachers. Devizes circuit had one minister and three local preachers for eight preaching places. The plan could be filled only with the help of 17 preachers from the adjacent Melksham circuit. St. Albans circuit was in a similar position and had to rely on 16 visiting local preachers to fill the appointments.

A survey of these 1825 plans confirms the impression that many village causes were served entirely by local preachers. John Vickers has analysed a sample of twenty circuits and finds that in 191 of the 398 places listed in these circuits, no ministers were appointed to preach on any Sunday. He further points out that this was not necessarily compensated for by weekday appointments. Devonport had two main churches at which services were predominantly, but not quite exclusively, conducted by ministers. One other church had occasional ministerial appointments and the remaining seven places were served entirely by local preachers, only one of which had regular ministerial appointments during the week. Dr Vickers concludes:

> . . . the initiative for pioneering new places and establishing new societies had largely passed, whether by deliberate policy or by default, to the local laity, while the circuit ministers gave themselves to the task of consolidating existing causes. Certainly in the years since Wesley's death, reduction in the size of circuits had been accompanied by decreasing mobility on the part of the [itinerant] preachers.[15]

A study of the Louth Wesleyan plans by Alan Rogers[16] shows a similar situation a few years earlier. In 1819 the ministers led worship in only six societies outside Louth itself, leaving nineteen others who did not see their minister for Sunday worship from one year's end to the next. As the century progressed however, the picture moderated, so that by 1866 only six very small societies did not appear on the full-time ministers' preaching plan. Yet through to the end of the century it remained true across the connexion that the circuit 'frontier' – the cottage meetings, the services in schools and makeshift premises, some of which would ultimately produce strong new causes – was almost entirely staffed by local preachers. This was as true in the town circuits, where new housing estates might provide opportunity for growth, as in the country areas.

CONGREGATIONAL CHOICE

'If any other person be present whom the congregation wishes to speak, the wish of the congregation must be complied with.'

A note on the first preaching plan (hand written) issued by the followers of Hugh Bourne and William Clowes after they had united in 1811 and were soon to take the name Primitive Methodists.

H. B. Kendall *The History of the Primitive Methodist Church* vol.i, pp.113 and 559.

W. G. Taylor, later to achieve fame as the superintendent of the Sydney Central Mission, Australia, tells in his autobiography how he started a series of early morning services in several of the Middlesbrough iron works while still 'on trial' in the 1860s,[17] and he was by no means exceptional in this regard. The intimate and informal prayer meetings and cottage meetings were an ideal training ground for mission bands and young preachers.

In the smaller branches of Methodism, especially the Bible Christians and the Primitive Methodists, the situation was very different. Both bodies were largely rural, particularly before 1870 and the local preachers shared the pulpits with the ministers on a more equitable basis. The distinction between minister and layperson was less marked than in Wesleyan Methodism and was further blurred among the Primitives by their use of 'hired local preachers', that is preachers who, though unordained, received an allowance, lived in a manse, and did all the usual work of a minister.[18]

It is impossible to generalise about the workload of local preachers at this period but a convenient bird's eye view of an average rural Wesleyan circuit is given by the Knaresborough plan of 1842 which prints by each preacher's name the number of his appointments. Which modern superintendent would dare to copy this idea? The circuit had two town chapels, Knaresborough and Harrogate, and preaching places in 28 villages, many of which had only one service – in some cases once a fortnight. There were 25 local preachers, *all* of whom preached during the six months covered by this plan. The two senior brethren took eight appointments between them, but the average for the rest seems to have been about 24 (i.e. 12 a quarter). The highest figure was 39. Most of the appointments were doubles: a morning service at one village followed by an afternoon service or more rarely an evening service at a neighbouring settlement.

Local preachers played a major part in the secessions from Wesleyan Methodism which marked the first half of the nineteenth century. We have already encountered the disgruntled preachers of Liverpool who nursed their grievances and exacted their revenge in a serious revolt in 1834, but the largest secession nationwide centred around the expulsion of three ministers at the Conference of 1849. Many localised quarrels were swept up into the widespread agitation that ensued. In Sowerby Bridge, near Halifax, a local preacher named Sammy Hoyle had established a reputation as a Yorkshire version of Billy Bray. A typical prayer of his, often quoted locally, was 'Lord, bless them leet-hearted milliners and them giggling lasses in t'gallery'. Despite, or perhaps because of, his popularity, he was expelled in 1849 following a sermon on 'The Danger of Riches' preached to a number of millowners at the circuit chapel. He and four other renegade preachers then issued their own plan, headed 'Plan of the Expelled Wesleyan Local Preachers in the Sowerby Bridge Circuit, 1850' on which the five preachers retained their former circuit plan numbers, suggesting perhaps that they did not intend the division to be permanent. When they finally built their chapel in 1854 they called it 'Wesley Chapel', to affirm their allegiance to John Wesley if not to the Old Body. But positions hardened and ultimately Wesley Chapel became part of the Free Methodist circuit. Similarly, in the same year the rebellious local preachers in Sheffield produced 'The Corrected Wesleyan Plan' which contained no ministerial appointments at all and which was issued, not by the superintendent minister, but by 'the authority of the local preachers' meeting'.

TENSION OVER TITLES

Revd W M Harvard, superintendent of Maidstone Circuit in the late 1840s, introduced a distinction in the way in which local preachers and ministers were referred to on the plan. The results were described in a letter to Jabez Bunting written 26 January 1848:

'I heard no objection until at our last local preachers' quarterly meeting when, with but one exception . . . it (the plan) was denounced as introducing novel and unscriptural distinction among "brethren equally called of God to the same work" . . .'

In a later letter (1 February 1848) Mr Harvard writes 'The people in the countryside say they are more indebted to the local preachers than to us and they will not sanction on our part any lording it over their oldest and best and most deserving friends, not to say "ministers", for so they speak of their apostleship.'

W. R. Ward, *Early Victorian Methodism*
1976 pp.185-6 and pp.358-9.

As the nineteenth century wore on, plans slowly became more elaborate and included more detail. Morning lessons became standard on Wesleyan plans along with regular fixtures such as the quarterly fast day ('it is shamefully neglected' several superintendents regularly complained). Primitive Methodist plans in particular were rarely without improving verses, or other exhortations very often aimed at the preachers. The Brandon (Suffolk) plan in 1854 was typical:

> Beloved brethren, never disappoint a congregation if you can possibly attend. Go to your important work in the spirit of prayer, choose the plainest text you can. In your discourse aim at the glory of God and the conversion of sinners . . . Resolve by Divine aid, every time you preach, to be instrumental in the salvation of undying spirits. Dip your sermons in the lightnings of heaven . . .

in the might of God grapple with the consciences of your hearers – exhibit the cross prominently – proclaim full redemption, pull sinners out of the fire . . . Up to your Master's work till the hand of death shall strike off your armour.[19]

Advice about the sermon was sometimes couched in verse:

A SERMON

1. It should be brief; if lengthy it will steep
   Our hearts in apathy, our eyes in sleep.
   The dull will yawn, the chapel lounger doze,
   Attention flag, and memory's portals close.

2. It should be warm, a living altar coal
   To melt the icy heart, and charm the soul:
   A SAPLESS, dull harangue, however read,
   Will never rouse the soul, or wake the dead.

3. It should be closely well applied at last
   To make the moral nail securely fast.
   'Thou art the man and thou alone' will make
   A Felix tremble or a David quake![20]

Primitive Methodism began in the open air and camp meetings continued to be a distinguishing feature of this branch of Methodism. On the London First plan in 1850 the following notice appeared:

No person to be taken on the plan as an accredited Local Preacher until he or she promise to take appointments in the Open Air when planned, or give a satisfactory reason to the Quarterly Meeting why they cannot.

The significant phrase 'he or she' is a reminder that among the Primitives (and the Bible Christians) women were welcomed as preachers. It is unfortunate that the use of initials rather than first names on the list of preachers makes it difficult to identify the women preachers. But women and men alike were expected to preach in the open and especially to take part in the popular outdoor festivals of prayer and preaching called camp meetings – an idea the Primitives had adapted from the American frontier. The prospect of hearing a woman preacher was an added attraction! (See Chapters 8 and 9.)

Camp meetings feature prominently on PM plans for the summer quarters and the local preachers provided the backbone of the organisation. A typical arrangement was for one minister and five, six or seven local preachers to be planned to attend, as, for example, at Stockport in July 1827: 'preachers to attend: 1, 4, 6, 9, 20, 21, 29' – a blend of experienced and younger preachers. This creative use of teams of preachers was employed also for Missionary Meetings and for 'Revival Meetings', a kind of indoor equivalent of camp meetings used in the winter. In October 1850 no less than sixteen local preachers and two ministers descended on Bollington, near Macclesfield, Cheshire to begin a week of nightly Revival meetings – a veritable evangelistic *blitzkrieg* which culminated in a meeting on Sunday evening at which every preacher in the circuit (nos. 2-28) was expected to be present.

The Bible Christians shared many of the characteristics of the Primitives but were largely confined to the south-west of England. They too, favoured verses printed in a spare space on the plan, written usually by one of the ministers. But in 1878, Joseph Turner, a local preacher in the St. Austell circuit produced a set of verses in which he described the preachers one by one. Perhaps it is as well that this idea did not catch on! Here is a selection:

> And the first of them is Brother LOBB,
> Who will soon be home to glory;
> For fifty years, through joys and fears,
> He has told the 'old, old story'.

> Then we have Father and Mother MINEAR,
> Who have faithfully laboured together;
> May their pilgrimage close in the calmest repose,
> May they triumph with Jesus for ever.

> In number six we've a BERRY quite ripe,
> Who has ninety years travelled below;
> He is washed in the blood of his crucified Lord,
> He is packed up and waiting to go.

> We've a PARSON among us, but not any Clerk,
> A BREWER, but the beer is all gone;
> And this I would say, ere I pass away,
> We are abstainers every one.

We've a HARPER, with no lack of courage and zeal,
Who with music is full, although vocal;
And Brother JOHN ROWETT, we all must allow it,
Is a very acceptable Local.

We have a little Sister, as Solomon said,
Brother CRISPIN has made her his choice;
But for family ties, enrapt in surprise,
You might list to her eloquent voice.

We've a COCK and a ROBINS, two providence birds,
Both are able to say or to sing;
There is ROBERTS and BIRT, t'will heal all your hurt,
To receive the glad tidings they bring.

HOOPER, POLLARD and BULLOCK are three youthful men,
Whose names are found with the others;
If I have not missed, I have finished the list,
And I pray God bless you, my brothers. [21]

Is there an idea here for a future *Epworth Review* competition?

Transport continued to be a major problem for preachers who did not own a horse. While urban circuits tended to become smaller in extent as a result of subdivision, the rural circuits did not contract in area in a time of rural depopulation after 1870. The railway network improved but Sunday travelling was frowned on. Many Wesleyan circuits held collections for the local preachers' horse hire fund. The Holsworthy circuit allowed horse hire 'for all journeys over four miles to those preachers only who have no horse of their own'. Presumably preachers could claim their costs from the circuit Treasurer. Many poorer preachers walked. So in country circuits preachers made a day of it, with two or three appointments in adjoining villages or two appointments at the same chapel and hospitality provided between services. In extreme cases Saturday night bed and breakfast was needed. There was, of course, a positive side to all this, with congenial fellowship around the dining table, at which all the circuit gossip was passed on, but it meant a long day for the preacher, often with a weary journey at the end of it and work next morning.

Emancipation came in the form of the safety bicycle and pneumatic tyres from 1888 onwards. The new county councils set about improving the main roads and for ten years or so cyclists had them to themselves in that magical period before the internal combustion engine began its remorseless advance. The adoption of the bicycle was rapid – it was cheaper and quicker than the horse and the Primitive Methodist Bookroom sold many hundreds of cheap cycles in the years before the Great War. In the towns the electric trams made it much easier to get to appointments, and early in the twentieth century the motor cycle began to disturb the peace of country lanes, so that by 1925 more than half a million were registered in Britain. There was also the country bus, but Cyril Rackett[22] recalls that as late as 1923 Sunday buses and trains on the Isle of Wight did not run until after midday. Not for nothing did many country circuits print the phases of the moon on the plan.

PRAYER AND THE PLAN

An old supernumerary and his wife used to sit with the Circuit plan before them each Sunday, and pray for blessing and help to come on ministers, local preachers and congregations.

'So they prayed together for those struggling village causes and the businessmen, schoolmasters, farmers, and farm labourers who had gone off willingly with their messages to spend the whole day, perhaps, away from home, on the other side of the circuit . . .

Lastly they prayed for the safe return home of all those hundreds who had been preaching the Gospel throughout the Connexion.'

Herston Travers 'The Circuit Plan'
LP Magazine 1932, pp.461-4.

The cycle was, of course, a solitary mode of travel but the car could be communal. By the 1920s most Wesleyan country circuits were using one or more cars to ferry preachers to outlying areas. The Bodmin Wesleyan plan for 1923 had a slightly mysterious note that a car was provided for preachers from the Stenalees end of the circuit on seven Sunday out of thirteen; one wonders why it could not have been available every week. At the same time preachers could still claim expenses from the circuit Horse Hire Fund. The Boston (Lincolnshire) plan for the last quarter of 1922 had an arrangement with a local garage which cost over £25 a quarter, more than the circuit paid in General Assessment. In addition £1. 4s. 0d (£1.20) was paid on the 'Cycle Account'. The Bude plan of 1926 marked certain Sundays with a star, explained at the foot of the plan: 'The Preachers' Motor Car will run on these Sundays from Bude'. Congleton preachers were told in 1927 to 'order a Cab as required

NORTH EASTERN RAILWAY.

Permit the Bearer, a Local Preacher on the Crook Wesleyan Circuit, to walk on Sundays over and along the Company's Railway between Stanley Colliery and Hedley Hill, near Waterhouses, in the County of Durham.

Dated the 7th day of February, 1893.

Secretary

NOTE. This pass is issued at the risk of the holder, and is subject to the terms and conditions contained in a Licence and Indemnity of even date signed by the Rev. C. Lumsden and the Rev. W. A. Phillips, and is to be exhibited when required and to be given up when the permission to walk on the Railway is withdrawn.

A local preacher's pass (nineteenth century) giving the right to walk along colliery waggonways to Sunday appointments.
(Acknowledgements to Ken Clark of New Brancepeth, Durham.)

Conveyances.

1.—The Car for Sibsey, etc., will start from Messrs. HOLLAND'S Garage, on the Sundays appointed, at 10.0 a.m.
2.—The Car for Swineshead, Kirton, etc., will start at 9.45 a.m.
3.—The Car for Holland Fen, etc., will start at 5.0 p.m.

The Preachers are requested to comply with these arrangements **punctually.**

Circuit Conveyances. — Preachers are requested to consult Mr. Langstaff if they require conveyances when none are appointed, and also if they do not require them when they are appointed. All these requests must be made to Mr. Langstaff not later than the first post on Friday morning.

No Car except those planned will run unless a written order be given by the Hon. Secretary.

The age of the motor car! Detail from Boston (Lincs) Wesleyan Circuit plan Oct-Jan 1922-3.
(With thanks to Alan Rose)

from Mr Latham, Spring Street'. As early as 1912, Douglas circuit had two cars every Sunday, one for Laxey and the other for the Baldwins.

A sampling of Primitive Methodist circuits over the same period (1907-30) shows no explicit references to travel arrangements, perhaps because PM circuits were generally smaller than Wesleyan ones, or perhaps because the Primitives could not afford to make such arrangements. Following Methodist Union in 1932 there was a gradual process of amalgamation of overlapping ex-Wesleyan and ex-Primitive circuits which produced still larger circuits. Until car-ownership became sufficiently widespread, a car plan remained essential outside the towns.

And so preaching plans continued to mirror the outward changes which enveloped Methodism in the twentieth century – the growing incidence of telephones, the greater numbers of women preachers, changes in hymn books (at least one plan was still referring to the 'new' Methodist hymn book in 1952, nineteen years after its publication) and now, the use of computers and desktop publishing. E mail and fax may one day replace the plan but for the present the quarterly preaching plan remains the local preachers' marching orders.

Mary Bosanquet (1739-1815) a woman of Huguenot descent,
an ardent Methodist, and a notable preacher. In 1781 she became the wife of
the saintly John Fletcher, vicar of Madeley.

8

WOMEN LOCAL PREACHERS

E. Dorothy Graham

The movement started by John Wesley had a profound impact on the lives of the men and women of his time and many lay people felt impelled to pass on their new-found faith and experience to their families, friends and neighbours. In the case of men there was no fundamental objection to this, but when women wanted to do the same there were reservations, though the giving of testimonies and even exhortations was not frowned upon as these mostly took place within the family or in classes, and from the earliest time women were appointed as class leaders, especially among their own sex. Even occasional speaking in services was permitted, but preaching a sermon was another matter altogether.

Wesley and Wesleyanism

John Wesley himself was not averse to the giving of short exhortations by women, but he would not countenance their preaching sermons. In 1761 he declared that 'the Methodists do not allow of women preachers'.[1] While there were, however, women such as Sarah Crosby, Sarah Ryan, Grace Walton and Ann Cutler to mention but a few, to whom Wesley gave guarded support in their ministry, because their work patently resulted in the salvation of sinners, nevertheless in 1780 he stated that he was not prepared to allow women to preach and wrote on the 25th March to George Robinson at Grimsby:

> 'I desire Mr Peacock to put a final stop to the preaching of women in his circuit. If it were suffered it would grow, and we know not where it would end.'[2]

However as time went on the matter was to a certain extent taken out of his hands and he was forced to give tacit, if reluctant, approval. Eventually, it seems, he was prepared to judge each case on its merits, rather than lay down a categorical rule.

Zechariah Taft says that in the case of Sarah Mallett not only Wesley, but also the Wesleyan Conference in Manchester of 1787, 'designates, authorises, and so to speak, *ordains* her as a preacher in his connexion',[3] and that this, therefore, opened the gateway for the approval also of other females. In fact in 1789 John Wesley gave Sarah Mallett advice on the conduct of her services:

> 'It gives me pleasure to hear that prejudice dies away and our preachers behave in a friendly manner . . . Never continue the service above an hour at once, singing, *preaching*, prayer and all. You are not to judge by your own *feelings*, but by the word of God. Never scream. Never speak above the natural pitch of your voice; it is disgustful to the hearers. It gives them pain, not pleasure. And it is destroying yourself. It is offering God murder for sacrifice.'[4]

This letter shows that if Wesley did not actually encourage women preachers, and never appointed one as an itinerant, several were travelling preachers in all but name.

Two women who were particularly notable for their preaching abilities were Mary Bosanquet and Mary Barritt (Barrett). Mary Bosanquet began her ministry when she was living with a family of children and poor people in Leytonstone. She continued it after she moved in 1768 to Cross Hall in Yorkshire, where people came from miles to her services, which in time developed so that a sermon was included, though she always refused to preach from the pulpit, preferring to stand on the stairs.

In 1771 Mary Bosanquet wrote a long letter to John Wesley about female preaching and her attitude to it, asking his advice. She explained that she and Sarah Ryan had been taking 'little kind of prayer meetings, etc.' which had been blessed, but some people had raised objections, based on scriptural injunctions about women keeping silence. Needless to say Mary put a different interpretation on these texts,[5] believing them to mean that women should not usurp the position or authority of men and that just as some women like Deborah in the Old Testament, and Mary and the woman of Samaria in the New, 'ministered' in certain circumstances, so she had an extra-ordinary call which was why she acted 'in an extra-ordinary manner'. In his reply Wesley agreed with her:

> 'I think the strength of the cause rests there, in your having an extraordinary call; so I am persuaded has every one of our lay-preachers; otherwise I could not countenance his preaching at all. It is plain to me that the work of God, termed Methodism, is an extraordinary dispensation of HIS providence. Therefore do not wonder, if several things occur therein, which do not fall under the ordinary rules of discipline. St. Paul's ordinary rule was "I permit not a woman to speak in the congregation", yet in extraordinary cases he made a few exceptions; at Corinth in particular.'[6]

Evidently some people asked Mary why she did not become an itinerant, but she said that was not her call; others wanted to know why she insisted on 'holding a meeting' rather than say that she was going to preach, to which she replied that it was less ostentatious, gave her more freedom and caused less offence. To those who asked why she did not become Quaker Mary answered that she felt 'that the spirit of the Lord is more at work among the Methodists . . . Besides I do nothing but what Mr Wesley approves'.[7]

After her marriage in 1781 to the Revd John Fletcher, Vicar of Madeley, Shropshire, Mary carried on with her ministry and regularly 'preached' to mixed congregations, among whom clergymen were frequently to be found. In fact John Wesley is said to have recorded that he 'heard the sainted Fletcher preach an excellent sermon in the church in the morning and Mrs Fletcher a more excellent sermon in the schoolroom in the evening'.[8]

In 1803 Mary Fletcher wrote to Mary Taft (née Barritt) telling her that although she was by then unable to travel far afield she had her own preaching room with large congregations. She went on:

> 'For some years, I was often led to speak from a text, of late I feel greater approbation in what we call *expounding*, taking part or whole of a chapter, and speaking upon it . . . I do look upon the call of women as an *extra* – not an *ordinary* call; therefore I strove, and do *strive now* so to act, not out of custom but only when I have a clear leading . . .'[9]

The Conference of 1803, which was held in Manchester, considered the question: 'Should women be permitted to preach among us?' and the following resolution was passed:

'We are of the opinion that, in general they ought not. 1. Because a vast majority of our people are opposed to it. 2. Because their preaching does not at all seem necessary, there being a sufficiency of Preachers, whom God has accredited, to supply all the places in our connexion with regular preaching. But if any woman among us thinks she has an extraordinary call from God to speak in public (and we are sure it must be an extraordinary call that can authorise it) we are of the opinion she should, in general, address her own sex, and those only. And, upon this condition alone, should any woman be permitted to preach in any part of our connexion; and when so permitted, it should be under the following regulations: 1. They shall not preach in the Circuit where they reside, until they have obtained the approbation of the Superintendent and a Quarterly Meeting. 2. Before they go into any other Circuit to preach, they shall have a written invitation from the Superintendent of such Circuit, and a recommendatory note from the Superintendent of their own Circuit.'[10]

So it is obvious that any woman who felt a call to preach needed to be very determined if she was to fulfil that call. Inevitably there were a number of 'irregular' preachers who ignored the regulation. One of the most famous, Mary Barritt (Barrett), started preaching in her early twenties, travelled many miles in the north of England, and was the instrument of the conversion of a number of later well-known Wesleyan ministers. In 1802 she married the Revd Zechariah Taft, a Wesleyan minister. In her memoirs, written in 1827, she emphasised that she never went into a circuit except by invitation from the superintendent and other friends, unless, on very rare occasions, she was absolutely convinced it was 'my duty and the will of God, for me to go, that I durst not at the peril of my soul neglect going'. From the second volume of her memoirs, which goes up to the end of 1805, it seems apparent that she worked virtually as another itinerant alongside her husband in the circuits to which he was appointed. In fact Joseph Benson was reputed to have written to

Taft that Conference had been ignorant that 'he was taking a female to assist him in the ministry'.[11]

TWO REACTIONS TO MARY TAFT (NÉE BARRITT)

In 1797 Mary Barritt met James Ridall the superintendent at Middleham, who enquired very kindly after her mother and brother; but when Mary's friends told him eagerly of her preaching and exhorting 'he appeared very distant and continued so all evening, so the next morning I took my leave . . . '

from *The Memoirs of Mary Taft,*
formerly Miss Barritt by herself, 1827.

'I have one favour to request, and that is that our sister Taft may not be hindered of her service in your Circuit. Our chapels are open to her at any time. I am witness of her usefulness in Yorkshire. I know not any one place that would object. I have those in my class at this day that were brought in by her instrumentality. Let us be gentle; and let the Lord make use of what he pleases. If He chooses to confound the mighty by weak instruments, let Him have the glory.'

Memoir of Richard Burdsall 4th ed.1884,
p.334 – the quotation is from a letter to his son
John Burdsall, a Wesleyan minister, October 19th 1809.

Although at first Taft paid lip-service to the Conference resolution he was convinced of the validity of women's preaching for its own sake and not just because of his wife's talents. He wrote several articles on the subject[12] and a two-volume work, *Biographical Sketches of the Lives and Public Ministry of various Holy Women.*

It is not possible to say how many 'unofficial' women local preachers there were in Wesleyan Methodism in the period after 1803, but probably the most famous was Elizabeth Evans (1776-1849) immortalised by George Eliot as Dinah Morris in *Adam Bede.* Elizabeth was converted in 1798 and began speaking in prayer meetings and sick visiting, but she really started to preach around 1802/3, and travelled from Nottingham into Derbyshire and Staffordshire on a missionary tour which lasted sixteen weeks. Then, finding much opposition and that all doors were closed to her, she returned to Nottingham. It must have been during this preaching tour that Samuel Evans, a local preacher from Roston Common, heard Elizabeth preach at Ashbourne and their marriage (in 1804) provided the opportunity for them to preach together. Elizabeth now faced much less opposition as she was no longer a female preacher on her own! Many villages experienced conversions and societies were formed. Samuel and

Elizabeth first lived at Roston, then in Derby, before finally settling at Wirksworth in Derbyshire in 1819 where Elizabeth formed a class of four members out of which grew four more classes. Their two names appeared as local preachers on the Cromford plan up to 1832, in which year the Wesleyan Conference apparently came to an understanding that women preachers should not be encouraged. It was therefore suggested that Mrs Evans, while allowed to take appointments, should be indicated on the plan by a simple asterisk. Mrs Evans declined the proposal, and she and her husband joined the recently-formed Arminian Methodists, but subsequently both returned to the church of their youth.[13]

Hugh Bourne was impressed by Elizabeth Evans, recording that 'I was much instructed by her' (21st March 1810). A little earlier he had written:

> 'Her voice was low and hoarse at first from having preached so much the week past and having caught several colds, but she got well into the Power. She appears to be very clear in Scripture doctrines and very ready in the Scripture. She seemed to speak fully in the Spirit, and from the very little I saw of her she seems to be as fully devoted to God as any woman I ever met with.' (25th June 1809)[14]

Memorial to Elizabeth Evans (the inspiration of George Eliot's 'Dinah Morris' who married Adam Bede in the novel of that name. See chapter 9 below). Now on view in the Crown Yard Heritage Centre, Wirksworth, Derbyshire.
(Photograph by Dorothy Graham)

Three other Wesleyan women worthy of brief mention are Mary Sewell, Sarah Mallett and Diana Thomas. The fact that they came from as far apart as East Anglia and the Welsh borders gives some indication that in all parts of the country there were able women who felt called to preach. Taft tells us that Mary began her public ministry at the age of twenty and continued to exercise it till her death, preaching widely in East Anglia and Lincolnshire with great effect, often in the open air. He comments:

> 'Her word was made "quick and powerful" to some, who are now ashamed to acknowledge that a feeble woman was the instrument of their salvation. But the day is at hand which shall declare it.'[15]

The oldest register of the Great Yarmouth Circuit (1785), when Yarmouth was part of the Norwich Circuit, recorded that among the five local preachers was 'Sister Mary Sewell,' a class leader at Thurlton. She died on October 19th 1786.

On October 27th 1787 Joseph Harper, an itinerant in Norwich circuit, wrote:

> 'We give the right hand of fellowship to Sarah Mallett, and shall have no objection to her being a preacher in our connexion so long as she continues to preach the Methodist Doctrine and attends to our discipline. – Josh. Harper.
>
> N.B. You receive this by order of Mr Wesley and the Conference.'[16]

Sarah's name is in the list of members at Loddon (in the Norwich circuit) 1785-7 so it seems that there were two female Wesleyan preachers in that circuit about the same time.

On the other side of the country was Diana Thomas, whose diary reveals that in 1809 she was authorised by the Kington quarterly meeting and William France, her superintendent minister, to preach in the circuit. According to the diary she travelled thousands of miles and preached in places stretching from Hereford in the south to Machynlleth in the north, from Aberystwyth in the west to Ledbury in the east. However, in spite of this her brief obituary notice in *The Methodist Magazine* of 1821 makes no reference to her preaching.[17] Perhaps the editor, a certain Jabez Bunting, suppressed this part of her story because of disapproval of women's preaching! If this was so then it is likely that there may be many more such omissions and consequently numerous 'hidden' women local preachers in Wesleyan Methodism.

A number of wives of travelling preachers became involved in the work, many of them exhorting, yet more 'prophesying', and some actually engaging in 'preaching'. So Mrs Hainsworth after her marriage 'continued to preach and exhort, as opportunities occurred' and often accompanied her husband to his appointments, speaking after he had preached. After his death she took occasional services.[18] Mary Wiltshaw sometimes took the place of her husband, assisting him with his work, particularly visiting villages in the circuit.[19]

Women preachers were also active in Ireland and the stories of two in particular are interesting, not only for the women themselves, but also for the comments which arise from them. Alice Cambridge joined the Society at Bandon in 1780 and soon began praying and preaching in public, visiting Kinsale, Cork, Limerick and Dublin. However in 1791 'many of the Methodists, including some of the preachers pronounced her public address irregular and such as ought not to be tolerated in the Christian church.'[20] She, therefore wrote to John Wesley for advice and in one of his last letters he replied:

> 'Mr Barber has the glory of God at heart; and so have his
> fellow labourers. Give them all honour, and obey them
> in all things as far as conscience permits. But it will not
> permit you to be silent when God commands you to
> speak: yet I would have you give as little offence as
> possible; and therefore I would advise you not to speak
> at any place where a preacher is speaking at the same
> time, lest you should draw away his hearers. Also avoid
> the first appearance of pride or magnifying yourself. If
> you want books or anything, let me know. I have your
> happiness much at heart.'[21]

This probably constitutes John Wesley's last word on female preaching. As we have noted, after his death opinon hardened so the story of Ann Lutton of Moira shows that local practice was not always in line with the official ruling. She was converted around 1815 and although she preached only to her own sex, many were converted. Apparently she received no opposition from the travelling preachers and indeed was appreciated and 'encouraged to proceed'. Taft comments that 'if female labours had always been properly countenanced amongst the Wesleyan Methodists, it is likely no other religious denomination would have produced such a number of eminently useful females. Miss Lutton was not only allowed, but also exhorted to use the talent committed to her care'.[22]

However, the 1803 Conference edict meant that women preachers in Wesleyan Methodism found it increasingly difficult to exercise their ministry and even though in 1804 the Conference was very short of male preachers it would not sanction the use of women. The 1803 regulation remained in force until 1910 when the phrase 'address only her sex' was deleted, though with an addendum restricting women to preaching in neighbourhoods in which there was no special opposition.[23] This was official Wesleyan policy up to 1918. A paragraph in the report of the 1885 Wesleyan Methodist Conference, Newcastle-on-Tyne reveals the tenor of Wesleyan thinking before these changes:

> 'The subject of 'female preaching' came up in connection
> with the printing of a woman's name as a Local-preacher
> upon a Circuit plan. While the Spirit of the Lord is
> poured forth upon his handmaidens as well as his
> servants, we may not close the mouths of holy women to
> whom the Spirit gives utterance; but to copy the example
> of the Society of Friends, and acknowledge the public
> ministry of women in precisely the same manner as that
> of men, is both inexpedient and unscriptural.'[24]

So within Wesleyan Methodism the subject of women preaching lay dormant till the twentieth century.

The non-Wesleyan Connexions

Things were very different in the non-Wesleyan traditions where women were widely used, both as travelling and local preachers. Briefly, women travelling preachers were used in Primitive Methodism from the very start until 1861 and in the Bible Christian itinerancy till 1874, with some continuing in China for many more years. Obviously before these women could become itinerants they were local preachers (though often only for a very short time) and after retirement, usually because of marriage or ill-health brought on by the strain of the work, they reverted to local preacher status and continued to work zealously. The greatest number of women travelling preachers in Primitive Methodism was twenty six (in 1834) and in the Bible Christian Connexion twenty six (in 1826). These women represented only a very small percentage of the women who preached locally in their own circuits throughout the nineteenth century. In many cases their stories cannot now be traced in any detail, and except for brief obituaries in the connexional magazines many have vanished without trace. We can only hazard a guess at the difficulties and dangers they faced and at the dedication which they showed in order to proclaim their faith in season and out of season, indoors and out of doors. Two stories from *The Primitive Methodist Magazine* paint a picture of the devoted work of these women local preachers.

The story of Elizabeth Elliott is a tragic one. Born in Bristol in 1810, Elizabeth was converted in 1824. Her story reads:

> 'It was not long before she made good use of the talents the Lord had given her. Having received a divine commission from above, she went out, with undaunted courage, into highways and hedges, to compel sinners to come in . . . The word of the Lord abundantly prospered in her hands; so that her labour of love was not in vain in the Lord. Through her instrumentality God raised up many living witnesses . . . She has left behind many mourning seals of her ministry, which are indeed "Living epistles, read and known of all men". She was an excellent speaker; generally short; but very powerful. She preached the Gospel with the Holy Ghost sent down from heaven. A great influence generally attended the word that dropped from her lips.'

We are told:

> 'At the beginning of her pious course she had to endure much persecution; but as her day was, so was her strength. Her will was swallowed up in doing and suffering the will of God. She was a most willing labourer for the Lord. I believe she never wilfully nor carelessly neglected an appointment. And if any other person's appointment wanted supplying, she would give all possible diligence to supply it, if in her power. In labours for souls she was abundant.'

Elizabeth preached at Porthywaen (Shropshire) at 2.00 pm on 17 April 1825 and one of the local preachers present reported that three times she said, – 'This may be the last time I shall speak to you in this place.' On

Saturday 23 April, just before 2.00 pm Elizabeth set off to walk to her Sunday appointment. She had to cross the river beyond Pant. There was a chain fence across the river to prevent cattle from straying and the ferry-man ought to have crossed below the chain, but set off above it. The force of the current drove the boat into the fence, upsetting it. Elizabeth and the ferry-man's wife were drowned. Although extensive search was made throughout Saturday night and all day Sunday her body was not found until Monday evening. Elizabeth was fifteen years and three months when she died.[25]

Around the time of Elizabeth Elliott's birth, at the other side of the country in Lincolnshire, another Elizabeth in her late thirties joined the Primitive Methodists. Elizabeth Swinton, born at Thurlby on 11 April 1776, had been brought up in a church-going family. Soon after becoming a Primitive Methodist, she

'began to hold forth to others the blessings of which she had herself become the partaker. Her zeal and courage were conspicuous from her first attempts to preach; and she was no less distinguished for labouring in the open air. She was in the habit of visiting the villages during the annual feasts, at which times not a few of the "baser sort" are gathered together for all kinds of mischief and wickedness. In the centre of a village, surrounded with scores of such characters, in different degrees of intoxication, making all sorts of noises, and missiles flying in all directions, she had stood firm and undaunted, and faced the rabble, and poured upon them, in no very measured terms, the awful truths of the Divine word. And it is a fact, that many of those characters felt the force of the truth as delivered by her, and became the fruits of her zealous labours.

Her appearance in the pulpit was somewhat singular, but very impressive. She generally wore a white or buff dress; and being of sallow complexion, her appearance was striking. The singularity of her dress and appearance induced many to come and hear her, or rather to see her, wherever she preached. And not a few who were actuated by mere curiosity in coming to see and hear her, were mercifully regarded by the gracious Saviour, and brought to a knowledge of himself.'

Elizabeth was buried in Lincoln and it is perhaps a remarkable tribute to Primitive Methodism and to the work of a woman local preacher that the *Stamford Mercury* reported her funeral:

'Mrs Swinton, the Primitive Methodist preacher, who for thirty-seven years devoted a large portion of her time to the teaching of the gospel, was interred in St. Botolph's, on Sunday last. How this humble woman was beloved, is shown by the fact that 1,500 people assembled to witness the funeral.'

A memorial tablet was erected in the Portland-place Primitive Methodist chapel Lincoln, to her and her husband:

'Sacred To the memory of ISAAC SWINTON, Who died October 11th 1852, aged eighty years. Also ELIZABETH his wife, Who died March 17th 1853, aged seventy-seven years. She was thirty-seven years a Primitive Methodist local preacher. "She hath done what she could." '[26]

Several points of interest arise from these two stories which are borne out by other Primitive Methodist obituaries. First, there is the very young age at which many of the early women preachers started their ministry, for example Sarah Mason (16), Hannah Hardy (18), and Ellen Cooper (19). Although it is not possible to give definite figures for local preachers, what was true of the women itinerants presumably applied also to the local preachers. Secondly, it was often remarked how the novelty value of a woman preacher drew crowds to hear her. The Primitive Methodists were only too willing to exploit this if it brought people to hear the saving Gospel, so when Primitive Methodism, in its wisdom, decided to 'side-line' its women travelling preachers, women local preachers, exhorters and evangelists were still readily accepted and widely used. In many cases women preachers suffered persecution in a variety of forms, but as this is equally true of the men I feel that it was more Primitive Methodism itself which was under attack, rather than women because of their sex.

The women local preachers whose obituaries were printed in *The Primitive Methodist Magazine* were presumably the tip of the iceberg and there must have been many more women up and down the country

---

COMMANDING A GOOD COLLECTION!

Horsforth
28 Feb 1855

'Dear Sister Scupham,

The Horsforth Society are wishful to have you to preach for them on the 11 of March. I trust you will do your utmost to oblige us. The person appointed for the day is the late Mr Reynard, and it being the time appointed for the Quarterly Collection, and our Circuit Funds being low, we wish to enlist your services as we know you can command a good congregation and collection.

Now do come for afternoon and evening and if you can't possibly preach twice, will you preach at night? I am told to say that you must not deny us. As it is getting so near the time will you please to write per return of post?

With kind regards to Mr S. and praying that you may have every needful supply of the Spirit of grace.

I am, Yours affectionately,
R. Baxter'

(Sister Scupham (died 1882) was a Leeds Primitive Methodist connected with the Quarry Hill society (Leeds First Circuit) for many years. She was the wife of Mr J. Scupham, both of them being local preachers. Beckworth comments that this was not uncommon 'in those days' (the middle decades of the nineteenth century) though the Scuphams stipulated that they should never be planned at the same time. Their son, Alderman William Scupham 1829-1896, was a successful Leeds businessman. See Wm Beckworth *A Book of Remembrance: Records of Leeds Primitive Methodism* 1910.)

Letter loaned by the late John Scupham of Hutton Rudby.

---

working faithfully, and without formal recognition. Several obituaries mention the fact that both husband and wife were local preachers, for example Mr and Mrs Dunn of Tidington in the Banbury Circuit, and Mr and Mrs Gardner of the Brinkworth Circuit, or other members of the family such as Mrs Eliza Beavan and her sister in the Monmouth area. Quite a number were local preachers for many years such as Hannah Hardy of Ripley who became a local preacher at eighteen and was on the plan for forty years till her death at the age of fifty-eight; Jane Gardner (Brinkworth Circuit) and Sarah Lawley (Prees Green Circuit) both served for twenty years.

The Bible Christian experience reflects closely that of the Primitive Methodists. Both connexions were prepared to make use of all means available to spread their message and to recognise women as equal workers with men. *The Minutes of the Bible Christian Connexion* of 1819 posed the question: 'What are our thoughts on women preachers?' with the reply 'We believe God can enable a woman as well as a man to speak to edification and comfort.'[27]

The earliest woman preacher of the connexion was Johanna Brooks Neale, who was a Bible Christian for forty-three years. Expelled from her local parish church in Morwenstow in 1816 for giving a public testimony, she left the church to find many of the congregation at the gate and spoke to them for about half an hour with great effect. William O'Bryan visited her and a society was formed. Johanna continued to preach and in 1823 joined with William O'Bryan in conducting a revival. One of the people affected by her address when she was expelled from the parish church was Miss Emily Cottle. The Cottle family were very supportive and became staunch members of the connexion. Emily herself was born at Brexworthy, Devon on the 10th June 1792. In 1803 the family moved to Youlston, near Morwenstow, Cornwall. On the 13th February 1816 William O'Bryan visited the area and came to know the Cottle family. Emily was one of the first to become a Bible Christian on the 23rd March and the rest of the family soon joined her. Before very long she started to pray in public, to exhort, then finally to preach:

> 'She also filled up a useful place in the church, as a local preacher, holding meetings on Sundays and week-day evenings, always embracing every opportunity of working for God. She has walked many miles (when she might have rode) to publish the glad tidings of salvation.'[28]

For a little while Emily had accompanied another female speaker as a volunteer in Devonshire, but in May 1818 for the first time she had 'an appointment to take a Circuit'. This was in the Michaelstow Circuit and so on 23rd she, with Mary O'Bryan, who was about eleven years old and already a preacher, set off. Her diary for that period shows that although she was not regarded as an itinerant she travelled considerable distances, taking many meetings in Cornwall and Devon. At the end of January 1819 Emily went to Devon to help look after her aunt and family who were suffering from a fever. Unfortunately she soon succumbed to the disease herself, and was taken home where she died on 21st February 1819 at the age of twenty-seven.

Another well-known family in the early history of the Bible Christians were the Reeds; four of them were preachers, of whom three, including Catherine, became itinerants. The fourth, Grace, was a very acceptable local preacher. Grace was born at Holwell, Devon on 30th

September 1802 and became a Bible Christian around the age of thirteen or fourteen. Apparently she felt a compelling need to tell others of salvation, and although she was well aware that she would be severely censured for preaching did not let this deter her from taking services and prayer meetings. A letter from Agnes Bear to Catherine Reed, dated 26th February, 1822, gives some indication of Grace's talents and usefulness:

> 'Her words were few, and seasoned with grace and such as ministered grace unto the hearers . . .'

> 'Her public discourses were generally such as suited the congregations which she had to address; and I believe they were delivered in demonstration of the spirit, and with power. I believe she always felt the importance of the subject on which she spoke; and it hath been made a blessing to many souls.'[29]

From June 1820 Grace's health deteriorated and she died on 1st October 1821. After the funeral at Holwell her coffin was carried by six preachers to Lake where she was buried in Ebenezer Chapel burying ground. Her grave-stone records that she

> 'was about five years a Member of the Society of Arminian Bible Christians, and some time a Local Preacher in which capacities she adorned her Profession, and sweetly fell asleep in Jesus, Oct. 1, 1821, Aged 19 years.'[30]

In *The Arminian Magazine*, later called *The Bible Christian Magazine* of 1823, there is an interesting account of the impact made by a female local preacher called Sophia Willis, who was working in the London Mission with William Strongman. Entitled 'The Female Field Preacher' it appeared in a weekly publication called *The Pulpit* and is an indication of the interest roused by female preachers:

> 'Passing through the fields, between the City-Road and Islington, on Friday evening, May 16th, my attention was drawn towards a number of persons collected together against the wall of the Britannia skittle-ground. I approached them, and found they were assembled around a young female, apparently about twenty-two or three years of age, who was standing behind a chair, and praying very earnestly. There was another young person

standing on the left side of her, most probably her sister, as they dressed nearly alike, and in the neat and simple habits of Friends . . . The auditory was not numerous, but it was attentive; and amongst others, I particularly noticed three countrymen with scythes on their shoulders, who seemed particularly so, I trust not without benefit. The preacher appeared very earnest, she delivered her observations without hesitation. – indeed with great fluency; with distinct enunciation, and generally, in very correct language. I know not who she is; but it was said, she lived somewhere near the place I heard her. The dress she wore was doubtlessly assumed merely on account of its simplicity, as I conceive she could not belong to the society of Friends.

'She needs great encouragement to undertake and persevere in such a task; and no doubt she will have it from Him who alone can give it her in this world of nothingness and vanity.'[31]

The second recorded meeting of the Chatham Bible Christian Circuit reveals the names of Mary Malyon and Sarah Clarke as local preachers on full plan. Mary continued till 10th August 1830. Sarah married in 1826 and appears to have taken an appointment for the Primitive Methodists because the minutes state that if she continued so to do her name should be taken off her own plan. As it continued to appear there until her death in 1828 she must have heeded the warning. There were at about the same time three other women 'on trial', but their work was brief.[32] Evidence from other Bible Christian circuits reveals women working as local preachers – e.g. Weare in Somerset, where the Bible Christian Circuit Book (1822-1853) shows for 1849/50 18 local preachers (14 men, 4 women) and for 1850/51 15 (13 men, 2 women).[33]

It seems unlikely that there were many official women local preachers in the Methodist New Connexion and indeed the Stalybridge Methodist New Connexion Local Preachers' Meeting, 25th December 1837, resolved that 'it is the opinion of this meeting that female preaching is unscriptural'.[34] Nevertheless Taft records the case of Miss Hannah Hunt:

'a native of Breaston, in the county of Derby, where she chiefly resides, except when for religious purposes she visits the different churches belonging to the people with whom she is united in Christian fellowship. She is a member of the New Methodist connexion, and has been preaching the gospel in many large towns and country villages in this kingdom, for the last twenty years. The Lord has taken away her natural sight, but he has continued her spiritual vision, so that she clearly sees the things that belong for her peace, and is likewise endued with gifts and talents to preach, to edification, exhortation, and to comfort, before any community of Christians . . .

'She has been in Lancashire, Cheshire, Yorkshire, Derbyshire, Staffordshire, and Nottingham, preaching the unsearchable riches of Christ – endeavouring to persuade the children of men to be reconciled to God. She has preached in various respectable chapels, to the astonishment of hundreds, and it is said she has been made the honoured instrument in the conversion of the many.'[35]

In a symposium on 'The position of women in the church' in *The Christian Ambassador* (1885) Thomas Parsons commented that 'The New Connexion and the United Methodist Free Churches permit women preaching, but to what extent we cannot say.'[36] It is not known if or how many women local preachers there may have been in the United Methodist Free Churches, but Oliver Beckerlegge says that in common with the Primitive Methodists and Bible Christians the Arminian Methodists used women preachers and cites the work of Elizabeth Evans, to whom reference has already been made. He further says that the Arminian Methodists 'altogether brought into the Union (with the Wesleyan Methodist Association in the mid-1830s) some 1,200 members and seventy local preachers'.[37] Some of these were probably women.

There is little detailed information available of the work of women local preachers in the later period to fill out the picture, but from references in the Primitive Methodist and Bible Christian magazines it is apparent that they were used in the circuits, particularly as evangelists and special preachers for anniversaries and chapel openings, throughout the nineteenth century. Again perhaps the novelty factor was evident here – it would be important to have a large congregation on such occasions and who knows what good might be done to those who came chiefly through curiosity. Many of the women preachers were ministers' wives whose work was really an extension of their husbands' ministry, for example Mrs Mary Hallam (née Hadfield) 'who was known throughout the northern circuits as a woman of exceptional gifts and usefulness. She frequently preached in all the circuits in which her lot was cast and with much acceptance'. Mrs Ann Hirst, when her husband was prevented by a snow storm from returning home to take a service, took his place by first reading a sermon and then expounding 'and revealed such surprisisng gifts that her name was soon placed upon the plan as a preacher. She became very popular as a 'special' preacher . . . Many in later years testified that she was the ablest woman preacher they had ever heard . . . For sixty years she preached the Gospel as the Spirit gave her utterance'.[38]

Primitive Methodism had a number of local preachers who were regarded as travelling preachers by their own circuits, if not by the Conference. More properly these should be designated as hired local preachers. The official distinction between the two was;

> 'one part are removable only by agreement of the circuits
> one with another or by agreement of one district with
> another, and these are called hired local preachers; the
> other part are removable by the Annual Meeting and are
> called travelling preachers. This is all the difference
> between them, in all other respects they are alike.[39]

Study of local circuit records show that when a circuit identified a missionary opportunity and had the necessary money to pay for an extra preacher it would 'take out' a hired local preacher (often one available locally) for a quarter or so. This means that such preachers appear along with the salaried, regularly stationed preachers, but then disappear from the accounts. Female examples are Hannah Petty (Cheshire); Ann Pugh (Shropshire); Hannah Summerlands (Burton upon Trent) and Mary Thatcher (Hampshire). Later well-known Primitive Methodist women local preachers were Miss Mary Bulmer, who commenced work as a young girl in the north of England in 1888 and conducted many missions, such as one at Tanfield, which resulted in five young people being converted.[40] She was born at Wylam-on-Tyne and accredited as a local preacher in 1891.[41] Obviously highly regarded, she acted at times as a hired local preacher and practically as a travelling preacher, as for example in 1899 when she was called upon to step into the breach in the Stanley circuit on the death of the superintendent minister, followed by the death of the second minister during the next year.[42]   She was also employed in the Chester-le-Street circuit for three years from 1903 and invited to stay for a fourth, but on 8th August 1906 she married the Revd J. E. Leuty and went with him to the Newcastle-under-Lyme circuit. 'Before that event her name had become connexional – indeed, had gone beyond the bounds of Primitive Methodism, for in 1904 she was elected to the National Executive of the Christian Endeavour Council, and visited the great centres of the country.   Her success in the (Newcastle-under-Lyme) circuit was remarkable . . . (and) will never be forgotten.'[43]

AN ANGLICAN CLERIC SPEAKS UP FOR WOMEN PREACHERS

'The Primitive Methodists' plea for employing women preachers is that their preaching has been blessed with success. And as this is the chief evidence for a Methodist preacher's call to the work, I do not see why the ladies, as well as the travelling preachers and the local brethren, should not stand up for the validity of their order.'

(The writer had heard a woman preacher himself and comments:)
'I assure you that I have heard many a worse sermon. There were certainly deaconesses in the Primitive Church; and as Philip the Deacon was an Evangelist perhaps so also was Phoebe the Deaconess. We read in the Acts of daughters that prophesied . . . I would like to establish the validity of ladies' orders . . . I have high hopes of being a successful pleader on their behalf.'

John Hunt (curate of St. Andrew's, Deptford, Sunderland.
Wesley and Wesleyanism; Three Lectures
London and Sunderland 1858, p.51.

Miss Bennett of Chester was a popular preacher greatly in demand in the north west where she conducted revivals with great effect in the 1850s and 1860s.[44]   Mary Ridley from West Cumberland was converted in 1829 and became a local preacher in 1831.   She acted virtually as a travelling preacher for fifteen years in the Alston area before doing evangelistic work throughout the Border counties.[45] Selina Jackson from Derbyshire (later to become Mrs Shimwell, then Mrs Llewellyn) became a local preacher in 1846 and acted as a hired local preacher from 1847-9. Her obituary describes her as

'a woman of vigorous thought, eloquent utterance, and godly life, and in great request for special services in many of the most important circuits in the Midland counties. She laboured with great acceptability and usefulness as hired local preacher . . .'.[46]

Patricia Powell (Mrs Mason) from Herefordshire became a local preacher in June 1847 and preached because of the travelling preacher's illness for five months in 1850 before her own health gave way. She acted as a hired local preacher in 1856-7, but finally had to retire through ill-health.[47] Finally mention must be made of Jane Spoor (Mrs Ralph Cook), from the north east, who was converted around 1827, became a Primitive Methodist member, an exhorter, then a hired local preacher, working with her itinerant brother Joseph, until the strain became too great. However she continued as a local preacher and a class leader, dying on 25th May 1878.[48] These examples indicate the geographical spread of women who were active in the ministry in local situations, showing that many were working energetically to spread the Gospel wherever they were.

The whole question of women preaching was never very far from the minds of church authorities, especially as the Methodist connexions became more settled, respectable and conformist, which usually meant toning down more extreme practices such as fervent evangelism and female preaching. *The Christian Ambassador* had a number of articles on the subject, usually dealing with women in the itinerancy, but much of the comment is relevant to all types of female preaching. In particular in 1885 there was the report of a symposium consisting of six papers on 'The position of women in the church'. Most of the contributors, who were all ministers, are rather ambivalent – they do not wholeheartedly approve of women preaching, but on the other hand they are not prepared to go so far as to deny the right of some women to preach. The most positive attitude was that of Thomas Parson (already quoted above) who submitted the fifth paper in which he stated that he agreed with the Wesleyans that women might be used 'but (they) make the conditions for admission into their pulpits so stringent that only women of unquestionable piety and talent can expect to occupy that position'. Parson's own view was that 'Female preaching will never be other than incidental, accessory, unreliable'. Then he went on to urge that female candidates for the plan should be examined as the men were and that they should be under 'circuit control' and not have a 'roving commission'. Parsons had alluded in his paper to the abuse of female preaching, so maybe this is a reference to the fact that when women ceased to be stationed as itinerants in Primitive Methodism many continued to act as evangelists, taking special services and missions, no doubt providing a novelty attraction, which was resented by some of the men whose congregations were being drawn away by the women preachers.[49]

Very often only the surname or initials of local preachers are given on circuit plans and records so it cannot be determined who, if any, were women. Several women are listed as 'Auxiliaries'. It is very interesting to analyse the plans of the Shefford Primitive Methodist Circuit (Andover Branch) for 18th January 1835 to 10th January 1836 which contain the name of 'Jane Farr' – presumably written in full to distinguish her from 'J. Farr snr.' (her father?). In the first quarter Jane had fifteen appointments on eight of the twelve Sundays and also was one of the speakers at a missionary meeting on 1st March at 2.00 pm; in the second thirteen on six out of twelve Sundays; in the third twenty on ten out of the thirteen and on the fourth fourteen on ten out of fourteen. In addition she took a service at Faccombe on Wednesday, 9th December. So her workload was considerable and certainly equal to the appointments taken by the preachers listed on the plan above and below her.

1818.	FEB.				MARCH.					APRIL.				NAMES.
PLACES.	1	8	15	22	1	8	15	22	29	5	12	19	26	1 H. Bourne
														2 W. Clowes
Derby 2 and 6	S K	17	8	27	45	10	9 T	7	36	28	17	19	8	3 J. Benton
														4 J. Buxton
Willeton 2 Normanton 6	W A	31	14	36	46	19	37 T	8	17	31	36	8	46	5 R. Weston
														6 J. Wedgwood
Nottingham 2¼ and 6	1	19	10 S	26	9 T	S K	15	TBL	26	18	10 S	9	19	7 W. Warren
														8 T. Hunt
Loughborough 2 and 6	19	M H	S K	17	42	9 T	44	42	10	26	H P	10	6	9 J. Harrison
														10 R. Winfield

A Nottingham Primitive Methodist plan of 1818 on which women preachers are
indicated by their initials, but not included in the list of preachers.
H.B. Kendall *Origin and History of the PM Church* c. 1905, (i) 208.

Full names were given on the 1835 (July 20 – October 12) plan of the Bolton Primitive Methodist circuit. Ann Noble was one of the four travelling preachers, and among the 33 local preachers two were women (16 appointments between them) plus six men and one woman 'on trial' (five appointments).

Twentieth century developments

As the turn of the century approached further debate about women preaching arose in Wesleyan Methodism, and an article entitled 'The place and power of woman in Methodism' by J. W. Walker in *The Wesleyan Methodist Magazine* of 1897 stated:

> 'As preachers they have not been numerous, and possibly may never become so. Long journeys into the country, exposure to rough weather and dark nights, and many other incidents . . . will probably prevent women from coming in large numbers on our plans. But if the question is to be answered in the abstract as to the general eligibility of women for this work, there can be little doubt as to the result . . . The fact remains that women have been and are being put on our plans, and that with the happiest results.'[50]

He goes on to impress on the women that as local preachers they had a seat on the circuit quarterly meeting, which gave them the right to vote on all important matters, a heavy responsibility which must be acepted. Walker concludes by saying that

> 'woman is beginning to share more equally in both the work and the rewards of the future, and this in the church as well as in the world . . . it is one of the many evidences of the adaptability of Methodism to modern times that it has . . . made such large opportunity for women to consecrate their talents to the highest service.'[51]

His comments are particularly interesting in that they appear to confirm that women had been and were being used by the Wesleyans up to the time at which he was writing, even if examples were rare and not only among the Wesleyans. Statistics of women local preachers in the various branches of Methodism are not easy to find but it seems that in London Primitive Methodism in 1896 there were only 11 women out of 432 local preachers.[52]

Significant official recognition of women local preachers after the 1910 resolution referred to earlier came in 1918 when the *Wesleyan Methodist Minutes* stated:

> '*Women Local Preachers*. The Conference declares that women are eligible to become fully accredited Local

Preachers on the same conditions and shall hereafter enjoy the same rights and privileges as men who are Local Preachers.'[53]

The following year there was a further development:

> '*Wesley Deaconesses and Women Preachers.* The Conference authorises Local Preachers' Meetings, in the case of Wesley Deaconesses and other women who have already been preaching under the sanction of the Regulations of conference of 1910, to receive them upon full plan without further examination.'[54]

The non-Wesleyan connexions never broke down their local preachers' statistics by sex, and neither did Wesleyan Methodism until 1927 when

---

WESLEYAN WOMEN PREACHERS AFTER WORLD WAR I

(i) 'We welcome the addition to the ranks of Local Preachers of three women, with three on trial. Now that women are taking such a keen interest in public affairs generally, we trust that more may be called to consecrate their gifts and graces to this higher work . . .'

(ii) 'The wish expressed last year that more women might hear the call to consecrate their gift and graces to this work has been realised, and we now report 9 as fully-accredited Local Preachers with 4 on trial. We trust that these numbers will be considerably augmented in the near future.'

Birmingham and Shrewsbury WM
District LP Committee, 1920 and 1921.

---

the numbers of women are given as 'Women fully accredited 442; women on Trial 68; women received on full plan 43'. The fully accredited numbers for the following years were: 1928 475; 1929 523; 1930 561; 1931 598; and 1932 642.[55] In the first returns after Union, those of 1933, there were 1,422 women in the Methodist Church who were fully accredited (110 placed on full plan that year) with 208 on trial.[56] These figures seem to imply that at Union 780 women came into the Methodist church from the non-Wesleyan traditions, although it is necessary to take into account those who would have become Wesleyan local preachers anyway (an average of 40 over the previous 5 years) and those who died or left.

Returning to the Wesleyan Methodist statistics the schedule for 1928 not only gives the total for the whole connexion, but also for each district. Sample percentages of women preachers by district are South Wales (7.36%); London First (4.2%); Devonport and Plymouth (3.59%); Halifax and Bradford (3.43%). At the bottom of the list come Manchester (1.55%); Portsmouth (l.53%); First North Wales (l.32%); Second North Wales (l.08%); and Isle of Man (0.60%).[57] Looking at the 1932 totals for Wesleyan Methodism there were 18,785 local preachers, 642 (3.42%) of these being women, while for Methodism as a whole in 1933 the figures were 34,948 with 1,422 women (4.1%).[58] Studying these district statistics and selecting districts which most nearly equate with each other, especially for those areas where non-Wesleyan traditions were strongest, it is found that there were increases in Scotland of 3.61%; Carlisle 2.92%; Newcastle-upon-Tyne 1.2%; East Anglia 1.1%; Lincoln and Grimsby 0.77%; and Stoke-on-Trent 0.69%; (Hull had a decrease of 0.57%). These increases must indicate the greater relative numbers of women local preachers in the non-Wesleyan branches.

According to *The Methodist Local Preachers' Who's Who, 1934* there were 106 women who were 'Fully Accredited' before 1910. Unfortunately it is not possible, in most cases, to tell from which branch of Methodism they came. Altogether there are 739 women listed in the survey, but few indicate their former connexion and so it is impossible to state categorically that at Union there were more women in one branch than another. However, of the 44 women preachers who were ministers' wives or widows 19 or 43.2% were Wesleyan and 25 or 56.8% were Primitive Methodists, but there were none from the United Methodist Church. No firm conclusion can be drawn from this small sample. 67 women were or had been deaconesses or missionaries.[59] Statistics of local preachers continued to be published in full until the late 1960s.

It is interesting to note that the Local Preachers' Meeting of the Jersey French Circuit reported on 10th May 1923:

> 'we have the happy satisfaction of welcoming Miss
> Susan Renouf after oral examination and trial sermon as
> the first lady local preacher in the Channel Islands.'[60]

And the Circuit plan of the same circuit in 1938 has the name of Miss Enid Le Feuvre, who was accredited in 1931, and another woman is listed under 'D'Autres Aides'.

Out of a dozen randomly selected 1994 plans, representing different parts of the British Isles, four have 50% or more women local preachers; six have 25% or over and the other two around 20%. Looking at the number of women 'Fully Accredited' since 1970 all but two of the circuits show that 50% or more women became local preachers after that date. Does this indicate a wider acceptance of women? Is there perhaps a link between women becoming local preachers and going on to enter the full-time presbyteral or diaconal ministry? There is room for further research here.

RESPONSES TO WOMEN PREACHERS IN MORE RECENT TIMES

'When on trial I was appointed to preach at Seacroft near Leeds. My father was a local preacher, and the old steward greeted me warmly. As the time went on he became agitated and when the vestry clock reached 10.30 said "Wheer's thi father?" I admitted to being the appointed preacher. He put on his glasses, inspected the plan, groaned, and opened the door into the chapel.'

The above is a memory of Margaret Batty. Mrs Dee Moss of Charlbury, Oxford, offers the following recollection:

'A steward some forty years ago in the Wisbech Circuit disapproved of women preachers. He invariably introduced me as "Brother Moss".' However, she also recalls the following:

'Much later in the Kidderminster Circuit a charming and sincere steward always prayed with me in the vestry thus: "O Lord, bless this 'ere 'andmaiden what 'as climbed thine 'oly 'ill to lead our worship."'

Women feature on the Bristol Road (Birmingham) Wesleyan Methodist circuit plan from 1937 and continued to play an increasing part, especially during the war years until the present day when about half of the total are women. The oldest local preacher in the circuit is Mrs Mary Worrall who was fully accredited in 1930 and remembers that

> 'I thought God was calling me to be a missionary . . . The circuit was very dependent on local preachers . . . I was put 'on note' and helped with services under the guidance of another local preacher. A close friend was accepted at the same time. I can only remember one other woman preacher . . . I don't remember any suggestion that we should *not* become local preachers because we were women, it never entered my head and we were welcomed wherever we went . . . I normally cycled, but sometimes borrowed my father's motor cycle.

'I can't remember having any training apart from the services 'on note'. In those days there did not seem to be any organised training and no written examinations, but I did take one or two Methodist correspondence courses. And eventually after two years, I had to preach a trial sermon and answer questions at the LP meeting before being put on to 'full plan' in 1930.'

Mrs Worrall preached in many parts of the country during the next 30 years and was readily welcomed by all the circuits and churches. Then in 1961 she and her husband moved to Northern Ireland where she found a very different situation:

'Most churches in Belfast had their own minister and there was little call on local preachers. But each church had an annual Methodist Womens' Association service for which they wanted a woman preacher! As a result I preached in almost every Methodist Church in Northern Ireland, and also was invited twice to the Cork District, three times to Dublin, also to Donegal, Sligo and two or three churches in the centre of Ireland.'[61]

On a final personal note I became a fully accredited local preacher in 1954, one of a family whose members can count over 350 years local preaching between them, and from 1955-1960 in Scotland I encountered much the same situation as Mrs Worrall did where a woman preacher was rather a novelty and so not only did I preach throughout the Wishaw and Motherwell Circuit but also in most of the Church of Scotland and Baptist churches in the burgh!

It seems that from the early struggles to gain acceptance women local preachers are now equally used alongside their male colleagues and in many circuits equal numerically too. So we can all honour the endeavours of the early women preachers and pay tribute to the countless faithful women who have sought through the years to proclaim the Gospel.

9

DINAH MORRIS PREACHES ON A VILLAGE GREEN

From the novel *Adam Bede*
by
George Eliot

[George Eliot (1819-1880), whose real name was Mary Ann Evans, was reared in evangelical religion, and though abandoning orthodox belief in her adult years she retained an admiring affection for some aspects of religion, including Methodism. Her uncle Samuel Evans was a Wesleyan local preacher in the Derbyshire area, and was joined enthusiastically in this work by his wife Elizabeth (née Tomlinson). George Eliot obviously learned her aunt's life story from her own lips, and was inspired to reproduce an imaginative version of it in her novel *Adam Bede* (1859). Dinah Morris (who becomes Dinah Bede) is, therefore, in many essentials Elizabeth Evans. George Eliot sets the novel around the year 1800 and conjures up the spirit of rural Methodism at that time. The revivalism which was soon to produce Primitive Methodism was affecting Wesleyanism profoundly, encouraging informal open-air preaching. In chapter 3 of the novel George Eliot recalls the character of such gatherings, where 'in an amphitheatre of green hills or the deep shade of broad-leaved sycamores a crowd of rough men and weary-hearted women drank in a faith which was a rudimentary culture', linking their thoughts with the past and lifting their imagination above the sordid details of their own lives. It is such an occasion which is described in chapter 2 of the novel, part of which is reproduced below.]

* * * * * *

George Eliot writes . . .

The stronger curiosity of the women had drawn them quite to the edge of the Green, where they could examine more closely the Quaker-like costume and odd deportment of the female Methodists. Underneath the maple there was a small cart which had been brought from the wheelwright's to serve as a pulpit, and round this a couple of benches and a few chairs had been placed. Some of the Methodists were resting on these, with their eyes closed, as if wrapt in prayer or meditation. Others chose to continue standing, and had turned their faces towards the villagers with a look of melancholy compassion, which was highly amusing to Bessy Cranage, the blacksmith's buxom daughter, known to her neighbours as Chad's Bess, who wondered 'why the folks war a-makin' faces a that'ns'. Chad's Bess was the object of peculiar compassion, because her hair, being turned back under a cap which was set at the top of her head, exposed to view an ornament of which she was much prouder than of her red cheeks, namely, a pair of large round ear-rings with false garnets in them, ornaments contemned not only by the Methodists, but by her own cousin and namesake Timothy's Bess, who, with much cousinly feeling, often wished 'them ear-rings' might come to good.

Dinah walked rather quickly, and in advance of her companions, towards the cart under the maple tree. While she was near Seth's tall figure, she looked short, but when she had mounted the cart, and was away from all comparison, she seemed above the middle height of woman, though in reality she did not exceed it – an effect which was due to the slimness of her figure, and the simple line of her black stuff dress. The stranger was struck with surprise as he saw her approach and mount the cart – surprise, not so much at the feminine delicacy of her appearance, as at the total absence of self-consciousness in her demeanour. He had made up his mind to see her advance with a measured step, and a demure solemnity of countenance; he had felt sure that her face would be mantled with a smile of conscious saintship, or else charged with denunciatory bitterness. He knew but two types of Methodist – the ecstatic and the bilious. But Dinah walked as simply as if she were going to market, and seemed as unconscious of her outward appearance as a little boy . . .

Dinah began to speak.

'Dear friends,' she said, in a clear but not loud voice, 'let us pray for a blessing.' She closed her eyes, and hanging her head down a little,

Dinah Morris preaching on a village green. A water colour by E. H. Corbould,
inspired by chapter 2 of George Eliot's novel *Adam Bede*.
(Acknowledgements to Royal Collection Enterprises, Windsor Castle, and Her Majesty the Queen.)

continued in the same moderate tone, as if speaking to some one quite near her:–'Saviour of sinners! when a poor woman, laden with sins, went out to the well to draw water, she found Thee sitting at the well. She knew Thee not; she had not sought Thee, her mind was dark; her life was unholy. But Thou didst speak to her, Thou didst teach her, Thou didst show her that her life lay open before Thee, and yet Thou wast ready to give her that blessing which she had never sought. Jesus! Thou art in the midst of us, and Thou knowest all men: if there is any here like that poor woman – if their minds are dark, their lives unholy – if they have come out not seeking Thee, not desiring to be taught; deal with them according to the free mercy which Thou didst show to her. Speak to them, Lord; open their ears to my message; bring their sins to their minds, and make them thirst for that salvation which Thou art ready to give.

'Lord! Thou art with Thy people still : they see Thee in the night-watches, and their hearts burn within them as Thou talkest with them by the way. And Thou art near to those who have not known Thee: open their eyes that they may see Thee – see Thee weeping over them, and saying "Ye will not come unto me that ye might have life" – see Thee hanging on the cross and saying, "Father, forgive them, for they know not what they do" – see Thee as Thou wilt come again in Thy glory to judge them at the last. Amen.'

Dinah opened her eyes again and paused, looking at the group of villagers, who were now gathered rather more closely on her right hand.

'Dear friends,' she began, raising her voice a little, 'you have all of you been to church, and I think you must have heard the clergyman read these words: "The Spirit of the Lord is upon me, because he hath anointed me to preach the gospel to the poor." Jesus Christ spoke those words – he said he came *to preach the gospel to the poor*: I don't know whether you ever thought about those words much; but I will tell you when I remember first hearing them. It was on just such a sort of evening as this, when I was a little girl, and my aunt, as brought me up, took me to hear a good man preach out of doors, just as we are here. I remember his face well: he was a very old man, and had very long white hair; his voice was very soft and beautiful, not like any voice I had ever heard before. I was a little girl and scarcely knew anything, and this old man seemed to me such a different sort of a man from anybody I had ever seen before, that I thought he had perhaps come down from the sky to preach to us, and I said, "Aunt, will he go back to the sky to-night, like the picture in the Bible?"

'That man of God was Mr. Wesley, who spent his life in doing what our blessed Lord did – preaching the Gospel to the poor – and he entered into his rest eight years ago. I came to know more about him years after, but I was a foolish thoughtless child then, and I remembered only one thing he told us in his sermon. He told us as "Gospel" meant "good news". The Gospel, you know, is what the Bible tells us about God.

'Think of that now! Jesus Christ did really come down from heaven, as I, like a silly child, thought Mr. Wesley did; and what he came down for, was to tell good news about God to the poor. Why, you and me, dear friends, are poor. We have been brought up in poor cottages, and have been reared on oat-cake, and lived coarse; and we haven't been to school much, nor read books, and we don't know much about anything but what happens just round us. We are just the sort of people that want to hear good news. For when anybody's well off, they don't much mind about hearing news from distant parts; but if a poor man or woman's in trouble and has hard work to make out a living, they like to have a letter to tell 'em they've got a friend as will help 'em. To be sure, we can't help knowing something about God, even if we've never heard the Gospel, the good news that our Saviour brought us. For we know everything comes from God: don't you say almost every day, 'This and that will happen, please God'; and 'We shall begin to cut the grass soon, please God to send us a little more sunshine'? We know very well we are altogether in the hands of God: we didn't bring ourselves into the world, we can't keep ourselves alive while we're sleeping; the daylight, and the wind , and the corn, and the cows to give us milk – everything we have comes from God. And he gave us our souls, and put love between parents and children, and husband and wife. But is that as much as we want to know about God? We see he is great and mighty, and can do what he will: we are lost, as if we was struggling in great waters when we try to think of him.

'But perhaps doubts come into your mind like this: Can God take much notice of us poor people? Perhaps he only made the world for the great and the wise and the rich. It doesn't cost him much to give us our little handful of victual and bit of clothing; but how do we know he cares for us any more than we care for the worms and things in the garden, so as we rear our carrots and onions? Will God take care of us when we die? And has he any comfort for us when we are lame and sick and helpless? Perhaps, too, he is angry with us; else why does the blight come, and the bad harvests, and the fever, and all sorts of pain and trouble? For our life is full of trouble, and if God sends us good, he seems to send bad too. How is it? how is it?

'Ah! dear friends, we are in sad want of good news about God; and what does other good news signify if we haven't that? For everything else comes to an end, and when we die we leave it all. But God lasts when everything else is gone. What shall we do if he is not our friend?'

Then Dinah told how the good news had been brought, and how the mind of God towards the poor had been made manifest in the life of Jesus, dwelling on its lowliness and its acts of mercy.

'So you see, dear friends', she went on, 'Jesus spent his time almost all in doing good to poor people; he preached out of doors to them and took pains with them. Not but what he did good to the rich too, for he was full of love to all men, only he saw as the poor were more in want of his help. So he cured the lame and the sick and the blind, and he worked miracles, to feed the hungry, because, he said, he was sorry for them; and he was very kind to the little children, and comforted those who had lost their friends: and he spoke very tenderly to poor sinners that were sorry for their sins.

'Ah! wouldn't you love such a man if you saw him – if he was here in this village? What a kind heart he must have! What a friend he would be to go to in trouble! How pleasant it must be to be taught by him!

'Well, dear friends who *was* this man? Was he only a good man – a very good man, and no more – like our dear Mr. Wesley, who has been taken from us? ... He was the Son of God – "in the image of the Father", the Bible says; that means, just like God, who is the beginning and end of all things – the God we want to know about. So then, all the love that Jesus showed to the poor is the same love that God has for us. We can understand what Jesus felt, because he came in a body like ours, and spoke words such as we speak to each other. We were afraid to think what God was before – the God who made the world and the sky and the thunder and lightning. We could never see him; we could only see the things he had made; and some of these things was very terrible, so as we might well tremble when we thought of him. But our blessed Saviour has showed us what God is in a way us poor ignorant people can understand ; he has showed us what God's heart is, what are his feelings towards us.

'But let us see a little more about what Jesus came on earth for. Another time he said, "I came to seek and to save that which was lost"; and another time, "I came not to call the righteous but sinners to repentance".

'The *lost!* . . . *Sinners!* . . . Ah! dear friends, does that mean you and me?'

Hitherto the traveller had been chained to the spot against his will by the charm of Dinah's mellow treble tones, which had a variety of modulation like that of a fine instrument touched with the unconscious skill of musical instinct. The simple things she said seemed like novelties, as a melody strikes us with a new feeling when we hear it sung by the pure voice of a boyish chorister; the quiet depth of conviction with which she spoke seemed in itself an evidence for the truth of her message. He saw that she had thoroughly arrested her hearers. The villagers had pressed nearer to her, and there was no longer anything but grave attention on all faces She spoke slowly, though quite fluently, often pausing after a question, or before any transition of ideas.   There was no change of attitude, no gesture; the effect of her speech was produced entirely by the inflections of her voice, and when she came to the question, 'Will God take care of us when we die?' she uttered it in such a tone of plaintive appeal that the tears came into some of the hardest eyes. The stranger had ceased to doubt, as he had done at the first glance, that she could fix the attention of her rougher hearers, but still he wondered whether she could have that power of rousing their more violent emotions, which must surely be a necessary seal of her vocation as a Methodist preacher, until she came to the words, 'Lost! – Sinners!' when there was a great change in her voice and manner. She had made a long pause before the exclamation, and the pause seemed to be filled by agitating thoughts that showed themselves in her features. Her pale face became paler; the circles under her eyes deepened, as they do when tears half gather without falling; and the mild loving eyes took an expression of appalled pity, as if she had suddenly discerned a destroying angel hovering over the heads of the people.   Her voice became deep and muffled, but there was still no gesture. Nothing could be less like the ordinary type of the Ranter than Dinah. She was not preaching as she heard others preach, but speaking directly from her own emotions, and under the inspiration of her own simple faith.

But now she had entered into a new current of feeling. Her manner became less calm, her utterance more rapid and agitated, as she tried to bring home to the people their guilt, their wilful darkness, their state of disobedience to God – as she dwelt on the hatefulness of sin, the Divine holiness, and the sufferings of the Saviour, by which a way had been opened for their salvation. At last it seemed as if, in her yearning desire to reclaim the lost sheep, she could not be satisfied by addressing her hearers as a body. She appealed first to one and then to another, beseeching them with tears to turn to God while there was yet time; painting to them the desolation of their souls, lost in sin, feeding on the husks of this miserable world, far away from God their Father; and then the love of the Saviour, who was waiting and watching for their return . . .

Dinah had that belief in visible manifestations of Jesus, which is common among the Methodists, and she communicated it irresistibly to her hearers: she made them feel that he was among them bodily, and might at any moment show himself to them in some way that would strike anguish and penitence into their hearts.

'See!' she exlaimed, turning to the left, with her eyes fixed on a point above the heads of the people – 'see where our blessed Lord stands and weeps, and stretches out his arms towards you. Hear what he says : "How often would I have gathered you as a hen gathereth her chickens under her wings, and ye would not!" . . . and ye would not,' she repeated, in a tone of pleading reproach, turning her eyes on the people again. 'See the print of the nails on his dear hands and feet. It is your sins that made them! Ah! how pale and worn he looks! He has gone through all that great agony in the garden, when his soul was sorrowful even unto death and the great drops of sweat fell like blood to the ground. They spat upon him and buffeted him, they scourged him, they mocked him, they laid the heavy cross on his bruised shoulders. Then they nailed him up. Ah! What pain! His lips are parched with thirst, and they mock him still in his great agony; yet with those parched lips he prays for them, "Father, forgive them, for they know not what they do." Then a horror of great darkness fell upon him, and he felt what sinners feel when they are for ever shut out from God. That was the last drop in the cup of bitterness. "My God, my God!" he cries, "why hast Thou forsaken me?"

'All this he bore for you! For you – and you never think of him; for you – and you turn your backs on him; you don't care what he has gone through for you. Yet he is not weary of toiling for you; he has risen from the dead, he is praying for you at the right hand of God – "Father, forgive them for they know not what they do." And he is upon this earth too; he is among us; he is there close to you now; I see his wounded body and his look of love.'

Here Dinah turned to Bessy Cranage, whose bonny youth and evident vanity had touched her with pity.

'Poor child! poor child! He is beseeching you, and you don't listen to him. You think of ear-rings and fine gowns and caps, and you never think of the Saviour who died to save your precious soul. Your cheeks will be shrivelled one day, your hair will be grey, your poor body will be thin and tottering! Then you will begin to feel that your soul is not saved; then you will have to stand before God dressed in your sins, in your evil tempers and vain thoughts. And Jesus, who stands ready to help you now, won't help you then: because you won't have him to be your Saviour, he will be your judge. Now he looks at you with love and mercy, and says, "Come to me that you may have life"; then he will turn away from you, and say, "Depart from me into everlasting fire!" '

Poor Bessy's wide-open black eyes began to fill with tears, her great red cheeks and lips became quite pale, and her face was distorted like a little child's before a burst of crying.

'Ah! poor blind child!' Dinah went on, 'think if it should happen to you as it once happened to a servant of God in the days of her vanity. *She* thought of her lace caps, and saved all her money to buy 'em; she thought nothing about how she might get a clean heart and a right spirit, she only wanted to have better lace than other girls. And one day when she put her new cap on and looked in the glass, she saw a bleeding Face crowned with thorns. That face is looking at you now,' – here Dinah pointed to a spot close in front of Bessy. – 'Ah! tear off those follies! cast them away from you, as if they were stinging adders. They *are* stinging you – they are poisoning your soul – they are dragging you down into a dark bottomless pit, where you will sink for ever, and for ever, and for ever, further away from light and God.'

Bessy could bear it no longer: a great terror was upon her, and wrenching her ear-rings from her ears, she threw them down before her, sobbing aloud. Her father, Chad, frightened lest he should be 'laid hold on' too, this impression on the rebellious Bess striking him as nothing less than a miracle, walked hastily away, and began to work at his anvil by way of reassuring himself. 'Folks mun ha' hoss shoes, praichin' or no praichin': the divil canna lay hould o' me for that,' he muttered to himself.

But now Dinah began to tell of the joys that were in store for the penitent, and to describe in her simple way the divine peace and love with which the soul of the believer is filled – how the sense of God's love turns poverty into riches, and satisfies the soul, so that no uneasy desire vexes it, no fear alarms it: how, at last, the very temptation to sin is extinguished, and heaven is begun upon earth, because no cloud passes between the soul and God, who is its eternal sun.

'Dear friends,' she said at last, 'brothers and sisters, whom I love as those for whom my Lord has died, believe me, I know what this great blessedness is; and because I know it, I want you to have it too. I am poor, like you: I have to get my living with my hands; but no lord nor lady can be so happy as me, if they haven't got the love of God in their souls. Think what it is – not to hate anything but sin; to be full of love to every creature; to be frightened at nothing; to be sure that all things will turn to good; not to mind pain, because it is our Father's will; to know that nothing – no, not if the earth was to be burnt up, or the waters come and drown us – nothing could part us from God who loves us, and who fills our souls with peace and joy, because we are sure that whatever he wills is holy, just and good.

'Dear friends, come and take this blessedness; it is offered to you; it is the good news that Jesus came to preach to the poor. It is not like the riches of this world, so that the more one gets the less the rest can have. God is without end; his love is without end –

> "Its streams the whole creation reach,
> So plenteous is the store;
> Enough for all, enough for each,
> Enough for evermore." '*

Dinah had been speaking for at least an hour, and the reddening light of the parting day seemed to give a solemn emphasis to her closing words. The stranger, who had been interested in the course of her sermon, as if it had been the development of a drama – for there is this sort of fascination in all sincere unpremeditated eloquence, which opens to one the inward drama of the speaker's emotions – now turned his horse aside, and pursued his way, while Dinah said, 'Let us sing a little, dear friends'; and as he was still winding down the slope, the voices of the Methodists reached him, rising and falling in that strange blending of exultation and sadness which belongs to the cadence of a hymn.

*Note: this is the fourth verse of Charles Wesley's hymn which begins 'Thy ceaseless, unexhausted love', number 48 in the Methodist hymn book *Hymns & Psalms* 1988.

10

SELF HELP AMONG THE LOCAL PREACHERS

C. Alan Parker

Christian faith has never safeguarded people from poverty and its effects. Public policy in England and Wales in the early nineteenth century was no more successful in that respect. The Poor Law, as it had developed from laws enacted at the end of the reign of Queen Elizabeth I (1597 and 1601), laid responsibility upon each parish to provide for its own poor.

There was great variability in the way the system worked, some laxity and a significant amount of corruption, and as the process of industrialisation gathered pace after 1800 – especially the rapid increase of population, the growth of towns and the expansion of factory industry – it was inevitable that political action would be taken to secure greater consistency and rigour in the administration of poor relief.

The Poor Law Amendment Act of 1834, based upon the work of a Royal Commission which reported in that year, left many people, some Methodist local preachers amongst them, destitute; their only recourse was to the parish Board of Guardians, upon which other Methodist local preachers were sometimes elected to serve. Out-door relief was strictly regulated, and for those in extreme necessity entry to the Poor- or Union-Workhouse was often the only option. This was the situation in which numbers of local preachers found themselves. The ultimate indignity was to be buried in a pauper's grave.

One means by which certain groups of working people were able to make some provision for their own needs in times of illness or injury was through the formation and membership of friendly societies. Such societies also commonly paid funeral allowances, so that members in good standing could be assured at the last of a decent burial. Many societies came into existence in the late eighteenth century and the early decades of the 19th century, following legislation of 1793 which afforded them some encouragement and protection, and removed some of the restrictions that had previously existed. It must be remembered, however, that the Combination Laws were not relaxed until 1824 and friendly societies were inhibited to some extent by the fear of being seen as 'cover' for illegal associations of workers. There were also difficulties for the societies resulting from the relatively undeveloped nature of the banking system at the time and the need to make secure and acceptable arrangements for the safe-keeping of members' contributions to the funds.

THE SHAME OF SEEKING POOR RELIEF

'A few years since, I was Poor Law guardian. The first man whom I ever remember hearing preach the Gospel was a poor local preacher. The sound of his voice is associated with my earliest impressions, and is continually, from such early remembrances, ringing in my ears. I sat at the Board one day, and who should come in to ask for relief but this brother? I felt ashamed when he came in. By my side sat a brother guardian, who was a Churchman, and I saw him, as I hung my head with something like confusion, quickening his gaze and looking with more attentiveness than usual. As the brother came to the table he said to me: "Is not this one of your people?" The inquiry deepened my confusion, but I was obliged to say: "Yes, he is." He made a second inquiry and said: "Is he not one of your preachers?" The truth escaped from me a second time, and I replied affirmatively. "Sir," said the Churchman, tapping me on the elbow, "this ought not to be. This brother of yours, this Methodist preacher, ought not to have come to this Poor Law Board for relief," and thrusting his hand into his pocket, he said: "I will give something to relieve him, if you will do so, and we will not enter his name here." From that day my mind was made up that some society ought to be formed for the relief of such cases.'

Told by James Walker of Halifax at the Preparatory Meeting of LPMAA, Birmingham July 1849.

F. H. Buss and R. G. Burnett,
A Goodly Fellowship London 1949, p.26-27.

In 1830, over 3,000 societies sought advice from a barrister appointed to give friendly societies guidance about their rules. In due course, he became the first Registrar of Friendly Societies. According to his evidence to the Poor Law Commission, the general level at which most societies paid benefit to members in need was approximately one-third of the current wage in the society's locality for the occupational group concerned. This became the basis of some of the Commission's recommendations for Poor Law Reform.

It was in this context and against this background that the first Wesleyan Methodist Local Preacher Friendly Societies were formed. Caring for fellow-Christians was clearly required by the faith that Methodist preachers proclaimed, though other influences both within Wesleyan Methodism itself and in society as a whole contributed to the development.

The growing pressures for democracy and freedom within the state were paralleled in the Wesleyan church by pressure for greater lay participation in its decision-making processes. At this time, and indeed until 1878, the Wesleyan Conference was exclusively ministerial, and the power to admit and expel members of the church remained with ministers. The tension was further manifest when the 1839 Conference declined to make money available from the Centenary Fund for the care and support of local preachers in need. As the church was not prepared to make this provision it was inevitable that the preachers themselves would feel the obligation to do so, to demonstrate both their concern for those to whom they were bound by faith and calling, and their determination that the proclamation of the Gospel should not be hindered. The decade of the 1840s was marked in Wesleyan Methodism by increasingly fierce strife leading to the withdrawal or expulsion in the early 1850s of many thousands of members (including local preachers) from Wesleyan congregations. The formation of the Local Preachers' Mutual Aid Association, also in 1849, was not directly attributable to this upheaval, but it could not avoid being affected by the events of that year and their consequences.

A MINISTER ALARMED BY LPMAA!

'I confess, I am more afraid of the result of this movement [LPMAA] than I am of the one by Messrs. Everett, Dunn and Griffith.' Revd Frederick Jobson, 25 September 1849.

W. R. Ward *Early Victorian Methodism: The correspondence of Jabez Bunting 1830-1858*, 1976, p.383.

The LPMAA was, in fact, the culmination of several initiatives by groups of local preachers in widely scattered parts of the country. The earliest local preacher friendly society so far traced held its 4th Annual

Meeting[1] in the Schoolroom of Rochdale Wesleyan Methodist Church on 5 August 1834. It must therefore be presumed to have been formed in 1830. The membership seems to have been drawn from a wide area of north west England. The report states that over 100 members (out of a total of 300) were present (from 21 circuits) and that the society had £250 in its funds. Its president that year was Thomas Taylor, of Manchester. Some Wesleyan local preachers had recently been excluded from the plan at Ashton and Oldham, which presented a problem of eligibility for membership. This was only a few years after the expulsions and resignations from the Wesleyan Church which had followed the Brunswick organ affair at Leeds, and was also evidence of continued discontent within Wesleyanism which was shortly to produce the secession of the Wesleyan Methodist Association. The friendly society arranged to hold its next meeting in Manchester.

Another early society held its first meeting in Rochdale, on 1 August 1836. This society is interesting not only because it pre-dates LPMAA by thirteen years, but because it continued in existence at least until 1866 (the last entry in the minute book is dated 1 July 1866) seventeen years after the national association began. A decision not to amalgamate with the Wesleyan Methodist Local Preachers' Mutual Aid Association is recorded in the minutes of a meeting in 1861.[2] Other similar societies had either ceased to exist or had become branches of LPMAA long before that time. Wesleyan Methodism in Rochdale was profoundly affected by the disputes and partisanship of that time, and there was a substantial secession of members, many local preachers amongst them. The local preachers' friendly society, however, chose to retain in membership those who left the Wesleyan connexion, and its name was amended accordingly. This practice was followed in later years, when the national Wesleyan Methodist Local Preachers' Mutual Aid Association resolved, soon after its formation (1849), to allow local preachers who left or were expelled from Wesleyan Methodism to continue their membership of the Association, though its title was not changed.

Further local preacher friendly societies are known to have existed in Bristol,[3] Cambridge and other places; most were concerned to meet the needs of members when unable through illness, injury or disability, to follow their normal employment, and to ensure that surviving relatives were able to pay for proper funerals for members upon death. The view was expressed from time to time during the 1840s that it would be preferable to have one combined national society for the relief of need amongst local preachers, rather than a number of local societies serving preachers in a single circuit, or a small group of circuits.[4] The first steps towards achieving this were not taken until the end of the decade. There was considerable enthusiasm at first, but because of the troubled state of Wesleyanism at the time, the new body developed slowly for some years.

Inauguration of the Wesleyan Methodist Local Preachers' Mutual Aid Association

Amongst others concerned for the adequate provision for preachers prevented by sickness, poverty or the frailty of old age from pursuing their call to preach, was Francis Pearson, commercial traveller and local preacher, in what was then the Cromford Circuit in Derbyshire. Pearson wrote letters to the Methodist newspapers of the day but only the *Wesleyan Times* published them (the first on 6 June 1849) and also supported Pearson's suggestion of a large-scale meeting of local preachers with favourable editorial comment. In the following weeks letters appeared from various localities, not all approving the idea.[5] However, a preliminary meeting of 24 local preachers was convened in Birmingham in July 1849 to arrange the inaugural aggregate meeting of a national local preachers' friendly society. This was held on 3 and 4 October 1849, when over 600 preachers from all parts of the country assembled in the Freemasons' Hall, Great Queen Street, London.[6]

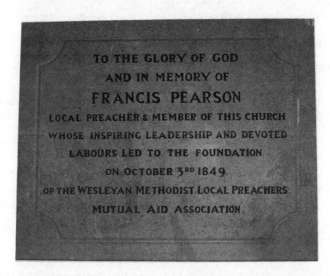

TO THE GLORY OF GOD
AND IN MEMORY OF
FRANCIS PEARSON
LOCAL PREACHER & MEMBER OF THIS CHURCH
WHOSE INSPIRING LEADERSHIP AND DEVOTED
LABOURS LED TO THE FOUNDATION
ON OCTOBER 3RD 1849.
OF THE WESLEYAN METHODIST LOCAL PREACHERS
MUTUAL AID ASSOCIATION.

Memorial to Francis Pearson, pioneer of the Local Preachers' Mutual Aid Association. (Wensley Methodist Church, near Matlock, Derbyshire. Photograph by Derek Byfleet.)

A London preacher, William Harris, who had been very active in preparing for the gathering, was elected to the chair, and must have impressed his colleagues with his ability in this role, for at the conclusion of the second day, upon Francis Pearson declining to be nominated, he was elected as the new association's first President. As well as becoming editor of *The Local Preachers' Magazine* (which began publication as the Association's official organ in 1851) he also served for a few years as Honorary Secretary. Under his chairmanship the Aggregate Meeting addressed itself to a score of resolutions, to give the body its name, to set down its objectives, define its membership with terms and conditions, to specify conditions of benefit, and to establish means of democratic government.

A LOCAL PREACHER PAYS THE PRICE OF CONSCIENCE

Joshua Dodgson of Elland was converted in 1820 and became a local preacher in 1823. In October 1829 his employer urged him to accept further responsibility, which would have meant working on Sundays...

'Joshua asked for time to think the matter over. At the end of a week he was asked for his decision. "I have been on my knees about it" he replied, "and He that said 'Thou shalt not steal' also says 'Thou shalt keep the Sabbath day holy', so that with my present views and feelings, I cannot be employed on any part of the Sabbath". He must have known what would be the result; his master would find someone without his scruples. So after a month's notice he left, on 14 Nov. 1829. Winter was looming ahead; he had no immediate prospect and a family of eight children.'

He set out on his preaching appointment the next day, knowing that in a real sense it had cost him his job.

Oliver A. Beckerlegge 'Like father, like son: the story of Joshua and Jonathan Dodgson of Elland' in *Preachers All* – Essays to celebrate the Silver Jubilee of the Yorks Branch of the Wesley Historical Society 1987, pp.34-5.

In spite of exhortations from the chairman, it proved impossible for speakers in the debates to eschew all reference to the troubles affecting Wesleyan Methodism; feelings ran high about the treatment of local preachers by Wesleyan authorities in some parts of the country, and there was determination that the newly-formed Association should not be subject to Conference control.[7] In fact some of its first leaders were either expelled or effectively forced to resign from membership of the Wesleyan church and thus lost their standing as local preachers, so that at an early stage the Association had to decide that 'reform' preachers could retain their membership in it. Francis Pearson, William Harris, and Isaac English (President 1850, later Honorary Secretary) were all in this category.[8] One consequence of the situation was that the proportion of local preachers joining the WMLPMAA remained low until the 1870s, in spite of the extent of perceived need. Indeed, as the Wesleyan Reform cause lost some support in the mid-1850s (leading to the negotiations that united the Wesleyan Methodist Association with some of the reformers to form the United Methodist Free Churches) the membership of LPMAA also declined.[9] It was not until the admission of lay people to the Wesleyan Conference in 1878 that the hesitancy of many local preachers was overcome, and the numbers joining the Association increased by the end of the century, to about half of those eligible.

During that half-century, however, the beneficent work of the Mutual Aid Association continued, and many ingenious ways were developed to increase income so that the scope of that work could be expanded. Subscriptions alone, originally fixed at 3d per week (approx. 12/- per annum – 60p in decimal currency, but at that time equivalent to a week's wages for many people)) were barely sufficient to meet weekly payments to sick and disabled members and death grants, but there were strong feelings that annuities should be available to frail, elderly, retired preachers, and benefits to those who were poor through unemployment, and to the families of deceased members. Honorary membership was accorded to anyone who subscribed the traditional charitable guinea, and recruitment through tea-meetings, then enormously popular, was urged upon members of local branches in Wesleyan and Reformed circuits. One enthusiast solicited one (old) penny from congregations for each sermon he preached; another gave up shaving and paid the money he saved to the Association. John Towne of Melton Mowbray, President 1858, devised the idea of special collecting cards, urging his colleagues to fill them up and pay in the money a quickly as possible, whilst his successor of 1863, James Arundale, made a special President's Appeal for £2,000, a figure much in excess of realistic expectation.

Some of these means may seem naive or oddly amusing, but they indicate the strength of feeling amongst some local preachers about the deprivation and desperate circumstances of many of their colleagues.[10] Something had to be done, and they did what they could. One major event was a bazaar in connection with the London Aggregate Meeting of 1860. The success of the Ladies' Committees who organised it was such that a supplementary event was possible a few weeks later. It is salutary to remember that hundreds of local preachers in the second half of the 19th century had to depend on initiatives of this kind for such material support as they needed to continue in the preaching work.

The consolidation of the work of local preachers in the non-Wesleyan branches of Methodism, together with continuing democratic pressures within the Wesleyan church and the widening of the democratic base in the state, created a climate in which major changes occurred in Wesleyanism during the later 1870s and 1880s. Attention was given to the training of local preachers (if only to improve the quality of candidates for the ministry in a period when public education was being expanded); in 1878 the first lay members were admitted to the Conference; and in 1883 the Wesleyan Church began to record the numbers of its local preachers. A year earlier – 43 years after the establishment of the Centenary Fund – a small sum was finally allocated to assist local preachers in need. The committee appointed to oversee this Necessitous Local Preachers' Fund included several men who were active leaders in LPMAA.

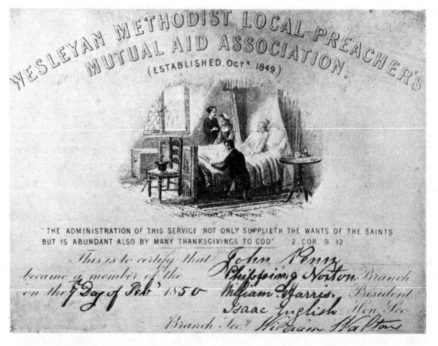

The original certificate of membership of the Local Preachers' Mutual Aid Association.
(F.H. Buss and R.G. Burnett *A Goodly Fellowship*, Epworth Press, 1949, frontispiece.)

One of the consequences of these changes was that laymen of substance and influence began to play a more significant part in both connexional affairs and the LPMAA. There were for example businessmen like William Kilner, whose family firm developed the famous 'Kilner' preserving jars; Kilner himself was a member of Conference in twelve of the fifteen years between 1878 and 1893, the year of his death, and served as President of LPMAA in 1888.[11] David Barr, whose story is told in the next section of this chapter, and Alderman W. H. Stephenson of Newcastle-upon-Tyne (the first member to serve twice as President – 1883 and 1895) are amongst a number of others. There were members of Parliament, such as Judge S. D. Waddy and Sir John Bamford Slack, and other loyal servants of Christ within Wesleyan Methodism, who gave generously of their time, energy and material wealth to support and sustain their less fortunate fellow-preachers. These enabled the WMLPMAA to move into the twentieth century enjoying the favour of official Methodism in a way that it had not in the earlier decades of its existence. The church was now recognising that its thousands of local preachers were indispensable to its work, worship and witness, and the Methodist people began to give them generous support through the preachers' Mutual Aid Association.

Homes for needy Preachers

Like most friendly societies, the Association had been unable, from its earliest days, to divert resources to tackling the need of many of its poorest members for free or low rent housing. Neither parish relief nor friendly society benefits were sufficient to cover both rent *and* basic subsistence, with the result that some local preachers who had fallen on hard times had no alternative than to enter a workhouse. At the same time other more prosperous local preachers were from time to time elected to Parish Boards of Guardians of the Poor and in that capacity became sadly aware of the plight of their poorer brethren. One such was David Barr, JP, a Birmingham businessman, and local preacher. He can be recognised as representative of a number of prominent Wesleyan laymen, also distinguished in the field of public service, who were active in pursuing the beneficent objectives of the Mutual Aid Association. David Barr was treasurer and vice-chairman of Wesleyan and General Assurance, a director of Birmingham Freehold Land Society, and served as chairman of Aston Local Board of Health, and as a member of Aston School Board, and of the Birmingham Board of Guardians. In Methodism he served as both society and circuit steward, and was a representative to Conference seven times. He was elected to the General Committee of WMLPMAA in 1892, having been a local preacher for over 30 years.[12]

Realising the inability of the Association at that time to address the housing need, Barr put his concern and intentions into a letter to the *Methodist Recorder* in December 1895. He gave a plot of land in his native village of Fillongley (a few miles north of Coventry) and an initial sum of money, inviting others who shared his hopes to contribute. The response was widespread and substantial: gifts came from some Wesleyan ministers (Hugh Price Hughes, F. Luke Wiseman), from an MP (Rt Hon Sir Henry Fowler, the future Viscount Wolverhampton), from supporters all over England and Wales, and from abroad. A Trust was formed from eleven laymen (including A. H. Barr – David's son – and John Barnsley, who became President in the Association's Jubilee year, 1899) and Revd William Harris, supernumerary, who had been president in the Association's first year. Harris had the honour of laying the principal commemorative stone. The right to nominate an elderly preacher who desired to be allocated a cottage was vested in those of the founders who had given £100 or more to the original fund.

The stone-laying ceremony took place on 27 August 1898; a local newspaper carried a report ahead of the ceremony and an account of the proceedings afterwards.[13] In 1899 the seven cottages were occupied, initially by elderly preachers from Hebden Bridge, Penarth, Coventry and four other midlands circuits, who expressed their appreciation in an illuminated address to the trustees in August of that year.[14] It is significant that the deed explicitly provided for local preachers from any Methodist tradition to reside in the cottages, if eligible and properly nominated. Philanthropy was not to be constrained by ecclesiastical boundaries.

As an experienced businessman, David Barr made provision for the trustees to receive income by way of rent from other properties in the area and further afield, so that the preachers' cottages could be maintained for the benefit of successive occupants without charge, and this continued until the end of the 1939-45 war. By the early 1950s the cottages were in need of considerable repair and improvement to bring them up to an acceptable standard, but the trust did not have the resources to do this. It was suggested that MLPMAA might take over the property, but since the war the Association itself had embarked on the provision of its own residential homes and did not require the Fillongley cottages. The trustees therefore disposed of them and realised their other remaining assets, the proceeds being divided between MLPMAA and local Methodism in accordance with the original deed. The cottages, in private ownership for forty years or more, with the foundation stone still prominent, stand as a reminder of, and a memorial to, the enterprise of David Barr and his colleagues. His election as president for 1906-07 was fitting recognition by the Association of what his charity and energy had achieved.

The development of the Association's residential care policy in the second half of the twentieth century is described in detail in the book *More Precious Than Rubies* by Alfred J. Gilliver (published to mark the 40th anniversary of Mutual Aid Homes in 1989).[15] The author had been an Honorary Secretary for eleven years, Senior Honorary Secretary for a further nine years, and travelled as President in 1976-77. His career in the civil service, including a senior appointment in the Registry of Friendly Societies and later as principal in the Department of Employment, enabled him to serve MLPMAA with great effect as both administrator and policy-former, and having been a member of General Committee for a great part of the Mutual Aid Homes era he was well-placed to record and interpret its history. Many legal and practical problems had to be overcome before the new policy could be implemented. In 1947 the Aggregate Meeting approved rule-changes authorising the establishment of rest and convalescent homes for sick, aged or infirm members, their wives, widows and dependants, but it was necessary to form, in 1948, a separate limited company (composed of 25 members of the General Committee) to have legal ownership of any land and buildings acquired for the purpose. The Association, not being a corporate body in law, could not do this.

The executive committee of the new company moved as swiftly as possible to obtain suitable premises for the first Mutual Aid Home. Recently enacted planning legislation gave rise to delay whilst questions of change of use were decided through application and appeal. The outcome was not known in time for the Centenary Aggregate of 1949, but two months later the official decisions were given that change of use was involved, but also that it was approved. After only a further three months, on 12 October 1949, the first home (named 'Westerley') was opened in Westcliff-on-Sea by the senior honorary secretary F. Harold Buss, in the midst of his year as Centenary President of MLPMAA, the second time he had been called to the Presidency. Having been elected to the Association's General Committee in 1912, subsequently serving as the magazine editor for nine years, and then as honorary secretary since 1926, it was very appropriate that he should carry out the formal opening. He was (and still is) only the third member to serve twice as President, and finally stepped down from his position as honorary secretary in 1956 after more than 40 years as committee member and officer of MLPMAA. The organisation and work of the Association and of Mutual Aid Homes owe a great deal to the influence and commitment of Harold Buss during those years. The last few years of his life were spent as a resident in the Westcliff Mutual Aid Home, where he died in 1964 at the age of 87. He was co-author, with R. G. Burnett, of the historical memoirs of LPMAA, *A Goodly Fellowship*, published in the Centenary Year.[16]

In the course of twenty years after the opening of the Home at Westcliff-on-Sea it proved possible to acquire and adapt suitable premises in various parts of the country to provide further Mutual Aid Homes. In March 1951 'Westerley' at Grange-over-Sands was opened, in May 1955 'Westerley' at Woodhall Spa, in May 1957 'Westerley', Minehead, and in July 1968 'Park View' at Rickmansworth. The growing need of members of the Association for residential care justified the building or acquisition of extensions at Woodhall Spa (1957), Minehead (1960), Grange-over-Sands (1972) and Rickmansworth (1980). At the peak of demand 120 residents have been accommodated in the five homes.

Three other initiatives must be mentioned, two successful and one whose success was short-lived. The latter was the venture into nursing care in the 1960s. This was first achieved in 1960, following the purchase of Barleythorpe Hall, Oakham, and its extension in 1963. Only two years later the decision was taken to establish a sixth home to meet the increasing demand for nursing care. This proved possible by the purchase of 'Park View' in 1966, along with the adjacent property which would house the Mutual Aid Homes head office, as well as the office of LPMAA. Sadly, because of additional costs arising from the need to register part of 'Park View' and of 'Barleythorpe' as nursing homes, difficulties in the recruitment and retention of properly-qualified and experienced staff, and the loss of local authorities' financial support (available only for residents not needing nursing care), by the end of the decade Barleythorpe Hall had to be run down and sold, whilst Park View henceforth operated as a normal residential home for elderly preachers.

As a consequence of the changing emphasis of the Association's work, from weekly allowances to residential care, action was taken in the mid-1960s to re-constitute Mutual Aid Homes Ltd as an Industrial and Provident Society, composed of all members of the General Committee of LPMAA for the time being. The effect was to bring the Homes more directly under the control of the General Committee, whose members have now a dual identity, and meet with a separate agenda as a General

Meeting of Mutual Aid Homes when considering Homes business. In this capacity they are a corporate body in law and own the Homes. The new Society was able to take the two longer-term successful initiatives mentioned above, first the purchase of two nomination rights in the Hanover Housing Association, later increased to four. This enabled members of LPMAA who were still able to look after themselves to take tenancies in various parts of the country. The scheme is now closed for new nominations. The second initiative was a partnership with Methodist Homes for the Aged, through which Methodism makes its contribution towards the national concern for housing old people regardless of religious persuasion. In 1977 MHA had set up a housing association, part of its role being the development of sheltered housing. As long ago as 1965 consultative contacts between LPMAA and MHA had been established, and during the 1980s details were worked out of a scheme under which LPMAA met the cost of five units in a sheltered housing development in Sheffield. This was opened, and the first LPMAA tenants took up residence in 1989.

LPMAA and Public Policy in the Twentieth Century

As indicated in the opening section of this chapter, both the limitations of public policy *and* the unwillingness of Wesleyan Methodism to provide help for local preachers in need, lay behind the various initiatives of local preachers in the mid-nineteenth century to establish friendly societies. The situation did not change materially until the early twentieth century, despite an Act of 1894 authorising Guardians of the Poor to disregard benefits up to 5/- (25p) per week paid to applicants by Friendly Societies.

Following the Liberal landslide victory in the 1906 election, Lloyd George (as Chancellor of the Exchequer) introduced legislation to provide old age pensions (1908) and national insurance benefits in sickness or unemployment (1911), with which Winston Churchill was also associated. These provisions, and other social legislation of the period, owed much to the work of charities and voluntary associations, which were often preferred as the avenues for administering publicly-provided benefits, because they were able to give a more personal, caring service than government departments could. For example, state health and unemployment insurance made use of friendly societies, insurance companies and trade unions, collectively termed 'approved societies', and bodies such as LPMAA had to decide whether to 'become approved' or to remain independent and modify the basis of their operation. The Association adopted the second alternative; there were several consequences.[17] To be eligible for state benefit its members had to join some other body which was 'approved'. The many who were enrolled as 'benefit members' (i.e. the local preacher members) were legally entitled to continue in that category and to receive benefits from the Association as of right, but from 1912 no new benefit members could be enrolled, and the local preacher category of membership became known as 'ordinary membership'. LPMAA could assist such members only if need could be proved, and only within stipulated limits without prejudicing the members' entitlement to state benefits.

PREACHING IN THE WORKHOUSE

'There used to be what was called the Workhouse at Wordsley, and preachers on the Stourbridge plan used to conduct services there every Sunday afternoon. The sexes were separated – about 200 men down one side of the Hall, and 200 women down the other, with nurses, attendants and porters seated at the ends of the rows . . . I never had so large a congregation anywhere else. Some had the intelligence of a normal chapel congregation, but others could only appreciate something very simple – and perhaps not even that. I cannot say I enjoyed these services, or the pitiful sight of many who seemed to think it an honour to shake hands with 'the minister' before proceeding back to their quarters. It makes me thankful that things are so different now.'

Memories of Francis Edward Lowe (1898-1990)
– typescript copy made available by
Dr E. Dorothy Graham, niece of Mr Lowe.

The approved society system was discontinued in 1946, in the wave of new social legislation that followed the 1939-45 war. During that war further changes in the way the Association operated became necessary. Legislation of 1940 provided supplementary pensions to help old people cope with increasing prices, and resulted in a limit of 7s.6d (37p) being imposed on weekly grants from friendly societies (later raised to 10s.6d.(53p)). LPMAA had no option other than to comply, and the 1943 Aggregate Meeting meeting at Nottingham approved the necessary rule-changes as recommended by General Committee.[18] One of these changes allowed the giving of single lump-sum grants, in preference to weekly allowances, where this would be a more appropriate way of meeting need, e.g. to meet the cost of a convalescent holiday after illness, to replace worn-out clothing or footwear, to pay for installation of telephone for an elderly member living alone. Another change made dependent relatives of deceased members eligible for assistance, in addition to widows who were already eligible. Some improvements were also made in the amounts payable to benefit members, over 1,600 of whom were still alive.

The role of voluntary associations and societies and their charitable provision within an expanding state welfare system underwent significant reappraisal during the post-war years. For LPMAA this reappraisal was also in the context of a contracting church. Steady decline in the numbers of Methodists, of congregations, of preachers, and of folk coming into membership of the Methodist Church provoked thought about the future basis and organisation of the Association. New charity legislation in 1960 encouraged action to secure the benefits of registration as a charity, principally exemption from the payment of tax. The process proved more difficult than was expected, however. Extended correspondence between the Association and the Charity Commission culminated in a letter in November 1963 stating unequivocally that registration as a charity could only be granted 'if poverty is an essential qualification for the receipt of relief'.[19] Under the rules as they then stood this was not the case, so the Commission helpfully suggested ways in which they might be amended in order to meet the requirements. The objects themselves had, in some cases, to be reworded so that *need* was made explicitly a condition for receiving benefit. The final complication was to find some way of protecting the position of the small and declining number of benefit members, fewer than 150 of whom were still alive in 1963, their membership dating from 1911 or earlier. This was done, the Aggregate Meeting of 1964 approved the revision of rules, and registration as a charity was granted in July of that year.[20]

The section of this chapter dealing with 'Homes for Needy Preachers' makes brief reference to the registration of Mutual Aid Homes as an Industrial and Provident Society. Its position in relationship to public policy has thus been clear and secure, but its operations in the development of high-quality residential care for members and dependants have inevitably been affected by changes in the legal framework of social provision, including that by voluntary and charitable bodies as well as by statutory agencies. Regulations governing the financial support of residents have also had to be reckoned with, and Mutual Aid Homes Ltd. is at the present time adapting to the latest legislation to bear upon its work, the Community Care Act which took effect in April 1993.

Public policy is now directed towards encouraging elderly people to live in their own homes as long as possible, as part of a shift from institutional to domiciliary and community-based care for all with special needs. The long-term effects cannot be assessed precisely at this relatively early stage, but as it has evolved to meet changes over nearly 50 years so the Society will adjust to new circumstances and needs in the future.

LPMAA and the Connexion

It has already been noted that both Wesleyan Methodist local preachers and those belonging to 'reformed' Methodism (i.e. preachers of the United Methodist Free Churches (after 1857) and of the Wesleyan Reform Union (1859)) were eligible for membership of LPMAA. It was only in time for the Centenary Year (1897) of the Methodist New Connexion that the WMLPMAA extended membership to the local preachers of that body, though it had been offered and declined some years earlier. Similar situations arose in 1907 when Bible Christian preachers were made eligible upon the amalgamation of Bible Christians, the Methodist New Connexion, and the United Methodist Free Churches to form the United Methodist Church, and in 1932 when Methodist Union united the Primitive, United, and Wesleyan Methodists. The 1896 incorporation of the MNC therefore established a pattern, whereby the connexion concerned paid an agreed sum to LPMAA to buy benefit rights for its preachers. This occurred again only 11 years later when the Bible Christians came in via the United Methodist Church. These two events added nearly 2,000 local preachers to the potential membership of the Association. The actual membership in 1914 stood at 8,993, approx. 35% of eligible local preachers, Wesleyan, United and Reform Union.

The 1932 Union had greater implications for LPMAA, as the Primitive Methodists had about 13,000 local preachers. A sum of £20,000 was agreed to entitle Primitive Methodist local preachers to join, and this was raised in a 'lightning effort' by September 1932. The word 'Wesleyan' was dropped from the Association's title, though it had become less widely used before that time. Ex-Primitive Methodist preachers were soon appointed to the General Committee, and several thousand took up membership by the end of the 1930s. One additional feature must be mentioned here. Primitive Methodism had, for many years, maintained a Preachers' Aid Fund, administered Connexionally with assistance from local preachers in the circuits. The balance of this fund was transferred to LPMAA, on the basis that the Association would be the body to provide financial help for all Methodist local preachers. By the beginning of the 1939-45 war, membership stood at 15,653, (approximately 50% of eligible local preachers) and nearly 1,400 local preachers and dependants were receiving financial help.

At the end of the war, Methodism – like all bodies and institutions – turned its attention to re-building for the future. Amongst concerns such as surplus chapels, and falling membership, attention was directed to the need for more and better trained local preachers. Numbers had fallen from about 35,000 at the 1932 Union to 28,000, recruitment had inevitably declined during the war, and the Connexional LP Department's funds allowed neither a major recruiting campaign nor a substantial training programme. The Connexional LP Secretary (Revd Fred Farley) therefore sought and accepted an invitation to address the General Committee of LPMAA, which held a special meeting for this purpose on 17 January 1944. Mr Farley suggested that collections on LPMAA Sundays might be shared between the Association and the LP Office.[21] Not surprisingly this evoked strong and diverse reactions. The Aggregate Meeting of 1945 was recommended by General Committee to approve a change of rules that would empower the Association to support financially the work of the LP Office. This did not receive a sufficient majority in the Aggregate Meeting. When this was reported, the correspondence columns of both *The Methodist Recorder* and *The Local Preachers' Magazine* contained many letters vigorously opposing the suggestion, while others expressed the view that Mr Farley's idea should be explored further.[22] The ground of the opposition was, of course, that the money given by the Methodist people for the Association's caring work was given in appreciation of the ministry of local preachers over many years, to help ensure that in time of need they should not be neglected. This had become the normal channel by which the church supported its army of lay preachers, and the money given for this purpose could not, morally or legally, be put to other uses. The contrary argument was that training and support in the preaching work was part of the care of local preachers; and that Methodist people would be happy to have their gifts used for developing the capability of those who led their worship week by week. The prevalent feeling was that the training of preachers was the clear responsibility of the Methodist Church and that separate and specific arrangements should be made for financing it. Methodism had declined to make adequate provision over nearly a hundred years for the care of those whom it commissioned to preach; local preachers had worked hard to make this provision for poor and needy sisters and brethren through their Association, and were determined to safeguard their resources for continuing to do it.

It is sad that these tensions were exacerbated, at a time when most of the old wounds had almost healed. It was 1963 before any fresh attempt was made to achieve new relationships between the Association and the Connexion, following a decision of Conference that the LP Department should take action to inform Methodism more fully about its role, and stress the need for more local preachers. The Connexional LP Secretary of the time, Revd David Francis, sought discussions with LPMAA national officers which resulted in agreement by 1967 that Conference should be recommended to endorse the suggestion for an official LP Sunday with a two-fold purpose. First, appointed preachers, whether ministers or local preachers, should explain something of local preachers' work and the function of the LP Department, and encourage people to consider the call to preach. Secondly, they should speak about the benevolent work of the Mutual Aid Association in caring for local preachers in need, by financial help and the provision of eventide homes, thanking congregations for past support and inviting them to continue it. Since 1967, LP Sunday has been jointly sponsored by the Association and the LP Office, through combined publicity material. Consultative links have been maintained by means of a standing joint committee. During this period of time many Methodist congregations have moved to envelope systems, covenanted giving, and stewardship schemes to meet their financial needs, and collections for special purposes (such as LPMAA) have been discontinued, but the level of grants and donations to the Association's caring work amongst preachers has continued to rise gradually, standing now (1995) at over £200,000 annually. Methodists generally still show gratitude for the ministry of their local preachers in this way.

The Annual Aggregate Meeting of LPMAA has from time to time over the years welcomed the Connexional LP Secretary as a guest speaker. Revd John Stacey, being invited to address Aggregate in 1979 at Derby, took the opportunity to suggest that the Association might consider 'taking Conference into its system', a phrase echoing Archbishop Geoffrey Fisher's phrase recommending the Free Churches to take episcopacy into their systems. Following John Stacey's speech, the standing joint committee gave careful consideration to the question, and in due time put forward some initial ideas for enabling LPMAA and the Connexion to relate more explicitly to each other, centred round cross-representation between the General Committee and the Board of the Methodist Division of Ministries, and the presentation of a brief LPMAA report for the information of Conference. These steps were implemented in 1983, and consultations continued.

In 1989 the LPMAA Aggregate Meeting (at Wimborne) adopted the recommendation of the General Committee that the Association should commit itself to explore, with the Division of Ministries, means whereby LPMAA could become part of official Methodist structures by the end of the century, whilst still safeguarding the use of resources accumulated or bequeathed over many years for the care and support of local preachers in need. The Methodist Conference of that year also endorsed this approach, and in May 1992 the Standing Joint Committee therefore published a discussion paper, *Becoming One*. Extensive consultation took place upon this, and the Standing Joint Committee prepared more detailed proposals for taking the matter forward. Meanwhile, the Connexional LP Secretary's annual letter to all preachers is being distributed in conjunction with the Association's magazine, LPMAA is administering grants made from the Connexional Necessitous Local Preachers' Fund, and the Association's honorary secretaries are discussing with the Secretary of Conference possible ways for it to become a discrete organisation within Connexional structures.

More To Be Told

A fuller account of LPMAA will be offered in the *History of Mutual Aid* planned for publication in the 150th anniversary year (1999).

From its foundation, LPMAA has always been concerned with the care of its members and, for many years, of all local preachers whether members or not, as *whole people*. For the founders, mutual aid meant helping each other in the preaching work as well as in times of material need. This was a prime reason why *The Local Preachers' Magazine* was begun in 1851. It included *The Mutual Aid Reporter* but for decades most of its pages (twelve monthly issues often exceeded 400 pages) were devoted to biblical and theological articles and other material useful to preachers. In later years, for a variety of reasons, including paper shortage in times of war, the size and frequency of publication were reduced. The magazine now appears quarterly and serves the purpose principally of a house magazine, with news from Districts and Branches, Head Office information and members' correspondence. Some space is still available for book reviews and other articles. Intellectual and spiritual mutual aid 'has remained an important part of Association activity, and in several Districts, including Cornwall, Cumbria, Lincoln, the former London South and South West Districts, and Nottingham & Derby, there has been a long

---

TWO GRAVESTONES TO LOCAL PREACHERS

In loving memory of
Leonard Dodd of West Slack
who departed this life
July 17th 1879 aged 69 years.
For upwards of forty years, as a Primitive
Methodist Local Preacher, he travelled
this and neighbouring dales, preaching
the Gospel of Salvation through Christ
Jesus to his perishing fellow men, many
of whom will doubtless be the crown of his
rejoicing in the day of the Lord.

In the churchyard of St. John the Baptist,
Garsdale, Cumbria.

Sacred
to the memory of
WILLIAM DIXON
who was for upwards of thirty years a
laborious and useful Local Preacher
and class leader in the
METHODIST CONNEXION.
He departed this life September 15th 1829
In him his family has lost one of the
kindest parents, the Poor
a Liberal Benefactor, and the Church
one of its brightest ornaments.

In the churchyard of St. Mary, Barnard Castle.

---

tradition of week-end courses and conferences to promote preacher-development. In other Districts study days with the same objective have been a regular activity, and quite often members who serve the Connexion as LP tutors have put their experience and expertise at the disposal of their colleagues by leading such events. General Committee members share in a residential study conference at Willersley Castle and make annual pilgrimage to the founder's chapel at Wensley nearby.

This chapter has shown how LPMAA has responded over the years to changes in Methodism and in the wider society of which we are all part. One aspect of this, not hitherto mentioned, is the role of women

in its life and activity. It was not until 1897 that women preachers, few as
they were at that time, were admitted to membership of the Association.
The Aggregate Meeting journal records the horror expressed by some
members on realizing that women might henceforth attend the Annual
Aggregate, and even be allocated preaching appointments on Aggregate
Sunday! In 1918, the year in which women over 30 were enfranchised,
the rules had still to include the explicit statement (acknowledged that
year by the Wesleyans for the first time in regard to the position of women
as local preachers in general) that women local preachers were entitled to
the same rights and privileges as men, though the rule book still contained
references only to 'brother'! The first woman member of General
Committee was elected in 1923;[23] it was over 20 years before another
woman was elected to the Committee. Harold Buss noted in 1949 that
'there are few who have dared to envisage the installation of a feminine
President'.[24] It was only one year later that the first woman candidate
was nominated for the Presidency but nearly 20 more years elapsed
before a female President was elected. This was Alice Nuttall, whose
husband Donald followed in that office some years later. He also served
the Association as honorary medical adviser and as Honorary Secretary
for Mutual Aid Homes. There have been three further women Presidents
in subsequent years, and women now comprise a substantial proportion of
General Committee members, and of the Aggregate Meeting.

Contrary to some opinions, LPMAA is not an inward-looking
body with a very narrow perception of its role and its members' needs,
though it holds tenaciously to its task of doing everything possible to
support local preachers in their preaching work and when they have
retired from it. For many years it exchanged fraternal delegates with local
preacher associations of Methodism in other parts of the world, and
continued to send and receive greetings long after it became difficult to
find suitable representatives to undertake the travelling.[25] It was one of
the first groups to memorialize the Conferences of the Connexions to
which its members belonged on the urgency of working for Methodist
Union – this was in 1887. It expressed strongly in resolutions to
governments the views of its members on current social issues, such as
Sunday newspapers (1907) and the extension of licensing hours in the
liquor trade (1874). The important COPEC Conference of 1924 on
Christian social concerns was fully reported in the LP Magazine for the
benefit of members. Its leaders have included men and women prominent
in Methodism and public life. Since 1932 three LPMAA Presidents have
served also as vice-president of Conference. R. Parkinson Tomlinson had

been President of the Association in 1928/29, and was elected Vice-President of Conference for 1938/39. He was called to be President of LPMAA again in 1942/43, serving all but two days of that second term. He died just before the 1943 Aggregate at which he would have surrendered office to his successor. There is a delightful memorial tablet to him in the Garstang Chapel, N. Lancs. Herbert Ibberson, a Barnsley lawyer, was Vice-President of Conference in 1942/43 and President of LPMAA in 1945/46. Albert Bailey, a Cannock (Staffs) businessman, was LPMAA President in 1961/62 and Vice-President of Conference in 1966/67. These and many others in different ways served the Lord through the Methodist Church, and their fellow local preachers through the Mutual Aid Association. A brief reference to the remarkable succession of General Secretaries who have headed the Association's administration over 145 years must conclude this chapter. Six men only, averaging 24 years in the post, have administered its affairs through changing and difficult circumstances. LPMAA stands indebted to Edward Cresswell, George Sims, John Harding, William Noddings, Squire Jones and Derek Bolton.

The beneficent work of LPMAA in caring for local preachers in need is done on behalf of Methodism and with the generous support of Methodist people. If worship is important, and no-one dare say it is not, then those whom the church commissions, in response to the call of God, to preach His Word in the context of worship must

    i) be upheld in training and preparation for that work,

    ii) be supported if at any time circumstances prevent them from exercising their call, and

    iii) at the last be cared for when no longer able to care for themselves.

It is a practical outworking, a demonstration, an application of the Gospel we preach. Without it our preaching is discredited.

11

THE METHODIST LOCAL PREACHER:
AN OCCUPATIONAL ANALYSIS

Clive D. Field

Although historians are slowly building up a picture of the social composition of British Methodist membership and congregations in the eighteenth, nineteenth and twentieth centuries,[1] and of the social background of the ordained ministry,[2] comparatively little is yet known about the origins of Methodism's lay leadership. Most attention has focused on chapel trustees, a group whose occupations are routinely recorded in the enrolled trust deeds available at the Public Record Office,[3] and very little primary work has been undertaken on the local preachers, despite the fact that they have always filled the vast majority of Methodist pulpits Sunday by Sunday. This chapter attempts to advance our understanding of the position regarding the occupational origins of the local preachers through, first, a synthesis of what little research has already been carried out and, secondly, an analysis of a random set of data drawn from *The Methodist Local Preachers' Who's Who, 1934*, the one and only occasion when an attempt has been made to publish biographical information about the whole community of local preachers.

Before Methodist Union

Representative evidence about the occupational background of the first generation of Methodist local preachers of the eighteenth century is particularly limited, although a number of twentieth-century historians of Methodism have been tempted to draw conclusions on the basis of isolated individuals. Wellman Warner, for example, writing in 1930, concluded that, whilst the majority were skilled artisans, small tradesmen

JAMES EVERETT RECALLS SOME SUNDERLAND LOCAL PREACHERS OF THE EARLY YEARS OF THE NINETEENTH CENTURY

'*Robert Spoor:* engaged in the manufacture of glass; like an old English squire; above the average size; robust, portly; features, as if chiselled in marble; inflexible, gravely austere; strict integrity; much respect; deliberate and sententious in the pulpit; more pompous in appearance than in reality; a full, strong voice, without modulation; the Northumbrian burr in perfection, hawked up in the windpipe, with its dialect, accent, and pronunciation slightly and awkwardly polished; without pathos; good judgement; instructive; and a good expositor of the Word of God.

Thomas Robinson: in the flax line; a kind, gentle spirit; fond of a good book; an easy, natural speaker; tender, a genial warmth; social; an inquiring mind; useful; and highly acceptable as a preacher.

William Rutherford: grocer and baker, a noble-looking man; fit, in appearance, to command a troop of horse; frivolous; talkative; forward; well-meaning; fluent in the pulpit; rather shallow; more like a brawling stream than a stately river.

Alexander Mathewson: a tallow-chandler, &c; belonging to Colliery Dikes; below the middle size; well-built; active as fire; acute; logical; well read; good expression; sermons full of instruction, and always embodying a subject; clear; convincing; telling; something for the hearer to carry away with him, and treasure up like spoil; his visits as welcome as the return of spring; an eye allied to that of the hawk tribe; a face beaming with intelligence.

John Burdon: a farmer, like a thick, dumpy Puritanic quarto, without its matter; gentle; "slow and easy"; deficient in reading; good character; commonplace; preaching like fireside talk.

John Foster: a sawyer; above the average height; muscular in his build, but often ailing in his chest; sterling sense; well read in the Word of God; an admirable textualist; a little too fond of spiritualising, which would have met with no disfavour from Benjamin Keach; but apart from this, an excellent preacher, combining useful matter with warmth of feeling; fluent; serious; earnest without rant.

Robert Adamson: a man whose character stood on a somewhat granite base; tall; muscular; dauntless expression; original; a little coarse; fluent; strong voice; in love with startling, quaint, bold figures and sayings; would have preferred the honest Tinker of Bedford for a model to the 'silver-tongued' Howe or Bates; much followed by persons of warm feeling.

James Irvine: tall; well favoured; from the lake districts; wordy; sermons too much beat out into leaf; never at a loss for something, though not always *the* thing; agreeable manner; useful; and acceptable in his turn.'

Coleman Collier *Gatherings from the Pit Heaps, or The Allens of Shiney Row* 2nd ed. 1868, pp.103-5.

and farmers, local preachers were recruited to a greater or lesser extent from all walks of life, including the professions and men of considerable wealth.[4] The best local evidence has been collected by Charles Wallace, for the Leeds and Wakefield areas between 1741 and 1801. Of the seventy-four individuals for whom he found occupational data, 14 per cent were professionals (including six schoolmasters, but also a surgeon, a physician, an alderman and an attorney), 45 per cent were merchants, manufacturers or retailers (mostly in textiles, amongst them eight clothiers, six clothmakers, five stuffmakers and three drapers), 27 per cent were skilled craftsmen (generally in textiles, shoes, wood, metal and pottery), 11 per cent were primarily or wholly farmers, and a mere four per cent were poor (two gardeners and a steward).[5] For the rest, it is occasionally possible to obtain details of the occupations of local preachers from circuit membership lists. In the Blackburn Circuit in 1790, for instance, all but one of the fifteen local preachers were either retailers (two ironmongers, a baker, and an upholsterer) or skilled craftsmen (five weavers, two shoemakers, two spinners, and a warper), the exception being a steward.[6] In the Bedford Circuit between 1796 and 1806, six of the 13 local preachers were skilled craftsmen (two tailors, a bricklayer, a flaxdresser, a shoemaker, and a weaver), but the remaining seven were drawn from a wide social spectrum, ranging from a gentleman to two labourers and a chimney sweep, and also including a clerk, a currier and a farmer.[7]

FARMER AND SCHOLAR

Joseph Watson of Kirkoswald (1800-1862) was a loyal son of the Church of England, a loyal Methodist local preacher, circuit steward and class-leader: 'A man of plain good sense, without crotchets.' 'Young farmer lads who went on the Plan had to get from place to place as best they could, more often than not on foot. On one occasion, after preaching at Brough, 24 miles away, Joseph reached home on Monday morning, just in time to join his brothers who were going out to the harvest field.'

'He was a great Bible student and his preaching ranged over every part of the Word. On the back of his plans he has written original poetry, and on one, texts in Greek and Syriac.'

H. K. 'A Fell Side Circuit' *Methodist Recorder*
Winter Number 1900, pp.33-34.

Passing to the early nineteenth century, we find claims appearing in at least three contemporary sources that Wesleyan local preachers were 'usually persons in business'.[8] These claims cannot be immediately reconciled with the concerns about proletarian preachers which surfaced at the time of Lord Sidmouth's bill in 1811, nor do they square entirely with the surviving evidence for this period, which suggests an altogether more complex reality. Thus in Sussex the local preachers tended to be either small tradesmen from the town societies or small-scale farmers and labourers from the country chapels; an annotated copy of the Rye Circuit plan for 1809 records occupations as diverse as apothecary, carpenter, itinerant vendor of yeast, labourer, and saddler.[9] Those who preached in

---

GOD MAKES THE PREACHER

'For God can mak' preeachers – hoo fearful the thowt! –
fra cobblers, er meeasons, er blacksmiths, er owt!'

From 'Wesleyanism at Easby' by John Castillo *Poems in the North Yorkshire Dialect* ed. and published G M Tweddell, Stokesley, 1878. Castillo (1792-1845) was a journeyman stonemason and Wesleyan revivalist.

---

the parish of Nuffield in the Diocese of Oxford in 1817 were categorized by the local clergyman, doubtless in deliberately pejorative tones, as 'of the lowest description, such as shoemakers, little grocers, poulterers etc.'[10] In the rural area of north Nottinghamshire, 28 per cent of eighty-nine Wesleyan local preachers between, approximately, 1820 and 1850 have been identified as farmers, compared with 30 per cent of the 212 class leaders and 44 per cent of the 166 trustees. Their farms were mostly of fewer than 300 acres. A further 19 per cent were shopkeepers or publicans (as against 13 and seven per cent of class leaders and trustees respectively). The proportion of craftsmen was 34 per cent (compared with 30 and 31 per cent for the other two groups of lay office-holders), and of labourers 16 per cent (with 21 and 11 per cent for class leaders and trustees). None of the local preachers was a gentleman, of independent means or a professional person, although three per cent of class leaders and five per cent of trustees were drawn from this category.[11]

In the Horncastle Circuit the Wesleyan local preachers are said to have been 'widely representative of all sections of the population' in the years before 1820, yet the accompanying sample list contains no labourers and is confined to professionals (a banker's agent, a schoolteacher and a solicitor), tradesmen (a draper, a druggist and an ironmonger), craftsmen (two farriers, two joiners, a breechesmaker, a bricklayer, a cooper, a saddler, a shoemaker, a tailor and a whitesmith) and two farmers.[12] In south Lindsey at mid-century 49 per cent of the 112 Wesleyan local preachers whose occupations could be identified were shopkeepers or craftsmen (including 13 grocers and ten shoemakers, but just two butchers), compared with 35 per cent of the 101 society stewards and 34 per cent of the seventy-nine class leaders; this high proportion has been thought to suggest 'a possible implicit protest against the ecclesiastical and social establishments, the claiming of a place in the social sun'. A further 33 per cent of local preachers were farmers (as against 58 per cent of stewards and 37 per cent of class leaders). Only 18 per cent of local preachers were labourers, more than the 8 per cent amongst stewards but less than the 29 per cent amongst class leaders.[13] In Bolton in the 1840s very few of the Wesleyan local preachers could be traced in the trade directories as manufacturers or retailers, just six out of thirty-nine in 1845, three out of forty-five in 1847, and three out of thirty-nine in 1849. The majority will presumably have been manual workers of some sort, mostly skilled.[14]

NO OVERLOOKERS IN HEAVEN

'The preachers, as I remember some of them, were very interesting spiritual men, and their preaching was racy and often humorous. I remember one who illustrated his view of heavenly life by saying that in heaven there would be no overlookers with their fat thumbs pinching the measure of the pieces as they took them from the weavers, and so cheating the workman out of the wages due to him for four or five yards on each piece. These homely illustrations were often apt, pointed and effective.'

Methodist Recorder Winter Number 1897
'Some West Yorkshire character sketches' p.61.

Although Wesleyan local preachers in the early nineteenth century were drawn from a broader social spectrum than might have been supposed, the Primitive Methodists probably had the greater success in recruiting from the lower reaches of the social scale. A study of the occupations of Primitive Methodist local preachers in Manchester before 1830 has revealed a preponderance (twenty-one of twenty-eight cases) of artisans, usually working in textile-based trades. There were also three retailers (bookseller, confectioner and salesman) and four labourers. The poor rate assessment of their dwellings ranged from £3 15s. to £18, five being assessed at under £5, twelve between £5 and £10, and eight at over £10 (with no information for the remainder).[15] In south Lindsey 51 per cent of fifty-eight Primitive local preachers active between 1825 and 1875 were labourers, approximately the same proportion as in the general population and 33 per cent more than for the equivalent Wesleyan sample. An additional 17 per cent were farmers and 32 per cent were craftsmen and others, both figures being appreciably lower than for their local Wesleyan colleagues, although the proportion of craftsmen and others was still higher than in the community as a whole.[16] The Primitive Methodist local preachers who preached in two Oxfordshire and Norfolk villages in the later nineteenth century were respectively 'farm labourers or small shopkeepers. With a very few exceptions they were poor, uneducated men'[17], and 'a cross-section of Breckland life, shorn of squires and professions', labourers, farmers and tradesmen.[18] In Great Yarmouth at the turn of the century it was said that 'our "locals" . . . have been, and are still drawn from the seaside, from the plough-tail, and a variety of other scenes of occupation. Our plans today contain the names of tinkers, tailors, soldiers, sailors, rich men, poor men, apothecaries – and many another, not forgetting carpenters, rope-makers, coal-merchants, butchers, postmen and what not!'[19]

A LOCAL PREACHER HERRING-CURER AND COOPER
JAMES TURNER OF PETERHEAD (b.1818)

'Each day at business, Turner assembled his employees, beginning and ending work with a psalm, a prayer and a reading from the scriptures. Any employee who was sick was visited personally. Illness meant no loss of wages, the "message" being given along with the creature comforts. Early on in his business life, determined to run his yard on Biblical principles, he introduced a profit-sharing scheme. At the end of each year, all profits were distributed equally so that the apprentice received the same as the fully-fledged tradesman. There was grumbling but Turner never argued. Opening his Bible he read to all the parable of the Labourers in the Vineyard. There the dispute ended.'

J. E. Hawdon, 'James Turner, Peterhead Cooper and Evangelist' in *Journal of the Scottish Branch of the Wesley Historical Society* Sep. 1975, pp.7-8.

By the early years of this century, however, the social gap between Wesleyan and Primitive Methodist local preachers was narrowing considerably, as it was also doing amongst the laity as a whole,[20] and there was a significant shift in favour of recruitment from non-manual backgrounds. Evidence for this is to be found, for instance, in Robert Moore's study of the four Durham mining villages of Esh

Winning, Cornsay Colliery, Waterhouses and Quebec-Hamsteels. Around 1900 only three of the ten Wesleyan local preachers pursued non-manual occupations (an official, a store departmental manager and a store clerk),

---

**PREACHER AND PATRON OF METHODISM
IN A RAILWAY COMMUNITY**

'One of Mr Timothy Hackworth's first acts on his removal to Shildon (County Durham) in 1825 was to open his own house at New Shildon for meetings, for prayer and for preaching. He often conducted services himself and secured the services of other local preachers as well. An office attached to his house was afterwards set apart for the regular worship of God, and proved truly a Bethel to many, and the spiritual birthplace of not a few. He soon gathered up a large society class which was afterwards several times divided. He watched over the little church with the affectionate solicitude of a parent over a child, and longed for the complete salvation of all connected with it.'

M. Braithwaite *History of Wesleyan Methodism in the Bishop Auckland Circuit* 1885, pp.74-5

(Hackworth was in charge of locomotive engineering on the Stockton-Darlington Railway and became a famous designer and builder of locomotives in his own right. He preached continually over many years, and had a heavy preaching load as the preaching plans shew : eg 22 appointments in 26 weeks from Nov.1834 to May 1835, 24 in 26 weeks from Nov.1841 to April 1842, and so on. He is said to have had a stately presence in the pulpit, 'gifted with powers of felicitous expression', and not reluctant to reveal emotion.)

---

as against seven in manual work (four miners, a coke worker, a signalman and a blacksmith). Of the twelve Primitive Methodist local preachers about this time whose occupations are known, five were in non-manual jobs (three mining officials, a school attendance officer and a shopkeeper), and seven in manual ones (five coal-hewers and two coke-yard workers). Just before the First World War five of the ten Wesleyan local preachers were in non-manual work (two mining officials, an insurance agent, a railway clerk, a store grocer), and five in manual (three miners, a coke-worker and a blacksmith). The corresponding figures for the twenty-two Primitive Methodist male local preachers were fourteen non-manual (six shopkeepers or shopworkers, two officials, an attendance officer, a stationmaster, a schoolmaster, a clerk, a missionary and a farmer) and eight manual (all miners). By the time of Methodist union in 1932 local preachers from the manual sector in general, and mining occupations in particular, were few and far between. Of ten Wesleyan local preachers six were shopkeepers, one a schoolteacher, one a store cashier, one a signalman, and one a miner. Of six Primitive Methodist local preachers one was an official, one an insurance agent, one a shopkeeper, one a greengrocer, one a checkweighman and one a miner.[21] Confirmation of this trend has been found in other areas, such as Nottinghamshire; here, in the 1920s, none of the twenty-two Primitive Methodist local preachers in Nottingham itself had a manual occupation, although the situation was not quite so bleak in the countryside.[22]

Thomas Bateman (d. 1897), born in Cheshire, farmer and land surveyor, said to have preached 10,000 sermons and travelled over 80,000 miles as a local preacher (first WM then PM). Twice president of the PM Conference, an unusual honour for a layman. ed. D. Whiteley *Illustrious Local Preachers* 1891, p.314

At Methodist Union

Coincidental with Methodist union, a unique primary source became available for the biographical study of the new Church's local preachers, *The Methodist Local Preachers' Who's Who, 1934*.[23] Prepared with the co-operation of the Methodist Church Connexional Local Preachers' Committee and the Methodist Local Preachers' Mutual Aid Association, this volume was issued, towards Christmas 1934, by Shaw Publishing Co., Ltd., publishers of a range of secular and religious reference works of this sort. Although it purported to be 'a complete record of the lives and careers of Methodist local preachers', it contained in fact the names and particulars of the 21,100 local preachers (20,660 accredited and 440 on trial) who had eventually (after three reminders) taken the trouble to complete the publisher's postal questionnaire, a response rate of approximately 57 per cent. This non-response by 43 per cent of the target population does not seem to have introduced any significant bias in terms of gender or region, when comparison is made with the connexional returns of local preachers for 1934, but there is some evidence to suggest that ex-Wesleyan local preachers may have been rather more likely than ex-Primitive Methodist ones to complete the questionnaire.[24]

A random 5 per cent sample (i.e. every twentieth name from a randomly-selected starting-point) has been drawn from these entries, to produce a nationally representative group of 1,055 individuals, information on whom was transferred to twenty-five-column analysis sheets.[25] In a very small number of cases supplementary biographical details could be obtained from the lay officers' section of *Who's Who in Methodism, 1933*.[26] In all instances *The Minutes of the Annual Conference of the Methodist Church and Methodist Church Buildings: statistical returns . . . as at July 1st, 1940* were consulted in an attempt to identify pre-union Methodist denominations (which respondents were not asked about in the questionnaire) from circuit and/or church names;[27] regrettably, this only proved possible to do with any certainty for 62 per cent of the sample. *Census 1951: classification of occupations* was used to assign occupations to the Registrar General's hierarchy of five social classes, which remains the preferred categorization scheme amongst historians for the analysis of late nineteenth- and early twentieth-century occupational data.[28] It should be noted, however, that occupations were not given for 199 (or 19 per cent) of the 1,055 local preachers. These 199 tended to have slightly different characteristics from the 856 for whom occupation was recorded; in particular, they included a disproportionately large number of women, people aged 70 and over (all presumably retired), persons who had been educated at secondary schools or privately, those with three or more children, and local preachers with forty or more years' service.

In his article in *The Methodist Local Preachers' Who's Who, 1934*, Arthur Button, Secretary to the Connexional Local Preachers' Committee, wrote:

> Local preachers are to be found in every walk of life, in the professions and among every grade of manual worker. Some are Members of Parliament, and some members of the judicial and magisterial benches. There are civil and municipal servants, university and college professors, heads of secondary and council schools, doctors, solicitors, authors, and prominent leaders in the world of commerce . . . Local preachers are workers in the factory and on the farm, in mine and mart, in shop and ship, in the office and at the forge, in the police force, on the railway and other transport services, in the officers' mess and in the ranks of the Navy, the Army and the Air Force.[29]

LUTON HATTERS

A hatter's heavenly crown: 'Mr Thomas Parker, an excitable and rather eccentric LP but a very true follower of the Lord Jesus was, like many of us, in the hat trade. He preached once on 2 Timothy 4 verse 8 : 'Henceforth there is laid up for me a crown of righteousness'. "Yes" he said, "there's a crown waiting, laid up for me, size six and seven eighths. The Lord knows my size. Hallelujah!"'

Gross darkness: 'Another local preacher was in the hat trade. It was a time when at the height of the season it was quite usual to receive an order for twelve dozen hats, referred to as a gross. One Sunday his text was Isaiah 60, verse 2 : "Behold, darkness shall cover the earth and gross darkness the people." He thought of those dark nights when he had to drive home after a service in the country, picture them to his congregation and added: "Think of the darkest night you have ever been out in. Well, gross darkness is 144 times as dark as that!"'

J. Douglas Tearle (of Luton)
An old local preacher remembers 1986
(compiled by his daughter, Dorothy Chapman.)

The data in Table 1,[30] by contrast, suggest that, whilst 'every walk of life' may certainly have been represented to some degree in the community of local preachers, its occupational profile was very different from that of the adult male population as a whole. In particular, there were more than twice as many local preachers from the professional class (I) as one might have expected, almost three times the number from the intermediate non-manual (lower middle) class (II), just half as many from the partly skilled manual class (IV), and a mere tenth as many from the unskilled manual class (V). Only for the skilled working class (III), comprising both non-manual and manual workers, were the proportions of local preachers and adult males similar. The preponderance (a combined figure of 83 per cent) of classes II and III amongst the local preachers appears to have been rather more pronounced than with rank and file worshippers, according to the evidence of Methodist marriage registers for the early twentieth century (where classes II and III together comprised 76 per cent in London, 68 per cent in Lincoln, and 75 per cent in Lancaster and Preston).[31]

A summary of the occupational groups represented in each social class is given in Table 2. It will be seen that there were five groups which, individually, accounted for more than five per cent of the local preachers and, collectively, for two fifths of them: dealers or retailers (12 per cent), farmers (eight per cent), clerical workers (eight per cent), teachers or lecturers (six per cent), and mineworkers (six per cent).

Disaggregated data are given in Table 3, which shows the distribution of local preachers by social class for no fewer than forty-six sub-samples. Although the number of cases involved for a handful of sub-samples is too small for analysis to be meaningful (for example, there were only twenty-eight local preachers in the sub-sample of women, twenty-seven who were resident in Wales, and sixteen who were on trial), some interesting trends do emerge from these data. Thus, the proportion of local preachers drawn from classes I and II increased with age, whilst there was a corresponding decrease in classes III and IV; Methodists evidently became more prosperous as they grew older. Similarly, and doubtless also a function of age, married or widowed local preachers had a slightly higher social status than single ones. The relationship between social class and fertility, however, was less certain; the mean number of children for married local preachers was highest in class II (2.51) and lowest in class III (2.29), the figures for classes I, IV and V being, respectively, 2.39, 2.46 and 2.30.[32] Education was clearly a powerful influence in determining social prospects; local preachers educated to tertiary level (whether degree or non-degree) were more than twice as likely to end up in classes I and II as those who received an elementary schooling. These two classes also boasted more material possessions, such as telephones. Of the three principal English regions, the Midlands had the lowest proportion of classes I and II, and the highest of III, IV and V.[33]

In denominational terms, ex-Wesleyans were more likely to come from the professional and intermediate classes than former Primitive or United Methodists, but there was otherwise surprisingly little difference between these three traditions, and certainly no evidence to suggest that Primitive Methodism was appreciably more working-class in its orientation than the other two. Age at appointment as a local preacher does not appear to have impacted significantly and consistently on the social class distribution, but local preachers with more than twenty years

---

AN ADVOCATE'S PRESENCE OF MIND IN THE PULPIT (S D WADDY)

'Mr Waddy is an extremely witty and ready speaker, alike in the law courts and in private conversation; and, if all we hear be true, he is also witty in the pulpit. When on circuit, he cheerfully takes preaching appointments, and Sunday almost invariably finds him in one or other of the Wesleyan pulpits. His professional brethren sometimes poke fun at him on this account, but, as he is particularly good at repartee, those seeking to indulge in "chaff" at his expense generally "come off second best." It is said that two well-known and distinguished advocates, who "took silk" about the same time, mischievously arranged to attend morning service together at a Wesleyan Chapel in the assize town, Mr Waddy having been announced as the preacher. These worthies, Messrs. L. and S., took seats in a front pew, purposely selecting a conspicuous position, calculated to disconcert the occupant of the pulpit. The moment Mr Waddy entered, his would-be tormentors caught his eye. He took in the situation at a glance and without hesitation solemnly called upon "Brother L. (QC) to offer prayer." The abashed counsel beat a precipitate retreat, and his equally crestfallen colleague was not slow to rid the amused congregation of his presence also.'

ed. D. Whiteley *Illustrious Local Preachers* 1891, p.196.

---

on full plan were more likely to belong to classes I and II, and less likely to III and IV, than those with less experience, albeit probably more as a function of their age than of their preaching. Social prejudice seems to have affected the pattern of office-holding by local preachers in the church or circuit, especially as regards the relative proportions of classes II and III. At the top of the ecclesiastical hierarchy were the positions of circuit steward and chapel steward, 65 and 59 per cent of which were filled by members of class II and only 26 and 29 per cent from class III. At its base, offices associated with children's and young people's work carried much less of a social cachet; thus, only 32 per cent of Wesley Guild or Christian Endeavour officers were recruited from the intermediate class, and only 36 per cent of Sunday school staff.[34] The same pattern is evident in respect of public offices, particularly with local preachers who served as councillors. Even the leisure life of local preachers was influenced by occupational factors to an extent; those interested in gardening, sports or games had a greater tendency to come from the skilled class, those who followed academic and cultural pursuits or who were active in religious, political or social work were rather more common in the intermediate class.

Two Wesleyan local preachers eminent in their professions.
Judge Samuel D. Waddy QC, MP, (1830-1902) and Arthur Henderson MP, labour leader and statesman (1863-1935). Henderson (on the right) won the Nobel Peace Prize in 1934.
F. H. Buss and R. G. Burnett *A Goodly Fellowship* 1949, p.48.
J. W. Bready *England: Before and After Wesley* 1938, p.353.

Since Methodist Union

The post-war evidence is far from systematic but tends to confirm an increasingly middle-class background for Methodism's local preachers, despite the occasional generalized statement which implied a rather broader recruitment pattern.[35] Thus, in the Okehampton area of Devon in the late 1950s the local preachers, mostly elderly or middle-aged, were mainly farmers with some business and professional men. Of the twenty local preachers in one rural circuit all but two of the men were farmers and the two women were the wives of farmers.[36] The thirty local preachers, twenty men and ten women, who were members of two Wolverhampton churches, one in a suburb and one on a corporation housing estate, in 1962-65 all belonged to the Registrar General's non-manual classes, twenty-four to II (intermediate occupations, many of them in teaching), and three each to I (professional) and IIIa (clerical and other non-manual workers). The proportion of what might be described as middle-class local preachers was therefore 90 per cent, far more than among society leaders (71 per cent), informal leaders (69 per cent), trustees (65 per cent) and youth leaders (63 per cent). It was also considerably higher than among the membership, 74 per cent of whom (in the suburban church) and 21 per cent (in the estate church) belonged to classes I and II, and infinitely higher than in the neighbourhood population (28 per cent in the suburb, 3 per cent on the estate).[37] The four local preachers resident in four Durham mining villages in 1968 were three retired miners and one self-employed baker.[38] Of the sixteen local preachers (including two on trial and one on note) in the Wallasey Circuit in 1990, four were university graduates and six others held professional qualifications. Five were or had been teachers, one was a chartered surveyor, one a retired manager of a retail store, one a former bus driver, and one a former factory worker. The remainder were in commercial or secretarial work.[39]

The most recent data derive from a postal survey of local preachers which was undertaken by David Burfield between March and May 1992 as part of his doctoral research at the University of Nottingham into pastoral care in Methodism. The questionnaire was sent to three hundred local preachers selected randomly from circuit plans or directories for seven Methodist districts (Bristol, the four London districts, Nottingham and Derby, and Newcastle-upon-Tyne), with the proviso that, as far as possible, only active preachers were targeted. Overall, 211 completed returns were received, equivalent to a response rate of 70 per cent. The majority of informants were male (63 per cent), married (79 per cent), educated to degree or post-degree professional level (54 per cent), and from suburban, country town or village churches (77 per cent). Their ages ranged from 23 to 87 with a mean of 57 years. A total of 58 questions was asked, many of them sub-divided, of which two specifically related to occupation.[40]

An enquiry about current occupational status revealed that 44 per cent of respondents were in paid employment (39 per cent on a full-time and five per cent on a part-time basis). An equal number were retired, eight per cent of whom were undertaking some form of voluntary work. A further five per cent were self-employed. Only one person claimed to be unemployed and there were no full-time students, but six per cent described themselves as home-makers. The attributes of occupationally active local preachers (in full- or part-time paid employment or self-employed) differed to a certain extent from those of the retired. In particular, as one would obviously expect, the former were younger (with a mean age of 47.4 compared with 66.6 years), with a marital status to match; thus the proportions of single local preachers were 17 per cent for the active and nine per cent for the inactive, and of widowed nought and 13 per cent. They also had a bigger component of men (74 per cent as against 53 per cent for the inactive) and of those educated to degree or post-degree professional level (60 and 45 per cent), with correspondingly fewer with just a basic schooling (five and 22 per cent). The active group had fewer years of accreditation as local preachers (16.6 against 31.1), and took slightly more appointments per quarter (5.1 compared with 4.8). But they were rather less likely to have had parents in Methodist membership (51 per cent against 68 per cent), to come from families with a tradition of local preaching (29 and 33 per cent), and to hold other offices in Methodism. The disparity in office-holding was especially evident in respect of class leaders (a position held by nine per cent of the occupationally active local preachers compared with 28 per cent of the retired) and pastoral visitors (19 and 41 per cent). At a district level, the Nottingham and Derby District had most occupationally active local preachers (62 per cent), and the Newcastle-upon-Tyne District the least (40 per cent); in the four London districts 50 per cent of the preachers were occupationally active and in the Bristol District 43 per cent.

Precise details of current or, in the case of retired people, previous occupation were also sought and analysed according to ten broad categories. This analysis reveals how overwhelmingly middle-class are the local preachers of contemporary Methodism. Especially noteworthy is the dominance of teachers and other educational staff, with 26 per cent of the sample active in the primary and secondary sectors and 12 per cent in the tertiary. A further 16 per cent were in the professions, 12 per cent in management and administration, seven per cent in health and social services, four per cent in church or charity work, three per cent in retail or other sales, and 11 per cent in lesser white-collar jobs. A mere four per cent were semi-skilled, with six per cent in other occupations (three technicians, three homemakers/housewives, two farmers, two journalists, one shipowner, one housekeeper). The relative smallness of the sample inhibits a systematic breakdown by demographic and other variables, but a few underlying trends can be detected. In respect of gender, for instance, women (44 per cent) were more likely to be active in primary, secondary or tertiary education than men (34 per cent), and far less likely to work in the professions, management or administration (nine per cent compared with 39 per cent). There were marked differences in the mean ages of the ten groups, ranging from 51.7 for local preachers working in management and administration to 66.0 for the semi-skilled; whereas 34 per cent of those aged twenty to fifty-nine and 36 per cent of the occupationally active came from the professions, management or administration, the figures were only 22 per cent for those between sixty and eighty-nine and 21 per cent for the inactive. Those educated to degree or post-degree professional level were, predictably, especially well represented in primary, secondary or tertiary education (64 per cent so qualified), the professions, management or administration (66 per cent) and in the health, social services, church and charity sector (74 per cent). Turning to Methodist variables, we find that the proportion of education-related occupations was particularly high amongst those with a tradition of local preaching in the family (46 per cent) and with either or both parents in Methodist membership (48 per cent, 26 per cent more than those without such a membership background). The number of appointments on the quarterly plan fluctuated between 4.4 for white-collar employees to 8.8 for church or charity workers. The Bristol District had the fewest local preachers engaged in education (27 per cent, compared with a high of 45 per cent in London) and the most in the professions, management and administration (37 per cent, as against a low of 22 per cent in the Newcastle-upon-Tyne District).

Conclusion

On the basis of the, relatively limited, evidence reviewed above, four propositions may be advanced. First, the earliest generations of Wesleyan local preachers had quite a varied occupational background, but tended to be recruited disproportionately from the ranks of farmers, retailers and skilled craftsmen; there were certainly few labourers or other unskilled persons in comparison with the general population. Second, for much of the nineteenth century (but far less so by the dawn of the twentieth), Primitive Methodist local preachers had more distinctly working-class origins, with significant numbers of labourers as well as of artisans.

Third, in the period immediately after Methodist union, when *The Methodist Local Preachers' Who's Who, 1934* was published, more than four fifths of local preachers could be characterized as lower middle class (Registrar General class II) or skilled working class (class III, many of these increasingly in non-manual positions). Especially noteworthy was the fact that there were almost three times as many local preachers from the lower middle class as in the male population as a whole (and only a tenth as many from the unskilled working class). Fourth, since the Second World War, further social elevation of the local preachers has taken place, with a growing dependence on teachers and others from the education profession and an almost complete elimination of manual workers. Although this process clearly mirrors developments in the Church's total lay constituency, members and adherents alike, it is probable that, given the combination of a very steep decline in the population of local preachers since the 1940s, and much higher congregational expectations of their performance in the pulpit, local preachers constitute much more of a social and educational élite in the Church than they did during the formative phases of Methodism.

TABLE 1

Occupations of Methodist Local Preachers in 1934
by Registrar General Classes in Percentages

		Methodist local preachers, 1934	Men in England and Wales, 1931
I	Professional occupations	5.5	2.4
II	Intermediate occupations	38.7	13.2
III	Skilled occupations	44.6	48.7
IV	Partly skilled occupations	9.3	18.2
V	Unskilled occupations	1.9	17.5

TABLE 2

Occupations of Methodist Local Preachers in 1934
by Occupational Groups within Registrar General Classes in Percentages

I	PROFESSIONAL OCCUPATIONS	
	Insurance managers	1.5
	Chartered accountants	0.7
	Chartered engineers or surveyors	0.8
	Others in professional occupations	2.5
II	**INTERMEDIATE OCCUPATIONS**	
	Farmers	8.3
	Teachers or lecturers	5.7
	Religious workers	1.3
	Clerical workers (higher)	2.8
	Officials	2.1
	Works or store managers	4.0
	Dealers or retailers	11.7
	Others in intermediate occupations	2.8
III	**SKILLED OCCUPATIONS**	
	(a) Mineworkers (higher)	5.4
	(b) Transport workers (higher)	2.7
	(c) Clerical workers (lower)	5.5
	(d) Armed forces	0.1
	(e) Insurance agents	2.9
	Commercial travellers or representatives	2.0
	Shopworkers or sales persons	3.3
	Textile workers	2.8
	Shoe or leather workers	1.1

continued . . .

III   SKILLED OCCUPATIONS continued

Wood workers	1.8
Metal workers	2.8
Food workers	2.6
Printing workers	1.5
Building or construction workers	0.7
Painters, decorators or furnishers	1.8
Engineers or mechanics	2.5
Others in skilled occupations	5.4

IV   PARTLY SKILLED OCCUPATIONS

(a)	Gardeners	2.1
	Agricultural workers	3.2
(b)	Transport workers (lower)	2.0
	Mineworkers (lower)	0.7
	Servants or caretakers	0.6
	Others in partly skilled occupations	0.8

V   UNSKILLED OCCUPATIONS

(a)	Building or dock labourers	0.1
(b)	Others in unskilled occupations	1.8

TABLE 3

*Occupations of Methodist Local Preachers in 1934 within
Registrar General Classes for Sub-Samples in Percentages (Across)*

	I	II	III	IV	V
GENDER					
Men	5.3	38.0	45.4	9.3	1.9
Women	10.7	57.1	21.4	10.7	0.0
AGE					
15-39 years	3.6	30.9	51.8	11.8	1.8
40-59 years	4.0	40.9	43.3	9.5	2.4
60 years and over	6.0	45.7	38.5	8.5	1.3
MARITAL STATUS					
Single	3.6	37.3	46.4	10.0	2.7
Married or widowed	5.1	40.2	43.4	9.7	1.6
CHILDREN					
None	5.4	33.8	47.7	12.3	0.8
One or two	4.0	41.5	43.1	8.9	2.4
Three or more	6.0	42.2	41.4	9.1	1.3
EDUCATION					
Elementary	2.7	31.6	49.9	13.1	2.7
Secondary	6.5	51.1	37.0	5.4	0.0
Tertiary	14.3	61.0	22.1	2.6	0.0

TELEPHONE OWNERSHIP					
Telephone number given	13.0	57.4	27.8	1.9	0.0
Telephone number not given	4.4	36.0	47.1	10.4	2.1
REGION					
Southern England	5.4	43.1	40.4	10.4	0.8
Midlands	3.7	31.5	49.8	12.0	2.9
Northern England	7.1	41.2	43.0	7.1	1.5
Wales	3.7	29.6	59.3	3.7	3.7
DENOMINATION					
Ex-Wesleyan Methodist	7.6	43.9	39.2	7.6	1.6
Ex-Primitive Methodist	5.5	37.6	46.7	9.7	0.6
Ex-United Methodist	3.0	37.3	44.8	11.9	3.0
FULL PLAN/ON TRIAL					
Full plan	5.6	39.0	44.3	9.4	1.7
On trial	0.0	18.8	62.5	6.3	12.5
AGE AT APPOINTMENT					
15-19 years	5.0	38.8	48.8	6.3	1.3
20-29 years	4.6	39.2	44.1	9.9	2.3
30-39 years	2.4	39.5	45.2	12.9	0.0
40 years and over	7.4	41.2	36.8	13.2	1.5
YEARS ON FULL PLAN					
0-19 years	5.2	32.4	49.7	11.3	1.4
20-39 years	5.9	44.8	38.1	9.1	2.1
40 years and over	6.1	42.6	42.6	7.4	1.4
CHURCH OR CIRCUIT OFFICES					
Trustee	3.5	41.3	46.9	5.9	2.4
Chapel steward	2.6	59.2	28.9	7.9	1.3
Society steward	3.3	45.9	40.2	9.1	1.4
Poor steward	2.9	47.1	44.3	4.3	1.4
Class leader	5.7	38.8	47.4	7.2	1.0
Sunday school teacher or officer	4.3	35.8	48.4	9.2	2.3
Wesley Guild or Christian Endeavour officer	7.5	32.1	50.3	8.8	1.3
Circuit steward	8.0	65.0	26.0	1.0	0.0
PUBLIC OFFICES					
Public office recorded	5.8	51.0	32.8	9.1	1.2
Public office not recorded	5.4	33.8	49.3	9.4	2.1
Parish, district, borough or county councillor	4.0	58.1	29.0	7.3	1.6
INTERESTS OR RECREATIONS					
Gardening	3.5	37.6	51.8	7.1	0.0
Sports or games	3.9	39.6	46.3	9.8	0.4
Academic or cultural pursuits	6.2	41.5	40.0	9.2	3.1
Religious, political or social work	4.7	47.1	38.8	7.1	2.4

12

PREACHING THE WORD:

Methodism and the Poor

Robert Colls

A little aside from the main road
becalmed in last-century greyness,
there is a chapel, ugly, without appeal
to the tourist to stop his car
and visit it. The traffic goes by,
and the river goes by, and quick shadows
of clouds too, as the chapel settles
a little deeper into the grass.

But here once on an evening like this,
in the darkness that was about
his hearers, a preacher caught fire
and burned steadily before them
with a strange light, so that they saw
the splendour of the barren mountains
about them and sang their amens
fiercely, narrow but saved
in a way that men are not now.

(R. S. Thomas, *The Chapel*)

In the beginning were the words of a man whom they imagined to
be something like them, even though he had been a Jewish peasant living
in Lower Galilee under the Roman Empire. He had told stories about a

kingdom of God which exists both within and without, and grows in the manner of mustard seeds, or dough. Entering this kingdom was worth everything you had. The poor were blessed. So too were the destitute, the reviled, the hungry, the robbed and the crying. First was last. Less was more. He taught that this temporal world was not the only world, and that repentance was necessary. He expressed love paternally, a love which the clever, the conceited and the rich would find hard to understand.

These stories were all of an ancient Mediterranean place of desert and lake, river and hilltop. They concerned rural people, living largely by their own labour, in families and villages, within a tradition. Whether magician or healer, mystic or Messiah, there were many ways to imagine the story-teller. He had lived as a local preacher who told his stories face to face, as a poor man who did not beg, but gave, and as a common man who did not listen so much as tell.

After him came the written Word, refracting his words through four of perhaps a dozen gospels in circulation after his death. Bound later with an older testimony to match the new, the Word flowed now through centuries of witness. Then there were the words of those who believed in the man, or who thought they might. Their words are not to be confused with Scripture because, like his, they were not simply learned from existing texts or ecclesiastical rituals. They broke free and sought to get beyond. Breaking free was something fundamental to Jesus and his followers.[1]

We find voices trying to get free in an English industrial village. This is from a Methodist prayer meeting at Winlaton, County Durham, in the 1850s:

> 'A score of voices of varying *timbre*, at the invitation of Matthew Pickering . . . join in singing "Thou Shepherd of Israel and mine," after which we are led to the Presence by simple heart language. Jackey Parker prays with open eyes, fixed on the ceiling, and his wheezy voice . . . William Armstrong, with the wooing note, gently and smilingly leads us . . . Then came the sonorous tones of George Spark . . . and how that voice rolled and swelled . . . then it broke as he told of those who had gone before . . . Then Tommy Warren, the singer saint . . . Ellison Clark, calm and judicial, and others less frequently heard . . . Women were there too, who came to keep their tryst

and meet their Lord . . . and young people were drawn
and held by the mystic contagion.'[2]

Words are contagious. Voices began on the inside and first
preaching was done unto self. One of the first 'Methodist' lay preachers,
Howel Harris, told himself in March 1735 that he had felt a quickening
under the Word – a conviction that great things were imminent. Then
came weeks of anxiety, bursting through on 25 May with a belief that
Christ had died for him, followed three weeks later by the fleshing of all
this inner agitation with great gusts of physical proof that it was true – 'I
felt suddenly my heart melting within me', crying out 'Abba Father!', his
soul 'filled and satiated': 'There was in me a well of water springing up
to everlasting life. John 4:14.' For Howel Harris, the preaching unto self
didn't end with assurance.[3] It continued in a form of self-disciplining
which later passed for 'Methodism', and went on to be translated by
Harris in over three hundred volumes organized by the power and
meaning of words: first, 'What passes between God and my soul';
second, 'Heads and substance of my public discourses'; third, 'An
account of what occurs in some conversation', and finally 'An account of
my journeys . . .' and what passed between him and those he met.

Somewhere between Wesley's and Hugh Bourne's ministries, the
Scriptures re-entered the life of a people who were being pressured by
history to understand themselves as a 'working class'. Though by no
means the only idiom, the Scriptures embedded themselves in the redoubts
of working-class consciousness some forty years before Karl Marx found
his English translation. Methodism found special favour in communities
of artisans, ironworkers, miners, small farmers, field labourers, knitters,
weavers and fishermen. From south-west to north-east, the Methodists cut
a diagonal swathe through the rural and industrial settlements of England,
with flanking movements, west into Wales and industrial Lancashire, and
east into the flatlands of East Anglia and north across the Humber.[4]

In one sense, we can hardly speak of 'Methodism' as a single
movement.[5] In another sense, in the sense of this chapter, it is indeed
reasonable to speak of Methodism as a common movement recognizable
by its chapel life, the words it spoke and those who spoke them. There
were great varieties of working and lower middle-class occupations and
even greater varieties of regional strength. The Wesleyans were always
the biggest and the most evenly spread, but they too had their strongholds
– particularly in Cornwall, in parts of the Midlands and right across
Norfolk, Lincolnshire, Yorkshire and Pennine Lancashire. The Primitives

were second, weaker in the south, stronger in the Midlands and northwards and eastwards right down to Norfolk, with a particular affinity for coastal, rural and mining villages. Other smaller denominations were much more regionally specific: the Bible Christians – almost exclusively in the south-west; the Wesleyan Methodist Association – mainly but not entirely in the southern reaches of the north-west, Manchester and Cheshire; the New Connexion – strong only in northern central England, with stations in Northumberland and Cornwall;   the Calvinistic Methodists – entirely in Wales and along the Mersey. By Scriptural quotation, allusion, analogy and metaphor, the texts spoke for an embattled class.[6] In a society whose economic dogmas caught 'labour' in the grip of the iron laws of supply and demand, and thereby denied the agency of working people, those people, seeing themselves like the Israelites in bondage, pitted the Bible against Political Economy. They rebuked the economists. What their employers denied, they affirmed:[7] that the labourer is worthy of his hire, that he shall receive the fruits of his labour, that it is wrong to oppress the poor, that not the sayer of the law but the doer shall be rewarded. Usually, these words were spoken aloud. At other times, they found their way into print and show historians theological ways of thinking about the Industrial Revolution. Occasionally, for high days and holidays, texts were stitched and woven into the reds and golds of trade union banners, the iconography of labour.[8]

To research the movements of the poor is to find oneself in dusty archives reading crumbling papers which reveal, with compelling clarity, certain pre-eminent concerns. First, the *names* of members, the human lists of organizations which only counted if they had people to count. Methodist membership was open.   Second, their *pennies,* the rent of organizations which could only exist if they were united in what they did. Third, *words,* the life-blood of organizations which could only associate democratically through networks of speech and writing.   Whether the research is into Primitive Methodist societies, or trade union lodges, or Cooperative stores, the bound volumes of names and pennies and words tell the same story. In the registers and accounts, regulations and minutes, we can listen to a movement looking for control. 'Questions to be answered by the Candidates for the Preachers' Plan' posed the questions with all the authority of print, and received the answers in a large and shaky hand:[9]

'1. How long have you been   *Over five years.*
    converted?

2. What means have you used to cultivate your religious life? — *I have attended the means of grace as far as possible.*

3. What books have you read since your conversion? — *The Bible, Farrar's Life of Christ, Pilgrim's Progress, and other good books.*

4. How long have you been a member of the Primitive Methodist Connexion? — *Nearly five years.*

5. Have you read the Rules of our Society? If so, what are your views of our form of Church Government? — *Yes, and I consider them equal to or better than I know.*

6. To what extent have you met in class, and what is your idea of the class as a means of grace? — *Regularly as far as practicable, and I believe it to be very helpful and soul inspiring.'*

Of course, there were words and there were words. Words of connexional control were one thing, Words out 'of Thy mouth' were another. To the poor, words such as these assumed the poetic mystery of what lay beyond and within their grasp. Special testimonies, they defined the moment when God had joined with them in a unique relationship. In that extraordinary encounter, no matter how much maundering had gone on beforehand, they had come face to face with the whole apparatus of

---

EXPERIENCING CONVERSION

'After being a member of the Bishop Auckland society at South Church for two years, my name was brought before the local preachers' quarterly meeting, whereupon I received a note from the superintendent minister, the Rev. Mr Haigh, informing me that I was to preach before Mr Matthew Braithwaite and Mr Buxton . . . Mr Braithwaite gave a good report of me, though there was a great difference of opinion respecting my fitness for the pulpit . . . I was put on the plan for twelve months on trial, and during that period I did my utmost to prepare myself for my appointments.' (At the oral exam for full plan) . . . 'One of the local preachers asked me which came first, regeneration or justification? I answered "Aw gat all mine in a lump".'

Hopper Joplin, *Thomas Harker* Jarrow 1900. Harker became a noted revivalist. He was born at Whaw in Arkengarthdale in 1828.

Pauline theology. Then it was Repentance – Justification – New Birth – Revelation – Sanctification – Purification. Theologians wrote about these things as if they happened in stages, but for the penitent in the moment of conversion they were simultaneous experiences. For a movement built so laboriously on words, when the means of grace was finally resolved it was a paradox that that resolution mustered only words which made no sense. Revd Colin McKechnie recalled the 1867 Northumbrian revival:

> The revival scenes at these places were often glorious. They cannot, indeed, be described without using language that would appear extravagant. Often when I have seen crowds, yea crowds of men and women flocking to the penitents' form, and with strong crying and tears pleading with God for mercy, I have felt utterly broken down. The whole countryside was moved. It almost seemed as if the Millenium was rushing upon us . . .[10]

Literacy – long the privilege of higher classes and their access to sacred knowledge – could not but be the ambition of poor Methodists. Because Protestantism put so much stress on texts, quite literally so, and because, of all the resources of labour, words cost least and mattered most, at times it seems as if literacy and grace went hand in hand. This had been the case in the seventeenth century and it became the case again in the nineteenth. George Edwards, later to become leader of the Norfolk agricultural labourers, first came on the plan in 1872:

> Up to this point I could not read, I merely knew my letters, but I set myself to work. My dear wife came to my rescue and undertook to teach me to read. For the purpose of this first service she helped me to commit three hymns to memory and also the first chapters of the Gospel according to St. John . . . When I returned home from work after tea she would get the hymn book, read the lines out, and I would repeat them after her.[11]

Methodists were strung together through language and particular forms and evaluations of language. In the early days, their object was the preaching of the Gospel and their only means were little more than a band of preachers, a heap of pennies, and some books and papers. They identified against a hostile world. Acts 28:22 provided the lines for the first Primitive Methodist class tickets, in 1811:

'But we desire to hear of thee what thou thinkest: for as concerning this sect, we know that everywhere it is spoken against.'

The Primitives had been expelled from the Burslem Circuit because of their field meetings – days and nights of steady preaching with spasms of unleashed emotion. The Wesleyan Conference had ruled against such meetings. But had not Wesley himself, albeit reluctantly, 'submitted to be more vile' when on 2 April 1739, at four in the afternoon, he had followed Whitefield out into the fields? Thereafter he had preached openly (including in other men's parishes) and wherever he could win a crowd. Yet he was always on guard against charges of unravelling public order and private decency, and he was particularly critical of 'those who are stiled mystick divines . . . [who] utterly decry the use of reason'. [12]

Wesley had always wanted his people to be a reading community but in his day reading was not necessarily a silent or private activity.[13] Reading in groups meant speaking, and speaking could provoke free speech. Before Methodism housed itself in chapels, free speech was easier. Chapel brought more order (who could speak and when) to the proceedings. Cottage religion, by contrast, encouraged a self-conscious sincerity and spontaneity which poor people were not supposed to show. What was said and sung in the home, or in barns and fields, was difficult to track and impossible to license. Women in particular found their tongue in these vernacular places. As feminists were to find half a century later, there was nothing like a self-absorbed free-speaking woman to incur the anger of her opponents.[14]

It was as a free speech community that Wesley worried about his people. So did the restored State, gagging free religious speech since the seventeenth century with its Acts of Test, Toleration and Uniformity. 'Toleration' in 1689 might denote official acceptance, but tolerated speech was registered and licensed, never encouraged. Once institutionalized, all of Methodism worried about state repression until from the late 1820s the State itself became more liberal and Methodism too big to be bossed. But before that, and for a long time after, the movement was wary of further distortion brought about by legal restraint. This put Methodist leaders in a cleft stick. On the one hand they tried to discipline their members not to speak in ways likely to incur repression; on the other hand, they led a movement which stood or fell on the freedom to preach *independently*.

Even if there had been no Jabez Bunting, the problem would have remained. Liberty was the fruit of discipline.

Politicians harboured few doubts about Methodism's deviancy, regardless of what it said or did. Any organization which allowed the poor their tongue threatened a state order whose instruments and offices were supported by a clerical intelligentsia. As an informer wrote from Bristol to the Home Office in 1821:

> Great numbers of Methodists have separated from the orderly and regular Westlean (sic) body and are forming plans for Preaching in *Tents* in the *fields this Summer* in all parts of England and it is *among these* that the seditious are directing their attention.[15]

To a ruling class who felt secure only when the poor had their heads bowed and their mouths shut, the Word and the words which dinned around it were potentially treasonable forces. From Robert Southey, who in 1820 called Methodist preaching 'disgusting', to the psychologist William James who in 1904 called revivalism 'that religion of chronic anxiety', St. Augustine's dictum 'Love God and do as you like' spelled nothing but trouble when on poor people's lips. Even the historian of the English poor, Edward Thompson, lost his great empathetic and dialectical gifts once in the presence of poor people's religious words and emotions. His treatment of Methodism is almost a Freudian history of repression and castration, completely at odds with other parts of his analysis. While Methodist tracts were full of nauseating tales of piety and psychic cruelty, the tract was less than the whole story.[16] It is, of course, part of Methodist folklore that it was pilloried and pelted. What is less well known is that local preachers were the main target. Poor men preachers reversed the order of society. Poor women preachers reversed both society and nature. It was alleged that the men were licentious, the women abandoned, and all were emotional to the edge of madness, taught as they were 'to snivel, groan, cant, whine and wheeze' while addressing their Maker in ludicrously intimate terms.[17] Enthusiasm was a dangerous genie. Once released from its bottle, who could tell where it would go? To 'A Professor', preachers were charlatans who crept about the byways of private gratification while espousing the narrow path of righteousness. Their nails were as long as their prayers. Their mouths were black holes of 'irrational bleating . . . larded with fine new words' – forgeries which they had minted for themselves.[18] Put in their own words, Christ

Jesusness's savingable Incarnation was carnal knowledge muchly, and the scoffers were not slow to scoff:

> 'In those soft Moments (all the Soul unbent)
> The Maid on heavenly joys intent . . .
> Say would she not in her New Birth
> Know some Part of her Heav'n on Earth?'[19]

Buck's *Theological Dictionary* of the 1840s categorized Primitive Methodism by its loose and impetuous tongue. They were known as *Ranters* and their illiteracy, noise, physical movement and widespread use of local preachers and permission for 'females to preach in promiscuous assemblies', attracted prurience as well as distaste.[20]

In spite of the avalanche of outside criticism, speech control was in fact, built into Methodist institutions. The Ranters, who had ignored strenuous Wesleyan efforts between 1800 and 1807 to control conferences, lovefeasts, band-meetings and camp-meetings, even they sought their own control almost from the beginning. In 1811 they proscribed 'free Gospelism'. In 1814 they published their first regulations. In 1819 they held their first Conference, which went on to ban women from certain offices in 1824 and generally from preaching in 1841, and which produced strict itinerancy rules in 1826. More well-connected movements than this could ignore the opinions of lesser members because greater members had sufficient say in higher places. Richer movements than this could not be bankrupted for £50. As an organization, Methodism could not afford the comfortable connections of the wealthy and nepotistic. Dependent on little more than the energies of its people, Methodism had to lay hold of their *will*, to encourage it but at the same time control it. There was nothing new in this. The Baptists had been doing it since the seventeenth century, but Methodism took it into hitherto untouched places.

From backsliding and unseemly liaisons to improper conversations and misuse of funds, there was always plenty to control. In 1849 the Primitive societies strengthened the bonds of the connexion with the General Consolidated Minutes – 176 pages binding the administration of the Word and the Fund into one system. Four years later, the 'Hymn Book Controversy' showed that these issues had not yet been satisfactorily resolved.[21] By the end of the century even the Ranters had college theologians for the finer sifting of the Word, and with over 16,000 lay preachers ministering at four-fifths of services, the Connexion had a lot of sifting to do. Until then, training had been informal, 'left . . . to their own resource', and learned largely on the job, with the note to preach. By 1896 they had a book which taught clarity, syntax, grammar and correct modulation of voice.[22] According to its authors, their intention was to get away from the worship of Scripture and back to the worship of God. Yet the danger was that God came through a Jesus who was himself mediated through college theology. There was always tension. For some, college scholarship was enabling; it put more authority in the preacher's hands and saved the Connexion from sectarian literalism. For others, there was not much difference between college and control. In 1902 William Mair's academic manual showed how detailed this control could be. The first half is nothing less than a physical science of lung and tongue. From first breath to last gesture, preachers should know that . . .

> . . . obstruction and compression of the breath required for an articulation take place in the mouth, and the compressed breath is between the point of obstruction and the glottis – that is, in the mouth and pharynx, both of which are contractile or elastic.[23]

Preachers were advised not to stand like a graven image, nor writhe, nor jerk their heads up and down, nor sway on the balls of their feet, nor hang their heads, nor pull at their attire, nor gaze dreamily into space. In particular, they should not end everything with Amen, or address Jesus too familiarly, or repetitiously, or without reflection.

If the academy directed that preachers' words should be more controlled, the unadorned Word directed that they could not. Not quite. This God and His People were talkers. Protestantism, especially, allowed Him to speak. Did not the Primitive Methodists proclaim the 'conversation ministry'? Was not the Wesleyan mode of taking Conference minutes by question and answer? Does not the Spirit blow where it listeth? How independent could a movement be and not instil a certain irregularity in its members? The entire Methodist economy – from extemporary sermons to open exhortation – encouraged talk as much as it distrusted it.[24] There was hardly a Protestant church in the world which had not found itself by losing itself from the orthodoxies of some other church. Luther had been only a successful heretic. To many contemporaries, Wesley himself had had a quick tongue and a dangerous tendency towards schism. Methodism found itself in a paradox of its own Protestant-Pauline making. How many Damascus Roads could it tolerate and still insist on one way only?

Preaching was the crucible. Preachers spoke of God, through Jesus. They spoke also for God's people, in their own dialect. Every service, therefore, mixed high epic with low naturalist modes of discourse. What was Godly came from on high, and was epic in its proportions. Godliness was offered through Scripture, the Word of God as revealed by a prophetic élite in literary English raised to ever higher emotional planes by hymns which sang their own language directly to the body, site of inner feeling. In general, therefore, epic discourse was a monologue, lined-out, speaking truths which could not be gainsaid, beyond contradiction and at least four steps higher than everyone else. Beneath this, and mixing with it, came what was natural, everyday, and anecdotal. Spoken in dialect, eschewing elaboration or ornament, taken from the heart and translated in broken sentences and scraps of theology, the natural yearnings of the many aspired to the epic verses of the few. Preaching was the crucible because through the preacher what was divine crossed paths with what was human. In the pulpit, what was controlled, and offered whole, mixed with what was free and offered in fragments. And when the two strains fused, as they were meant to do, then who could deny the freedom of that moment to have rendered whole what was once in pieces? 'At liberty', they called it.

A PREACHER'S MODELS

John Wilson MP (1837-1915), the leader of the Durham miners, acknowledged two particular models for his local preaching. One was a fellow preacher, Mr J. Featonby of Haswell, at whose feet he sat. The other was the description of a preacher in William Cowper's poem *The Task* (1785), part of which he quotes in his autobiography:

> He that negotiates between God and man,
> As God's ambassador, the grand concerns
> Of judgment and of mercy, should beware
> Of lightness in his speech. 'Tis pitiful
> To court a grin when you should woo a soul;
> To break a jest when pity would inspire
> Pathetic exhortation; and to address
> The skittish fancy with facetious tales
> When sent with God's commission to the heart.

'In this way I tried to shape my preaching. No one knows better than myself how far I have fallen short of my ideal.'

Memories of a Labour Leader: The autobiography
of John Wilson, JP, MP. London, 1910 p. 213.

In these ways, between the epic and the natural, between what was divine and what was human, and becoming *one*, little miracles were born. What was everyday became sacred. Squat black chapels became holy places. Brick and dust streets became Galilee. Men were enrobed metaphorically as disciples, the women as 'Mothers in Israel'. Standing before the Lord demanded only wonder, and wonder, silence. But silence would have merely to affirmed the earth-bound nature of the human enterprise. The Gospel demanded that the preacher speak, and in the move from silence to speaking the Kingdom of God was at hand, and Canaan and Kedron and Jerusalem were rendered in Welsh Bethesdas and English Zions.[25]

Preachers were apprenticed to speech and charged to make weekly miracles. Once on the plan, what may have started as something personal was forced into the public gaze. The uses of literacy began: books were acquired, reading and writing was mastered, concentration and a certain capacity for conceptual thought was fostered. For poor people, these were among the greatest gifts they could possess and took some of them way beyond chapel life. Thomas Burt had been brought up in a family of pitmen preachers and was elected, in 1874, as one of the two first working-class MPs. He eventually became a junior minister in Gladstone's 1892 government. When high ranking civil servants wanted to shield this know-nothing former miner from confidential information, they retired to talk in public school Latin. But Burt had learned some Latin after he had mastered English. Like so many labour leaders of his generation, Burt regarded the intellect with all the respect of a man who had had to make his own. Two chapters of his autobiography were devoted simply to the books he valued. People like him didn't read texts so much as absorb them. When they came to shape the pattern and meaning of their lives they did so, above all, by drawing on the Bible and Bunyan. Burt remarked on two mentalities of hewing:

> A reflective, contemplative man is driven inward upon himself, and in self-communion and meditation is made strong. The unreflective, superficial man becomes a mere machine for hewing coals.[26]

Local preachers must have started nervously, capping their own words with 'Hosanna' to give them credence. And they certainly harboured too great a respect for the 'Lord's Book' – 'always dressed in inverted commas and deeply underlined and sprinkled with star dust'.[27] Many got no further than this and used Scripture like a hand-rail. Some, however, found their own tongue by practising others. For these, knowing the Bible, and knowing it as the source of other men's authority, was a first faltering step towards their own.

Historians have called the confidence this authority bestowed 'spiritual egalitarianism'. It may have started with words but it took believers deeper than the sound of their own voices. For an earlier context, Max Weber referred to it as an 'ethic', a power within.[28] Spiritual egalitarianism was not just theological. It was historical too, validated through a long gallery of men and women who also had stood up to speak. The office was ancient. Depending on how sacerdotal a view one took of the ministry, the prophetic tradition could run from Moses to Samuel to Jahaziel to Elijah and Amos, Miriam and Deborah, or it could flatly claim that all the Old Testament prophets except Ezekiel were preachers rather than priests. Methodism claimed, moreover, that the New Testament knew of no clerical priesthood. From Jesus and the twelve, to the great Pentecostal outburst, to Stephen and Philip, first deacons of a New Church, to Justin and Origen up to the Friars' revival and into the Reformation – it was held that declines in preaching were coincidental with declines in the Church, especially in the Roman Church. After the Reformation, and even before it with the Lollards, the egalitarian line became clear again through Puritanism and Dissent and into Methodism which, it was believed, revived preaching on a scale commensurate again with the first days of the Apostles.[29]

Such histories put flesh on theology. Spiritual egalitarianism emerged as an old activity, with precedents. Methodism always had more manual workers and fewer middle class people than its detractors – those who stressed the 'sleek grocers, sponging preachers' side – supposed. That Jabez Bunting, dominant figure in early nineteenth century Wesleyanism, wanted his ministers 'on the same pecuniary level with the middle class of [their] own members' did not change the fact that the vast majority of all Methodists were working people who toiled with their hands.[30] Primitive registers in particular reveal an astonishing proportion of the unskilled. Wesley had believed that the poor carried a special dispensation. They were more gracious because their lives were lived closer to the edge. If, as he said, faith was the eye, the ear, the palate and the feeling of the soul, then only the Poor were poor enough not to have had their senses dulled.

Ministries came to be judged by their power to incite grace. No religious movement was more socially-denying and yet more caught up in social crisis than poor people's Methodism. From the 1790s to the 1840s, the movement grew as social crises grew. There appeared to be some linkage between economic transformation and religious revival. Under such circumstances, one woman's rant could be another woman's means of grace. When Primitive Methodist travelling preachers marched down

---

RELIGIOUS CHEEK OF THE MINER-PREACHERS!

'And I remember as a child, I used to wonder over the curious sense of self-glory which one felt in the uneducated leaders, the men especially of the Primitive Methodist Chapels. They were not on the whole pious or mealy mouthed or objectionable, these colliers who spoke heavy dialect and ran the "Pentecost". They certainly were not humble or apologetic. No, they came in from the pit and sat down to their dinners with a bang, and their wives and daughters ran to wait on them quite cheerfully, and their sons obeyed them without overmuch resentment. The home was rough yet not unpleasant, and there was an odd sense of wild mystery or power about, as if the chapel men really had some dispensation of rude power from above. Not love, but a rough and rather wild, somewhat "special" sense of power. They were so sure, and as a rule their wives were quite humble to them. They ran a chapel, so they could run their household. I used to wonder over it, and rather enjoy it. But even I thought it rather "common". My mother, who was Congregationalist, never set foot in a Primitive Methodist chapel in her life, I don't suppose. And she was certainly not prepared to be humble to her husband. If he'd been a real cheeky chapel man, she would no doubt have been much meeker with him. Cheek, that was the outstanding quality of chapel men. But a special kind of cheek, authorised from above, as it were. And I know now, a good deal of this special kind of religious cheek was backed up by the Apocalypse.'

From D. H. Lawrence *Apocalypse* 1931 (In *Apocalypse and other Writings on Revelation* by D. H. Lawrence, ed. Mara Kalnins (1980) p.64).

---

the dales into a Durham coalfield locked in industrial conflict, there was little love lost by colliery owners for their 'large proportion of cunning, mixed up with an abundance of Cant, and Pure Brass'.[31] But in later, more stable days, it was not only Methodist obituaries and Jubilee publications which looked back on all that cant and brass as the mark of a great preacher and a ministry of grace. Indeed, late Victorian and Edwardian Methodism so much judged itself by a redemptive power that it was neurotic about its failings to recapture former days. Some blamed the colleges and their professors, others blamed a new prosperity, but the truth was that just as the old preachers had not understood their success, the new did not understand their failure.

How can we explain those early days? There is a view, for which there is little evidence, in this country, of religious revivalism being 'sold' to the poor by their betters, or their employers, as a way of keeping them quiet. The employing classes were quite capable of understanding the quiescent side of Methodism and how it could work to their advantage, but only in exceptional cases can we see them plotting to supply it as a kind of class-opiate. They understood also that if poor people's Methodism could be pietistic, then it could also be militant, and middle-class sensibilities were never really comfortable with either. Although business élites did give substantial sums to the movement, especially during the twentieth century, they usually donated as believers, not as manipulators.

Perhaps the words of the preachers scorched the simple minds of the crowd in a way that was exploitative? This was the side which drew so much of the anti-Methodist venom. While it is true that the preachers could speak inspirationally on and to the meagre life chances of the poor, it is true also that the preachers knew that their success depended as much upon the unction of the crowd as upon their own rhetorical skill. Hugh Bourne was a shy and inarticulate man given to preaching with his hand over his face and yet he could stumble upon a Staffordshire fervour which he could not explain and did not know how to control. Thomas Batty was, by all accounts, a great preacher who toured Weardale in the steps of five other great preachers and yet was there six months before revival came and 'the country was opening before us.'[32] The theory of dynamic preaching has much to commend it, not least to a Methodism whose own myths are founded on dynamic preaching, but it doesn't explain the 'dry seasons' and 'barren places' of failure. We need to take into consideration the preached as well as the preachy. We have to dig deeper into a popular culture notorious for its turbulence and its distance from the polite culture of the rich. Wesley and his preachers entered that world with mixed results. Any deeper analysis of what actually happened as the two sides collided must get out of the pulpit and into the crowd.[33]

Can the new manufacturing districts be seen by way of American analogy as 'burned-over districts', hungry for meaning and stability? Did Methodism supply factory workers with those disciplines and character transformations, both equally unpleasant, which a capitalist class required? Again, there is something to commend this interpretation but it condescends to the working class as a people who could not know their own minds or trust their own feelings. If the poor did indeed submit, then we need to consider *which* 'poor' (for only a minority were factory workers) as well as the strategies and limits of their submission, and the degree of choice that was open to them. And if their Methodist self-discipline was forged to repress deep psychological damage, as William James would have it, then there must have been other movements which did the same. It is hard to see why religion should be blamed for damage that was not of its own making. Whatever working-class Methodists did and believed they were not just victims because they did it and believed it for themselves. What happened to the children, of course, is another matter. While there can be no doubt that connexional government could intrigue against its members – 'sneaks and slanderers' as Bunting called them – there is also no doubt that many Methodists were too democratically-minded to stand for it, as the history of breakaways and expulsions shows. Similarly, some historians have judged Methodist preaching as if they would have preferred it to have been a version of political radicalism, with deeper realities than religion to lay hold of. But the movement cannot be judged for failing to be what it patently was not. As John Walsh has remarked, we cannot suppose that there were more real levels of reality to address just because the religious level is not to the taste of its critics.

These are all moot points. They probably exaggerate the degree of political excitement and overplay the level of personal torment. Even if they do not, one has to identify the causes and look at the alternative organizational forms. Not only revival religion, but revival politics and revival trade unionism also traded in poor people's anxieties, and none of them could survive without discipline. The political radicals of 1817-23 organized themselves into 'classes', paid their pennies, read their texts and channelled their energies through those classes. The National Union of the Working Classes between 1831 and 1835 self-consciously modelled their association on the Methodist system. Chartists copied the camp meeting. The Independent Labour Party had its 'plan'. Miners' lodges and agricultural labourers' branches were not averse to sacred texts and social hymn-singing. Methodist local preachers can be traced through all these movements, making the short step from religion to politics, pulpit to platform.[34] Thomas Paine, once a local preacher, took not so much a short step as a gigantic stride. Although he preached for only a short time, in Sandwich and Dover through 1759, his biographer makes much of the 'revolutionary democratic potential' which this master staymaker learned from Wesley's movement.[35] Paine, truly a great Englishman and influential in two mighty revolutions, the American and the French, was followed in his path by many others. In Leicestershire, John Skevington and Thomas Cooper made the step into Chartism. In the Potteries, Joseph Capper made it too – and indeed, in the earlier phase of Hanley radicalism, in 1820, the Home Secretary learned more about local preachers Yates and Ridgeway, father and son-in-law, than he ever wanted to know. There were other less famous preacher radicals like Robert Pilkington of Bury and James Grundy of Manchester in 1818-19, and those more famous like Sam Bamford of Middleton and Joseph Rayner Stephens of Manchester, eye-witnesses of the Peterloo massacre.[36] In 1831-32 Tommy Hepburn led the Northumberland and Durham miners against the most powerful capitalist combination in Britain. Assisted by a cadre of young pitmen-preachers, Hepburn said he would meet the owners and show them 'how very far he would beat them, at all points, in reasoning and argument'.[37] Here was a man who made Lord Londonderry bend the knee and pray before negotiation. At the end of the strike seven young Jarrow miners were arrested, tried for conspiracy and transported to Botany Bay. Five were Primitive Methodists.[38] Of the six Dorsetshire labourers who were transported in 1834 – 'The Tolpuddle Martyrs' – four were Methodists and three of them, the Loveless brothers and Thomas Stansfield, were local preachers. George Loveless was identified by his voice for his part in earlier, nocturnal protests. During the 1830s the former Wesleyan local preacher and minister, J. R. Stephens, became the most famous orator of northern radicalism. It has been estimated that half of Joseph Arch's union speakers were local preachers.[39]

In fact, Methodism is another example of a nineteenth-century mass movement trying to come to terms with the *absolutely unprecedented* problem of an active, mass membership. The chapels, along with the CWS stores, the producers' co-ops, the friendly societies, the trade unions, the CIU clubs, the teetotal 'tents' and socialist parties, *all* shared the same problem of how to associate, within the law, in ways that were stable as well as coherent.[40] We can see from their names that association had to be democratic if it was going to be strong enough to be independent. So many guilds and congresses, leagues and unions, federations and *connexions* held them together. Against their enemies who wanted other kinds of social relationship – relationships based on individuals, markets and contracts, or relationships based on deference or worse – these associations maintained a moral, collective and, above all, an independent stance.[41] For the task of holding people together, allowing them to imagine themselves as a community, the press was central and Methodism was very early drawn into associational journalism.

GEORGE LOVELESS AND THE 'SONG OF FREEDOM'

'The judge told us "that not for anything that we had done, or, as he could prove, we intended to do, but for an example to others, he considered it his duty to pass the sentence of seven years' transportation . . . As soon as the sentence was passed, I got a pencil and a scrap of paper and wrote the following lines:

> God is our guide! from field, from wave,
> From plough, from anvil and from loom;
> We come our country's rights to save,
> And speak a tyrant faction's doom:
> We raise the watch-word Liberty,
> We will, we will, we will be free!
>
> God is our guide! no swords we draw,
> We kindle not war's battle fires;
> By reason, union, justice, law,
> We claim the birthright of our sires:
> We raise the watch-word Liberty,
> We will, we will, we will be free!

While we were being guarded back to prison, our hands locked together, I tossed the above lines to some people as we passed; the guard, however, seizing hold of them, they were instantly carried back to the judge; and by some this was considered a crime of no less magnitude than high treason.'

George Loveless, *The Victims of Whiggery,*
being a statement of the persecution experienced
by the Dorchester labourers, London
The Central Dorchester Committee, 2nd edition, 1837.

It is, of course, easy to make the point that institutional Methodism disciplined its members and, in the case of the Wesleyans at least, was not much interested in democracy. The harder point is to understand the painstaking efforts to build bureaucracies which could still do the Lord's work and maintain connexional association while at the same time preserving the strength and integrity of a single movement. Right up to Methodist Union in 1932, these constitutional problems persisted and needed both enterprise and patience in their handling. The Labour Party took from Methodism its 'Conference'. It also took the techniques of manipulating that Conference. The Cooperative Wholesale Society, like Methodism, sought to make its structures open to all and, in so doing, they both had to think creatively about the meaning of membership. They also had to impose order. Seen in this light, all of these mass movements represented extraordinary attempts to build new ways of being human in society. It would be no exaggeration to see Methodist association as about the common ownership of the powers of spiritual production, distribution and exchange.

As early as the 1870s, preachers from all Protestant bodies were worrying about their fading evangelical powers. Moody and Sankey missioned, but it was always understood that their work was largely with interdenominational assemblies of the already converted, a model for American road-shows ever since. They rose without trace. Since then, and with occasional outbursts of 'drop-dead' preaching in fortuitous circumstances – notably Evan Roberts' 1905 Welsh revival[42] – the churches' preaching power has become ever weaker. It is no longer possible to see Methodism as a 'movement'. This barren season has lasted a long time.[43]

The major cultural problems which will follow us into the next century cannot be dealt with here. Technology and its uses, global capitalism and its licence to plunder, the erosion of forms of social ritual, the growth of private life, the decline of community, the fracture of work as a meaningful activity, are all problems which have damaged Methodism as well as other forms of associational life and certainly go beyond their resources to tackle. Some commentators have bundled these problems together and called them 'post-modernist' dilemmas. Whatever we call them, it is certain that nineteenth-century cultural capital is all but played out. The post-modern rejection of the big moralities and single explanations pierce right to the heart of all future relationships, especially religious ones.

And even in their most heroic phase, the preachers' efforts never went entirely according to plan. Earnestness was not for all and not even for the majority. Other groups spoke just as effectively, if not as numerously, to working-class people and the most plebeian church of all, the Roman Catholic, was definitely not the most welcomed. Away from the religious camps, in everyday life, other speech communities prevailed which took their meanings from less rigid notions. To these communities life was best represented by ironies and ambiguities rather than by fixed wills and divine commands. The Word gushed too strong for most people and, it has to be said, carried with it more conceit and humbug than many could bear. Once Methodism had softened its plain speaking in pursuit of other 'languages', and a growing concern with church architecture and accountancy spring to mind, then the charge of hypocrisy gained in force.

And yet, and yet, the privilege of history is to know how things can be different in other contexts. In the recent times the power of the Word has shifted to black American preachers. Spiritual egalitarianism there showed no sign of fatigue in the civil rights struggle. Martin Luther King went to prison seventeen times but never shut up. Black hymns and music, camp meetings, freedom walks and electrifying preaching mixed rights with religion and all with a personal discipline of the sort that many people considered in this volume would have understood. In the autobiography of Malcolm X one can see a spiritual education in the tradition of working-class Methodism in this country. Malcolm was moved first by words while in prison in 1947. As ever, first preaching was done unto self:

> The very enormity of my previous life's guilt prepared
> me to accept the truth. Not for weeks yet would I deal
> with the direct, personal application to myself, as a black
> man, of the truth. It was still like a blinding light.[44]

In Britain, whatever Methodism's shortcomings, it did find voice for those who had no case. If the national culture can be seen as a sort of conversation, then Methodism allowed a significant number of poor people into the debate. In turn, finding that voice helped shape our culture in democratic ways. For women, for a time, Methodist preaching flew in the face of 1 Corinthians 14:34-35. If God called women to make them whole, who could argue? Many men did, of course, and Victorian Methodism put women firmly on the margins. Nevertheless, Miriam, Deborah, Hannah, Abigail, the women who followed Jesus and those who testified to his resurrection were inspirational to the preachers like Mary Barritt, Ann Cutler and Ann Carr with her Leeds 'Female Revivalists' who, in turn, have inspired the feminization of the Word in this century. Galatians 3:28 is back on the readings. Similarly, while it was once convenient for superior persons to depict the English landscape as devoid of people and who, when chancing upon those people, depicted them as mute, dumb and ignorant, the babble of Little Bethel voices gave the lie to that. These were poor people who *had* spoken. The English agricultural labourer, 'Hodge', was represented as stupid as he was silent. Joseph Arch, founder of his first union and a local preacher of renown, explained the trade of teeth locking:

I could speak, but I knew how to keep my mouth shut and my teeth locked up tight. Teeth-locking was a trade I learned early in life . . . like scores of my class, I might have got lock-jaw when in the presence of my 'betters' . . . The timid labourer did, and his masters thought that he was so dull and slow that he had next to no wits, and so had nothing to say . . . A man with the weight of many masters on him learns how to be dumb, and deaf, and blind, at a very early hour in the morning.[45]

On a wet morning of 7 February 1872, three labourers came knocking on Arch's door in Barford, Warwickshire, and requested that that evening he address a body of men in nearby Wellesbourne. Aged forty-six and trained to speak, Arch felt ready. He went to Wellesbourne and spoke beneath the lantern-lit tree and founded the Union. Like so many other poor men and women before him, he had found words.

Joseph Arch MP (1826-1919), Wesleyan local preacher, and one of the principal founders of the National Agricultural Labourers' Union in 1872. He began his life as an itinerant farm labourer, and did more than any other man of his time to improve the working and living conditions of agricultural workers.
(A 'Spy' cartoon from *Vanity Fair* 26 June 1886,
reproduced in Pamela Horn *Joseph Arch* 1971, p.59.)

Professor Arthur Samuel Peake MA, DD, (1865-1929), son of a PM minister, local preacher, biblical scholar, tutor at Hartley P M College Manchester (1892), first Rylands Professor of biblical criticism and exegesis Manchester University (1904), author of many books and editor of the famous Bible Commentary (1920) bearing his name.

13 (i)

LOCAL PREACHERS AND THEOLOGICAL CHANGE IN THE LATER NINETEENTH AND EARLY TWENTIETH CENTURIES

The impact of Arthur Samuel Peake

John Banks

Arthur Samuel Peake was born into the Primitive Methodist Church. His grandfather had been converted under Primitive Methodism and his father was one of its ministers. He had the best of educations in Ludlow, Stratford-upon-Avon and Coventry. In 1883 he went up to St John's College, Oxford, where he took a third in Classical Moderations and a first in Theology. He won a number of prizes in Biblical studies and became familiar with German theological ideas. In 1889 he became a lecturer at Mansfield College and a Fellow of Merton College [both at Oxford]. In this period he came under the influence of five scholars who were in the forefront of biblical and historical studies: Cheyne, Driver, Sanday, Fairbairn and Hatch. It was while Peake was at Mansfield that William Hartley (later Sir William) found him and persuaded him to train men for the Primitive Methodist ministry at the PM theological institute in Manchester which, under the name of Hartley College, was to become known affectionately as 'the jam factory'. Fairbairn (Principal of Mansfield) was loth to let Peake go but wrote to him: 'It seems to me as if you had been specially raised up and trained for the very work . . . and in many ways you are the only person who can do it.'[1]

Peake's advent initiated a quiet revolution. The leading article of *The Primitive Methodist* for February 1892 states: 'What shall we do to amend the rules on the working of the Theological Institute to adapt them to the appointment of Mr A. S. Peake MA as tutor?' and it added 'The tutor shall teach Old and New Testament Introduction, Old and New Testament Exegesis, Old and New Testament Doctrine and the History of Doctrine.' [2]

There were only twenty-eight men in the college at the time and their courses were too short and too inappropriate to afford much help. They were examined in Genesis, Mark, Theism, Stanley, Calderwood and Green [text books available at the time]. In complaint about this a letter appeared in the issue of May 5th 1892 signed 'A Probationer':

> 'The men sent into the work are grievously unprepared . . .
> their education is below that of many of the congregation
> . . . a radical change will be needed in the mode of
> teaching. The time spent in the lecture room . . . was most
> often most unpractically and monotonously spent. The
> knowledge given direct from books, without being properly
> digested, often made the student exclaim: "thank heaven
> another class is over".'[3]

The point was made.

Conference in June 1892 was held at Queen's Road PM Church, Norwich. On the evening before his appointment Peake, and his Oxford friend Dr Fairbairn, spoke to a crowded meeting. Peake's comments were short. He said that 'until last year biblical studies [at the Manchester College] had been entirely neglected. It is impossible to have a sound theological education without going back to the source of theology in the Bible'. He added 'the aim of the course would not be to produce showy men but plain, practical, hard-working men and good Primitive Methodist preachers'.

Judging by the indications of applause in the text Dr Fairbairn was the star of the evening. He asked:

> 'When we plead for an educated ministry what do we
> mean? We plead for a ministry which is capable to the
> very utmost of apprehending the truth of God, presenting
> that truth, and living that truth . . . Don't tell me that the
> first ministers were only fishermen, tent-makers and
> publicans. Do you think that because the first were so the
> present ought to be?' [4]

Next day Peake was unanimously appointed and a gloss was added to the event in a comment in the Conference edition of the paper the next week:

'Mr Arthur Peake MA is quite youthful in appearance and withal extremely modest. Nearly all that is dear to a scholar and an Oxford man he is prepared to surrender at the behest of conscience and in the interests of his father's Church. If we fail to appreciate such splendid loyalty and such noble self-sacrifice, and neglect to profit by it to the utmost, it will be to our everlasting shame, and men may well despair of our connexional future.'5

A S PEAKE AS LOCAL PREACHER

'Before becoming a candidate for the ministry I had the good fortune to be a member of the Great Western Street Circuit, Manchester, with which Dr Peake was in active association. Frequently I heard him preach and was impressed by his quiet, unassuming but penetrating interpretation of the Word. His rich devotional spirit pervaded every part of the service. One worshipper was heard to say on leaving "I would walk ten miles to hear that man pray." In those days a prayer meeting always followed the Sunday evening service and never once did Dr Peake make a breach in that habit. His conduct of that after-meeting made one recognise how real was his belief in the priesthood of believers and it gave proof of his sensitiveness in seeking to follow the lead of the Spirit in supplication.'

W. E. Farndale 'Impressions of an early student'
in J. T. Wilkinson ed., *Arthur Samuel Peake 1865-1929*,
Essays in Commemoration, 1958 p. 58-9.

Peake, by his calm dissemination of the latest and best biblical knowledge through his lectures, articles and books, trained Primitive Methodist ministers, and laymen, in a new way of looking at the Bible. By doing so he helped his own denomination, and other churches in Britain, to avoid the worst effects of fundamentalist controversies of a kind which split the Church in America and had repercussions in Britain also. Indeed, echoes may still be heard of the tragic and foolish debate about natural selection and evolution in which the victory went to the scientists, and Bishop Wilberforce was routed by Professor Huxley. Had it not been for Peake our Church could have been among the losers and Sunday School children might still be singing the chorus to the American ditty which went

Come down, come down, out of your family tree;
Let higher critics, Darwinites, teach their philosophy.
Come down, come down, come off, come off,

And let the baboon be;
They may be apes, but they can't make
A monkey out of me. 6

Such fundamentalism persisted when I was a candidate for the ministry. The eleven farmers who formed the quarterly meeting in 1944 discussed me for a long time as I waited outside the room. The superintendent told me afterwards that they had no real objection to make except that 'He'll go to college and that'll ruin him'. They still had not come to terms with what Peake had done.

Samuel Horton wrote in 1937:

> 'Peake's advent into Primitive Methodism meant a theological revolution by permeation. In its theological outlook it was the most conservative of all the larger divisions of Methodism . . . the bulk of the ministry had not moved from the position of the Founders and looked on the modern approach to the Bible with suspicion, if not with decided antagonism. Primitive Methodism's contribution was in heat rather than light . . . Petty's *Theology*, the first of its standard books, was really a simplification of Watson's *Institutes* . . . the outlook was the same rigid orthodoxy. Peake, while loyal to the accepted tenets of the Church, widened the horizons . . .'7

Peake settled down to thirty-seven years at Hartley, becoming Rylands Professor of Biblical Exegesis in the new Faculty of Theology at Manchester University in 1904, and a constant contributor to learned journals. My father, who left the pit face in 1911 to become one of 'Peake's men' at Hartley, told me 'It seemed to us that we were getting a university education.' It was not ministers alone who attracted Peake's best endeavours. He wrote also in the *Primitive Methodist Leader* and the *Holborn Review* [the P.M. quarterly] so that the worshipper in the pew, the teacher in the Sunday School and the local preacher in the country pulpit could benefit from what he knew. In an article entitled 'Unshaken Truths' Peake wrote:

> 'The local preachers supplement the work of the ministers. Among these are men drawn from different classes, capable of enlarging the outlook of the congregation, and bringing different types of thought before them. Such men, who are

going in and out – men in business, office, workshop, mingling every day with their fellow men – are in a position to understand the problems that vex the common mind in a way which is not possible to the settled minister. That is a great advantage to a church served by a good staff of local preachers.' And he added 'we are called to preach to men of the twentieth century and not to men of the early part of the nineteenth century.'[8]

Peake died on August 19th 1929. John T. Wilkinson in *Essays in Commemoration* quotes an unascribed tribute written shortly after his death: 'If the Free Churches of England have been able without disaster to navigate the broken waters of the last thirty years, it is largely due to the wisdom and patience of trusty and trusted pilots like Arthur Samuel Peake that they owe it.'[9]

It was not to be expected that even so quiet a revolution would be achieved without comment or protest. In the Peake archive at the John Rylands Library are many letters he received throughout the years. Most of those he treasured were from his peers, the teachers in other universities. Some were from ministers and a few were from laymen. We have no means of knowing whether these were local preachers or not, but it is worth remembering that every minister began his preaching as a local preacher. Consider this cry of the heart:

> 'Sunday 21st Nov: Sir, I must thank you for your grand book upon *Christianity its Nature and Truth* for I got it from the Hulme Library . . . I have been ill 4½ years and my faith in my Saviour was tried many times in my poverty & pain and sickness and I renewed it for another 14 days I cannot part with it yet for I am not able to buy one for myself for I get relief from the Guardians at All Saints No 1 District . . . I am only or was a working man but it lifts one up out of self to Higher things . . . John Lister, 6 Thornhill Street, Hulme.'[10]

In 1914 the Revd J. Lindley wrote from St. Ives about his father . . .

> 'a Methodist of the old type. Having a large family he had little time for books and his one book was the Bible . . . he devoted a great deal of time to the Old Testament and I remember when he was at least eighty-six years old how perplexed and confused he was over the history of the

barbarous wars with the so called divine commission to slay women and children. He knows nothing about 'Higher' or 'Lower' criticism but his own human instincts revolted against these conceptions of providence. He did not stand alone in this and I think your book giving as it does the main facts of the case so far as they are understood will have far reaching results.'11

J. H. A. Hart of St. John's College, Cambridge, wrote on November 12th 1913: 'All your work ... tends to the reconciliation of old and new views and I don't wonder that people trust you. For your own folk you must have saved the whole situation . . .'12

Of course, he had his detractors. He once wrote: 'It has been my fortune now for a number of years to be exposed to many criticisms and misjudgements. Generally I meet them with silence.'13 When he decided to reply he was devastating. Lt Col Mackinlay wrote a critique of Peake's book on Job in the *Bible League Quarterly* of July/September 1921 and said 'The Higher critics have given an illustration of the old saying that a little knowledge is a dangerous thing.' Peake showed up the poverty of the man's argument and added: 'It is less perilous to write with a little knowledge than with no knowledge at all.'14 There were, of course, other critical letters. Someone who hid under the name of ONE WHO LOVES THE TRUTH wrote to the *Sunday Strand* magazine:

'We always looked upon this hitherto charming book as suitable to give to children and servants, and to enjoy ourselves on a Sunday Afternoon, or if unable to get to a place of worship . . . but now that such articles of this type have been allowed to creep in to what has always been looked upon as a helpful religious magazine one hesitates.15

Peake's *Commentary* was published in 1919. W. Taylor of Heaton Moor complained about a statement that chapters 40-66 of the book of Isaiah 'includes no Isaianic matter'. 'How can these statements be made in view of Matt. 8:17, Matt. 12:17, Luke 3:4, John 1:23 . . . can it be that modern critics are wiser than the evangelists?'16 As late as 1925 a letter from Mr Edward Geo. Varnish of London commented:

'I had long wanted a catholic minded commentary on the scriptures . . . I read a laudatory review in the *Church Times*, . . . and forthwith bought it . . . I was simply horrified at its tone . . . Jonah, Esther, Ruth "story books", St. Paul's "allegory" of Melchizedek, Elijah "powerful poetry rather than balanced history" . . . the "legend" of David the Psalmist. Magnificat . . . "ascribed not to Mary but to Elizabeth" . . . every time I think of the book it is with a mental shudder.'[17]

A PIT-VILLAGE PREACHER AND A CRITICAL LISTENER

'Jack Willis ses, "Aa hed te preach at such a chapel. There's a chap at that place, whe, if ye got byuks and put them side by side fra heor te the Cathedral, he's read them aal. He's a fine skoller and a critic. Aa couldn't get ma eye off that man aal neet. Aa'd written ma sermon oot se that Aa couldn't make any mistyeks. Aa lyuked doon at ma notes, and it wes aal a blot. Aa dinnet knaa hoo Aa got through. Syun efter, Aa meets this critic's brother. He ses Aa's come te thank thoo for what thoo's dyun te wor brother on Sunday neet." As ses "Aa nivvor did owt te him." "Oh yes, thoo did", the mon said, "he's a great skoller, thoo knaws, and he's getten away fra the track, and thoo's browt him back to the beginning of things. He's never prayed in the meeting for months till that Sunday neet".'

John Salisbury *Me and Jake: The experiences of some Durham Miners* 1916, p.177. The book is based on true experiences, but the author says that the dialect has been toned down to make the sketches more readable in the South!

I wonder why, among the letters, he kept the following – an unsigned letter in a crabbed hand which looked as if it was written by an old man, without much education. Perhaps Peake felt the hurt of those whose Christian world was crumbling because of what he wrote. I give it 'warts and all':

'Sir, it may be the oppion of you and a few, that the old Methods won't do for the Present time it is a Concolation to know that neither you nor your oppions have much weight with the Public. But the old Methods will answer when your Bags of wind are burst and vanished in the air, you insult our Worthy Farthers that are gone to rest. and our Best Men and weomen in the connexion. What bit of learning you have is some old Dry Church History that you got from other men's Labours, Prosition is no honour to a man unless he honouors tat prosition, it is a question if you have not go over the wall into the Church and not through

Christ, you are not going to get over the wall into heaven, be careful that you are not with the number that Christ will sat [say] at the Last Depart from me I never knew you, Better to go to Hell a Drunkard than a Methodist Preacher, you having the title of Professor Peake goes for nothing with God it is clear that Methodism is drifting from God and from Holiness, it is made use of for some to have a idle life much more than get sinners Converted, woe to the Man that Makes religion a Trading Consers [concern?] for a easy life. One that would not like to see you at the left hand at Last.[18]

In 1905 Peake had agreed to write a succession of leading articles for the *Primitive Methodist Leader*. It was the first of many he was to write for laymen and women. He wrote:

'We are tempted to undervalue knowledge ... few things may be more mischievous than good intentions misdirected by ignorance' and he added 'our methods of religious training leave much to be desired ... the duty incumbent on the Church of giving its ministers the best theological training it can command was never taken more seriously than today.'

In this he had not forgotten children and local preachers for within six months he had added eight articles on the work of the Sunday School, and wrote 'We can do no other than rejoice that the work of helping local preachers to a more thorough theological equipment goes forward.'[20]

In the issue of the *PM Leader* of June 22nd 1905 it had been proposed that the PM College should be affiliated with the Theological Faculty of Manchester University. Peake had become a professor there and the approach had come from the Vice-Chancellor of the University. Principal Johnson of Hartley was glad at 'the compliment paid to Professor Peake' and added 'it is just possible that in the matter of Biblical scholarship his equal is hardly to be found.'[21]

It had been the custom to send bright young men, local preachers, directly into circuit and let them train themselves on the job, making up for what they lacked in knowledge by enthusiasm. A correspondent, called ZETA, commenting on the local preachers' report in the July issue of the *PM Leader* wrote: 'we want consecrated intellect as well as emotion', and described how he had introduced the local preachers of a country circuit to

Peake's new commentary on Job. 'Some of the locals were evidently perturbed by uncertain things in the commentary . . . it seemed as if this was their first introduction to the critical view of Old Testament literature and they did not know what to make of it.'[22]

REPETITION IN THE PULPIT

'The Bible was Tommy Wanless' one book; he could quote more scripture than the majority of preachers. He knew it so extensively that his sermons seemed very much alike.

At Seghill he said, one morning "Noo lads. I've a brand new horse for ye this morning" (by "the horse" he meant his sermon) then announced his text.

"Aye," thought an old friend of Tommy's, "we've not had that before." However, Wanless had not gone far before he was on old lines. When the congregation dispersed, his friend said, "Tommy, the saddle's new, the saddle's new, but it's the same awd horse".'

J. B. Wilson *A Primitive Methodist Diamond Field*
(Seaton Delaval Circuit, Northumberland) 1909, P.38

Peake's response, as ever, was to pour out his lucid scholarship not only in the pages of learned journals but also in the ephemeral sheets of the PM connexional newspaper intended for the man or woman in the pew and the local preacher in the country chapel. His titles were learned enough: *Religion and Theology* ; *The Construction of Theology* ; but his speech was direct and his illustrations were homely. In one passage he quoted an Anglican clergyman who said: 'Don't put me down as a thinker, put me down as a believer' and Peake asked: 'What is the value of belief without thought . . . what lies at the basis of this pestilent talk about the mischief of thought?' Elsewhere he compared the old-style theologians to medieval men looking at their maps: 'Everything was mapped out with complete precision (but) they were speculating on disastrously imperfect data.' Illustrating the way Biblical investigation did not destroy what it looked at he quoted Thiersch:

'. . . if a certain great painting, which had been assigned to Raphael, turned out not to be by Raphael, but by another unknown painter there would not be one great picture the less, but there would be one great painter the more.'[23]

An early Christian apologist once wrote: 'I did not think I would get as much good from a book as from a living and abiding voice' so I searched for those who, even at this distance might remember him. A letter in the *Methodist Recorder* brought a number of responses. Some of them were second-hand in that people told me what their father had told them. Mr Maurice Morgan of Hebden Bridge wrote that he had heard Peake preach when he was a teenager and quoted a story of a local preacher who approached him after a service and asked 'Are you the man who says there are three Isaiahs?' Dr Peake agreed that it was so. The preacher said 'I say there is only one Isaiah.' Dr Peake gave him the soft answer: 'If you say so that settles it.' Another response came from a local preacher, now aged 95, in the words of her daughter:

> 'My mother remembers reading some of Dr Peake's books from the age of 15 (1914) and wishing she had someone of her own age to discuss them with . . . they influenced her thinking greatly as she prepared to become a local preacher in 1921 and remained an active preacher for 60 years. When planning to read from the Bible in a service my mother would invariably study what was said about the passage in Peake's Bible commentary. This became the usual practice in our household where all of us eventually became preachers . . .'[24]

Albert Harvey, who trained at the Wesleyan Theological College at Didsbury in the 1920s, told me how Samuel Chadwick wrote generously on Peake's death in *Joyful News*, paying tribute to his dedication, scholarship and humility despite their differences over fundamentalism. The Revd Leonard Duchars wrote from the Isle of Man:

> 'I arrived at Hartley College in 1923 and left in 1926, to be ordained in 1927 . . . Dr Peake gave the charge to the Church . . . His influence has remained to the present day, seventy years later. He taught me how to read the Bible. I entered College like many others with the vague idea that the Bible must be interpreted literally. Dr Peake led me through lower and higher criticism to a new and more intellectually satisfying understanding of the Bible. But he did more than that. It was his aim . . . to make the scriptures more helpful to his readers as a means of grace. His scholarship was unquestioned; his confidence that biblical

criticism, rightly understood, enhanced the value of the Bible was convincing. He was a humble man. He never paraded his learning, and he treated his students with the utmost respect. He was totally dedicated to Christ, and fully committed to serving the Church. I will never forget his prayers in the College Chapel. Spoken quietly they showed us a man in the presence of God who knew Christ and was utterly dependent on Divine Grace. He had a sense of humour and would relieve a sustained argument with a story. When he came to the punch line his whole body would shake with laughter . . .'[25]

I visited the Revd Frank Ward, who was born in 1898, and who at the age of twenty three was sent as a pre-collegiate candidate for the Primitive Methodist ministry to be the acting superintendent of the Appleby circuit. He had been working double shifts in the coal mine (ninety hours a week) to earn the money with which to go to College, and his two year stint at Appleby was a considerable undertaking for a young local preacher. He had left school at 13 to work on the screens of the Darfield Main colliery in Barnsley but his real spiritual education had never been interrupted. Those who taught him were the local preachers of the Barnsley second circuit,

---

MODIFIED VIEWS OF HELL!

'My husband's grandfather preached in the Grimsby Circuit for over 60 years and kept a note book. Grandfather Collins' notebook has several items under prayer meetings held after services at which he preached. At one a petitioner spoke of sinners and of the fires of hell: "Lord, hold them over the flames. Singe them Lord, but don't burn them".'

Mrs Dee Moss of Charlbury, Oxford, writing in August 1993.

---

many of them miners like himself. They were 'a wonderful set of men' who involved him in the Christian Endeavour and the Temperance movement. They were versed in theology and English literature. They opened up to him the world of Ruskin, Tennyson, Browning, Dickens and Victor Hugo, but above all 'they introduced me to Peake . . . and, as soon as it was available, I bought a copy of his *Commentary*'. Their schooling, like his, had been in short supply but they had taken advantage of the Workers' Educational Association and Correspondence courses, and they took him to summer schools. 'They were' he added 'all socialists and many of them became leaders in the Labour movement. They were more evangelical than we are now, their preaching was expected to bear fruit.' Mr Ward recognised that he was 'born lucky'. Had his home been in the Yorkshire Wolds, or the East Riding, instead of Barnsley, the influence of conservatism would have been stronger and that of Peake weaker.

The example and encouragement of this group of 'well-read men' meant that he needed no persuasion to take the teaching and writings of Peake seriously when he arrived at Hartley. On the first night the students were welcomed by the Principal who asked Dr Peake to say a few words to them. He responded 'Mr Principal, and fellow students, at least I hope so . . .' After that they were determined to make every effort to study because they knew what a privilege was theirs.

In 1924 an American lady, returning by ship from the USA, asked the cabin boy to bring her an entertaining book from the library. 'He returned with a bulky volume saying: "This is a grand book, Miss." It was Peake's Commentary.' [26] In 1947 I was working in Brighton. Near me was a local preacher who wished to offer as a candidate. He had left school at 13 to work in a London restaurant and described his education as 'being kicked in the backside by an Italian head waiter'. I asked how he was preparing for his candidature? 'I'm reading my way through Peake's *Commentary*' he said. He was accepted.

13 (ii)

LOCAL PREACHERS AND
THEOLOGICAL CHANGE

The 1960s and 1970s

John Stacey

I arrived at Westminster on 1 September 1967, as General Secretary of the Local Preachers' Department, though there were no other secretaries over whom to be general. I stayed there until 1985. After six years and much travail, divisionalisation arrived, now apparently soon to be dismantled. It reduced the Connexional Committee from around 80 to 21, and although the lines of communication to the circuits were much less workable, the new committee under Margaret Siebold, and then Judy Jarvis, was a success story right from the beginning. Happily, the Studies Board was left alone and, under Margaret Siebold and Gordon Simmons, it became the instrument through which theological change was mediated to the world of local preachers and local preachers on trial. Divided into its four panels, Old Testament, New Testament, Christian Doctrine and Worship and Preaching, the Board both made up for my lack in these various fields and gave me shelter when the winds of controversy whistled in my ears. I gladly acknowledge the debt.

There are clearly two ways of treating the word 'theological' in the heading to this half-chapter. The normal way would be to include under its umbrella all four areas in which local preachers on trial were instructed to study by the Conference. Biblical and liturgical studies may be subsumed under 'theology'. The practice brings wholeness and cohesion into the enterprise. And change is not an isolating factor, for in each area there has been change. In New Testament studies, for example, one of the set books for 1971, and subsequently, was Dennis Nineham's commentary on St. Mark's Gospel, published in 1963 and hardly a tame regurgitation of previous commentary material. So too, Morna Hooker, Lady Margaret's Professor of Divinity at Cambridge, provided *Study Notes on the New Testament* from 1972, and she is scarcely a fundamentalist. And as for the subject 'Worship and Preaching', Richard Jones had edited a book, *Worship for Today* (1968), which was full of liturgical change ('experiments in worship' they were called in those days) and in which the Local Preachers' Department cooperated, until it came up with its own *In Church* (1971) which was by no means averse to what were then new ideas.

LOOKING BACK TO THE TURN OF THE CENTURY: AN INSIGHT INTO THE LONG HISTORY OF LOCAL PREACHERS' TRAINING

'For the local preachers' connexional examination, 167 names were sent to the examiners. Last year 251 names were handed in, but only 137 brave bold men faced the fiery ordeal. At the moment of writing no one can tell how many of the 165 who have entered their names as candidates for this year's examination will, to use the common phrase, "funk" at the entrance door. If the withdrawals be on the same extravagant scale as twelve months since, little heart will be left for continuing the examination any longer.

It is a pity local preachers cannot be brought to see the benefit these examinations would be to them. The textbooks are of the kind they ought to read, while the careful reading of them, followed by strict examination, would prove an incalculable advantage. Men, especially young men, ought to be eager to reap the benefit thus freely offered; the comparative indifference shown is absolutely incomprehensible, for it costs them nothing, and for their convenience is brought to their very door.

Seventy circuits are represented in the examination, a miserably small percentage of the total number in the Connexion, and twenty-six synods of the thirty-two English-speaking districts. The largest number of any circuit is from Lancaster, which sends fifteen: Hull Great Thornton comes next with eleven and is the only circuit in the district furnishing candidates.'

Wesleyan Methodist Church Record Vol IX No. 100 April 1900.
(Inset in the Easingwold Circuit Methodist Record)

But nevertheless, we shall not treat the subject in this comprehensive way, but rather confine ourselves to 'Christian Doctrine' or 'systematic theology' as it is known at a higher level. There are two reasons for this decision. One is a matter of space. To deal adequately with change in all four subjects, and how local preachers on trial came to terms with it, would require more space than we have. The second, and determinative, reason is that Christian Doctrine engendered a *cause célèbre*, the famous or, as some would say, infamous *Doing Theology*, published in 1972, which was the catalyst for exposing the attitude to change of local preachers and local preachers on trial, and opened up again within Methodism the conservative/radical debate in theology.

But first it is necessary to digress for a moment to point out that *all* local preachers on trial were required to study the books which the Department and the Conference prescribed. Before 1972, circuits had the right, 'in very exceptional circumstances', to make local preachers without any connexional tests at all, and this was in a few cases somewhat liberally interpreted. (In 1967 there were 117 exemptions from LP examinations, of which only 49 were for people with 'comparable academic qualifications'.) If we were to make progress on training, we knew that this loop-hole had to be blocked. All local preachers on trial had to be trained. Our strategy for presenting this reform to Conference was to offer the choice of written examinations, continuous assessment course or (carefully safeguarded) connexional oral examinations, and the reform was accepted. So when change came about in the study of Christian Doctrine, or theology, everybody had to come to terms with it.

Doing Theology

I remember well that morning in September 1967, when I began work in the Local Preachers' Department. My first visitor was my brother, alas no longer with us, who had come to celebrate the first, and in all probability the last, Stacey to be made a Connexional Secretary. Then followed George Sails and Sinclair Walker, two boffins from the Home Missions Department, who had come to welcome me to the club. After that I was just about to launch into a massive signing of Local Preachers' Long Service Certificates when I noticed a neat pile of typescript at the end of the desk. It was the new Christian Doctrine book to be studied by local preachers on trial which, for some reason or another, had not been able to be cleared by my predecessor. I took it home that night, and in the study at Makepeace Avenue, Highgate, its window looking out across the lights of London, I read it.

I knew immediately that I could not publish it. That the author was a highly competent scholar I had good reason to know, and his scholarship was evident. But those were the years when the Anglican-

Methodist Conversations were at their height and their reception in the two churches was the stuff of ecclesiastical politics: meetings, addresses, articles, letters to the religious press galore, consumed the attention of both Anglicans and Methodists. This book, without question, rubbished the claims that the Church of England was making about the Christian ministry, and in doing so allied itself with those determined to reject the proposals that had emanated from the Conversations. That people had a

---

UNION PROPOSALS DISCUSSED BY PREACHERS

'There was a discussion about the proposed Anglican-Methodist union, particularly as it affected local preachers . . . Lay Readers (of whom there were 700) corresponded roughly to local preachers. Their standard of training, however, was lower. Appointment was by bishop, on a diocesan basis. They are looked upon basically as emergency stand-in preachers and normally act as assistants to priests in conducting services. The President believes the local preacher has a distinct, independent contribution to make to the life of a united church. However, after union, which would result in many churches being closed because they served the same district as others, the local preacher might find that all appointments could be taken by ordained ministers. The differing interpretations of the priesthood, especially in relation to the administration of the Sacraments, were discussed.'

Edinburgh Circuit Local Preachers' Meeting, 25 May 1964.

---

perfect right to reject them I did not for one moment question, just as I assumed the right to support them. But a local preachers' text-book, published at the behest of the Conference, was a different matter. An official sanction would have been given to views of which the Conference itself had not approved and which would certainly have offended our Anglican partners in the negotiations, not by their publication, for the 'Voice of Methodism' never ceased to publish them, but by the Conference Resolution which was required before a book could be prescribed for compulsory study by local preachers on trial. So the book had to go. The question then was: what is to be put in its place? And time was short, for supplies of the current book were running out.

At this point the Studies Board met for consultation. Its first decision was a negative one: that no one author could do the work in time. And it must be done in time for the Conference would show no pleasure on hearing about local preachers on trial with no Christian Doctrine book to study. The second decision of the Studies Board was that every existing basic theology book was lacking in some way. Biblical studies, yes: the Bible was the same, one supposed, for Methodists and everybody else. But Christian Doctrine, with its required spicing of 'Methodist Doctrine' had nothing ready-made. The only way through seemed to be the way of the symposium, which would place no impossible burden upon a single author. Once this had been agreed the Board began to suggest names. Obviously competency was a high factor, but not the only one. Two other factors, I remember, came into our considerations. One was a sensitivity to the preaching office: it should be remembered throughout that the theology was to be *preached*. The other was that the authorship should cover as wide a cross-section of Methodist theological life as could reasonably be done. We have to confess that though our intentions were laudable enough, our performance could have been better. In the event, we chose David Deeks, Ivor Jones, Roland Wilson and Neville Ward, four good and learned men, but not one of them boasting the name of conservative evangelical. They shared chapters on religious experience and language, God, Christ and the cross and resurrection, the Holy Spirit, man (as it would not now be called), ethics, the kingdom, the church and the sacraments. I wrote the Preface.

So much for the outline of the book and the reason behind it. Before we come, however, to the deeply-felt objections and the angry debates of the Conference, we ought to take a little time to notice what was, theologically speaking, going on in the world at the time.

The Context

During the 1960s and 1970s changes on the theological scene came thick and fast and it is impossible to describe them all. One has to select, and as a convenient package I have chosen a handful of books from theologians in the Church of England. The obvious candidate for the first place is *Honest to God*, published in 1963. With Tillich standing behind him, Robinson taught us to replace the image of the Father with 'our ultimate concern' so that 'he who knows about depth knows about God'. Bonhoeffer's 'Christianity without religion' was assumed in *Honest to God* and God was delineated as 'the ground of our being'. Christ was not so much the Son of God but the man for others. With this slim volume of less than 150 pages, change had arrived in theology. Local preachers tended to divide between those who saw this as enlightenment and those who saw it as outer darkness: but we anticipate. In 1972 came *True Resurrection* from Harry Williams and with it the closer possibility of preaching, not simply about the first Easter morning and the empty tomb, but the profound meaning of resurrection in human experience. That powerful first chapter laced many a Methodist sermon. Of course there were some who complained that Christ was being locked out of his throne room, but the human understanding of resurrection exalted rather than diminished him. Whatever happened, things were different. Then I take *The Human Face of God* from 1973. There is nothing outrageous about

---

PREACHERS' CONCERN FOR SINCERITY AND CLARITY

'In presenting the Christian message today, we need to avoid religious-sounding words, which amount sometimes to jargon.'

'A useful discussion was held centring on the 'fear' of the Lord. Whilst it was felt there were dangers in minimising the impact of the meaning of the word 'fear' thus leading to complacency, nevertheless the discussion brought out the great need for an up to date translation of Biblical words and terminology.'

Minutes of the Edinburgh Circuit Local Preachers'
Meeting 7 Dec 1965 and 2 June 1966.

---

this book. Though Robinson does say that Christ 'had a dark side as well as a light', the fact that he comes through as 'God for us' makes the new insights more readily acceptable. My next book of change is Maurice Wiles *The Remaking of Christian Doctrine* (1973). I can best comment on this book with a quotation from a piece by Bishop F. R. Barry in *The Times* one February morning in 1975: 'Thus, step by step, Professor Wiles builds up the case for non-incarnational Christianity and a wide (though still Christ-orientated) Theism. It will be severe shock to the man in the pew, who may well ask, as the author himself remarks, whether this is not the un-making of Christian doctrine rather than its remaking.' Not everybody is as cautious as Barry, but my place is not to approve or disapprove, but simply to indicate a context of change. And that I can do with no difficulty. Geoffrey Lampe's Bampton lectures *God as Spirit* must be taken into account, for to the person who thinks solely in terms of the saving work of Christ as 'a kind of invasion from outside, a personal descent, from heaven to a "world below"' there is presented instead the position that 'All divine revelation to us and all God's activity are apprehended and mediated through human minds and emotions and wills', and then finally, the clear decision: 'I believe that the Trinitarian model is in the end less satisfactory for the articulation of our basic Christian experience than the unifying concept of God as Spirit.' I am tempted to add to my list of theologians of the Church of England, the authors of *The Myth of God Incarnate,* some of whom were not Anglicans. But really the point is the same. The book was published in 1977 and it would be hard to find a more unsettled home for theology.

These theologians were not the only ones writing at the time, of course, not even the only ones in the Church of England, but they were indicative of the kind of radical theological change that was abroad in the 1960s and 1970s, forming a context within which *Doing Theology* would have to find a place. Inevitably, therefore, the way in which local preachers reacted to what they found in *Doing Theology* both conditioned, and was conditioned by, their attitude to the theological change of the kind we have noticed in these Anglicans.

Level of difficulty

We have to admit that *Doing Theology* was not as easy reading as we would wish. I recall at the Conference of 1974, when the debate was at its height, Rupert Davies, ex-President of the Conference, took a copy of *Doing Theology* away at night and returned the next morning to tell me that he thought parts of it were too difficult for local preachers on trial. And I must admit that some sections – religious language and eschatology for example – were hard going for them. Given time, we might have made these section more easily readable, but we did not have time. Conference shared Rupert's view and insisted we take time. John Munsey Turner was invited to produce some simple, basic material – *Introducing Theology* – for use until a completely new Christian Doctrine book could be written unhurriedly, by a single author. This was achieved by my writing *Groundwork of Theology* (1977, 1984). By this time we had the level more or less right.

But we return to our main question: what does the reaction to *Doing Theology* have to tell us about the attitude of local preachers to theological change? We have to resist the temptation to quote from the letters and utterances of ordained ministers. They have a built-in theological interest (or should have) and certainly in this controversy they were not slow to throw their weight in on one side or the other. But we shall disregard what they said, no matter how wise, for this book is about local preachers and we must confine ourselves to them.

What the local preachers said

      It is simple, and obvious, to divide the comment into three groups. The first group consists of some of the comments of those who found *Doing Theology* helpful. A local preacher, for example, wrote from Sheffield:

> 'I found much food for thought in *Doing Theology* . . . I felt that it set me on the path of re-thinking out many aspects for myself – just what many of us needed. As usual, I was in the minority!'

Even this first sentence reveals that there was more to this book than simply the imparting of information and the communication of simple, basic truths. Not that previous Christian Doctrine text-books had been reduced to that: but this one was more evidently a raiser of questions. As a local preacher on trial wrote from the Isle of Wight:

> 'As a local preacher on trial, I am 'doing theology' and would like you to know how much I am learning from the course. . . I am learning to think honestly and (I hope) clearly, and not to shut away the difficult questions.'

There is space for one more, this time from a preacher in his prime:

> 'I feel I must write to you, having just read *Doing Theology*, and receiving a real boost to my faith. What is all the fuss about? The text-book I studied eighteen years ago, *An Approach to Christian Doctrine*, was never criticised as far as I remember, but it was not more "fundamental" than *Doing Theology*. After all, this is stated on the cover to be "An Introduction for Preachers" which suggests to me immediately that here is a book for those whose faith is now well-rooted as against a book for those searching for faith. In several places I have had to stop and read over a sentence, a paragraph or even a page or two again and then again before being satisfied that I understand the point being made. On pages 29 and 30 you state that it is your intention that the reader should do exactly that, since such is the purpose of the book. For anyone to allow the reading of such a book to be the

cause of resigning from Methodism, he would have to be
looking for an excuse to desert his denomination.'

So wrote a preacher from Southport, almost twenty years ago. Local
preachers who thought like him did not make a big issue out of *Doing
Theology* since they did not feel outraged or disgusted, the strong
motivation for writing to ecclesiastical officers or the religious press. But
they said enough for us (the Local Preachers' Studies Board and
Connexional Committee, now within the Division of Ministries) to realise
with gratitude that when it came to theological change, such local
preachers did not reject it out of hand but brought to it the consideration of
open, but discerning, minds, and found that it then stimulated and
enlivened their preaching.

The second group of local preachers consisted of those who were
not totally averse to change in theology, but they were cautious about the
change they would allow. Their approach to *Doing Theology* was not to
demand its withdrawal but to ask for what they considered to be
improvements. For example, I received the following comment from the
secretary of the local preachers' meeting of a West Midlands circuit:

'This meeting considers that the book *Doing Theology* is
not suitable as a first study book for local preachers on
trial. The book *An Approach to Christian Doctrine* gives
better instruction to young local preachers about what the
doctrines of the Methodist Church are. *Doing Theology*
is a good follow up book to encourage preachers to think
more for themselves about Doctrine.'

Something similar came from the secretary of a District local preachers'
committee:

'They were almost unanimous that it was not a good
book for guidance in Christian Doctrine, it was too broad
and could be confusing, but it was an excellent study for
the mature preacher – it was a radical book with
insufficient doctrine and should be treated as such. There
was a need for a rock, and ABC of Doctrine.'

This letter specified some theological dissatisfactions: the Ascension, the
Second Coming, the uncertainty over Satan, the Resurrection and
(unacceptably for a church whose Doctrinal standards declared 'The
Methodist Church recognises two sacraments namely Baptism and the

Lord's Supper as of Divine Appointment and of perpetual obligation') complained that

> 'the chapter on the Sacraments gives only one school of thought, with for example, no reference to the attitude of Quakers and the Salvation Army.'

A further letter appeared in the *Methodist Recorder* from 'three university graduates and members of the teaching profession in North Yorkshire asking for both *An Approach to Christian Doctrine* (or *Christian Foundations* – the book I studied myself when I was, long ago, a local preacher on trial) and *Doing Theology,*

> 'the first to provide a sound basic knowledge of the subject and the second to stimulate further thought'.

I would also include in this section a letter from an Essex preacher which said:

> 'I understand that Methodism is a denomination in which it is possible to hold liberal and conservative evangelical views. Therefore I should have expected that a set text book should contain both these views.'

She was asking for alterations rather than burning, as was another local preacher from the South West: he complained about the emphasis put on Macquarrie's definition of religion and the need to give more prominence to the work of grace. He had difficulty with 'myth' because

> 'it fails to appreciate the importance of historical accuracy to the Hebrew mind, particularly Hebrew prophecy.'

Then comes his parting shot:

> 'In conclusion, I feel this book gives a good introduction to the new liberal theology but fails to do justice to those scholars who are no less a part of the contemporary scene for having the label "conservative".'

Letters of this kind seem to me to consist of reasonable disagreements. Misunderstandings abound: for example, the notion that we are advocates of liberal theology, and in such matters the way is open for fruitful discussion with the local Christian Doctrine tutor. But as far as theological change is concerned, these minds are not closed. They may want changes other than those immediately presented to them, but they are not opposed to change as such.

We come to the third group, consisting of those who opposed *Doing Theology* from the first word to the last and who would be satisfied with nothing less than its complete withdrawal. I must confess that it gives me no joy to go raking over the cold ashes of this controversy of over twenty years ago, but it has to be done if we are to give a comprehensive view of local preachers' attitudes to theological change. Let a Midlands local preacher begin, for he resigned from local preaching as a result:

> 'I wonder if it makes sense to preach the evangelical faith in Methodist pulpits when, with the official approval of the church, the man or woman next week will be doing his or her own thing. Pluralistic theology is now welcomed.'

This preacher then quotes specifically:

> 'Chapter 7 (Ivor H. Jones) concerning the Resurrection – "they are speaking of the resurrection as an historical event, and we may not share their confidence that it is possible to speak of the resurrection in this way." In the same chapter, concerning the Ascension, "has Luke created the story?", and concerning the Emmaus story, asking "whether it is the record of an actual journey or the expression in narrative form of the early Christian experience of encounter with the risen Lord." '

> 'Chapter 11 (J. Neville Ward) "We do not think that Christ left the world at his ascension and is to have a second visible coming at some future date."

A local preacher from Oxfordshire, who issued long duplicated sheets of theological invective, can be quoted, though a modest distillation will suffice:

> 'I am not convinced that the writers of this text book believe in the Supreme Revelation recorded in Holy Scripture . . . how can these authors believe the Bible to be supreme in faith and practice . . . the Resurrection need not be accepted as history, doubt is cast on the

> Ascension history, doubt is cast on the Virgin Birth history, the Second Coming can be rejected . . . the unbiblical statements of the text books must be displaced and in their place positive Biblical Truth . . . I believe these books (*Introducing Theology* is included) have been written by Liberal Modernists and the Fundamental Evangelicals have been left out in the cold . . . Pardon for length of letter but what I have said is a burden.'

I believe this last to be the case, as we shall see. But we must first let the secretary of the local preachers' meeting of a Nottinghamshire circuit have his say:

> 'I have read the dreaded book and as a result would unhesitatingly call for its withdrawal . . . It seems to me that you are in danger of joining the thought-group which is very common outside of Christianity today. Their main tenet is that all opinion is of equal value and that to hold any 'dogmatic' view is just not acceptable . . . This is not only nonsense but very dangerous nonsense at that.'

In a letter to the *Methodist Recorder* the same gentleman invokes John Wesley's sermon on 'The Catholic Spirit':

> 'Surely Wesley would have referred to these modern advocates of theological pluralism as among those having . . . "no settled, consistent principles, but are for jumbling all opinions together." '

Our last quotation is from a letter in the *Methodist Recorder* from two local preachers in Lancashire who took exception to a paragraph in *Doing Theology* which is worth quoting in full:

> 'The doctrinal clauses of the Deed of Union are anything but precise: the statements of Faith and Order accepted by the Conference are models of comprehensiveness: and other official publications, like the Methodist Hymn Book and the Book of Offices, express theological views of bewildering variety. The hard-liner who believes in "truth" and "heresy" just has no home in Methodism. That, of course, is not something to be sorry about. Exclusiveness in theology has cloaked more spiritual

pride and done more harm to Christendom than any of us will ever know. We have great cause to be grateful that our founder did not hang this mill-stone round our necks.' (W. David Stacey, 'The Gospel and Theology' *The Preacher's Handbook* No.2. New Series *About the Gospel* pp.12-13.)

The correspondents' comment on this paragraph is:

'The writer clearly believes that "truth" is anathema to the true Methodist and must be sought outside our denomination.'

Having failed to grasp the meaning conveyed by the inverted commas, they announce to *Recorder* readers:

'A memorial is being sent to the 1974 Conference calling for the withdrawal of the book because of its unscriptural and heretical content. We call on all true Methodists to ensure that their voice is heard at Conference this year, before any more people find that they have no home left in Methodism.'

Local Preachers and Theological Change

It is clear from the above quotations that local preachers were deeply divided. Their differing views on *Doing Theology* in fact reveal their differing views on theological change. And here they are no different from any other body of committed Christians. It is sometimes hard to believe that what one group of Christians regards as the stimulus of a new understanding of truth, and therefore the work of the Holy Spirit, another group, in fellowship with them, will regard as a denial of the biblical revelation and a monstrous contradiction of 'our doctrines'. Sometimes, in this situation, dialogue is useful, enabling those of opposite persuasions to understand each other better, but sometimes it is not, and only drives one to the conclusion that here we have virtually not one religion but two. And it is idle to suppose that at the end of a chapter of this kind one can perform some kind of rescue act which will bring conservatives and radicals together (I use the terms as they were used in the 1960s and 1970s) in a mutually agreed understanding of what we believe and what we are to preach. Not at all. The divisions go too deep for that. Nevertheless, there is something positive and constructive to say about Methodist local preachers, whatever their theological convictions.

THE HARASSED PREACHER

Now that summer has brimmed on the uplands
White mine-crusts seed in the sun,
And around each pit and its outcast grit
A gabble of green is spun.
Soon silenced by bomb and gun.

Bushes have bragged into blossom,
Flicked by the teasing sand;
Milk-wan streams vein the valley's dreams;
Larks lilt where the tip-beams stand.
Faith's dream and song are banned.

Our forefathers dug in the field here,
Built us a preaching-place,
So that truth might spread from the ringing bed
Ruled by the Galilee base.
Too distant now – no trace.

A hundred summers have panted
Along our zigzag lanes
Since the first raw crowd of converts bowed
Inside these window panes.
But the analyst explains . . . .

The seats were rough bare benches;
No organ spun a tune;
The squeaky hymns and unwashed limbs
Made a meagre mock at June.
The new age mocks the boon.

Grains from the towering scriptures
Were flicked by the winds of prayer:
In our grit-ringed nook those drab lives took
Fresh shape in Wesley's air.
Now shapeless atoms wear . . . .

We toil in a fevered season;
Soul-crusts lie hard on the hill.
Do our tools ring true? Don't we signal through
To a ruling Potter still?
Our super-egos spill . . . .

A plague on the heckling voices
That would check my sermon's flight!
It's eleven o'clock and here's my flock –
Five villagers, old and bright,
Knowing their faith is right.

Jack Clemo

First, preaching for them is a vocation and they have to fall back again and again on the vocational nature of the work they are doing. They are preachers, not because of idiosyncratic gifts they possess or bright ideas they wish to purvey, but because God has called them into his prophetic ministry. The ground of their unity, therefore, is no theological uniformity or identity of biblical interpretation, but a common vocation straight from the living God.

Second, there is throughout the discussions and arguments we have been describing, a concern for theology. It matters to the local preachers. The editor of the *Methodist Recorder* would not have been bombarded with letters and the Methodist Conference would not have held debates that went on for hours if it did not. For the preacher it is indispensable, involved in every sermon. And the fact that he or she understands it differently from the preacher who will be occupying the pulpit next Sunday, though it does not lessen the tension, does not lessen its importance either. It drives the preacher on to deeper and wider theological exploration which must not stop as long as that preacher is given appointments on the circuit plan.

Third, these preachers, who differ so much on how to handle theological change, have nevertheless to play their part, and in Methodism it is an important one, in holding the Christian community together. They are charged with both the preaching and the practice of love and peace. This does not mean that they must be silent on the issues we have been discussing, but it does mean that the context within which they are discussed must be both a concern for the truth and a readiness to treat seriously – which may of course lead to sharp rejection – the attitude to theological change which is different from their own. The Christian community is itself a theological community and the theological community is a community of love.

My last word, like my first, is personal. During my eighteen years as connexional Local Preacher's Secretary I met local preachers of all theological persuasions, from flaming radicals to rock hard conservatives, and, believe it or not, of no theological persuasion at all. I can say this of them all: the combination of a vocation to preach, the modest theological training which we were able to give and the discipline of the working world was, in my judgement, a rare gift to the church. The preaching ministry of the Methodist Church has depended, and still depends, in large part upon the local preachers. It is good to have a book which acknowledges the debt.

Tom Hall (Sunderland South Circuit)
celebrated fifty years as an accredited local preacher in 1995, and is still in service.
Tom's photograph, taken in Ewesley Road Methodist Church, Sunderland, is printed as
representative of all those who are carrying on the work of local preaching today.
(With Acknowledgements to Northeast Press Ltd., *Shields Gazette*, and Tom Hall)

14

LOCAL PREACHERS' RECOGNITION SERVICES

Norman Wallwork

The earliest known order for a local preachers' public recognition service was published in the 1913 *Book of Services for the Use of the United Methodist Church* (a denomination which had come into being only six years earlier) prepared by the direction of the United Methodist Conference. The outline of this *Order for the Public Recognition of Fully Accredited Local Preachers* was as follows :

```
 1 Hymn
 2 Declaration of purpose
 3 Invitation to prayer
 4 Act of thanksgiving
 5 Prayer for forgiveness
 6 Scripture lesson
 7 Printed charge
 8 Questions
 9 Commissioning collect
10 Giving of Bible
11 Hymn – 'O Thou who camest from above'
12 Thanksgiving for Departed Saints
13 Prayer of blessing on new preachers
14 Hymn
15 The Grace (Benediction)
```

The officiant at this service was to be 'the Superintendent, or other Presiding Minister'. The congregation was informed that the candidates had satisfactorily passed through their period of probation, had been duly examined and approved, and were now to be set apart for 'this important service in Christ's Church'. In the charge the candidates, described as having 'the great advantage of being in close touch with human life in its daily business and activities', were 'consecrating' themselves 'as preachers of the Gospel and as interpreters of the Word of God'.

In their answers to the Questions, the candidates were required to relate their conversion to God and their present experience, to state why they believed they were called to the work of a preacher, and to declare that they believed and would teach 'the doctrines of the Holy Scriptures as they are generally believed and taught in the United Methodist Church'.

They were urged moreover to seek the salvation of souls and diligently to devote themselves to prayer and study, giving special attention to the Word of God, and to work affectionately and zealously with other preachers rendering 'due respect and loyal co-operation' to the quarterly meeting, to the preachers' meeting and to the superintendent minister.

There then follows the collect from the *Book of Common Prayer* used at the end of the Questions put to the candidates both in the Ordering of Priests and in the Consecration of Bishops. In Methodist liturgy the collect occurs at this same point in both the United Methodist and the Wesleyan Methodist services for the ordination of ministers as well as in the recognition services for local preachers.

The collect runs as follows:
> Almighty God, who hath given you this will to do these things;
> Grant also unto you strength and power to perform the same;
> that he may accomplish his work which he hath begun in you;
> through Jesus Christ our Lord. Amen.

The Presiding Minister was then to present each local preacher with a Bible as a token and memorial of the preacher's dedication and appointment to the 'office of a Preacher'.

Charles Wesley's hymn 'O Thou who camest from above' (three verses only) was a happy choice and no other was offered. The hymn corresponds to the '*Veni Creator*' offered (via *The Book of Common Prayer*) in both the United Methodist and the Wesleyan Methodist Ordination Services and in the Wesleyan Local Preachers' Recognition Service. It was to be used in the Local Preachers' Recognition Service of the Methodist Church (reunited in 1932) in the *Book of Offices* (1936). The Prayer of Blessing on the new local preachers fell into three sections. The first part gave thanks for the cloud of witnesses 'who gaze on the race-course of our mortal life'. The second part asked for God's blessing on those who had just taken their place in the 'noble succession' and the third part consisted of a collect, again from the Consecration of Bishops in *The Book of Common Prayer*. The collect appeared in both the United Methodist and in the Wesleyan Ordination Services and in the Wesleyan service for the Recognition of a Local Preacher. In each of the four Methodist cases there are slight variations. The 1913 United Methodist Local Preachers' Recognition Service version runs thus:

> Almighty God, Giver of all good things, we beseech Thee so to replenish Thy servants with the truth of Thy doctrine and adorn them with innocency of life, that both by word and good example they may faithfully serve Thee in this office, to the glory of Thy Name and to the edification of Thy Church; through the merits of our Saviour Jesus Christ, who liveth and reigneth with Thee and the Holy Ghost, world without end. Amen.

After a hymn the service closed with the 'Benediction' in which the third line refers to 'the communion of the Holy Spirit'. The United Methodist and Wesleyan Methodist practices of basing local preachers' recognition Services on their ordination services for ministers testifies both to the early parity (of sorts) between the travelling and the local preachers and to the need to reaffirm the status of local preachers in the early part of the present century.

THE PRIMITIVE METHODISTS SPOKE OF THEIR LOCAL PREACHERS' RECOGNITION SERVICES AS 'ORDINATIONS'

'A deeply impressive service was held recently in the Wellington Road Church, Stockport, when Messrs H. B. Langley and D. S. Malbon were ordained into the lay ministry of the Church. After they had related their Christian experience and call to preach, the ordination charge was given by the Revd William Upright who also presented each candidate, on behalf of the circuit, a copy of Dr Weymouth's translation of the New Testament. The Charge of the Church was given by Mr T. Molloy, Circuit Steward and district secretary of the LP Training Committee. The ordination prayer was taken by Revd Mr Willings of Australia. A pleasing feature of the service was the attendance of the Boy Scouts in recognition that their Assistant Scoutmaster, Mr Langley, was one of the ordinands. The service will be remembered as one of the finest circuit gatherings in the Stockport 1st Circuit.'

Primitive Methodist Leader 22 August 1929 p.630.

A Wesleyan minister, J. A. Clapperton in *A Manual for Local Preachers* (1910) ended his section on the Final Examination with the sentence: 'It is recommended that all local preachers after being thus received on Full Plan should be recognised at a public religious service.' (p.13)

No doubt as a result of such hopes there was published in 1921 *A Form of Service for the Public Recognition of Wesleyan Methodist Local Preachers*. The service was as follows:

```
 1  Hymn
 2  Prayer for blessing on the service
 3  Reading of candidates' names
 4  Scripture lesson(s)
 5  A printed charge
 6  The questions
 7  Collect for strength and power
 8  Silent prayer
 9  Hymn: 'Veni Creator' ('Come Holy
       Ghost,our hearts inspire')
10  Prayer of blessing for the candidates
11  Hymn
12  Declaration of recognition
13  Charge at the giving of the Bible
14  Prayer for the Spirit
15  The Lord's Supper
16  An address
```

The opening prayer in the service was to be extempore. Four readings could be read, or fewer. The printed passages were Matt. 28:18-20; Luke 12:35-38; John 21:15-17; and Eph 4:7-13, and are a selection from those in the Wesleyan Ordination Service. The long printed charge, with a few variations, is that in the Wesleyan Ordination Service, deriving in turn from the charge in the Ordering of Priests in *The Book of Common Prayer*. The charge raised such questions as the dignity of the office; the calling to be messengers and prophets; the need to bring God's children to ripeness and perfection in Christ; the application to study; the necessity of continuously praying for God's assistance and the summons to fashion both the life of the preacher and his household after the rule and doctrine of Christ.

Significantly, the last paragraph of the charge insists that the new local preachers should 'confirm' those assurances 'already given in a more private manner' on the preacher's 'acceptance' by his brethren 'as Local Preachers in our Church'.

CIRCUITS' RESPONSES TO THE 1921 WESLEYAN SERVICE FOR THE RECOGNITION OF LOCAL PREACHERS

1. 'We are surprised to find that, although thirty local preachers have been received on full plan during the year, only two public religious services have been held for the recognition of same. This is much to be regretted, as the Connexional Local Preachers' Committee has prepared a beautiful form of service for this purpose, with the presentation of a Bible and a letter from the President.'

Birmingham and Shrewsbury District LP Committee Report 1922-3
(By 1938 the report shows a more general use of the service.)

2. 'Bro. Henry Brown was examined after tea by the superintendent . . .and all being satisfactory was recommended as a fully accredited local preacher. It was resolved to hold a Recognition Service early in the New Year for four local preachers. Bibles would be presented to them on this occasion.'

Shildon (Co. Durham) WM Circuit LP Minutes,
14 Dec 1921. (Durham County Record Office.)

A constant tension and theme in Methodist local preachers' recognition services concerns at what point one *becomes* a local preacher. Is it during the service or during a meeting prior to the service or even, at one time, on the written authority of the superintendent?

The five questions are all taken from those in the Wesleyan Ordination Service which again are closely modelled on those for the Making of Deacons and the Ordering of Priests in *The Book of Common Prayer*. When Wesley revised the *Ordinal* in his 1784 revision of the Prayer Book (The *Sunday Service of the Methodists*), he kept the threefold ordinal, but changed bishops, priests and deacons to superintendants (sic), elders and deacons. As this ordinal was rarely used, and then fell into disuse, the Wesleyan Conference eventually produced a one-order ordinal for 'ministers' using elements from all three services. The three collects for God's blessing on the newly accredited local preachers are also from the Wesleyan Ordination Service but are closely based on the forms in *The Book of Common Prayer* for the Ordering of Priests and the Consecration of Bishops.

The declaration of Recognition includes the fact that the official meetings of the circuits have 'cordially received' the candidates 'into the brotherhood of Local Preachers in the Wesleyan Methodist Church'. The presiding minister says that 'it is fitting that there should be a wider and more public Recognition' of an appointment to 'so important an office amongst us', reflecting an increased awareness within Wesleyanism (and indeed Methodism as a whole) of the value of local preachers.

The charge at the giving of the Bible, and the blessing before the service moves to the Lord's Supper, are again based on prayers in the Wesleyan Ordination Service and again they are directly borrowed from *The Book of Common Prayer*. This time it is from the charge and the blessing which the Archbishop gives to the newly consecrated bishop as he delivers to him the Bible and blesses him. So the new Wesleyan local preachers are to 'hold up the weak, heal the sick, seek the lost'.

As part of the worshipping life of the Methodist Church, after the re-union of 1932, there was published on the authority of the 1936 Methodist Conference *The Book of Offices* of The Methodist Church. The outline of the 1936 service was as follows :

1	Hymn: 'Come, Holy Ghost, our hearts inspire'
2	Brief invocation or Collect for Purity
3	Lord's Prayer
4	Declaration of Purpose
5	Scripture passage(s)
6	Hymn: 'Lord, in the strength of grace'
7	The questions
8	Recognition and blessing
9	Right hand of fellowship
10	Delivery of a Bible
11	Reading and presentation of President's Letter
12	Hymn: 'Lord of the living harvest'
13	Prayer for gifts of the Spirit
14	Prayer for guidance in study and preparation
15	Prayer for divine power in public worship
16	Prayer for the coming of God's kingdom
17	Charge in the form of a sermon
18	Hymn: 'O Thou who camest'
19	The Lord's Supper

The Declaration of Purpose was publicly to recognise the new brothers (and also by this time sisters) as 'members of the 'Order' of Local Preachers'. (The issue of an 'order' is discussed in chapter 6.) They were to exercise the ministry of God's Word for the calling of many to repentance, for the edifying of God's Church, and for the glory of God's name.

The selection of scripture passages were to be taken from Matt. 28:18-20; Is. 6:1-8; Is. 52:7-10; Mark 3:13 and 14; Luke 10:1 and 2; Eph. 4:7,8,11-13 and 2 Cor. 4:5 and 6.

In their answers to the Questions the new preachers acknowledged Christ as Saviour and Lord; and pledged themselves to be faithful members of Christ's holy church; to preach the truth revealed in the Scriptures; to make known the gospel; to be diligent in prayer, Scripture reading and related studies; and to exercise a ministry in harmony with the doctrines and discipline of the Methodist Church.

In the name of Christ and his church the new brothers and sisters were 'joyfully' recognised as Local Preachers. A blessing was asked on them in the name of Father, Son and Holy Spirit in the fellowship of ministers and local preachers 'in the Gospel'. The 'right hand of fellowship' was a 'token' of their welcome 'by the Church' and 'in recognition' of their place and office as preachers in the church. The new preachers knelt to receive a Bible and stood to hear and receive the President's letter. The concluding collects were in 'prayer-book' language but were clearly written for the 1936 service and bore no pride of ancestry.

The first draft of the Commissioning of Local Preachers for publication alongside the 1975 *Methodist Service Book* was published by the Faith and Order committee in 1971 along with the Commissioning of Class Leaders and the Commissioning of Sunday School Teachers and Youth Workers. The argument was that the new *Methodist Service Book* was a 'shorter Book of Offices' and would not contain the midnight-blue booklet of 'Commissioning Services' though they were to have the 'same status' as the services in the bound service book. There was however a perceived loss of status in this move. In later editions of the Methodist Service Book, the Commissioning Services were included.

The 1975 version of *The Recognition and Commissioning of Local Preachers* (within the context of *The Sunday Service)* was, in outline, as follows:

1	(Opening hymn)
2	(Opening prayers)
3	Collect
4	Collect of the day (before or after 3)
5	Scripture reading(s)
6	Hymn: 'Come, Holy Ghost, our hearts inspire,' or some other
7	Gospel: Luke 8:4-15
8	Sermon
9	Hymn: 'Eternal Son, eternal Love', or some other
10	Declaration of purpose and duties
11	Questions
12	Prayer for the Holy Spirit
13	Delivery of a Bible
14	Question to the congregation
15	Reading and presentation of President's letter including the giving of right hand of fellowship
16	(The rest of 'The Sunday Service' including intercessions)

Because the 1975 Recognition Service was within the content of the *Sunday Service*, printed elsewhere, it was in appearance the thinnest with regard to its own material. Discounting the general opening collect and the provision of scripture readings, and apart from the Declaration of Purpose and Duties and the Questions, there are only seven lines of prayer, before we come to the general intercessions and, presumably, the Thanksgiving in the 1975 order for the Lord's Supper. The preamble to the commissioning is merely a summary of the Standing Order about the duties of a local preacher.

The third and last of the questions to those to be 'recognised and commissioned' lists the primary work of a local preacher as the leading of worship, prayers, and the preaching of the gospel, and this they do 'in the light of their experience in the world where they work and witness for Christ'.

As part of the process of preparing a successor to the 1975 *Methodist Service Book* the Faith and Order Committee was authorised by Conference to produce draft orders of service, to be available for photocopying and trial use.

The General Directions within the proposed order include an invitation to other local preachers to be invited to read lessons, preach the sermon, lead the intercessions and assist with the distribution of holy communion. One of those to be admitted as a local preacher may be invited to speak briefly about his or her call.

In outline the 1994 *Draft Order for the Admission of Local Preachers* was as follows:

1	Declaration of Purpose				
2	Hymn	3	Invocation	4	Act of penitence
5	Collect	6	Old Testament	7	Psalm
8	Epistle	9	Hymn	10	Gospel
11	Sermon	12	Hymn		
13	Presentation of candidates				
14	Re-affirming of vows by other preachers				
15	Printed Charge				
16	The questions				
17	The admission				
18	Delivery of a Bible				
19	Declaration of admission and request for support				
20	Reading and Presentation of President's Letter				
21	General exchange of right hand of fellowship and invitation to applaud				
22	Prayers of Intercession				
23	The Lord's Prayer (if not later in Lord's Supper)				
24	The Peace (if not later)				
25	The Lord's Supper (from the preparation of gifts and setting of the table)				

The opening prayers, including the collect, are all related to the ministry of the word in the life of the church. The Bible passages offered are Ex. 3:1-7a and 10-12; Is. 52:7-12; Is. 55:6-11; 2 Cor. 5:14-20; Eph. 4:7-8 and 11-16; Jas. 1:16-25; Matt. 25:14-24 and John 12:20-26.

The presentation, to accord with the procedure under new standing orders (carefully agreed by the Conference and the Local Preachers Office), now includes the phrase 'on the *recommendation* of the Local Preachers' Meeting, they have been *approved* by the Circuit Meeting, for *admission* to the *office and ministry* of a local preacher'.

As result of requests from local circuits, the presiding minister now invites the existing local preachers of the circuit to re-affirm their ministry as follows :

Sisters and brothers in Christ do you re-affirm your call to the ministry of a local preacher?

We do.

Will you continue to fashion your life according to the way of Christ, and be diligent in your preparation for worship through your prayers and your studies?

With God's help, we will.

The Preface to the Questions is a new composition and includes the words 'You will bring the message of salvation to all, in season and out of season. As you lead worship, and offer good news to others, your own life will be shaped and transformed.'

The Admission takes place during a Prayer of Thanksgiving which includes the petition to God: 'Give your Holy Spirit to A, B and C, whom we now admit to the office and ministry of a local preacher that they may fulfil their calling.' (The phrase 'Order of Local Preachers' which was used in 1936, and which was not included in 1975, has not re-appeared. See discussion of Standing Order, above).

Of the five *Recognition Services* examined both the United Methodist and the Wesleyan orders looked over their shoulders to the shape, content and style of the ministerial ordination services. Indeed the Wesleyan Local Preachers' Recognition Service, as we have seen, leant very heavily indeed on the Wesleyan ordination service. As indicated earlier, this perhaps implies that Methodism has never shaken off the inherited parity (of sorts) between travelling and local preachers. The strong theology of the Wesleyan 'pastoral office' in the 1850s and the desire to enhance the status of the local preacher is *one* possible explanation of this heavy reliance on the ordination service. Another explanation is that the compilers were in a hurry and had no other model or lacked liturgical inventiveness!

The 1936 service was a recognition of something that had already happened in a meeting, before the service took place and similarly, the 1975 Recognition Service was recognising and commissioning as local preachers those who had already been 'tested and approved'.

As we have already noted, the question of *when* a person becomes a Methodist local preacher was not spelt out in a new way until the Standing Orders were changed prior to the drafting of the 1994 experimental order. Now the new local preacher is *recommended* by the Local Preachers' Meeting, *approved* by the Circuit Meeting and *admitted* to the office and ministry of a local preacher during the service itself.

TWO TAILPIECES!

'Do you think' asked the preacher eagerly 'that they approved of my sermon?'

'Oh yes' was the reply, 'did you not see them all nodding?'

Found in the *Primitive Methodist Leader* 10 Jan 1919

A local preacher lost his way in his sermon:

'Nay Aa's lost.' We'll sing another 'ymn and then gan yam'.

A memory recalled by Mr Wilf Bainbridge
from a service long ago at the former Primitive
Methodist Chapel, Hutton Rudby, North Yorkshire

REFERENCES

Abbreviations used in the references (and in some cases in the main text also)

WM	Wesleyan Methodist (to 1932)
PM	Primitive Methodist (to 1932)
MNC	Methodist New Connexion (to 1907)
BC	Bible Christian (to 1907)
WMA	Wesleyan Methodist Association (1834-1857)
UMFC	United Methodist Free Church (1857-1907)
UM	United Methodist (1907-1932)

Minutes	Minutes of Conference (published annually for the various Methodist Connexions.
Agenda	Conference agendas (as above)
WHS	Wesley Historical Society
WHS Proc.	*Proceedings of the Wesley Historical Society*
WMHS	World Methodist Historical Society
AM	*Arminian Magazine* (title of the *WM Magazine* 1778-1797 and of the *BC Magazine* 1822-1828)
MM	*Methodist Magazine (WM Magazine* 1798-1821)
WMM, PMM etc	The magazines of the Wesleyan, Primitive and other Connexions.
JWW	*The Works of the Revd John Wesley* ed. Thomas Jackson, 14 vols., London 1872.
JWJ	*The Journal of the Revd John Wesley* ed. N. Curnock, 8 vols., London 1909-16, reprinted by the Epworth Press 1938. (Known as the Standard Edition.)
JWL	*The Letters of the Revd John Wesley* ed. J. Telford, 8 vols., Epworth Press 1931. (Standard Edition.)
EMP	*Lives of the Early Methodist Preachers* ed. T. Jackson 1837-8, 3 vols., and republished in 6 vols, 1865 and 1871. (The lives were later edited by J. Telford 1910-14 in a different sequence and in 7 vols., as *Wesley's Veterans)*
LPMAA	Local Preachers Mutual Aid Association
LPMag	*Local Preachers Magazine and Mutual Aid Register* 1851 to present.
HMCGB	*A History of the Methodist Church in Great Britain,* ed. R. Davies, G. Rupp and A. R. George, 4 vols., Epworth Press, 1965-1988. Vol. iv contains an extended bibliography of Methodism by Clive Field.

ed.	edited by
ibid. (ibidem)	in the same place
idem	the same
op.cit. (opera citato)	in the work quoted
passim	throughout

CHAPTER 1

1. H. J. Foster, 'Portland Chapel, Bristol', *Proceedings of the Wesley Historical Society* (hereafter *WHS Proc*), xvii p.144; *The Journal of the Revd John Wesley AM* ed. N. Curnock, standard ed., 8 vols., Epworth Press 1938 (hereafter *JWJ)*, ii, p.174n; iii, pp.124n, 151 and n, 152, 241n.

2. *The Letters of the Revd John Wesley AM* ed. J. Telford, standard ed., 8 vols., Epworth Press 1931 (hereafter *JWL*), i, p.353.

3. H. Moore, *Life of the Revd John Wesley*, 2 Vols. London 1824-1825, i, p.507.

4. J. Trapp, *Observations upon the Conduct and Behaviour of a certain Sect usually distinguished by the name of Methodist*, 3rd ed. London 1744, p.24.

5. J. Wesley, 'Farther Appeal to men of Reason and Religion', 1745 *The Works of the Revd John Wesley AM,* ed. T. Jackson, 14 vols., London 1872, (hereafter *JWW*), viii, p.244.

6. Anon., 'Aberdeen, June 2 1763. A Short account of the Rise and Progress of Methodism in this City' *The Scots Magazine* XXV, pp.421-423.

7. *JWL* i, p.285.

8. *JWW*, 'Sermon on Bigotry', v, p.488.

9. *Methodist Recorder Winter Number*, 1895, p.65; *JWL* v, p.257.

10. *JWL*, iii, p.186.

11. *JWW*, 'Farther Appeal', viii, pp. 219, 221.

12. W. J. Townsend, H. B. Workman and G. Eayrs, *A New History of Methodism*, 2 vols., London 1909, i, p.293.

13. J. Wesley, *Standard Sermons*, 2 vols., London 1921, ii, p.119, and *JWL* ii, p.148.

14. *JWL*, iv, p.151-2.

15. A. F. Hall, 'Charles Wesley and Lay Preaching' *WHS Proc,* xv, p.70.

16. *JWL*, iii, p.146.

17. T. Jackson, *Life of Revd Charles Wesley M.A.*, London 1841, ii, p.85.

18. *JWW*, 'Large Minutes', viii, pp.311-12.

19. Townsend, Workman and Eayrs, *op.cit.* p.294.

20. *The Journal of the Revd Charles Wesley MA*, 2 vols., London 1849, introduction and notes by T. Jackson. i, p.420.

21. *ibid.* p.422.

22. *JWJ*, ii, p.307.

23. *ibid.* p.354.

24. C. Wesley, *Journal*, ii, p.95.

25. *WMM*, 1823, p.572.

26. *MM*, 1815, p.117.

27. Anon., *Early Methodism in the Easingwold Circuit*, London 1872, p. 24.

28. D. Whiteley, *Illustrious Local Preachers*, Bradford 1891, p.57.

29. *JWL*, v, p.130

30. *MM*, 1811, pp.11, 12.

31. *MM*, 1812, p.6.

32. *Minutes*, 1862, i, p.94.

33. 'The Life of Christopher Hopper', in *The Lives of the Early Methodist Preachers*, ed. T. Jackson, 6 vols., 3rd ed., London 1866, (hereafter *EMP*) i, pp.190, 197. *et passim.*

34. *Keighley Circuit Book* quoted in J. W. Laycock, *Methodist Heroes of the Great Haworth Round*, Keighley 1909, p.349.

35. C. Hopper, *op.cit.* p.200.

36. John Bennet's 'Minutes', *WHS Proc*, i.

37. 'Headingley' Minutes, *WHS Proc*, i

38. *ibid.*

39. *ibid.*

40. *ibid.*

41. An agreement of November 25 1750 shows that the Wesleys' confidential friend Vincent Perronet, the vicar of Shoreham, helped them to frame these regulations. L. Tyerman, *The Life and Times of the Rev. John Wesley, MA, Founder of the Methodists*, 3 vols., 4th ed., London 1878, ii, pp.129-130, *Publications of the WHS* i, pp.39-51; *Minutes* 1751; *WHS Proc* xxiii, p.183.

42. *Minutes* 1752, London 1862, i, pp.708-9; 1753, i, p.719, Wesley's ms. *Minutes* 1758, *WHS Proc*, iv.

43. *Minutes*, 1763, London 1862, i, p.626.

44. See 27 June 1768 in *An Account of the Monies received and Disbursed at the Quarterly Meeting of the Leeds Circuit 1768-1777* (ms) by William Hey, Steward. (He was the senior surgeon at Leeds Infirmary.) (Leeds District Archives.)

45. *EMP* v, p.82.

46. *Minutes* London 1812, i, p.73, 1767; *ibid.* p.79, 1768; *ibid.* p.88, 1769.

47. *JWJ*, vi, p.178.

48. *Ibid.* p.322.

49. *Ibid.* vii, p.467-8.

50. e.g. *JWJ* iii, pp.109, 368; iv, p.227*n*; v, pp.177, 372, 460, 479; vi, p.8; vii, pp.185, 257, 300; viii, p.56.

51. *JWJ* iii, p.109 and *AM* 1778, p.531.

52. *JWJ* vi, p.155.

53. *AM* 1785, p.199; G. Lester, *Grimsby Methodism (1743-1889)*, London 1890, pp.42-44; *Methodist Recorder* 8 Dec 1898, *JWL* iii, p.97, *JWJ* iv, 227n, and v, p.479.

54. J. Burdsall, *Memoirs of the Life of R. Burdsall of York*, 3rd ed. Thetford 1823, p.110 and *JWJ* v, p.177n.

55. *MM* 1816, pp. 5-8 and *JWJ* vii, pp.64, 257, 300; viii, p.56.

56. *JWL* vi, p.374.

57. Tyerman, *op.cit.*, vol ii pp.144-6 and 239.

58. *JWJ* v, p.460 and n; vi, p.8; *JWL* vi, pp.104, 114, 117, 130, 241 and viii, pp.97, 216, 252; *WMM* 1827, p.359.

59. *JWJ* iv, pp. 201, 248.

60. *JWJ* v, p.497; vi, pp.295, 452.

61. e.g. *JWJ* vi, pp.115 and *n*, 240, 413; vii, p.113, and many others; *JWL* vi, pp.355, 377; vii, pp.33-4, 47, 113, and many others.

62. *JWJ* iii, p.151.

63. *JWJ* iii, p.371.

64. *JWJ* v, p.479.

65. *WMM* 1826, pp.580-1.

66. T. Evans, *The History of Modern Enthusiasm, from the Reformation to the Present Times*, 2nd ed. London 1757, p.119.

67. W. Cowper, *The Task* (1785), book ii 'The Timepiece', quoted in *AM*, 1794, p.501-2.

68. O. Goldsmith, *Miscellaneous Works* Philadelphia 1872, p.130.

69. 'The Life of Duncan Wright', in *EMP* ii., pp.121-2.

70. *The Connoisseur*, March and July 1755.

71. *MM* 1813, pp.834-837; A. Clarke *Commentary on the New Testament*, 2 vols. London 1836, ii; S. Tuck, *Wesleyan Methodism in Frome*, Frome 1837, pp.87-93; A Somersetshire Preacher, *Memorials of Josiah Gregory, an early Methodist Local preacher and Class Leader*, n.p. London 1870.

72. *WHS Proc*, ii, p.72.

73. W. H. H. Lecky, *History of England in the Eighteenth Century*, 6 vols. London 1872, ii, pp.545, 560, 582.

74. *JWL* v, p.45.

75. *JWL* iv, p.163; vi, p.224; vii, pp.68, 88, 94.

76. *JWJ* vii p.128, *JWL* vi p.363

77. *JWL* viii, pp.188 and 249.

78. *Minutes* 1862 i p.94, 1787.

79. *Minutes* 1862 i p. 570, 1790.

80. Reproduced in *JWJ* viii, pp.335-341.

81. *MM* 1817, p.133.

82. *JWJ* vi, p.279.

83. M. Batty, *Gunnerside Chapel and Gunnerside Folk* Barnard Castle 1967, pp.9-10, and see *JWL* ii, p. 94.

84. ed. J. C. Bowmer and J. A. Vickers, *The Letters of John Pawson* 3 vols., (*WMHS* 1994-5) i, p.96 to Charles Atmore, 9th March 1791.

85. *Minutes* 1793, London 1862, i, p.276.

86. *Minutes* 1795, London 1862, i, pp.322-325.

87. A. Kilham *Free Enquiry, Mutual Deliberation, and Liberty of Conscience, proved to be the only bonds of lasting union among the Methodists* (Leeds 1795 and Bristol 1796) passim. See also his *Progress of Liberty, amongst the people called Methodists. To which is added the Outlines of a Constitution. Humbly recommended to the serious consideration of the preachers and people late in connection with Mr Wesley.* (Alnwick 1795).

88. J. Crowther, Bristol 1796.

89. *Minutes* 1862 i p.344, 1796.

90. e.g. ms. *Account of the Monies Received and Disbursed at the Quarterly Meeting of the Leeds Circuit 1768-1777* by William Hey, Steward; *The Life of Samuel Drew* by his eldest son, London 1834, pp.94-97; Panton mss. III 1794-5, quoting *Sunderland Circuit Records*, Local Preachers' Meeting Minutes, 29 December 1794.

91. *Minutes* London 1862, i p.349. 1796.

CHAPTER 2

1. M. Batty *Stages in the development and control of Wesleyan Lay Leadership 1791-1878*, Methodist Publishing House (WMHS) 1992 p.42.

2. J. C. Bowmer *Pastor and People* 1975, pp.71ff. (Band Room Methodists). W. R. Ward *Early Correspondence of Jabez Bunting*, 1972 p.81. Also see J. L. Baxter 'The Great Yorkshire Revival' in M. Hill (ed.) *Sociological Year Book of Religion* 7, 1974. R. Carwardine *Translantic Revivalism: Popular Evangelicalism in Britain and America 1760-1865*, Greenwood, 1978. J. F. C. Harrison *The Second Coming: Popular Millenarianism 1780-1850*, RKP, 1979.

3. Julia S. Werner, *The Primitive Methodist Connexion: Its Background and Early History*, Madison U.S.A., 1984. Deborah Valenze, *Sons and Daughters of Prophecy*, Princeton, 1985.

4. S. G. Hatcher, 'The Sacrament of the Lord's Supper in Early Primitive Methodism.' *WHS Proc.* xivii, May 1990, pp.221-5. R. W. Ambler, 'Preacher and Plan: Patterns of Activity in Early Primitive Methodism', *WHS Proc.* xlvi May 1987, pp.21-31. G. F. Nuttall, *The Puritan Spirit*. Epworth Press, 1967 ch.xx. 'Early Quakerism and Early Primitive Methodism'. I presided at Holy Communion at an ex PM chapel in the Cym and Kingston Circuit which did not celebrate Holy Communion until the 1970s.

5. For the Sidmouth affair see: D. Hempton, *Methodism and Politics in British Society 1750-1850*. Hutchinson 1984, ch.4. idem: 'Thomas Allan and Methodist Politics 1790-1840', *History* 67. No. 219 (1982), pp.119-36. The Allan papers are in the Methodist Church Archives (MCA), John Rylands University Library of Manchester. D. M. Thompson, *Nonconformity in the Nineteenth century*. Selected Documents, Routledge 1972, pp.29-38. W. R. Ward, *Faith and Faction* Epworth Press 1993, ch.14. idem: *Religion and Society in England 1790-1850*, Batsford 1972, ch.4. R. W. Davis, *Dissent in Politics 1780-1830: The political Life of William Smith MP* Epworth Press 1971, chapter on the Sidmouth Bill. B. L. Manning, *The Protestant Dissenting Deputies*. Pt.2. CUP 1952 part 2, ch.3. F. C. Mather, *High Church Prophet – Bishop Samuel Horsley and the Caroline Tradition in the late Georgian Church*, OUP 1992 pp.64ff. pp.186ff. J. M. Turner, *Conflict and Reconciliation*. Epworth Press1985, ch.7.

6. D. W. Lovegrove *Established Church and Sectarian People: Itinerancy and the Transformation of English Dissent* OUP 1988. W. R. Ward, *Faith and Faction*, chs.ll, 15. R. W. Dale, *History of English Congregationalism*, Hodder 1907, p.593. M. Batty, *Stages* pp.51ff. pp.110ff.

7. *HMCGB* (iv) p.351. cf. p.390 from William Cobbett.Turner, *op.cit.* p.122

8. M. Batty, *Stages*. p.51

9. W. R. Ward, *op,cit.* pp.55ff. the text of Sidmouth's Bill. Parliamentary Debates XIX pp.1-128ff.

10. A. R. B. Robinson, *The Counting House: Thomas Thompson of Hull 1754-1828 and his family* York 1992.

11. Thomas Jackson, *Recollections of my own Life and Times* London 1873, p.203.

12. Hempton *op.cit.* p.101.

13. W. R. Ward, *Religion and Society* p.60. *WMM* 1811. pp.553-5.Turner *op.cit.* p.125.

14. *Minutes* 1812. pp.318ff. 51 George III c.155.

15. Hempton *op.cit.* p.103.

16. *Op.cit.* p.102.

17. e.g. H. B. Kendall, *History of the Primitive Methodist Church* 2 vols. c.1905 (i) pp.342-3.

18. P. N. Dale, *Many Mansions: The Growth of Religion in Bolton 1750-1850*, Bolton 1985, based on Bangor Ph.D. 1984.

19. D. A. Gowland, *Methodist Secessions: The Origins of Free Methodism in three Lancashire Towns, Manchester, Rochdale, Liverpool.* Manchester, 1979. An important book showing how difficult any generalisations are in this area.

20. C. D. Field, 'The Sociology of Methodism' *British Journal of Sociology.* July 1977. pp.199-225. A. D. Gilbert, *Religion and Society in Industrial England* London, 1976 pp.59ff.

21. The present writer checked this when the Minutes of both groups were in his possession in 1968. For the Leeds Organ Case see J. C. Bowmer *Pastor and People op.cit.*pp.108-118. M. Batty, *Stages op.cit.*pp.117ff. The MS evidence in (Leeds) District Archives deposited by the then minister Revd John Banks in 1969. O. A. Beckerlegge, *The United Methodist Free Churches* Epworth Press, 1957 pp.13-79.

22. Cited from the *Nottingham Review* December 14, 1827 in R. F. Wearmouth *Methodism and the Working Class Movement in England 1800-1850.* Epworth Press, 1937 p.195. W. R. Ward, (ed.) *The Early Correspondence of Jabez Bunting 1820-1829*, London, 1972, pp.156ff. esp. p.164, p.203.

23. D. A. Gowland, *op.cit.* The chapter on Rochdale.

24. O. A. Beckerlegge, *op.cit.* p.70. J. C. Bowmer, *The Lord's Supper in Methodism 1791-1960* Epworth Press, 1961

25. W. H. Jones, *History of the Wesley Reform Union* Epworth Press, 1952

26. cf J. M. Turner, *op.cit.* ch.5. John Kent, *The Age of Disunity* Epworth Press, 1966. chs.2- 5. *HMCGB* (ii) ch.6 by John Kent.

27. R. Currie, *Methodism Divided.* Faber 1968.p.53 and footnotes 1,2.

28. John Kent, *Holding the Fort* Epworth Press, 1978

29. E. V. Chapman, an article in the *Halifax Evening Courier*, 14 October 1978.

30. B. Wilson, *The Struggles of an Old Chartist* Halifax, 1887, p.3. Thompson *The Making of the English Working Class.* Pelican ed. 1968.p. 438

31. David B. Clark, 'Local and Cosmopolitan Aspects of Religious Activity in a Northern Suburb' in D. Martin and M. Hill (eds.) *A Sociological Year Book of Religion in Britain* SCM Press, 1970 pp.45-64.

32. *HMCGB* (i). ch. 8. *HMCGB* (ii) ch.3. F. Baker, *Methodism and the Lovefeast* Epworth Press, 1957. cp P. Bradshaw, *The Search for the Origins of Christian Worship.* SPCK, 1992. 67ff.

33. W. F. Swift, 'The Sunday Service of the Methodists' *WHS Proc.* xxxi June 1958, pp.133-143.

34. Murdoch first used this lighting in Birmingham in 1804.

35. T. Jackson, *Recollections,* pp.64-5.

36. C. N. R. Wallwork, 'Wesley's Legacy in Worship' in J. Stacey (ed.) *John Wesley Contemporary Perspectives,* Epworth Press, 1968. pp.83-98. *idem. Origins and Developments of the Methodist Preaching Service* Birmingham University M.A. Thesis. 1984. Adrian Burdon, *The Preaching Service, the Glory of the Methodists. A study of the Piety, Ethos and Development of the Methodist Preaching Service.* Grove Books, 1991. L. F. Church, *More about the Early Methodist People* ch.6 'Worship – Public and Private'. Epworth Press, 1949. James F. White, *A Brief History of Christian Worship* Abingdon, 1993. pp.145-152. *HMCGB* (ii). p.127.

37. T. Shaw, *The Bible Christians* 1815-1907, Epworth Press, p.85ff. Burdon *op.cit.* though beware minor errors.

38. D. Hempton, *op.cit.* p.95. cf Ward *Early Correspondence* pp.8-14. *PMM* 1850. p.298.

39. Batty, *Stages* pp.49ff. T. Jackson, *op,cit.*p.144. F. H. Cumbers, *The Book Room* Epworth Press, 1956, pp.144-9. H. F. Mathews, *Methodism and the Education of the People 1791-1851.* Epworth Press, 1949. p.79. *HMCGB* (ii). ch.2. esp. pp.98,104.

40. T. W. Laqueur, *Religion and Respectability: Sunday School and Working Class Culture 1780-1850,* Yale, 1976.

41. W. R. Ward, *Early Correspondence of Bunting,* pp.61-3.

42. E. P. Thompson, *op.cit.* p.411ff.

43. B. Moore, *Wesleyan Methodism in Burnley and East Lancashire* 1899. p.80.

44. Batty, *Stages* pp.54-5. Ward, *Early Correspondence* p.21.

45. R. F. Wearmouth, *Methodism and the Working Class Movements of 1800-1850* Epworth Press, 1937. pp.213ff. A.Briggs, *Chartist Studies* MacMillan, 1959. ch.4. East Midlands.

46. J. Marlow, *The Tolpuddle Martyrs* Panther, 1974. E. J. Hobsbawm and G. Rudd, *Captain Swing* Lawrence and Wishart, 1969. pp.281ff. R. F. Wearmouth, *Some Working Class Movements of the Nineteenth Century* Epworth Press, 1948. pp.277ff.

47. S. Y. Richardson, 'John Skevington of Loughborough: Primitive Methodism and Chartism,' in *From Mow Cop to Peake 1807-1932,* Essays to commemorate the 175th anniversary of the beginnings of Primitive Methodism. WHS Yorkshire Branch, 1982, pp.47ff.

48. John Kent, *The Age of Disunity* Epworth Press, 1966 pp.132ff.

49. A. R. B. Robinson, *op.cit.*

50. J. H. Drew, *Life of Samuel Drew* Longmans, 1834. J. R. Gregory, *A History of Methodism* vol.i, Kelly, 1911. pp.288-9. L. F. Church, *More about the Early Methodist People* Epworth Press, 1949 pp.53,110, 134.

51. J. Everett, *Memoirs of the Life, Character and Ministry of William Dawson* London, 1842. L. F. Church, *op,cit.* p.131. J. R. Gregory, *op.cit.* p.295. W. R. Ward, *Early Correspondence* p.207. J. L. and. B. Hammond, *The Age of the Chartists* London, 1930. pp.243-4.

52. L. F. Church, *op.cit.* pp.105,116,125,272. J. Everett, *The Village Blacksmith* 1875 (First published 1830). S. Hick, *Memoirs* Halifax, 1858. J. R. Gregory, *op.cit.* p.297.

53. John Kent, *The Age of Disunity* pp.x, 137.

54. For clear statements of the tension here see A. Barrett, *An Essay on the Pastoral Office* 1839. J. Beecham, *An Essay on the Constitution of Wesleyan Methodism* 1st Edition 1829. W. Vevers, *Observations on the Power Possessed and Exercised by the Wesleyan Methodist Ministers* 1828. J. Everett, *Methodism as it is* 2 vols. 1863-5. Pamphlets listed in M. Batty, *Stages*, p.254ff.

55. M. Batty, *Local Preachers* p.81, from D. Simpson as quoted in J. Warner *The Wesleyan Movement in the Industrial Revolution* 1960 p.261.

CHAPTER 3

1. George Lawton's lively and commendable book *Reader-Preacher* 1989, pp.92-129, offers interesting material related to this chapter. For Wesleyan local preachers in the nineteenth century up to 1878 see Margaret Batty's scholarly study *Stages in the development and control of Wesleyan Lay Leadership 1791-1878* published 1992, esp. chapter 12. For more detailed and extended references on Wesleyan local preaching Dr Batty's M.A. thesis (Leeds University 1969) should be consulted: 'The Contribution of local preachers to the life of the Wesleyan Methodist Church until 1932, and to the Methodist Church after 1932, in England'. Dr John Bowmer covers the ground briefly but usefully within 'The Local Preacher in Methodism 1791-1964', *The Preacher's Handbook* ed. D. N. Francis, No.9. 1965. pp.1-19. For a vivid account of local preaching in one area in the nineteenth century see chapter 14 of Rowland C. Swift *Lively People:Methodism in Nottingham 1740-1979* 1982.

2. ed. G. E. Milburn, *The Diary of John Young, Sunderland Chemist and Methodist Lay Preacher 1841-43*, Surtees Society Vol. CXCV, 1983.

3. Original in the writer's possession.

4. A useful guide to these trends is in D. Gilbert *Religion and Society in Industrial England:Church Chapel and Social Change 1740-1914* Longmans 1976.

5. Table compiled from information in the *Wesleyan Methodist Minutes* for 1907, *United Methodist Church Minutes (First Conference)* 1907, and *PM Magazine* for 1907.

6. ed. W. J. Townsend, H. B. Workman and G. Eayrs, *A New History of Methodism,* 1909 (ii) 532-3.

7. John Kent, *The Age of Disunity* 1966, pp.34-5.

8. *WMM* 1850 pp.712ff.

9. W. B. Pope, *The Methodist Local Preacher* 1879, an address delivered in the Grosvenor Street Chapel, Manchester, 25 March 1879 at the request of the Wesleyan Methodist Local Preachers' Mutual Aid Association.

10. The lay representatives are listed, with brief biographical details, in the *Watchman and Wesleyan Advertiser* 24 July and subsequent weekly issues. I owe this information to Dr Margaret Batty.

11. *Proceedings of the Oecumenical Methodist Conference held in City Road Chapel, London, September 1881* 1881 pp.119-120. On Waddy see D. Whiteley (ed) *Illustrious Local Preachers*, Bradford 1891, pp.181-196, which includes the text of one of his sermons. Also J. L. Waddy, *The Waddy Family* 1985.

12. H. B. Kendall, *History of the Primitive Methodist Church* (one volume) revised edition 1919 p.93ff. passim. H. B. Kendall, *Origin and History of the Primitive Methodist Church* 2 vols. c.1905, ii p.358 ff.passim. G. E. Milburn, 'Tensions in Primitive Methodism in the 1870s' *WHS Proc.* XL, parts 4 and 5, February and June 1976.

13. Kent *op. cit.* p.7.

14. Milburn, *op. cit.* (*WHS Proc.* 1976) and also *The Christian Lay Churches, Their Origins and Progress,* Sunderland, 1977.

15. *WHS Proc.* June 1976 pp.136-7.

16. ed. A. Binney and J. A. Vickers, *A City Road Diary by Helen G. McKenny 1885-88,* 1978 p.45.

17. *HMCGB* (iii) p.156.

18. H. J. Martyn, 'The Local Preacher in his relation to the future of our churches' *LPMag.* 1893, pp.77-80.

19. I owe my access to this source to Dr Dorothy Graham.

20. e.g. 'May the day be far distant when in Methodism education shall be preferred before piety, when showy parts shall be more attractive than spiritual power.' W. D. Lawson, *Wesleyan Local Preachers* 1874, p.22.

21. Quoted Batty *op. cit.* p.208.

22. *Proceedings of the Oecumenical Methodist Conference* 1881 p.115.

23. *Journals of William Clowes* 1844, pp.42-3.

24. G. E. Milburn 'Michael Longridge of Sunderland', *WHS North East Branch Bulletin* 23 March 1975, pp.22-28.

25. *Bible Christian Magazine* 1851, pp.69-70.

26. J. Atkinson *Life of Revd Colin M'Kechnie* 1898 pp.79ff. G. E. Milburn *A School for the Prophets* 1981 pp.10ff.

27. W. B. Pope *op. cit.* p.36.

28. Hetton-le-Hole Primitive Methodist Circuit Local Preachers' Examination Committee Minutes 1896-1913, Tyne and Wear Archives, ref.MC/He.1/2.

29. *Wesleyan Conference Report* 1914 p.55.

30. *Preachers' Magazine* August 1914. pp.383-4.

31. *Methodist Recorder* 27 June 1918. Sir Henry Lunn thought the figures to be more like two thirds. *Recorder* 13 June 1918.

32. *Recorder* 13 June 1918.

33. *Ibid.*

34. *Recorder* 17 February 1916, p.5.

35. *Recorder* 8 August 1918, p.6.

36. *Recorder Ibid.*

37. *Recorder* 25 August 1918, p.7.

38. Documents related to Victor Murray's conscientious objection are deposited in the Liddle Collection (World War I Archive), Edward Boyle Library, University of Leeds.

39. On the work of the Local Preachers' Commission set up by the Wesleyans in 1918 see Dr. Batty's MA thesis pp. 287ff.

40. *The Methodist Leader*, the weekly journal of the Primitive Methodist Church, 23 June 1932, pp.1-2.

CHAPTER 4

1. *Preachers' Magazine*, September 1932, p.8.

2. General Statistics of Methodism, 1932 in *A History of the Methodist Church in Great Britain*, iv, p.648.

3. *Preachers' Magazine*, November 1932, p.3.

4. J. Munsey Turner, in 'Methodism in England 1900-1932', *A History of the Methodist Church in Great Britain*, iii, p.340.

5. Table of statistics in the *Local Preachers' Affairs Report*, p.2 in the Conference *Agenda* 1943, p.177.

6. See my WHS Conference lecture, 'Practical piety or lettered learning: objections to ministerial training', *WHS Proceedings, October 1995*.

7. *Preachers' Magazine*, September/October 1946.

8. Report on Local Preachers' Affairs in the Conference *Agenda* 1948, pp.209ff.

9. eg. in vol. 9 of the *Preachers' Handbook*.

10. Aricle appearing in October 1937 in the *Preachers' Magazine*.

11. see *HMCGB*, iii, pp.338-339.

12. See Standing Orders 263-5 of *Constitutional Practice and Discipline* in the 1940s.

13. See the statement in the *Minutes of the Methodist Conference*, 1946, Appendix II on 'Lay Administration of the Sacraments', pp.203-204.

14. Oral recollection of Revd J. M. Turner.

15. *Preachers' Handbook* , No.1, 1950.

16. *Minutes of the Methodist Conference*, 1947, p.168 : SO 65 (4) 9.

17. *LP Magazine*, April 1936, p.150.

18. *LP Magazine*, February 1938.

19. *LP Quarterly*, December 1955.

20. *LP Magazine* 1953.

21. W. E. Sangster *Power in Preaching* Epworth Press, 1958, p.34.

22. Oral recollection by Revd J. M. Turner.

23. *Preachers' Magazine*, November 1934.

24. *Local Preachers' Quarterly*, December 1954, on 'Team Study and Team Preaching'.

25. D. Francis, *The ABC of Preaching*, 1968.

26. A. Hastings, *A History of English Christianity 1920-1985*, 1987 edition (pb) p.129.

27. See John Stacey's comments in the *LP Magazine*, April 1968, p.45.

28. See the *Annual Report of the Local Preachers' Department,* 1966, p.7.

CHAPTER 6

1. *Agenda*, 1983, p. 86.

2. *Agenda*, 1982, p.270.

3. *Agenda*, 1986, p.57.

4. John Stacey in a letter to the writer, 10 September, 1993.

5. *Agenda*, 1972, p. 351.

6. *Let the People Worship*, Methodist Publishing House, 1988.

7. See, for example, the series *God's People at Worship*, DEY/MPH 1990- and the regular weekly feature in *Worship and Preaching* entitled 'All-age Worship' or 'All Together'.

8. *Agenda*, 1993, p.141.

9. *The Book of Offices*, Methodist Publishing House, 1936, p. 74

10. *Ibid* p.77.

11. It is sometimes debated as to whether or not ordained ministers (presbyters) are still local preachers. It was argued by the Local Preachers' Office, when new disciplinary procedures were being considered by the Law and Polity Committee, that a person's office/status as a local preacher was subsumed into another order of ministry on ordination. This view is supported by the fact that, if ministers resign or are dismissed by the Conference they can, with consent, still *retain* their local preacher status.

12. *Agenda*, 1967, p. 399

13. *Agenda*, 1968, p. 430.

14. *The Recognition and Commissioning of Local Preachers*, Methodist Publishing House, 1975, p. 4.

15. *The Constitutional Practice and Discipline of the Methodist Church*, Methodist Publishing House, 1992, p. 660.

16. *Agenda*, 1993 p. 139.

17. *Bishops' Regulations for Reader Ministry*, ABM Publications, 1991, pp.4-6.

18. *The Constitutional Practice and Discipline of the Methodist Church*, Standing Order 568.

CHAPTER 7

1. J. B. B. Clarke, *An Account of the Life of Adam Clarke* (1833) i, p.179.

2. *Journal of Revd John Wesley* ed. N. Curnock (Standard Edition) 8 vols. 1938, vi, p.322.

3. J. Entwistle, *Memoir of Joseph Entwistle* (1848) p.15.

4. T. Jackson (ed), *Lives of the Early Methodist Preachers* (3rd ed. 1866) iv, p.24.

5. Preserved in the WHS Library, Westminster College, Oxford.

6. *Minutes* (1862 ed.) I, p.361.

7. MS letter, W. Thom to Alexander Kilham, March 17 1798, at the Methodist Archives, John Rylands University Library of Manchester.

8. For the complete version, see *Cirplan* 15 (1962).

9. Retford Wesleyan LP Minute Book 1830-65 quoted in B..J. Biggs, 'The Disciplined Society . . . ' in *Transactions of the Thoroton Society* 1971 p.99.

10. Tadcaster Quarterly Meeting Minutes quoted in *Cirplan* 41 (1975) p.13.

11. W. Robinson, *An Essay on a Lay Ministry* (1832) p.159.

12. *Ibid.* pp.161-2.

13. WHS North East Branch *Bulletin*, 63 (March 1995) p.18. The plan is printed in G. E. Milburn, *The Travelling Preacher* 1987 p.89,

14. The Marriott Collection, now at Drew University, Madison, NJ, USA.

15. J. A. Vickers, 'Circuit Life in 1825' in T. Macquiban (ed.) *Methodism in its cultural milieu* (Westminster Wesley Series, No.2, 1994) p.165.

16. Alan Rogers, 'When city speaks for county . . .' in D. Baker (ed.) *The Church in Town and Countryside* (Studies in Church History, 16, 1979) pp.336-341.

17. W. G. Taylor, *Taylor of 'Down Under'* (1920), p.48.

18. See R. W. Ambler 'Preachers and the Plan . . . in Early Primitive Methodism' in *WHS Proc.* xlvi (May 1987), pp.21-31 for a detailed study of part of a PM circuit in 1821.

19. Quoted in J. M. Turner, *The People's Church* (1994) p.9.

20. The complete poem of nine verses is reproduced in *Cirplan* 17 (1963) pp.13-14.

21. Transcription supplied by O. A. Beckerlegge.

22. C. G. Rackett, *According to Plan* (1986) p.5.

CHAPTER 8

1. *The Letters of the Rev. John Wesley*, AM (hereafter *JWL*) ed. John Telford, 1933, Standard Edition, 8 vols. iv p.133.

2. *Ibid.* vii p.9.

3. Zechariah Taft, *Biographical Sketches of Holy Women* 2 vols. (vol. I 1825; vol. II Leeds 1828) Preface, i p.iv and p.84.

4. *JWL* viii p.190.

5. I Timothy 2:12; I Corinthians 14:34; 11:5; Z. Taft, *The Scripture Doctrine of Women's Preaching*, (1820), pp.19-21.

6. Taft, *op.cit.* i pp.21-23; *JWL* v p.257.

7. *Ibid.* p.25; Henry Moore, *The Life of Mrs. Fletcher* (1867 – 17th ed.) p.125.

8. Joseph Ritson, *The Romance of Primitive Methodism* (1909) p.133.

9. Taft, *op.cit.* i p.20.

10. *Minutes of the Wesleyan Methodist Conference (hereafter WM Mins.)* 1803 (1862 ed.) p. 187.

11. See 'A Famous Lady Preacher' by Dr Waller and the Editor, an article from the *Wesleyan Methodist Magazine* (hereafter *WMM*) (1907) pp.538-44. The same day John Pawson wrote to the church at Dover commending Mrs. Taft.

12. Zechariah Taft, *Thoughts on Female Preaching* (Dover, 1803); *The Scripture Doctrine of Women's Preaching: stated and examined by Z. Taft* (York, 1820); a reply to an article inserted in WMM for April 1809 entitled 'Thoughts on Women's Preaching' extracted from Dr. James McKnight; 'Thoughts on a Proper Call to the Christian Ministry' in *The Bible Christian Magazine* (1826); MSS correspondence in the Taft Collection in the Methodist Archives and Research Centre.

13. H. B. Kendall, *The Origin and History of the Primitive Methodist Church* 2 vols. (n.d., c.1905), i, p.142.

14. H. Bourne, MSS *Journal*, 25th June 1809; John Walford, *Memoirs of the Life and Labours of the late Venerable Hugh Bourne* (1855), p.216; Kendall, *op.cit.* pp.142-4; cf. J. T. Wilkinson, *The Life of Hugh Bourne 1772-1852* (1952).

15. Taft, *op.cit.* i, pp.326-8.

16. J. Conder Nattrass, 'Some Notes from the Oldest Register of the Great Yarmouth Circuit'. *WHS Proc.* vol.3 (1902) p.74.

17. William Parlby, 'Diana Thomas, of Kington, Lay Preacher in the Hereford Circuit 1759-1821', *WHS Proc.*, vol.14 (1924, Part 5) pp.110-11.

18. Taft, *op.cit.* ii, pp.224-7.

19. *Ibid.* pp.184-193.

20. Taft, *op.cit.* i, pp.269-70; C. H. Crookshank, *History of Methodism in Ireland* (Belfast, 1885-88) 3 vols. ii, p.400.

21. *JWL* viii p.259.

22. Taft, *op.cit.* i, pp.326-8.

23. *WM Mins.* (1910) pp.365-6.

24. *WMM* (1885) p,712.

25. *Primitive Methodist Magazine* (hereafter *PMM*) (1825) pp.409-13.

26. *PMM* (1853) pp.444-6.

27. *Minutes of the Bible Christian Connexion* (1819) pp.4-6.

28. Taft. *op.cit.* i, pp.271-90.

29. *Ibid.* pp.52-64.

30. *Ibid.* pp.52-64.

31. *The Arminian (Bible Christian) Magazine* (1823) pp.281-86.

32. Minutes of the Chatham Bible Christian Circuit Local Preachers' Meeting 1822-62.

33. Weare Bible Christian Circuit Book, 1822-53.

34. Stalybridge Methodist New Connexion Local Preachers' Minute Book 1837.

35. Taft, *op.cit.* ii, pp.250-2.

36. Thomas Parsons, 'The Position of Women in the Church in *The Primitive Methodist Quarterly Review and Christian Ambassador'* (3rd series) 1885, p.682.

37. Oliver A. Beckerlegge, *The United Methodist Free Churches: A study in Freedom* (1957) p.27.

38. Ritson, *op.cit.* pp.154-7.

39. *Primitive Methodist Minutes of Conference* (1821) p.4 (Question 9)

40. W. M. Patterson, *Northern Primitive Methodism* (1909) p.221.

41. *The Methodist Local Preachers' Who's Who* London, 1934 p.328.

42. Patterson *op.cit.* p.224.

43. *Ibid.* pp.275-6.

44. *Ibid.* p.175.

45. *Ibid.* p.143.

46. *PMM* (1888) p.242.

47. *Ibid.* (1887) pp.177-8.

48. *Ibid.* (1880) p.118.

49. Parsons *op.cit.* – reference as in note 36 above.

50. *WMM* (1897) pp.174-6.

51. *Ibid.* pp.174-6.

52. E. C. Rawlings *London Directory for the Primitive Methodists* (1896) pp.23-37.

53. *WM Mins.* (1918) p.85.

54. *Ibid.* (1919) p.271.

55. *Ibid.* (1928) (gives 1927 numbers). pp.388-9: (1928) pp.388-9: (1929) pp.404-5; (1930) pp.390-1; (1931) pp.386-7; (1932) pp.250-1.

56. *Minutes* (1933) pp.450-1.

57. *WM Minutes* (1928) pp.388-9.

58. *Ibid.* (1932) pp.250-1; *Minutes* (1933) pp.450-1.

59. *The Methodist Local Preachers' Who's Who* 1934 passim.

60. Minutes of the Jersey (French) Circuit Local Preachers' Meeting, 10th May 1923.

61. Memories of Mrs Mary Worrall, February 1994.

CHAPTER 10

1. Stephens's *Methodist Magazine* vol.1 (September 1834). John Stephens, editor, was brother of Revd J. Rayner Stephens.

2. The Society's minute book is at present in the care of the writer of this chapter.

3. There is an account of one of its public meetings in *The Wesleyan Times*, 30 January 1849.

4. *Wesleyan Times* 30 January 1849.

5. More than 20 letters appeared during June and July 1849, four of them from Francis Pearson.

6. A full report of its proceedings has been preserved and is in the care of the writer of this chapter.

7. The report contains details of the debate on this question.

8. Cromford Circuit LP Meeting Minutes of September 1850 record the Superintendent's statement that he would bring charges against Pearson.

9. LP membership of LPMAA rose to 2,648 by 1854, fell to 1,674 in 1866, not reaching the 1854 figure again until 1880.

10. These and other instances are recorded in the *LP Mag* during the 1850s and early 1860s.

11. *Methodist Recorder* of 24 August 1893 carried a detailed report of Kilner's funeral, with full summary of the address.

12. David Barr's autobiography *Climbing the Ladder* (1910) gives interesting insights into his career and religious life.

13. Birmingham *Daily Gazette* 23 August 1898 and 29 August 1898. (Birmingham Central Reference Library).

14. In Coventry Record Office, with minute book of Fillongley Cottage Homes Trust.

15. A. J. Gilliver, *More Precious than Rubies,* LPMAA, 1989.

16. F. Harold Buss and R. G. Burnett, *A Goodly Fellowship,* Epworth Press, 1949.

17. The minutes of the General Committee are in the Methodist Church Archive (MCA) at John Rylands University Library, Manchester.

18. The minutes of the General Committee and Aggregate Meeting of LPMAA for 1943 are in MCA.

19. From letters held in LPMAA files of the period.

20. From letters held in LPMAA files of the period.

21. The text of Mr Farley's address is included in General Committee Minutes for 1944, in the Methodist Archive at (MCA).

22. More than 20 letters appeared in the *Methodist Recorder* during June, July and August 1945, and over a dozen more in the *Local Preachers' Magazine* during the winter of that year.

23. She was Lady Newbold Kay, wife of Sir Robert Newbold Kay, MP, Lord Mayor of York.

24. *A Goodly Fellowship* p.73.

25. *The Local Preachers' Magazine* in the later years of the 19th century and the early years of the 20th century records many such exchanges.

CHAPTER 11

1. See, especially, C. D. Field, 'The social structure of English Methodism: eighteenth-twentieth centuries', *British Journal of Sociology*, xxviii (1977), 199-225 and 'The social composition of English Methodism to 1830: a membership analysis', *Bulletin of the John Rylands University Library of Manchester*, 76: 1 (Spring 1994), 153-78, and the sources cited therein.

2. See, in particular, K. D. Brown, *A social history of the Nonconformist ministry in England and Wales, 1800-1930* (Oxford: Clarendon Press, 1988), 19-55.

3. The most systematic studies to date have been C. I. Wallace, 'Religion and society in eighteenth-century England: geographic, demographic and occupational patterns of Dissent in the West Riding of Yorkshire, 1715-1801' (Duke University Ph.D. thesis, 1975), 249-347, 433-75 and R. W. Ambler, 'The social composition of church leadership: Nonconformist trustees in Lincolnshire, 1800-1870', *Bulletin of the John Rylands University Library of Manchester*, 75: 1 (Spring 1993), 133-56. Cf. Field, 'The social structure of English Methodism', 213-15.

4. W. J. Warner, *The Wesleyan movement in the Industrial Revolution* (London: Longmans, Green and Co., 1930), 259-61. Cf. L. F. Church, *More about the early Methodist people* (London: Epworth Press, 1949), 99-135.

5. Wallace, 'Religion and society in eighteenth-century England', 362, 511-15. The status of eighteen Methodist New Connexion local preachers in the West Riding at this time (1797-1801) was broadly similar; *Ibid.*, 362, 370, 517-18. See Field, 'The social composition of English Methodism to 1830', 164-5, 176-8, for details of the scheme used here to classify occupations, which differs somewhat from Wallace's approach.

6. Membership book of the Blackburn Wesleyan Methodist Circuit, 1788-1808 (Blackburn Circuit Archives, Wesley Hall, Blackburn).

7. *Bedford St. Paul's Methodist Circuit class book* (Bedford: Bedfordshire County Record Office, 1977), passim.

8. J. Sutcliffe, *A review of Methodism, in a discourse delivered on laying the foundation-stone of New Street Chapel, York, on January 1 1805* (York: printed and sold by T. Wilson and R. Spence, 1805), 22-3; D. Bogue and J. Bennett, *History of Dissenters from the Revolution in 1688 to the year 1808* (4 vol., London: printed for the authors, 1808-12), iv. 338; W. Jones, *A dictionary of religious opinions; or, Concise account of the various denominations into which the profession of Christianity is divided* (London, 1815), 140.

9. R. C. Swift, 'Methodism in Sussex and its influence in the life of the community (1756-1900)' (University of Sussex M.Phil. thesis, 1984), 53.

10. Oxford Diocesan clergy visitation returns, 1817 (Oxfordshire Archives, MS Oxford Diocesan Papers, d.576-7), d.577, fo. 29.

11. B. J. Biggs, 'Methodism in a rural society: north Nottinghamshire, 1740-1851' (University of Nottingham Ph.D. thesis, 1975), 426, 429.

12. J. N. Clarke and C. L. Anderson, *Methodism in the countryside: Horncastle Circuit, 1786-1986* (Horncastle: F.W. Cupit (Printers), 1986), 103.

13. J. Obelkevich, *Religion and rural society: south Lindsey, 1825-1875* (Oxford: Clarendon Press, 1976), 195-6, 202.

14. J. M. Reed, 'Wesleyan Methodism in Bolton, with gleanings from other Methodist associated chapels (1820-70)' (University of Birmingham B.A. dissertation, 1983), 30-1.

15. M. R. Sheard, 'The origins and early development of Primitive Methodism in Cheshire and south Lancashire, 1800-1860' (University of Manchester Ph.D. thesis, 1980, 3 vol.), iii. 1125-6.

16. Obelkevich, *Religion and rural society*, 239.

17. F. Thompson, *Lark Rise to Candleford: a trilogy* (London: Oxford University Press, 1951), 214.

18. M. Home *pseud.* [i.e. C. C. Bush], *Autumn fields* (London: Methuen & Co., 1944), 90.

19. A. H. Patterson, *From hayloft to temple: the story of Primitive Methodism in Yarmouth* (London: Robert Bryant, 1903), 114.

20. Field, 'The social structure of English Methodism', 210-11.

21. R. Moore, *Pit-men, preachers & politics: the effects of Methodism in a Durham mining community* (London: Cambridge University Press, 1974), 249, 251.

22. G. M. Morris, 'Primitive Methodism in Nottinghamshire, 1815-1932' (University of Nottingham Ph.D. thesis, 1967), 172, 174.

23. *The Methodist Local Preachers' Who's Who, 1934: a complete record of the lives and careers of Methodist local preachers* (London: Shaw Publishing Co., [1934]). A projected 1935 edition mentioned in the publisher's foreword never seems to have materialized. The data cited in this paper derive exclusively from a random 5 per cent national sample. However, the present author has also undertaken an analysis of a sub-set of London local preachers in connection with an earlier study; C. D. Field, 'Methodism in metropolitan London, 1850-1920: a social and sociological study' (University of Oxford D.Phil. thesis, 1974), 63-5.

24. In the 5 per cent national sample derived from *The Methodist Local Preacher's Who's Who*, 1934, 58.2 per cent of local preachers whose former denomination could be deduced were Wesleyan, 29.4 per cent were Primitive Methodist and 12.5 per cent were United Methodist. In 1932, by contrast, the proportions for all local preachers appear to have been 51.9, 35.6 and 12.5 per cent respectively.

25. The principal column headings are: gender, year of birth, age, education, marital status, number of children, occupation, social class (Registrar General's scheme), year of appointment as a local preacher, age at appointment, years on full plan, pre-union Methodist denomination, Methodist circuit number, Methodist district number, region, church/circuit offices held, public offices held, interests, recreations, publications, telephone ownership.

26. *Who's Who in Methodism, 1933: an encyclopaedia of the personnel and departments, ministerial and lay, in the united Church of Methodism* (London: *The Methodist Times and Leader*, 1933).

27. *The Minutes of the Annual Conference of the Methodist Church, held in Leicester, July 1934* (London: Methodist Publishing House, 1934), 107-57; *Methodist Church buildings: statistical returns including seating accommodation as at July 1st 1940* (Manchester: Department for Chapel Affairs, 1947).

28. General Register Office, Census 1951: *classification of occupations* (London: Her Majesty's Stationery Office, 1956).

29. *The Methodist Local Preachers' Who's Who*, 1934, 24.

30. The data for men in England and Wales in 1931 derive from the population census of that year, as summarized in D. C. Marsh, *The changing social structure of England and Wales, 1871-1961* (revised edition, London: Routledge & Kegan Paul, 1965), 198.

31. Field, 'The social structure of English Methodism', 206, 210-11. It should be noted that a slightly different methodology was applied in this earlier study for the allocation of occupations to social class than in the current paper. Although the *combined* totals for classes II and III are directly comparable, the figures for each class separately are not.

32. It will be appreciated that these figures do not necessarily relate to *completed* family size, since a good many local preachers were still of an age when they could reasonably be expected to have further children.

33. Methodist district numbers for 1934 have been allocated to regions as follows: southern England – 1-6, 9, 11, 16, 20, 34-6; Midlands – 7, 15, 17, 19, 25-6, 33, 38, 40; northern England – 8, 10, 13, 18, 21-2, 24, 27-32, 37, 39, 41; Wales - 12, 42-4.

34. It should be noted that the church or circuit offices concerned may not necessarily have been held in 1934. Some may have been held in the past, but not contemporaneously. The inclusion of retrospectively-held offices may possibly have had a distorting influence on the data.

35. For example: 'The brotherhood of 25,000 local preachers includes men of every calling, of all degrees of ability, and of every variety of temperament and gift: Members of Parliament, trade-union leaders, scientists, labourers, business-men, teachers, miners, tradesmen, doctors . . . '; F. H. Everson, *This is Methodism* (London: Epworth Press, 1957), 88.

36. E. W. Martin, *The shearers and the shorn: a study of life in a Devon community* (London: Routledge & Kegan Paul, 1965), 179-80.

37. L. Burton, 'The social stratification of two Methodist churches in the Midlands in respect of leadership, membership and adherence: a study of the social structure of the local church' (University of London Ph.D. thesis, 1972), 205-7, 215-17, 227-9 and 'Social class in the local church: a study of two Methodist churches in the Midlands', *A sociological yearbook of religion in Britain, 8*, ed. M. Hill (London: SCM Press, 1975), 19-20, 23. Five of the local preachers were single and twenty-five were married. Three were in their twenties, four in their thirties, seven in their forties, ten in their fifties, four in their sixties, and two in their seventies. Nine had left school at the statutory leaving age, nine stayed on after that age, and twelve had been to college or university.

38. Moore, *Pit-men, Preachers and Politics*, 252.

39. P. S. Richards, 'The call to local preaching', *Worship & Preaching*, 20: 1 (February 1990), 22.

40. The data used in this essay are all hitherto unpublished. They derive from a special computerized analysis of the replies to selected questions in the '"Pastoral care in Methodism" Local Preachers' Survey', an analysis which was generously arranged for the author by Dr Burfield. I am most grateful to him for allowing me to use the data in this way, although he is in no sense responsible for my interpretation of them. The only publication arising from the survey to date is: D. R. Burfield, 'Survey of local preachers: interpreting the response to the sexuality report', *Methodist Recorder*, 15 April 1993, 13.

CHAPTER 12

1. 'You are healed healers, he said, so take the Kingdom to others, for I am not its patron and you not its brokers. It is, was, and always will be available to any who want it': John Dominic Crossan, *The Historical Jesus*, T. and T. Clark, (1992) p.xii.

2. W M Patterson, *Northern Primitive Methodism,* London (1909) pp.207-208.

3. Eifion Evans, *Howel Harris. Evangelist 1714-73*, University of Wales Press, (1974) p.9.

4. David Hempton reckons that Methodism thrived 'in areas of Anglican parochial weakness': *Methodism and Politics in British Society, 1750-1850,* London, (1984) p.15. One reason among many for Primitive Methodist growth, according to Julia Werner, was its 'lay apostolate and . . . pastoral techniques which Wesleyan preachers were beginning to ignore': *The Primitive Methodist Connexion,* University of Wisconsin Press, (1984) p.14.

5. In particular, *Welsh* Calvinistic Methodism was very distinctive in its relative strength, and theology. I am grateful to my colleague, Keith Snell, for pointing this out to me, and for helping me with the geographical spread of the various connexions.

6. See, for instance: Nigel Scotland, *Methodism and the Revolt of the Field,* Gloucester, Alan Sutton, (1981) pp.147-59.

7. A National Miners' Association leaflet put it this way in an imagined conversation between coalowners Mr D and Mr F -

    'Well, sir, you see it is now as in the year 1831 . . . contrive what plan we will, they are sure to lay a deeper one . . . Then they have a few tallented (*sic*) fellows amongst them that if we had to enter into public discussion with them, they would be sure to make fools of us.'

    'I quite agree with you Mr D . . . there is a number of their Delegates, who are local preachers, and some of them can ransack the Bible between backs; another thing is that they carry on their financial affairs that the most ignorant of them may understand . . . '

    (*Dialogue between Three Coal Viewers,* 1844)

    The Parliamentary Commissioner fully concurred with these sentiments: Report of the Commissioner . . . into the State of the Population in the Mining Districts, *Parliamentary Papers* 1846, p.8.

8. The classic work here is: John Gorman, *Banner Bright* (1976). On trade unions as Good Samaritans, and the banner's proclaiming message, see Jack Lawson, *A Man's Life* (1949) pp.121-22.

9. Hinckley Primitive Methodist Circuit, no date/early 20th century: Leicestershire County Record Office, N/M/142/96

10. Revd H. B. Kendall, *The Origin and History of the Primitive Methodist Church,* London, (c.1905) vol ii, pp.185-6. On Pauline theology: John Kent, *Holding the Fort – Studies in Victorian Revivalism,* Epworth Press, (1978) pp.11-23.

11. Alun Howkins, *Poor Labouring Men,* Routledge, (1985) p.49.

References

12. R. E. Davies, *Methodism,* Epworth Press (1964) p.69, pp.80-83; John Wesley, *Earnest Appeal to men of Reason and Religion* (1771) p.14.

13. Stephen Dawes, *Adam Clarke, Methodism's First Old Testament Scholar* (Cornish MHA paper 26, 1994) pp.3-5. John Wesley's *A Collection of Hymns for the Use of the People called Methodists* (1780) was intended to replace 'the round' mode of singing for a more literate and theologically acceptable collection: John Telford, *The Methodist Hymn-Book Illustrated* (1906) pp.9-10.

14. Deborah M. Valenze, *Prophetic Sons and Daughters. Female Preaching and Popular Religion in Industrial England,* Princeton University Press, (1985) pp.101-83. For the Primitives, chapels did not outnumber other places until 1868 (p.274). Early nineteenth-century feminist Christians swapped text for text, historical precedent for precedent, and never surrendered their right to preach. Hugh Bourne joined them in his *Remarks on the Ministry of Women* (1808), refusing to give privilege to ecclesiastical habit or convenience, and giving Joel 2:28, Acts 2:18, 1 Cor 1:27 as his texts. See chapter 8 for this theme.

15. Letter, 'J. S.' to Home Department, 6 April 1821, Home Office papers HO/40/16. See also: Alan D. Gilbert, 'Methodism, dissent and political stability in early industrial England', *Journal of Religious History,* 10, 1978-79.

16. Robert Southey, *The Life of Wesley and the Rise and Progress of Methodism* London, 2 vols, (1820) p.298; William James, *The Varieties of Religious Experience* (1904) p.95; E. P. Thompson, *The Making of the English Working Class,* Penguin edition, (1968) chapter eleven. Thompson hated the tracts and over-emphasized their importance, but here it is easier to sympathize with his attitude: 'I shall not be here long; and if I die as I am, it will be awful, if the Bible be true', 'Dear Mother ... do what you know to be right, and prepare to meet me in heaven.' (*The Power of Divine Grace exemplified in the last illness of William Chapman,* Darlington 1844).

17. Albert M. Lyles, *Methodism Mocked,* Epworth Press, (1960) p.74.

18. 'A Professor', *Confessions of a Methodist* (1810) pp.iii-viii.

19. Lyles, *op.cit.,* p.71.

20. Werner, *Primitive Methodist Connexion, op.cit.,* p.142.

21. 'A lawless, ill-governed family, or one that is rebellious against good laws, is its own cankerworm': *The General Consolidated Minutes of the Primitive Methodist Connexion: approved by the thirtieth annual conference thereof* (1850). Robert Currie sees the foundation, within Wesleyanism, also in 1849, of the Local Preachers' Mutual Aid Association, as a blow for the dissidents against the bureaucrats: *Methodism Divided* (1968) pp.51-53. See chapter 10 above. Kendall says of the hymn book controversy that its opponents considered the new book to be too 'authorized, stereotyped', with not enough consultation before its introduction: *Origin and History, op.cit.,* vol ii p.371.

22. Revd J. Travis and Revd H. Yooll, *The Local Preacher's Manual* (1895).

23. William Mair, *Speaking* (1902) p.19. Mair's book was originally written for Church of Scotland candidates. As early as 1835 James Everett had challenged those Wesleyans, like Bunting, who wanted academics: 'Whence are the people to look for their REVIVALISTS? Not, alas! to a college.' (Currie, *Methodism*

Divided, op.cit., p.76). The 'Warrenite Controversy' fought over the Wesleyan decision to build a theological institute, led to the Wesleyan Methodist Association secession. Everett and the dissidents could not stem the flow. Ten years later 'A Wesleyan Local Preacher' advocated grammar, elocution, and logic: *Remarks on Preaching addressed chiefly To The Lay Preachers* (Manchester 1844). For studies of such tensions in Primitive Methodism see: G. E. Milburn, *The Christian Lay Churches* (1977), and *A School for the Prophets* (1982) – 'Expansion gave way to consolidation, and connexional and ministerial interests became increasingly dominant over those which were local and lay' (p.4).

24. On a talkative God, Colin Morris, Fount Publications, *Wrestling with an Angel* (1990) pp.11-29. For the manifold opportunities to talk in public, on a range of topics, in ways which demanded different deliveries, see: Valentine Ward, *A Miniature of Methodism; or a Brief Account of the History, Doctrines, Discipline, and Character of the Methodists* (1829). Asked about 'irregular' preaching in Leicestershire in 1821, Revd Robert Hall responded – 'Was not the course of the apostles, and of Stephen, and of many of the Evangelists very irregular? Were not the proceedings of Calvin, Luther . . . Whitefield and Wesley very irregular . . . ? Revd John Petty, *The History of the Primitive Methodist Connexion* (1860) p.62.

25. On the Protestant uses of speech and silence, Richard Bauman, 'Speaking in the Light: the Role of the Quaker Minister', in R. Bauman and J. Sherzer, *Explorations in the Ethnography of Speaking, C.U.P.,* (1974). D. H. Lawrence remembered the power of hymns in his 'Hymns in a Man's Life', in, W. T. Roberts and H. T. Moore, eds, *Phoenix II,* Heinemann (1968).

26. The government story comes from Revd J. Cuthbertson, 'The First Pitman in Parliament', *Wesleyan Methodist Magazine,* 1908, pp.864-69. Burt talks of contemplation in Aaron Watson, *A Great Labour Leader. The Life of Thomas Burt MP* (1908) p.71. There are many examples like these from the labour movement, and the Methodist press recorded some of them. See, for example: Interview with Mr W. E. Harvey MP, 'From Pit to Parliament', *Primitive Methodist Magazine,* 1907, pp.236-37; Revd Arthur Wilkes, 'The Methodist in Parliament', *Primitive Methodist Magazine,* 1921, pp.252-56. A story of true Bunyanite morality is that of Durham's 'Labour Leader', John Wilson: *Memories of a Labour Leader. The autobiography of John Wilson, JP, MP* (1910). Robert Moore has studied coalfield Methodism in depth: *Pit-Men, Preachers and Politics* (1974), Cambridge University Press.

27. Harold Heslop, *Out of the Old Earth,* Newcastle (1994) p.65.

28. 'For the kingdom of God is not a matter of talk but of power': 1 Cor 4:21. (*New English Bible* 1961)

29. There were differences of emphasis across the Methodist denominations. At Union in 1932, Wesleyans tended to see ordained preachers as divinely instituted; Primitives and United Methodists did not. Clause 30 of the Deed of Union lined up with the latter: 'They hold no priesthood differing in kind from that which is common to the Lord's people and they have no exclusive title to the preaching of the gospel or the care of souls . . .'

30. 'It is too possible that to some of my readers Methodism may mean nothing more than low-pitched gables up dingy streets, sleek grocers, sponging preachers and hypocritical jargon': George Eliot, *Adam Bede* (1859), quoted in Hempton, *Methodism and Politics, op.cit.,* p.224. On class composition: Clive D. Field, 'The

social structure of English Methodism', *British Journal of Sociology*, 28, 1977, p.216 and chapter 11 above. On Bunting: W. R. Ward, *Early Victorian Methodism. The correspondence of Jabez Bunting 1830-1858 OUP* (1976) p.9.

32. Letter, John Buddle to Lord Londonderry, 28 September 1821, Durham County Record Office, D/LO/C 142.

32. J. W. Fawcett, *Memorials of Early Primitive Methodism in the County of Durham 1820-29* (1908) p.20.

33. 'Indeed the very mob of Newcastle, in the height of their rudeness, have commonly some humanity left. I scarce observed that they threw anything at all': *JWJ*, ed Nehemiah Curnock (1938) iii, p.81. John Munsey Turner has written a useful introduction to this collision in, *Primitive Methodism. From Counter-Culture to Transformer of Values* (Chapel Aid Lecture, 1994), and E. P. Thompson's essays on eighteenth-century popular culture are indispensable: *Customs in Common*, London, (1993).

For a close analysis of revivalism in its full social context see: Robert Colls, *The Pitmen of the Northern Coalfield*, Manchester University Press, (1987) part 2.

34. The classic work on this remains Robert F Wearmouth, *Methodism and the Working Class Movements of England 1800-50*, Epworth Press (1937) Part 2, chapters 1 to 3.

35. John Keane, *Tom Paine. A Political Life*, London, (1995) p.49.

36. Wearmouth, *Working Class Movements, op.cit.*, Part two, chapter six.

37. Letter, Buddle to Londonderry, 27 June 1832, DCRO D/LO/C 142.

38. W. H. Walton, *Centenary Celebration, Primitive Methodist Church, Jarrow* (1922) pp.14-15.

39. Wearmouth, *op.cit.*, pp.266-67., p.270. On Stephens: Michael S Edwards, *Joseph Raynor Stephens 1805-1879* (Lancs and Cheshire WHS, 1968) pp.11-12, p.20.

40. In an age when '. . . it was difficult for the common law to distinguish between private association and conspiracy', Methodism established itself as a free association with a mass membership: Frederick Dreyer, 'A "Religious Society under Heaven",' *Journal of British Studies*, 25, 1986, p.81.

41. Association yielded its rewards early. As Rev. T. D. Whitaker told Elland Clerical Society in 1813 – 'Accordingly, the parish minister now stands single against a host of bands, classes, and nameless authorities all acting with the compact and uniform force produced by combination': quoted in John Walsh, 'Methodism at the end of the Eighteenth Century', in R. Davies and G. Rupp, eds, *History of the Methodist Church in Great Britain*, Epworth Press, (1965) vol i, p.312. For new ways of understanding the history of association, which can include Methodism, see: Stephen Yeo, ed, *New Views of Cooperation*, Routledge, (1988) and *Who Was J. T. W. Mitchell?* (1995).

42. '". . . popular, non-clerical, unlearned, unsophisticated, enthusiastic, organic in the community and Welsh in language",' quoted in Gwyn A. Williams, *When Was Wales?* Penguin, (1985) p.240.

43. Membership has nearly halved since 1931. For comment on decline of membership, and preaching, see chapters by Davies, 'Methodism', and Mervyn Willshaw, 'The Decline and Rise of Preaching?' in Rupert Davies, ed, *The Testing of the Churches 1932-82. A Symposium,* Epworth Press, (1982).

44. *The Autobiography of Malcolm X,* with the assistance of Alex Haley, Penguin, (1968. 1992 ed) p.189. Malcolm converted to a version of Islam.

45. Joseph Arch, *Joseph Arch. The Story of his Life,* London, (1898) p.147.

I would like to thank Ron Greenall, Dick Ellis and Jean Shaw for their help in the making of this chapter. It is dedicated to my friend Peter Gaddes.

CHAPTER 13(i)

1. Letter from A. M. Fairbairn, 3 June 1891. Quoted in W. B. Selbie *Life of Andrew Martin Fairbairn* 1914, pp. 244-5.

2. *The Primitive Methodist*, February 1892.

3. *op.cit.* May 5 1892.

4. *op.cit.* June 1892.

5. *op.cit.* June 1892.

6. *Sunshine Songs*: a collection of Gospel Specials sung by the Sunshine Duo, Johnson and Gustafson. Chicago 1929.

7. Samuel Horton, *Little Books of the Kindly Light*, 1937, Dr A. S. Peake. pp. 4-5

8. 'Unshaken Truths', Notes of an address delivered in connexion with the the Primitive Methodist Conference held in Wesley's Chapel June last. Revised for the *United Methodist Magazine* Vol. (i) 1908 by Dr Peake.

9. Arthur Samuel Peake: *Essays in Commemoration*. Ed. J. T. Wilkinson 1952, p.12.

10. Methodist Church Archives: John Rylands University Library of Manchester; Peake material MA PR VIII D 93.

11. *idem* Peake MA PR VIII 75.

12. *idem* Peake MA PR VIII D70.

13. *idem* Peake MA PR VIII D 263.

14. *idem op.cit.*

15. *idem* MA PR VIII D32.

16. *idem* MA PR VIII D 314.

17. *idem* MA PR VIII D 316.

18. *idem* MA PR IV 1826.

19. *Primitive Methodist Leader* June 15, 1905.

20. *op.cit.* 1905.

21. *op.cit.* June 1905.

22. *op.cit.* July 1905.

23. *op.cit.* July 1905.

24. Letter from Pamela Taylor on behalf of her mother, Mrs E. Howe.

25. Letter from the Revd Leonard Duchars.

26. Methodist Church Archives: Letter from Revd E. B. Storr, December 22 1924.

OUR CONTRIBUTORS

DONALD ENGLISH

Born and brought up in the north east of England and was ordained into the Methodist ministry in 1962. Spent six years in circuit ministry in Cullercoats, and has had several spells of teaching in theological colleges, including four years in Nigeria. He became General Secretary of the Methodist Church Home Mission Division in 1982, a position he held until his retirement in August 1995. He is also Chairman of the World Methodist Council (until August 1996). Has written several books, including a work on preaching due to be published late in 1995. He can be heard quite frequently on BBC Radio 4's Thought for the Day. Lives near Chipping Norton, Oxfordshire.

MARGARET BATTY

Brought up and educated in Leeds. Became a local preacher in 1951. Married to a Methodist minister. After a few years in what was then British Guiana, lived and worked until retirement in the North Riding of Yorkshire. Was head of the languages department in a comprehensive school. Member of the Wesley Historical Society and author of books and articles on Methodist history in the Yorkshire dales, and also in its wider aspects, including *Stages in the development and control of Wesleyan Lay Leadership 1791-1878*, a doctoral thesis submitted 1988 and published by MPH on behalf of the World Methodist Historical Society 1992. Lives in Edinburgh.

JOHN MUNSEY TURNER

Brought up in Wolverhampton. Read history at St. Catharine's College Cambridge 1949-1952, and trained for the ordained ministry at Didsbury College Bristol. Circuit ministry at Colchester, Burton upon Trent, Sheffield, Leeds. Tutor in Church History at Queen's College Brimingham 1970-1981. Superintendent Minister at Halifax (1981-9) and Bolton (1989-1995). Author of articles and books on Methodist history including *Conflict and Reconciliation: Studies in Methodism and Ecumenism* (1983). Lives at Horwich, near Bolton.

GEOFFREY MILBURN

Brought up in North Yorkshire and studied history at Manchester University. His working life has been spent within education, formal and informal, including teaching history in schools and (from 1970 to 1988) at the Polytechnic (now University) of Sunderland. Active in the Wesley Historical Society, especially its north eastern branch, whose Bulletin he has edited for twenty five years. Author of a range of studies on local and religious (especially Methodist) history with a particular interest in Primitive Methodism. Co-editor of *River, Town and People*, a history of Sunderland (1988). A local preacher for 37 years. Lives in Sunderland.

TIM MACQUIBAN

A native of Chester and educated there and at Cambridge and Liverpool Universities. Spent ten years working as an archivist in local government. He started preaching in 1975 and later became a minister, serving in the Halifax circuit. Went on to become Tutor in History at Wesley College, Bristol, and is presently serving as Director of the Wesley and Methodist Studies Centre at Westminster College, Oxford. Editor and Contributor to *Methodism in its Cultural Milieu* and *Pure Universal Love*, Applied Theology Press, Westminster College, 1994 and 1995.

T. FRANCIS GLASSON

Born and brought up in Derby, leaving school at 15. Trained for the Methodist ministry at Richmond College 1930-33 and served in several circuits while also establishing himself as a Biblical scholar. Appointed Lecturer in New Testament Studies and Biblical Theology at New College (then Congregational), London, in 1960. Author of a number of publications on N.T. themes, including *The Second Advent* (1945).

JOHN S. LAMPARD

Qualified as a solicitor before training for the Methodist ministry at Wesley College, Bristol and Phillips University, Oklahoma. After fifteen years in circuit ministry in Yorkshire, Lancashire and Sussex (1970-1985) he was appointed to the Division of Ministries with special responsibility for local preachers' affairs. In 1994 he resumed circuit ministry as superintendent of the South London Mission, based in Bermondsey.

E. ALAN ROSE

Was born and educated in Manchester. Following teacher training in Durham he taught science and then history in secondary schools in Tameside until his retirement in 1989, since when he has divided his time between selling antiquarian books and writing. He has written a number of local histories of Methodism and has been editor of the Wesley Historical Society Proceedings since 1980. He has been a local preacher for 32 years. Lives in Mottram, Cheshire.

E. DOROTHY GRAHAM

From a family with a strong local preaching tradition. Brought up in Warwickshire, educated there and at Leeds and Birmingham Universities. Taught in Scotland and Yorkshire and latterly in a Birmingham school as Head of Religious Education. General Secretary of the Wesley Historical Society since 1980 and Connexional Archives Liaison Officer since 1989. Author of various publications and articles on local history, Methodist women and church membership including *Chosen by God*: a list of the female travelling preachers of early Methodism, 1989. A local preacher for 42 years. Lives in Birmingham.

C. ALAN PARKER

Native of Birmingham, where he received his early Christian education at High Street (then Primitive) Methodist Church, Erdington, and attended King Edward VI School. Following military service he studied at Manchester and London Universities, graduating in Economics. A spell in local government finance led to a career of over 30 years in further education, which culminated in the principalship at Stockton, were he now lives in retirement. Local preacher for 45 years. Member of LPMAA General Committee since 1982, and served as President of the Association in 1988-89.

CLIVE FIELD

Born at Luton in 1950, and educated at Dunstable Grammar School and Wadham College, Oxford, where he read history. Has held a number of posts in university libraries: as Assistant Librarian (1977-87) and Sub-Librarian (1987-90) at the John Rylands University Library of Manchester, and as Deputy Librarian (1990-1995) and Librarian (since 1995) of the University of Birmingham. He has published widely in the field of the social history of English religion from 1689 to the present day, and is the author of a number of standard bibliographies of the history of British Methodism, including that in vol. iv of the *History of the Methodist Church in Great Britain*, 1988.

JOHN BANKS

Retired Methodist minister. A junior member of the Primitive Methodist Church at the time of Union! Served as Chaplain to Methodist students in both Manchester and Leeds, and as Superintendent of the Manchester and Salford Methodist Mission. Founder (in 1972) and still the Chairman of the Manchester Methodist Housing Association. Has written a number of books including *Nancy, Nancy* the story of Ann Bolton, friend and confidante of John Wesley and published by MPH on behalf of the World Methodist Historical Society, 1992.

JOHN STACEY

Brought up in Bristol and educated at Queen Elizabeth's Hospital, Handsworth College and London University. After ordination he served in the following circuits: Leigh-on-Sea, Altrincham, Ealing, Hoylake and West Kirby. He was Connexional Local Preachers' Secretary 1967-1985, and Editor of the *Epworth Review* 1974-1991. He is the author of *John Wyclif and Reform, About the Ministry, The Common People of the Old Testament, Preaching Reassessed* and *Groundwork of Theology*. Awarded a doctorate in 1995 for a thesis on Wyclif.

ROBERT COLLS

Teaches history at Leicester University. His next book is *The Identity of England* (1996 Oxford University Press). From the age of twelve to twenty he came under the remarkable ministry of the Revd R. H. Ellis, at Westoe Methodist Church, South Shields.

C. NORMAN R. WALLWORK

Brought up in Cumbria where he also taught, after training in Sunderland. Trained for the Methodist ministry at the Queen's College and the University at Birmingham. In addition to circuit ministries in Cheshire, London, Cumbria and Exeter he has written and lectured on liturgy, Methodism and spirituality. A member of the new Methodist Service Book Committee and of the Joint Liturgical Group. Author of *A Book of Vestry Prayers* Epworth Press 1976, and *Blackbirds and Budgerigars: A critical history of Methodist Liturgical dress 1786-1986* Methodist Sacramental Fellowship, 1986.

READING LIST

and guide to further study

(See also chapter references for some works not included here)

A. General Works on Methodist History

Because local preachers have played such an integral part within Methodism their story cannot be separated from that of the wider movement. Our list therefore begins with some sources (in reverse chronological order) on the history of Methodism as a whole and of its various divisions:

Barrie Tabraham, *The Making of Methodism*, Epworth Press 1995.

Rupert E. Davies, *Methodism*, 2nd revised edition, Epworth Press 1985.

R. E. Davies, A. R. George and E. G. Rupp, *A History of the Methodist Church in Great Britain*, Epworth Press 1965-1988, 4 vols. Vol. iv of *HMCGB* contains a detailed and extensive bibliography by Clive Field of books on Methodism.

C. J. Davey, *The Methodist Story*, Epworth Press 1955.

F. Baker, *A Charge to Keep*, Epworth Press 1947.

A. W. Harrison, B. A. Barber, G. G. Hornby and E. T. Davies, *The Methodist Church: Its origins, divisions and reunion*, Methodist Publishing House 1932.

W. J. Townsend, H. B. Workman and G. Eayrs, *A New History of Methodism*, Hodder & Stoughton 1909, 2 vols.

Clive Field edits an annual *Bibliography of Methodist Historical Literature* published as a supplement to the *Proceedings of the Wesley Historical Society*. See also the *United Methodist Bibliographic Series* by O. A. Beckerlegge and E. A. Rose, published as 5 pamphlets, 1988, and covering all those branches of Methodism which united in 1907 (omitting therefore the Wesleyan and Primitive Methodists); S. Hatcher, *A Primitive Methodist Bibliography*, Glasgow 1980; also Roger Thorne, *Methodism in the South West - an historical bibliography*, Exeter 1986, and J. S. English, *A Bibliography of Lincolnshire Methodism*, Gainsborough 1994.

B. Works directly related to the history of local preaching:

M. Batty, 'The contribution of local preachers to the life of the Wesleyan Methodist Church until 1932, and to the Methodist Church after 1932, in England'. University of Leeds MA 1969.

J. C. Bowmer, 'The Local Preacher in Early Methodism' and 'The Local Preacher in Methodism 1791-1964' in *The Local Preacher's Handbook* 8 (1963) pp1-14, and 9 (1965) pp1-19.

F. H. Buss and R. G. Burnett, *A Goodly Fellowship: A history of the hundred years of the Methodist Local Preachers' Mutual Aid Association, 1849-1949*, Epworth Press 1949.

D. Coomer, 'The Local Preacher in Early Methodism' in *WHS Proc.* xxv, pp32-42 (1945).

G. Lawton, *Reader-Preacher, a lay ministry ideal*, (esp. chapters 11-13) London, Churchman Publications 1989.

J. Telford, *A History of Lay Preaching in the Christian Church* (from Biblical times to the 19th century) C. H. Kelly, London 1897.

N. B. Harmon et al. *The Encyclopaedia of World Methodism*, (two articles on local preachers) Nashville 1974, 2 vols.

The Methodist Local Preachers' Who's Who, 1934: a complete record of the lives and careers of Methodist local preachers, London [1934].

C. Some Lives of local preachers:

(a representative selection only)

A Somerset Preacher, *Memorials of Josiah Gregory, a Somerset collier, and an early Methodist Local Preacher and Class Leader*, London, 66 Paternoster Row 1870.

T. H. Bainbridge, ed. G. France, *Reminiscences*, with a short sketch of the life and character of T. H. B. by the editor, London, C. H. Kelly 1913.

J. Burdsall, *Memoirs of the Life of R. Burdsall of York*, 3rd edn., 1797 and later editions.

J. E. Coulson, *The Peasant Preacher, memorials of Mr Chas. Richardson,* London, Hamilton Adams 1867.

J. H. Drew, *The Life, Character and Literary Labours of Samuel Drew AM, of St. Austell,* London, Longman 1834.

J. Everett, *The Village Blacksmith* (Samuel Hick), first published 1830, London, Newton, 18th edn. 1879; and *Memoirs of the Life, Character and Ministry of William Dawson*, London, Hamilton Adams 1842.

S. Foot, *My Grandfather Isaac Foot*, Bossiney Books 1980.

T. F. Glasson, *Thomas Glasson, Lay Preacher*, Epworth Press 1943.

S. Hick, *Memoirs of Samuel Hick, in his own dialect, by himself,* Halifax 1858.

W. D. Lawson, *Wesleyan Local Preachers: biographical illustrations of their position in the Connexion, utility in the Church and influence in the world*, (short biographies of S. Drew, W. Dawson, S. Hick, T. Hackworth, T. Bush, P. Embury), Newcastle-upon-Tyne 1874.

J. W. Laycock, *Methodist heroes of the Great Haworth Round, 1734-1784*, Keighley 1909.

H. Longden, *The Life of Henry Longden of Sheffield, from his memoirs and diary, by himself*, 7th ed. London, J. Mason 1839 G. E. Milburn ed., *The Diary of John Young, Sunderland Chemist and Methodist Lay Preacher, 1841-1843*, Surtees Society, vol. CXCV 1983.

G. E. Milburn ed., *The Diary of John Young, Sunderland Chemist and Methodist Lay Preacher, 1841-1843*, Surtees Society, cxcv, 1983.

H. Moore, *The Life of Mrs Mary Fletcher*, 11th edn., London, J. Mason 1844.

Preachers All: Essays to commemorate the Silver Jubilee of the Yorkshire Branch of the WHS, 1987. (Chapters by J. M. Turner and O. A. Beckerlegge are relevant to local preachers.)

C. G. Rackett, *According to Plan: years of memories . . . of a Methodist Local Preacher*, Milford on Sea 1986. A. R. B. Robinson, *The Counting House: Thomas Thompson of Hull 1754-1828*, York 1992.

Z. Taft, *Biographical Sketches of Holy Women*, London, Kershaw 1828, 2 vols. Reprinted 1992.

G. Thomas *Mr Speaker*, (autobiography) the memoirs of Viscount Tonypandy, Guild Publishing, London 1985.

S. Told, *The Life of Silas Told, written by himself, with a note to the serious and candid reader by John Wesley AM*, [1786] Epworth Press 1954.

G. P. White, *A Half-Century of Cornish Methodism 1925-1975: A local preacher's experience*, Redruth 1975.

D. Whiteley, *Illustrious Local Preachers*, Bradford 1891 (21 short biographies, from all branches of Methodism, mainly in Lancashire and Yorkshire).

J. T. Wilkinson ed., *Arthur Samuel Peake, 1865-1929: Essays in commemoration and selections from his writings*, Epworth Press 1958.

D. Connexional Minutes, Periodicals etc.

The *Minutes* and/or *General Rules* of the Methodist Connexions (published annually) are a valuable record. On Methodist constitutional matters and policy since 1932 see G. Thompson Brake *Policy and Politics in British Methodism since 1932*, Edsall, London 1984.

Also helpful is *Statements of the Methodist Church on Faith and Order 1933-1983*, Methodist Publishing House 1984.

The branches of Methodism all published their monthly magazines, and in some cases weekly papers also. These constitute a very rich source especially for the 19th and early 20th centuries. A useful guide to them is E. A. Rose, *A Checklist of*

British Methodist Periodicals, Methodist Study Guide No.1, World Methodist Historical Society 1981, (currently out of print and under revision).

Local collections of some of these magazines occur but the fullest runs are in the Wesley Historical Society Library at Westminster College, Oxford, and especially at John Rylands University Library, Manchester, as part of the enormous archive of Methodist materials deposited there.

It is useful to point out here that circuit and chapel records are to be found in county and city record offices, or still in safes and cupboards in the circuit chapels.

The Wesley Historical Society has published its *Proceedings* since 1897 (3 numbers a year) and its local branches up and down the land produce their own journals. For information on the WHS nationally contact the Secretary, Dr E. D. Graham, 34 Spiceland Road, Birmingham B31 1N1, and on the local branches Mr R. F. S. Thorne, 31 St Mary's Park, Ottery St Mary, Devon, EX11 1JA.

Local branch secretaries of the WHS are useful sources of information in their own areas.

On the WHS Library contact Mrs J. Banks, 23 Oaklands Court, Somertown, Chichester, West Sussex, PO19 4AF.

Cirplan, published twice a year by the Society of Cirplanologists, contains detailed information on circuit preaching plans and related matters, and also holds a large number of old plans. The Secretary is Mr E. A. Rose, 26 Roe Cross Green, Mottram, Hyde, Cheshire, SK14 6LP.

E. Works addressed to local preachers or defining their role:

'An Old Local Preacher', *Thoughts on the case of the Local Preachers in the Methodist Connexion*, Bristol 1820.

Anon., *One of them: Local Preachers and their work*, 1875.

Dr Aldom, *Methodist Local preachers and their work*, [c.1858]

B. Bailey, *The Wesleyan Local Preacher's own book, or choice baits for spiritual fishermen, with directions how to use them*, London, J. Mason 1841.

J. H. Carr, *The Local Ministry, – its character, vocation and position considered*, London, J. Kaye 1851 [an apologia].

J. A. Clapperton, *A Manual for Local Preachers*, 1st edn. 1910, revised edn. 1920, 6th edn. Epworth Press 1926.

C. O. Eldridge, *The Lay Preacher's Handbook*, London, Kelly 1894, and *Local Preachers and village Methodism*, Joyful News, Rochdale and London 1895.

W. Hatton, *A Brief Account of the Rise and Progress of Local Preachers and of Local Preaching among the Methodists*, Leeds 1817.

W. B. Pope, *The Methodist Local Preacher, an Address published at the request of the Methodist Local Preachers' Mutual Aid Association*, London, Wesleyan Conference Office 1879.

A. W. Robinson, *An Essay on a Lay Ministry, particularly on that of Wesleyan Local Preachers*, London, J. Mason 1832.

J. Travis and H. Yooll, *The Local Preacher's Manual*, London, Mitchell 1876. [PM]

H. Strawson, *The Lay Preacher*, (Little Books of the Kindly Light No.27) Epworth Press 1936.

J. W. Whittome, *The Local Preacher's Efficiency Course*, Stockwell c.1920.

Compendium of Rules and regulations relating to Local Preachers.. WM Bookroom 1902. See also relevant sections of PM *Consolidated Minutes*, BC *General Rules*, UM *Free Church Manual* (Askew), MNC *General Rules* etc.

The Report of the High Leigh enquiry on 'Doctrinal Preaching', Local Preachers' Department 1951.

The Report of the Eastbourne enquiry on 'The Local Preacher and Evangelism', Methodist Local Preachers' Department 1950.

F. Examples of books and journals intended to assist local preachers in their studies and in the work of preaching:

The Local Preachers' Magazine and Mutual Aid Reporter, 1851 to the present.

The Preacher's Handbook, 1949 to 1969. Epworth Press.

The Preacher's Handbook, new series, all ed. J. Stacey, 1. *About Preaching* 1970, 2. *About the Gospel* 1971, 3. *About Faith* 1972, Epworth Press.

The Preachers' Magazine (monthly, Wesleyan) 1884-1932, then as a Methodist publication to 1954. (Called *The Local Preacher's Treasury* 1884-1889, and from 1928 *The Local Preachers' and Class Leaders' Magazine*.)

The Preachers' Quarterly 1954-1969. The successor to *The Local Preachers' and Class Leaders' Magazine*, succeeded by *Worship & Preaching*.

F. A. Farley, *Preparing to preach: A guide to local preachers*, Epworth Press 1939/1945.

G. Fletcher, *Chapters on Preaching*, London, Kelly 1902.

D. N. Francis, *The ABC of Preaching*, Epworth Press 1968.

Faith and Worship, the Local Preachers' Training Course, Methodist Publishing House 1991.

M. D. Hooker, *Studying the New Testament*, Epworth Press 1979.

R. G. Jones, *Groundwork of Worship and Preaching*, Epworth Press 1980, and *Groundwork of Christian Ethics*, Epworth Press 1984

H. McKeating, *Studying the Old Testament*, Epworth Press 1979.

J. Stacey, *Groundwork of Theology*, Epworth Press 1977.

W. D. Stacey, *Groundwork of Biblical Studies*, Epworth Press 1979.

Many other relevant works could be listed if space allowed, especially those relating to the local history of Methodism. Readers can glean some idea of the wealth of this literature from the references to the chapters in this book.

G. The wider context (a few examples of works on the general social and ecclesiastical background in which Methodism and its preachers were operating, and on the role of lay people in the life of the Church).

O. Chadwick, *The Victorian Church*, 2 vols. London A.& C. Black 1966/1970

D. Clark, *Between Pulpit and Pew: folk religion in a North Yorkshire fishing village*, Cambridge University Press 1982.

A. D. Gilbert, *Religion and Society in Industrial England: Church, Chapel and Social Change 1740-1914*, Longmans 1976.

A.Hastings, *A History of English Christianity 1920-1985*, Collins 1986.

K. S. Inglis, *Churches and the Working Class in Victorian England*, London/Toronto 1963.

T. R. Morton and M. Gibbs, *God's Frozen People*, Collins, 1964, Fontana edition 1971.

S. Neill and H. R. Weber, *The Layman in Christian History*, SCM Press, 1963.

W. R. Ward, *Faith and Faction*, Epworth Press 1993.

E. R. Wickham, *Church and People in an Industrial City*, London Lutterworth 1957.

SOME IMPORTANT DATES IN LOCAL PREACHING

1712	Susanna Wesley held house meetings at the Epworth rectory (in Samuel's absence) for prayer, sermon readings and religious conversation.
1739	Thomas Westell, a carpenter, began to preach around Bristol.
1741	John Nelson, a stonemason, began to preach around Birstal.
1742	Susanna Wesley warned John Wesley not to stop Thomas Maxfield's preaching in London.
1743	Charles Wesley prevented a woman from preaching, in Evesham.
1745	In *A Farther Appeal to Men of Reason and Religion* John Wesley set out his reasons for allowing laymen to preach.
1746	The term 'exhorter' used to describe lay persons who addressed meetings or congregations but without expounding a text in a formal way. (Much later the term was used to describe LPs on trial.)
1747	Reference made to 38 Methodist preachers who 'assist in one place', i.e. were not itinerant and full-time, but preached in their own localities.
1751	First use of the term 'local preacher' in Wesley's Minutes of Conference.
1754	Wesley made out 17 weekly preaching plans for the London circuit. It became a required work of the assistant (superintendent minister) in the years following.
1755	15 'chief local preachers' attended the annual Conference of preachers arranged by Wesley.
1769	Wesley commented 'I am a centre of union to all our travelling, as well as local preachers'.
"	Wesley told Sarah Crosby not to give the appearance of preaching, therefore never to take a text (in effect to remain an exhorter rather than aspire to being an expository preacher).
1777	Earliest known preaching plan (for the Leeds circuit) – it has handwritten entries on a printed grid, and shows the initials of the preachers. (See p.145)
1780	Wesley instructed one of his itinerants to stop preaching by women in his circuit.
1787	Wesley received Sarah Mallet as a preacher in the Methodist connexion.

1789	Evidence suggests that by this date Wesley was holding quarterly meetings with the London LPs.
1791	Death of John Wesley.
1795	Alexander Kilham, an itinerant of radical views, proposed in his *Free Enquiry* that LPs should be better trained and selected more democratically.
"	The Plan of Pacification endorsed by Conference. (An attempt to resolve some of the tensions within Methodism and a major step towards Methodism becoming a separate Church.
1796	Conference authorised the general introduction in all circuits of quarterly meetings of LPs, under the chairmanship of the superintendent.
"	Kilham expelled from the itinerancy for advocating lay involvement in administration at all levels of Methodism.
1797	The Methodist New Connexion established under Kilham and others.
"	The WM Conference insisted that all itinerants should first have served as LPs.
1803	LPs told by the Wesleyan Conference that they did not come within the safety-net of the Toleration Act of 1689, because they were not 'wholly set apart', and that if they applied for a preacher's licence they would be expelled.
"	Women's preaching restricted by the Wesleyan Conference to those with an 'extraordinary call' and only to other women.
1806	First annual meeting of the Independent Methodists, whose origins date from a year earlier. They employed a completely lay ministry.
1807	First Camp Meeting organised at Mow Cop by Hugh Bourne, a Wesleyan LP soon to become the founder of Primitive Methodism with William Clowes, who shortly afterwards also became a LP.
1808	MNC began annual records of the number of its LPs. It had 174 LPs that year.
1810	Clowes expelled from Wesleyan Methodism for attending Camp Meetings. Emergence of Primitive Methodism.
"	William O'Bryan (soon to become founder of the Bible Christians) became a local preacher.
1811	Sidmouth's Bill, attempting to suppress local preaching, defeated in Parliament.

1812	Primitive Methodism fully established by this date under Bourne and Clowes.
"	Wesleyan Conference told LPs not to meddle in politics.
1815	Bible Christian societies were formed in the south west under William O'Bryan and James Thorne. Used both men and women preachers.
1819	Some radical Wesleyan preachers expelled for attending political gatherings, in the year of Peterloo.
1825	Zechariah Taft (Wesleyan itinerant and husband of Mary Barritt, a preacher) published *Holy Women* and urged that women be recognised as LPs.
1827	Revolt of WM LPs in Leeds as a result of the Leeds Organ Dispute and its aftermath. Formation of the Protestant Methodists.
1829	PMs began annual records of the numbers of their LPs. By 1832 there were 3,156.
1832	Arminian Methodists formed in the Derby area – result of local tensions between LPs and itinerants.
1834	In Rochdale, earliest known LP Friendly Society held its first annual meeting.
"	Wesleyan Methodist Association formed as a protest against the autocracy of the WM Conference, particularly towards LPs. In the years following a number of smaller break-away groups united with the WMA.
1837	The WMA began annual records of the number of its LPs. By 1837 it had 824, not counting those on trial.
1839	WM Centenary Fund raised £220,000 but requests for aid from the fund for old, poor or disabled LPs were refused.
1840s	Renewed restiveness and rebellion within the WM Connexion over the controlling authority claimed by ministers in Conference and in circuit life.
1849	Formation of the Wesleyan Local Preachers' Mutual Aid Association – it had no financial links with the WM Connexion and in due course was to admit LPs of the non-Wesleyan connexions into membership.
"	The build-up of the Fly Sheets controversy led to the expulsion of three WM itinerants, followed by the expulsion or departure of 100,000 lay members over an extended period.

1850	First meetings of the Wesleyan Reformers – a new Methodist grouping resulting from the above.
1851	Start of the *Local Preachers' Magazine* (organ of the LPMAA). The following years saw an increasing output of publications (articles and books) offering help and advice to LPs.
1852	WM local preachers of 3 years' standing given a seat on the circuit quarterly meeting.
1857	After some years of negotiation the Wesleyan Reformers and the WMA came together to form the United Methodist Free Churches. In some places local unions were formed earlier. The UMFC had 1,739 LPs this year, about one quarter of them from the Wesleyan Reformers.
1859	George Eliot's novel *Adam Bede*. Set in the 1790s it contained descriptions of a Methodist woman preacher, Dinah Morris, based on George Eliot's memories of her aunt Elizabeth Evans.
"	A minority of Wesleyan Reformers who had not joined the UMFC formed the Wesleyan Reform Union.
1860	Primitive Methodism's jubilee year: 11,384 LPs in the PM connexion by this date.
1861	The *Methodist Recorder* (weekly newspaper) launched.
1877	Christian Lay Churches established in the north east – a breakaway movement from Primitive Methodism in the Sunderland area. Had a completely lay ministry and soon joined forces with the older Independent Methodists and took their name. Ex-PM LPs were among the Lay Church pioneers.
1878	Lay representatives attended the WM Conference for the first time – many LPs among them.
1879	Revd Dr W. B. Pope (WM) delivered an important and influential address on LPs, describing them as an 'order' and encouraging the strengthening of training and morale.
"	A WM Conference committee set up to plan the training of LPs.
"	The PMs introduced for the first time a question paper to be answered *in writing* by those being examined as exhorters or LPs. It was intended as a supplement to the standard oral examination, and covered matters relating to candidates' religious life and knowledge of basic doctrines.
1881	First (decennial) Methodist Ecumenical Conference. The representatives included some leading LPs.

1883	WMs began annual records of the numbers of their LPs. 14,183 this year (not counting those on trial).
"	First issue by Thomas Champness of *Joyful News* from which Cliff College was eventually to develop.
1885	WM Connexional and District Committees set up to deal with LP affairs.
1889	Joyful News Mission founded by Thomas Champness at Rochdale. Champness opened Castleton Hall, Rochdale as a place of training for evangelists.
1890	*The Preachers' Magazine* (WM) began. From 1914 it combined a PM Supplement. (Not to be confused with the *Local Preachers' Magazine* published by LPMAA from 1851.)
1892	Arthur Samuel Peake (a layman and LP) appointed as tutor to the PM Theological Institute in Manchester. Peake's books and articles which appeared from the late 1890s onwards introduced Methodist preachers to modern Biblical scholarship, though not without controversy.
1893	Launch of the WM Union for Biblical and Homiletical Studies.
1897	Women admitted as members of LPMAA.
1899	Seven LPMAA cottages for elderly LPs opened at Fillongley, near Coventry.
1903	Cliff College opened under Methodist auspices to carry on the work begun by Thomas Champness. Thomas Cook was the first principal.
1904	New PM legislation for Training and Equipment of LPs.
1906	Mention of 33 recognition services in WM annual *Minutes* (the practice must have begun earlier).
1907	The United Methodist Church formed from the union of the New Connexion, the Bible Christians and the United Methodist Free Church, after years of negotiation. Numbers of LPs this year (not counting those on trial) WM 19,672, PM 16,259, UM 5,621.
1909	First reported decrease in the numbers of WM LPs.
1910	J. A. Clapperton, (WM) published *A Manual for Local Preachers* in which he advocated the use of public recognition services for LPs.
"	The WM Conference gave permission for women to preach both to women and men but only where there was no local opposition to it.

1913	The United Methodist *Book of Services* included a public recognition service for LPs.
1914-1918	World War I highlighted the importance to Methodism of its LPs.
1918	WM women LPs put on an equal footing with men.
"	WM Local Preachers' Commission set up. Its Report (1919) shocked the Connexion.
"	Start of union negotiations between the WMs, PMs and UMs. Intense debate over following years.
1919	Peake's *Commentary on the Bible* published – became a standard work of reference, much used by preachers.
1921	WMs introduced an order for a public recognition service for LPs.
1923	Arthur Button (a layman) became first Connexional LP Secretary for the WMs.
"	First woman member of LPMAA General Committee.
1932	Methodist Union (based on the Act of Union passed in 1929) created the Methodist Church by uniting the WMs, PMs and UMs. Almost 35,000 LPs in the united Church, not counting those on trial. Just over half were WMs. The Methodist Local Preachers' Department came into being, with Arthur Button as Secretary.
1934	*The Methodist Local Preachers' Who's Who* published.
1936	The *Book of Offices* for the Methodist Church contained a new recognition service for LPs.
1937	Connexional written examinations for LPs compulsory for the first time. Revd Fred Farley replaced the layman Arthur Button as Connexional LP Secretary – an appointment not without controversy, owing to the replacement of a layman by a minister.
1939-1945	World War II (like its predecessor) brought home to Methodism the vital importance to Methodism of its LPs, as well as the need to equip them better to preach to the needs of the modern world.
1941	Deaconess Bessie Higgins began work as the first travelling tutor for LPs. Others joined in the work later.
1946	Revd Greville Lewis Connexional LP Secretary (to 1958).
1949	First of the *Preacher's Handbooks* published – eleven in all between 1949 and 1969. 14,000 of vol.i sold.

1950   Report by the LP Department on *The Local Preacher and Evangelism* based on a retreat held at Eastbourne.

"   First LPMAA Home (Westerley) opened at Westcliff on Sea. Others soon to follow.

1953   24,387 LPs (not counting those on trial).

1955   Worship and Preaching added to the subjects in which LPs were examined.

"   *Epworth Commentaries* began to be published.

1958   Report on *Rural Methodism* severely criticised the quality of much Methodist preaching, while acknowledging the magnificent work done by LPs.

1963   *Conversations between the Church of England and the Methodist Church*. A report.

1964   Report to Conference on *The Place and Functions of the LP*.

1967   Revd John Stacey Connexional LP Secretary (to 1985).

"   Local Preachers' Sunday henceforth to have a double purpose – to make better known the work of LPMAA, and to explain the work of LPs and offer an invitation to consider the call to preach.

1972   *Doing Theology* (a handbook for LPs) caused some controversy. (See chapter 13(ii)).

"   End of right of circuits to exempt LPs, in special circumstances, from connexional examinations. LPs offered choice of written exams, continuous assessment, or an oral exam.

1973   The LP Department changed its name to the LP Office.

"   17,291 LPs (not counting those on trial).

1975   A new *Methodist Service Book* published – did not at first include the new order for the commissioning of LPs.

1977   John Stacey's *Groundwork of Theology* published to replace *Doing Theology*.

1979   Beginning of discussions to bring LPMAA institutionally within Methodism.

1983   Report by Prof. David Bartholomew: *Methodist Local Preachers – a Statistical Review*.

1985   Revd John A. Lampard Connexional LP Secretary (to 1994).

1988   'Auxiliary' preachers to be phased out, or train as LPs.

1990   *Faith & Worship* (the new LP training course) introduced, based on study units integrating biblical study, theology and liturgical practice.

"   Beginning of plans to celebrate Methodism's LPs in 1996.

1992   Introduction of report on CLPD (Continuing Local Preacher Development) at Conference.

1993   13,126 LPs (not counting those on trial).

1994   Revd Peter Barber Connexional LP Secretary.

1995   Handbook on CLPD published; the programme to be introduced in September 1995.

INDEX